Tragic Magic

The Life of Traffic's Chris Wood

Dan Ropek

Oakamoor
Publishing

Published by Oakamoor Publishing, Bennion Kearny Limited
6 Woodside
Churnet View Road
Oakamoor
ST10 3AE

www.BennionKearny.com

Cover Image: © Dick Cooper

I dedicate this book to my wife, Ramona Ropek, for her love, support and incredible patience for a project which ended up spanning more than a decade. I promise not to do it again! Special thanks also to Lucas Ropek, a fellow writer (and my son) for his continual encouragement.

A huge 'Thank You' goes out to all of the people listed below (in a non-alphabetical but sensible-to-me order) who gave their time, expertise and memories to help tell the story. Each person added an important piece to the mosaic of Chris Wood's life, allowing an otherwise lost portrait to re-emerge. All of you have my deep gratitude.

Jim Capaldi, Dave Mason, Roger Hawkins, David Hood, Jimmy Johnson, Mick Weaver, Chris Mercer, Malcom John 'Mac' Rebennack, Ritchie Crooks, Michael Johnstone, Pete York, Mike Kellie, Andy Bown, Trevor Burton, Junior Marvin, Tyrone Downie, Phil Ramacon, Paul Rodgers, Tony Branagual, Poli Palmer, Gordon Jackson, Jorge Spiteri, Charles Spiteri, Steve Alpert, Remi Kabaka, Keith Bailey, Doug Fieger, Bob Greenfield, Russ Gibb, Don Carless, Andy Silvester, David 'Rowdy' Yeats ,Roger Bruton, Jim Simpson, Frank Devine, Dave Pegg, Phill Brown, Eleanor Barooshian, Holly Beth Vincent, Ann (Bird) Stockdale, Moogie Klingman, Steve Hyams, Pete Bonas, Randall Bramblett, Bobby Messano, Tony Curtis, Richard Feld, Candace Brightman, Christopher 'Noggy' Nolan, Suzette Newman, Andy Cahan, Steve Hadley, Ed Davis, Perry Foster, Stuart Carr, Vinden Wylde, Mick Lee, Tony Wright, Terry Barham (interviewed by Neil Storey), Stephanie Wood, Nina Parkes, Brenda Harris, Peter Harris, Bob Paul, Hugh Fraser, Mike Lewis, Becky Lewis, Robert Edwards, Paul Medcalf, Trevor Jones, John Walker, Gloria Wheeler, Brenda Bryan, Syd Bryan, Damien Jay, Anna Capaldi-Gilbey, Penny Massot, Lorraine Mason, Christie Nichols, Helen Hamilton, Dian Melzer, Marsha (anonymous), Rosie Roper, Shirley Sheldon, Patricia Boyd, Nick Cannon, Graham Broadbent, Philip Edwards, John Priest, Jim Conway, Gordon Davidson, John Barnett, Peter Nokes, Theo Travis, Pete King, Elena (Iglio) Woontner, Alan Woontner, Yvonne Haynes, David Dalton, David Rensin, Dick Polak, Keith Altham, Burt Muirhead, Larry Geller, Richard Breese, Tim Schell, Neil Storey, Paul Minkinnen, Louis Farace, Cheryl Gallegos, and Jayne Gould.

I also thank James Lumsden-Cook at Bennion Kearny for giving this story a chance to be known, and his always insightful editorial work with the manuscript.

And last but not least, a very special thanks must go to Stephanie Wood and Brian Withers for their unflagging friendship, assistance and support – the book would have been impossible without you.

ABOUT DAN ROPEK

Dan Ropek has previously written for *Goldmine*, *Record Collector*, and *Crawdaddy!* magazines. He also designed the cover and wrote the liner notes for Chris Wood's *Vulcan* album (2008). Excerpts from this book are slated to be included in the forthcoming (2016) Chris Wood box-set retrospective, *Evening Blue*. When not teaching at Columbia Gorge Community College, Dan plays music and tends a small patch of forest in nearby Mount Hood, Oregon.

CONTENTS

PROLOGUE: TRAGIC MAGIC   1
CHAPTER 1: THE BLACK COUNTRY   3
CHAPTER 2: THE MUSIC OF EMOTION   11
CHAPTER 3: A KID NAMED STEVIE   15
CHAPTER 4: 'HE JUST BELIEVED IT…'   17
CHAPTER 5: THE SPELL OF WITLEY COURT   27
CHAPTER 6: PAINTING WITH MUSIC   33
CHAPTER 7: PAST MIDNIGHT AT THE 'ELBOW ROOM'   37
CHAPTER 8: 'QUITE COOL, SLIGHTLY HIPPIE'   41
CHAPTER 9: BOB DYLAN'S GHOST   49
CHAPTER 10: THE 'DREAM OF TRAFFIC'   51
CHAPTER 11: MELODIES OF A HAUNTED COTTAGE   59
CHAPTER 12: STUDYING MUSIC   65
CHAPTER 13: 'THE EGO WENT MAD'   71
CHAPTER 14: DEAR MR FANTASY   77
CHAPTER 15: POINTS OF DEPARTURE   81
CHAPTER 16: THE TRAIL OF THE HEADLESS HORSEMEN   87
CHAPTER 17: THE END OF THE BEGINNING   107
CHAPTER 18: BLIND FAITH AND A WOODEN FROG   117
CHAPTER 19: DR. JOHN'S TRAVELING MEDICINE SHOW   127
CHAPTER 20: JOHN BARLEYCORN MUST DIE!   133
CHAPTER 21: FAREWELL JIMI   145
CHAPTER 22: 'ALABAMA MEETS GHANA'   157
CHAPTER 23: NOTES FROM THE EDGE   161
CHAPTER 24: THE SHADOW OF MARBLE ARCH   171
CHAPTER 25: THE BEGINNING OF THE END   191
CHAPTER 26: THE RISE AND ECLIPSE OF VULCAN   199
CHAPTER 27: RETURN TO THE MIDLANDS   207
CHAPTER 28: SEASON OF THE SULLEN MOON   217
EPILOGUE: A NEW 'TRAFFIC' AND VULCAN'S RELEASE   231

PROLOGUE: TRAGIC MAGIC

Spring, 1967: Chris Wood was on the verge of becoming a 'rock star' – and he didn't like the looks of it. Having relocated with his band to the English countryside to musically find themselves, away from the gaze of prying eyes, they were just beginning to find their footing when a photographer named Linda Eastman discovered the hideout in the village of Aston Tirrold. With a camera full of black and white film, she reeled off candid shots as the band drank in their favorite pub, surrounded by locals. While the others were happy to oblige, Chris, unable to muster a smile, squirmed and fumed, his face reddening before he finally had enough and bolted, muttering oaths as he stormed out the door.

Outside he glanced up to notice a girl, Rosie Roper, walking her dogs. He did not know her, but she knew him. Having previously seen Chris and his friends roaring through the usually quiet village in a sports car, the sight of him on foot was cause for a sly comment, "*Oh*, what are you doing out by yourself – *walking?*" Chris paused, "Aaargh, they've sent some blooming woman down – taking photographs…" Together, Chris and Rosie walked back to the country cottage where the band lived and practiced.

Little more than a year before, Chris had been a student in one of London's premiere art schools. But instead of a quiet career in painting, he quit college and cast his lot with the burgeoning music scene of the mid 1960's – all of the energy was focused there, and he couldn't resist. It would have been a truly crazy move except for one thing: the group he eventually formed included Steve Winwood. Barely eighteen, Winwood was already a star with the highly successful Spencer Davis Group – his vocal and instrumental skills unmatched in the UK. Having just quit that band, Winwood's options were nearly limitless; Eric Clapton and other superstars vied mightily for his attention.

Yet, Winwood would start again with a ragtag set of unknowns: Dave Mason – a guitar player whose most recent job had been as a band roadie, Jim Capaldi – a drummer whose first aspiration was to be a priest, and Chris – an introverted woodwind player. From the start they were quirky and unorthodox, and yet also capable of making amazing sounds. And this was before they finally settled on the name that would fit like a glove – 'Traffic'.

The challenges for Traffic were significant. Tasked with coming up with music that would satisfy a teenage audience while still meeting Chris's high standards proved difficult. Assuming the role of the band's conscience, he was constantly reminding the others to hold to the right road, to not lose their artistic integrity. But, before long, his anxiety skyrocketed as personality issues and soul-killing compromises threatened the enterprise. There was more – something even his band mates did not fully comprehend: Chris suffered from sometimes paralytic stage-fright. For someone intending to make a living performing music, this was of course a problem – one he was attempting to solve with alcohol and other drugs.

Meanwhile, Linda Eastman had recently crossed the Atlantic Ocean from her native New York with the goals of photographing the Beatles and Steve Winwood. Although only a minor figure in that world, she would charm her way into the press event for the *Sgt. Pepper's Lonely Hearts Club Band* album launch (attracting Paul McCartney's undivided attention).

But first she'd come to Aston Tirrold, taking Traffic to several locations and posing them in ways Chris deemed contrived. Envisioning the photos splashed across any number of teeny bopper magazines, he blanched. For Chris, fame by mere image was the worst, a form of artistic death; hence the abrupt departure from the pub.

Back at the cottage, he and Rosie settled onto cushions in front of a cold, blackened fireplace and talked about a chilling subject – the resident ghost. Rosie knew all about it and began by relaying the source of the haunting – a stable boy from early in the century; a lonely teenager, depressed by rural isolation, who finally committed suicide just yards away. She pointed her finger, "The bloke hung himself down that well. They had to destroy his dog too, 'cause it was tied to the well – howling for its master. They say that you can still hear the dog at times. Have you heard the dog howling yet?"

Chris, a man for whom the paranormal was merely 'normal', shook his head, "I haven't heard that, but we've got things that move around." Nodding toward the fireplace, above which a small ornament sat, he said, "It'll start in a minute – on the mantelpiece… it'll move in a minute." In the tense silence, the pair stared expectantly at the roughhewn block of wood until Rosie broke the tension, laughing, "No, it won't – 'cause *I'm* here!" Chris smiled back, "Are you frightened?" Summoning up something like her usual self-confident demeanor, Rosie responded, "No…but it *is* getting dark."

Soon a large cargo van, incongruously painted bright pink and bearing a strange wheel-like symbol on the side, rattled up the ruts and stopped next to the house. Out poured those Chris had left at the pub, Eastman included. She came over to Chris and Rosie, camera in hand, "What have you two been up to?" Still annoyed, his response was terse, "Nothing, we've just been sitting here, talking." But Eastman finessed a way around the impasse, asking to take a picture of Rosie and Chris together. Something shifted in Chris and he agreed. His guard suddenly down, the shudder clicked just as the two smiled with genuine warmth.

With night approaching, it was time for Rosie to go. Chris walked her and the dogs back to the path toward the village, as behind them cigarettes and candles were lit, and instruments tuned. Standing for a moment in the rutted tracks, Chris listened as she fretted that her dream of becoming a nurse might have to be cancelled due to issues at home. Like a knowing big brother, he leaned forward to leave her with an emphatic request, "Don't throw your life away Rosie – go back to school."

Returning to the others, Chris picked up his flute. Illuminated only by candle flame and then moonlight, shadows would soon dance around them with every movement. Initially formless and meandering, the sound eventually coalesced into *Morning Dew*, Bonnie Dobson's vision of a world broken by nuclear war. Eyes closed, Chris's raw emotions were gradually transformed to bittersweet notes, fluttering like a moth into the night.

Shifting from mood to mood, tune to tune, they would play until the dawn – as they often did. Despite the conflicts and contradictions, an undeniable synergy gripped these four whenever the music took hold; a strange amalgamation capable of conjuring magic. In the end, for Chris, it would come down to just that. Whatever the hassle and personal risk, Traffic's music was worth it all. For better or worse, he wasn't going anywhere.

CHAPTER ONE

THE BLACK COUNTRY

If you were a bird, and lived on high,

You'd lean on the wind when the wind came by,

You'd say to the wind when it took you away:

"That's where I wanted to go today!"

From *When We Were Very Young*, by A.A. Milne

(Taken from a forty third edition, published in 1946. Inscribed
in red ink on the first page by "Sir Christopher GB Wood")

*

Christopher Gordon Blandford Wood was born on June 24th, 1944, in Quinton, a suburb to the west of Birmingham, England. The first child of Stephen and Muriel Wood, his first dwelling was a small terraced home, only a few miles from still smoldering rubble left from the Nazi blitz which had pounded Birmingham for almost three full years.

A dimple-cheeked butterball as a child, Chris's brown hair and incredible blue eyes were a legacy of Stephen, while his facial features – revealed as the baby fat melted away – closely resembled Muriel's. Once ambulatory, family tales describe Chris as a four and then two legged explorer; a child seemingly bent on testing the limits of his boundaries.

The Woods were a middle class family when that stratum of society was still quite thin. Stephen Wood held a degree in architecture and his love of design and beautiful buildings would lead to a career as the Surveyor (Municipal Engineer) for the Borough of Rowley Regis. Even rarer for the time, Muriel was also college educated and professionally employed as a teacher of shorthand, typing and business skills at the local adult education center in nearby Dudley. Personality-wise, the couple were a study in contrasts; vivacious and quick-witted, Muriel sized up people and situations quickly, responding as she thought necessary, while Stephen was a typically reserved, quintessential Englishman, content to observe and analyze rather than immediately react.

With the birth of his sister, Stephanie Angela, when Chris was three, the family would be complete. Steph would share many of Chris's physical features as well as his sensitive, artistic nature – a younger, female near-twin. Chris would dote on his little sister, as well as being watchful and protective of her wellbeing as they grew up.

When Chris was about eight, momentous change came to the young family. With the need to rebuild post-war England from the ground up, new projects were sprouting throughout the country. As the Borough's Head Surveyor, Stephen's responsibilities included planning and the design of the county's infrastructure. In partial compensation for an otherwise marginal salary, the Woods were given use of a county-owned residence situated further west in Cradley Heath, across the M5 motorway near the town of Stourbridge.

Known as Corngreaves Hall, the residence was actually a huge nineteenth century dwelling built by one of the leading industrialists of the day. Taken over by the county in recent years, the three story, multi-roomed property topped with a single octagonal-shaped battlement held a view over the countryside. Surrounded by woods, fields and a nearby orchard, the evocative setting inspired the imagination and would stoke Chris's fantasy life. But outside the secure grounds of the Hall, another, more complex and sometimes dangerous world waited; a land known as 'The Black Country'.

Inspiring J.R.R. Tolkien's hellish vision of Mordor from the *Lord Of The Rings* books (written during this period), the Black Country easily invoked both imagination and dismay. In earlier days, the Industrial Revolution's earth-rending savagery had incalculably altered the landscape. With above ground seams of coal providing an abundant energy supply, the mix of mines, filth-belching factories, and back-breaking labor created the unique, if inhumane, environment which Tolkien would later shape into literature. An American visiting the area in the 1860's succinctly described a nightmarish visage of a land dominated by metal foundries running twenty four hours a day, "Black by day and red by night."

Post World War II, amid bomb craters and nearly depleted coal deposits, the region entered an uncertain twilight. Once proud (if soot covered) superstructures now fell into decay. Amid the surrounding farm fields and forested tracts, abandoned factories, derelict open pit mines, and still smoking slag heaps dotted the landscape.

Whatever the changes, the local working people quietly persevered; they'd been there a long time. The dialect spoken in the Black Country retains words and phrases popular since the Middle Ages, and embedded in the old culture were equally ancient traditions. It would also be one of the last places in England to give up the vestiges of a deeply superstitious past. Less than one hundred years before Chris's birth, a woman known as the 'Cradley Witch' still lived in a stone dwelling at a place called Dungeon Head. On the road leading to the local ironworks she spent mornings casting curses and threatening workers heading to work with spells of impending doom should they refuse to pay her 'protection fee'. Afterward she would turn her glare across the street toward the home of the factory owner – a place destined to become Chris's home – Corngreaves Hall.

Invariably, people who remembered Chris's childhood, recall him possessing two pronounced qualities – sensitivity and curiosity. Dissatisfied with pat or superficial explanations to nearly anything, from early on Chris would dig – either figuratively or literally – for answers. His need to uncover hidden truths likely arose within his own family, particularly in relation to his mother. A pale-skinned beauty, Muriel was by all accounts a generous and giving woman with an easy laugh. But her other side, especially her 'cutting' sense of humor, was one seemingly wielded as a form of self-protection. Muriel's barbed comments, emerging whenever she felt threatened, proved an effective means to put some emotional distance between herself and others – her own children sometimes included.

The roots of Muriel's complex personality were, of course, formed within her own childhood, which were by any measure extraordinary. Raised in a deeply religious home, her father was a Protestant minister, James A. Gordon. Incredibly, one day Gordon announced that the family would be moving to China with the intent, as Muriel later described it, of "converting the heathens." Swept away from her home and culture, the young girl soon found herself in an utterly alien environment. As exciting as it could have been, her years as part of the missionary service of the Plymouth Brethren Church (an ascetic sect believing in the imminent return of Jesus) proved more akin to captivity. The English children were expressly forbidden to make social contact with their Chinese counterparts, who, newly Christian or not, were considered very much inferior. As a result, Muriel's isolation was extreme. Perhaps hardest of all, when finally returning to England, the now teenage girl once again found herself considered a foreigner, this time in her own country. The period of readjustment was, to say the least, difficult.

The only artifact of that early era, one that served to inflame Chris's imagination, was a photograph of his grandfather. Taken sometime after the family's arrival in China, it showed a still youthful James Gordon dressed in Asian robes; sporting a traditional Chinese haircut with a frontally shaved head and braided pony tail, looking nothing at all like a proper Englishman. Although the photo would be examined many times over the years, in the end the enigmatic face – noticeably similar to Chris's own – would reveal no secrets.

If religion overshadowed Muriel's childhood, she and Stephen consciously chose to lighten the effect on their own children. Adopting the more mainstream Methodist approach to Christianity, henceforth church would be contained and partitioned. With the horror of war behind them and brighter days ahead, the children were encouraged to shape their own individuality and given nearly free reign to play and create – as long as they were within the safe sphere around Corngreaves Hall.

Chris's father encouraged the local birds with feeders, and Chris from an early age was fascinated by the singing creatures which possessed the ultimate state of freedom. Stephanie recalled that even then, the avian world was an important refuge for Chris, "It was wonderful; Chris was very keen on birds, a bird watcher from very young days onward. Maybe it was the fact that he was so shy and quiet – I think I can understand that. The animals and trees, they don't talk back, you can have a lovely relationship with them, and you've got no hassle. Whereas, the world that we live in…" Having developed a practiced eye and ear for the various species via bird books and binoculars, over time the fascination would only deepen. In their calls, songs and behaviors, Chris seemed to understand something about birds that most did not.

One of Chris and Steph's earliest friends was a girl named Nina Parkes. Having been a neighbor from Quinton, Nina's family kept in touch, and frequently visited Corngreaves Hall. She recalled the various strands of life there, "As kids, it was a super place to play – like living in a castle when you were little, it seemed enormous. There were always two dogs – two golden Labradors – the first were called Suzi and Caesar, they were followed by Apple and Cider. Stephanie got a pony that was called Macaroni, and that came from London. On Sunday we had to go to a kind of Sunday School – 'Crusaders', which Mrs. Wood ran. She was religious, but not as one would think today particularly religious – it was just part of her life. She was sociable, gregarious, a very strong woman, extremely vivacious, open speaking. And I think that the kids were a bit shy, as a reaction against that really."

The inspiring setting and lack of parental oversight unleashed a creative streak. Nina Parkes explained, "It was amazing, great big stone stairs, a great big hall with a stone floor…they had antique furniture, all the rooms were enormous – it was a bit like Hogwarts really, in Harry Potter! Chris sometimes had a friend who would stay the weekend, and they would wait until Steph and I were asleep and they would play 'ghostie games'. They would make 'wooh, wooh' noises and then wave a mop over the top of the door. It was a very nice childhood; we were left alone a lot. We were really close. We used to do Puppet Theater in the attic at Corngreaves Hall, and we'd sell tickets to the neighbors, and give a performance. That was good fun."

While sometimes shy and skittish around people he didn't know, among friends Chris was the opposite – gregarious, and quite mercurial, full of joy and exuberance, but also quick to react when slighted. Nina Parkes noted that the two sides were seemingly inseparable, "Chris was very temperamental – he used to fly off the handle for nothing at all. It was quite scary really – terrible, really oversensitive, very touchy. He would lose his temper for nothing, wouldn't speak for hours and sulk. Then, after hours or the next day, there'd be a twinkle in the eye, and a smile and a story. He had a most beautiful smile, it just transformed his face – a lovely smile from a very young age – it was magic, and he'd be alright again."

Another childhood friend, Peter Harris, also recalled the outbursts, but didn't always take them at face value, "He was always an actor. There were times when he really wanted his own way, and the rest of us kids weren't going to give it to him. It could have been as simple as something over where we were going to play or what we were going to do next – that sort of thing. He was one of the most expert people at putting on a stamping, screaming fit – tremendous theatrics, and high dudgeon: 'I'm never gonna play with *you* again', and this and that. He could do them like nobody else – they were very good! He was totally involved in it. When he decided to do this he was convinced, and mortified when you didn't believe him. He began to realize in the end that we were on to him, but it was wonderful while it lasted…"

The theatrical quality didn't come out of thin air – or perhaps it did. His favorite radio program, *The Goon Show*, mixed the wild, over-the-top acting of Spike Milligan, Peter Sellers and others with a deranged comedic style utterly unique for the time. Chris found the freewheeling madness gloriously funny – often dissecting episodes with friends. With his well-orchestrated fits of fury likely modeled on them, his acting skills would come in handy in the less safe outside world, beginning with school.

*

After primary years spent at Garry House School in Edgbaston, Birmingham, Chris attended Harborne Collegiate. It was a private, all-boys facility and the main advantage of Harborne seemed to be that it was a shade better than the local state schools. One of Chris's good friends there (and mostly likely the visitor mentioned by Nina Parkes) was a boy named Hugh Fraser. A successful movie actor in adult life, Fraser recalled little to commend the place, "We ended up in a sort of fee-paying school for the sons of the well-to-do, who didn't want them to go into the bottom end of the state system, which was really sort of horrendous, sort of 'Blackboard Jungle' kind of places. We were in this private school in the west end of Birmingham, in a fairly dilapidated old house. The staff were sort of dubious; outcasts who wouldn't last five minutes educating small boys these days."

Chris's initial reaction to the education provided by his inadequate teachers seems to have been a mental withdrawal. Becoming a diffident dreamer prone to looking out the window during class may have helped him cope, but problems would arise. Most telling was his penmanship – typically the pride of a proper English education, which never progressed much beyond a semi-intelligible scrawl. Worse, even rudimentary spelling and grammar remained stubbornly haphazard. He was, however, an excellent reader, and when interested in a given subject consumed books as if his life depended on it. Sparked by subjects related to history, biology and geology, at one point he was especially fascinated by metamorphosis, the mysterious process allowing creatures such as tadpoles and butterflies to utterly transform themselves upon maturity.

While utterly uninspired by his school, Chris did find a way to redeem his self-respect, and in his own way, fight back. Having already refined the art of play in the upper floor of Corngreaves, Hugh Fraser recalled that he and Chris teamed up to consciously, and very publically, skewer their instructors. "We survived it by taking the piss out of the teachers and doing impressions. We used to organize end of term shows where we would do impressions of them. Chris was very good at that – an extremely good mimic, and very witty. These end of the term shows that we put together hadn't really been done before. It was a dangerous thing to do, but we got away with it – mostly because Chris was so talented at the whole thing."

Music was also near the top of the list of things he loved, although his first attempt at playing didn't go well. Having always had a piano in the house (Muriel could play a little), Chris's banging attempts were interpreted as a serious interest and lessons were arranged. Apparently, the combination of a very young age (about 5), and his somewhat shorter than average finger length, made it an exercise in pure frustration for little Chris. His attitude deteriorating to the point of tantrums such that, ultimately, he would refuse to continue. Although he would later learn to play on his own, the lessons left a bitter and surprisingly lingering aftertaste. Driving by the teacher's house many years later with a friend who inquired about the lessons, Chris, who had neither forgotten nor forgiven, would only mutter, "I fucking hated it."

But listening was another matter. Methodically going through stacks of the family 78's, Chris put one after another on the huge gramophone as he intently absorbed the sounds. Big Band and crooners like Bing Crosby were often played, but Stephen also loved classical, so Beethoven and Brahms echoed through the corridors as well. As for the radio, while the diversity of music wasn't tremendous, by the mid-fifties the BBC was playing classical and light pop as well as some new sounds. In later years, he would recall hearing Bill Haley and the Comets this way – one of the first rock 'n roll bands.

Electronic devices in general proved fascinating, and he took joy in manipulating the invisible energy that flowed in and out of them. Peter Harris lived in a much smaller house situated within feet of Corngreaves Hall and was a friend from nearly the day the Wood's arrived. Harris recalled that Chris reveled in creating havoc with the walkie-talkie set he got for his birthday, "Almost from the first he found that it interfered with the VHF television that was currently being used for black and white at the time. It would either interfere with the sound or the pictures depending on how you tuned your walkie-talkie. So Chris's trick was to interfere with the picture – make it break up – and then actually if you just tuned it a little bit, you could make an apology for the picture on the sound channel of the T.V.! It was a good trick from the next room and for the neighbors as well. We got in a lot of trouble for that obviously."

The two would have many adventures in the coming months and years. Once, like an English Huck Finn and Tom Sawyer, they made a ramshackle raft to float the Avon River, which flowed past Corngreaves Hall. Unfortunately, dubious design and poor environmental quality made the travel far less romantic than envisioned, "We overturned more than once without drowning…it was an industrial sewer really; people dumped anything they wanted into it – industrial waste."

On solid ground, bicycles were the preferred mode of transport. Away from the protected grounds of home, the derelict legacy of the Industrial Revolution proved a huge attraction. Peter Harris recalled, "I don't know if we noticed the poverty, but what you did notice was the old factories. A lot of them would have a big wooden bar, right through the factory – from one end to the other – carrying pulleys, and a steam donkey engine driving that sort of machinery. The machinery would probably be gone, but outside you might see the rusty steam engine. And there were piles of foundry sand, piled up where the buildings were or where they'd been." Compelled to capture the impressions, Chris began carrying a sketchpad with him, stopping to furiously scribble outlines of the buildings and landscapes around him as they caught his fancy.

The need to understand, to discern 'truth' became an important, if often elusive goal during this period. At home he would silently wriggle into the ceiling crawlspace of the huge house and stealthily move around, observing and literally 'eavesdropping' on the habits and conversations of his family and the neighbors. This sly vantage point allowed him to develop a keen awareness of the dissonance between public and private discourse. The intimate knowledge of the house led him to believe that other types of entities might be living there as well. "We always believed that the house was haunted" Nina Parkes recalled, "We used to go in together and huddle! After dark, we used to dare each other to go up to the attic…we would usually go up in twos and threes."

The darkest aspect of a curious nature was revealed in what Chris was willing to ingest. Even in the earliest days, he would try almost anything just to see what would happen. His first experience with mind-altering chemicals began with the most accessible source. His father, Stephen, recalled Chris casually collecting half empty glasses after cocktail parties, and gulping down the remaining contents when he thought no one was looking. The initial childhood experiments with alcohol were only the first step. Peter Harris observed, "If there was some substance we weren't sure what it was – the person that would stick his finger in it and taste it was Chris. It's a wonder he wasn't poisoned. There wasn't any hanging back – it would be 'Oh what the hell let's do it.' Yeah, he always wanted to explore things."

Another profound life lesson would soon present itself. The tiny town of Padstow on the rocky coast of Cornwall quickly became first the family's holiday place of choice. In 1958, the Woods shared the trip with the Harris family. The intersection of the earth, sky and ocean was formative to Chris's psyche, inspiring his imagination. On this particular trip, the time was thoroughly enjoyed by all – at first – until the idyllic spell was broken when the families learned of a horrific accident that had occurred. Traveling too fast around a bend in the road a car driver had lost control and veered into a group of four girls waiting to be taken home from Sunday school. The two younger girls were killed, while the older two received severe injuries, including broken legs. Hearing of the tragedy Chris was horrified, and insisted on visiting the hospital, where he bonded with one of the girls. Peter recalled a compassionate side emerging, "This kid was having a hard time coping with it all, and Chris spent a long time with her on holiday. I think he ended up drawing all over her plaster cast – he was trying to make it humorous, to cheer her up. He was basically, underneath, as soft as a lamb."

*

As the 1950's played out, the teenage Chris Wood was maturing as well. Aided by his family's relative affluence, his tastes became increasingly sophisticated. Always well dressed, Chris now developed his own fashion sense. A Harborne class-mate, Bob Paul, recalled, "He was definitely sort of a leader, people gathered around him. He had that sort of personality that you came around. He did what he wanted to do. One morning he came in with a big cloak, like Batman! I remember going around with him to Birmingham, his mother had an account – 'cause they were quite well off, to the big clothing shops, and he had a credit card, and he bought a black and white striped jacket – in that period it was fashionable. He always stood out, clothes-wise – always very smart."

Hugh Fraser too recalled that Chris could be quite critical of those he thought on the wrong track – regardless of current trends, "We went to the pictures after school – I think we had a half day or something, and we'd arranged to meet a couple of people at the cinema. We arrived on the bus; we were in our school uniforms. We saw this other boy who'd been able to go home and change into this sort of 'Teddy Boy' outfit – which was the 'Elvis look', swept back hair and this overcoat with the broad shoulders, narrow waist, drainpipe trousers and crepe shoes. I said, 'God he looks good, doesn't he? And Chris was outraged – 'Oh *my god*, he looks dreadful, he looks awful!"

Local Birmingham music stores, like The Diskery on Hurst Street, became frequent haunts. There Chris voraciously listened to, and then accumulated records of all sorts and formats. He was particularly intrigued by imported 45's from obscure American companies. But it was his discovery of jazz – music from a universe impossibly distant from his own – which would change his worldview forever. Hugh Fraser observed, "We used to go to Birmingham city center after school and lurk around the record shops. Chris was interested in jazz – bebop, Miles Davis, Cannonball Adderly, Dave Brubeck. East coast and west coast jazz was his thing at that stage. *Nobody* else was interested in that sort of jazz at school. This was definitely something that he heard and discovered himself, and introduced me to it. Jazz and blues, Howling Wolf, Muddy Waters… He was always very interested, that and classical music. What he wasn't interested in was the pop music of the time."

In modern jazz, Chris found a musical style he could viscerally relate to. The African American Bebop style of Charlie Parker, Miles Davis and Dizzy Gillespie broke away from the obsolete WWII era Big Band/Swing and Dixieland jazz, creating an innately 'cool' approach with long, exploratory solos and introspective themes. U.S. jazz was different in another crucial way – by enfolding the emotions of long repressed Black culture into musical notes, the artists could convey every thread of their people's pain and joy with the utmost skill and sophistication. And yet it was all done in an instrumental *code* – telling all – but only to those truly in tune with the vibe.

CHAPTER ONE

Already steeped in the passions of European classical music, Chris's exploration led to a breakthrough of understanding: the musical expressions of the black jazz artists were fully equivalent to those of Beethoven and Mozart. Seeing all emotion-based music as part of a common human language, it now also became clear that race, time and geography were false divisions. The lesson would prove profound and life altering.

The inspiration to join this exclusive club – to play – now asserted itself. If the instrumental virtuosity of the jazz greats was intimidating, a specific performer and his instrument called to Chris's heart. Primarily the guitarist for Dizzy Gillespie's late 50's band, Les Spann also played the 'C' flute in a way that was mellow, lyrical and free spirited. Despite the limitations, Spann understood that the flute could be used to effectively paint contrasts. Woven around Gillespie's emphatic and much louder trumpet in songs like "Moonglow" and "I Found a Million Dollar Baby in a Five and Ten Cent Store", Spann's flute lines were the coolest part of a band that already defined 'cool'.

Interestingly, Chris would later declare that it was actually the *sound* of the flute, as opposed to any specific stylistic concerns that first attracted him. Indeed, the flute has perhaps *the* primordial place in the human expression of music: flute-like instruments made of bone have been found dating back at least 32,000 years. Like others before him, Chris understood that it mirrored the voice of nature, especially birds. He also intuited that the instrument was capable of hinting at another area he was very interested in – the supernatural.

Chris got his first flute in 1959. While loving the instrument, he still had to learn how to play it, a process which was not as smooth as he'd imagined; for those within earshot, his initial efforts bordered on excruciating. Nearly fifty years on, family friend Nina Parkes had no trouble recalling, "He used to practice, and he used to play jazz – and it was sounded ghastly – it was dreadful! We used to scream out: 'Oh no, don't do it again!' It was very painful, and he used to get very upset about it." Stung by the criticism but desperate to play, lessons were hastily arranged. His music teacher (from Harborne Collegiate) didn't actually play the instrument himself, so could offer only theory as to proper technique. But unlike the earlier hated experience with the piano, Chris's keen interest assured that he stuck with it. Hugh Fraser recalled, "There was a great deal of discipline in Chris at that time. He was very rigid about his scales and chords; he didn't just pick it up and start playing tunes. He really learned his instrument properly; he was a very serious musician."

Certain non-musical uses were discovered as well. By the late 50's the local pub used a television to lure locals with supper programming consisting of scary mystery stories. Densely wooded, the grounds of Corngreaves Hall sat perched above the main road to the pub. Awaiting their return, Chris would sit quietly amid the trees, instrument in hand. Peter Harris witnessed, "So, people would be seeing these kinds of dramas, and he'd wait until they were on their way back from the pub. Chris would sit there with his flute and start playing some really, really ghostly music. He'd play the flute and watch these people sort of look around, pull their collars up and their hats down, and scurry on up the road. He used to think it was tremendous fun – making it as ghostly as possible to frighten the wits out of them."

This ability to see comedic elements embedded in mundane life was impressive to close friends. As an adult Hugh Fraser would become a professional actor who worked with some of Britain's best comedians. Regarding Chris he said, "He was one of the warmest people I've ever known. And he was the funniest man I've ever known – without a doubt, the funniest human being I've come across – with a wonderfully lateral take on life, and people. We'd be in a department store after school, and we'd ask an assistant to demonstrate a record player or something, and Chris would pick up what was funny about this bloke and just riff on it. And then the impressions would start. It was at a time when humor wasn't like that – it was all about, 'Have you heard the one about the bloke that walks into the pub with a gorilla?' It was all jokes. Chris was able to do what Monty Python and people like that did, much later, and very successfully – a sort of lateral humor. Chris was extremely talented in that way."

While the mix of interests and talents in his mid-teen years were all well and good, a quandary also emerged. With adulthood approaching, a career path needed sorting out and his father's line of work was initially somewhat appealing. As a municipal planner, Stephen's job required both creativity and a fine hand to create detailed plans for government-owned buildings. Perhaps wanting to placate his parents, Chris indicated that architecture and civil engineering was indeed the direction he wanted to go.

But there was a problem; while genuinely interested in architecture, Chris's eye was actually drawn toward the opposite end of the spectrum from his highly disciplined father – with the crumbling, decaying Black Country buildings proving the most interesting of all. How this could be parlayed into a career was unclear. Despite the conflict, there was still time to sort it all out – or so he thought.

In 1960 a tidal wave, in the form of a movie, swept over England. An unlikely success, Bert Stern's *Jazz On A Summer's Day*, a documentary of the 1958 Newport Jazz Festival, proved a hit with musically-oriented teens almost immediately upon release. A photographer and jazz lover but merely a novice film maker, Stern approached the festival impressionistically. Juxtaposing the nearby Rhode Island coastline (and an ongoing yacht race) with frequent shots of smiling, appreciative fans, for the first time the true context of a great jazz event had been captured on film. With artists ranging from iconic old jazz masters – Louie Armstrong, Anita O'Day and Dinah Washington, to the young turks of the next generation such as Gerry Mulligan, Chico Hamilton, and Sonny Stitt, to R&B (Big Maybelle), and even rock 'n roll (Chuck Berry), *Jazz On A Summer's Day* was groundbreaking – and eye opening. With nearly every performance stellar – if not outright definitive, the movie portrayed American jazz at its most attractive and compelling. For many English youth, *Jazz* proved a siren's call, not just to the music, but to lifestyle that looked to be the hippest of all.

Seemingly timed to have a maximum effect on Chris's developing psyche, *Jazz* had the whole package – the setting, the clothes, the music, and an implicit sense of knowing. Especially significant was the performance of "Blue Sands" by the Chico Hamilton quintet. Based around percussion and flute (played by Eric Dolphy), the music was absorbing to the point of entrancement, allowing Chris to visualize the power of the instrument he himself was learning. With the full gravity of the performance demanding multiple viewings, he dragged friends along to share the experience. Hugh Fraser was one, "He took me. That was a kind of dawn at the wall-to-wall grayness of Birmingham in the late '50's. It's impossible to describe how drab and bleak the whole experience was. The film was a kind of beacon of possibility, and I think he was attracted to that sort of lifestyle."

While the burning desire was real, the reality of life in the Midlands in 1960 forced it back into a smolder – Chris's career path was one likely to land him in a starched shirt. But then, one day, it was announced that his reviled school, Harborne Collegiate, had collapsed into bankruptcy and would close. An unforeseen gift from the gods now in his lap, Chris pushed his parents to allow a left turn – he wanted to go to art school. If initially unmoved by his emphatic, then emotional pleadings, he had an ace in the hole. Emerging from his room with his sketch books, he let them flip through the pages. Muriel appreciated the passion, while Stephen noticed the talent – and the path was opened.

His available option was the Stourbridge College of Art. While not especially prestigious, its emphasis on glass allowed graduates to find employment at the local glassworks – a working class, or sometimes better way to make a living. It was also a place where misfits and counter-culture kids came to sort out their less certain futures.

In the Fall of 1961, suited up in his best sport coat and tie, briefcase in hand, Mr. Christopher Wood stepped off the bus and walked in the front door of the Stourbridge College of Art. Primed by his exploratory sketches of the Black Country, an innate aptitude soon emerged, one which came as a bit of a shock to his classmates. Bob Paul recalled, "He was better than we thought. He had several of his paintings hung up around the College – of industrial scenes, the local industry. They were very good. I was quite surprised, because I didn't really think he was that good at art – fine art, but he surprised us."

Working as if he had something to prove, by the end of that year Chris's paintings were not just good, in the sense of figurative accuracy, but memorable and distinctive. One classmate remembered, "His work was quite unique really – they were very, very direct." Paul, too, recalled a character to the art that defied a narrow category, "He developed a peculiar style, I can't explain it - it was realistic, not abstract. I remember one that he did of the butcher's shop at High Street in Stourbridge – with the meat hanging up. There was another industrial scene that he did – local industry, with chimneys – very vivid colors that he used – reds, greens, yellows, and burnt umbers, sienna's. I don't know if they still exist, but they were hung around the college in the corridors – I think the lecturers were quite impressed."

Regardless, Chris was often – even typically – unhappy with the final product. As prolific as he was, many of his works (early and later) were sooner or later scraped off the canvas, painted over or simply thrown away. As a result, almost none exist today.

One of the few that did survive (also against Chris's wishes) is an early painting of the woods next to Corngreaves Hall. Using earthy colors – mostly greens, and browns, he created a close-view frame – branches and leaves, with small patches of light filtering through to dapple the trees. While unsophisticated at first glance, he did manage an interesting trick – in the arrangement of the foliage, the dimensionality of the space is somehow suggested. Viewed up close, it feels as if one is actually standing among the trees.

That *this* particular painting exists today was only due to Brenda Harris's instant attachment to it. Watching Chris create it, she loved that the piece actually captured the essence of the place where they all lived. Pointing to it on her wall she said, "There's dear Christopher's picture. He painted that. He sat down the drive there, and (pointing) looked across, and there were all these trees. I love it. My dear, he was going to scrape it all off and re-use the canvas! And I said: 'I'll buy it off you, don't do that!' Her affection for the painting had not dimmed with time – it hung on the wall of her living room for fifty years.

THE MUSIC OF EMOTION

Steve Hadley arrived at the college the year before Chris. Working toward a teaching degree in art instruction, the slightly built, blond-headed Hadley also happened to be a 'natural' musician, capable of listening intently and then playing what he heard on a keyboard. By the age of fifteen, he had been deemed proficient enough to serve as the organist for his church, Causeway Green Methodist, in Stourbridge. But his ears were open to the secular world as well. Against the grain of his conservative Christian upbringing, Hadley was impressed by modern jazz and R&B. Worse yet, he harbored a secret love for the frenetic rock 'n roll of Jerry Lee Lewis.

Chris first met Steve downstairs in the Students' Common Room, which contained a decrepit piano set in the corner. While anyone could, and did, bang on it – Hadley's impromptu twelve bar blues romps caught Chris's ear. He listened for a bit before approaching Steve, motioning for some room on the bench. With Steve sitting on the left, and Chris on the right, the hated piano lessons suddenly paid off as stomping blues echoed across the room. Steve Hadley remembered that first session, "He had a reasonable command of the piano with his right hand. I did accompaniment – both hands – on the lower half, and he'd play the top half. The other students enjoyed it, it became a party piece around every break – we would entertain them. We made, for then, a respectable sound; of course it all rotated around the blues. And from this we grew very, very close musically."

Bonding over a common lexicon of R&B and jazz, Chris had already begun to take a stand, partly on principle and occasionally just to be contrary, against popular music. His passion, 'Modern Jazz', was defended at every opportunity. Discovering tastes very much in sync, soon Steve would accompany him on the bus after school to Corngreaves Hall, where they pored through the record collection. Here the bluesy American piano jazzers – Thelonius Monk, Dave Brubeck, Horace Silver, and Oscar Peterson, were listened to then discussed, as well the saxophone greats, especially Cannonball Adderley, and the British sensation – Tubby Hayes.

But above all, one artist captivated them both – Ray Charles.

The impact of the blind American was hard to overstate. A musical dynamo, Charles was a force of nature – singing, as well as playing piano and alto sax. He also he wrote and arranged the music, all the while managing to look impossibly cool with his ever present black shades, and sequined jackets. At the top of his game in the early 1960's, his unique blend of R&B, Soul, and Gospel was pure musical intoxication. Chris had Charles albums, but had recently gotten hold of a 'live' recording, the seven inch EP – *Ray Charles at Newport*, which they played incessantly. Songs such as "The Night Time Is The Right Time", and "I Got A Woman", and "Talkin' Bout You" hit hard with a bluesy, funky sound. Just as important was Charles's voice – alternately low and sexy, or wailing to a joyous shout. The emotional appeal overlaid by a flat-out coolness proved irresistible – Ray Charles had it all.

As the afternoon trips to Corngreaves continued, they gravitated to the Woods' piano – a fine Steinway sitting in the living room. It was there that Hadley discovered Chris's more serious instrument, "He was playing flute, and he was accomplished enough to play jazz, and to improvise quite freely." In short order, a nascent though purposeful musical duo emerged. Though inexperienced, as Hadley recalled, their ambitions were high – to somehow crack the musical magic of their hero. "He (Charles) gave us a tremendous appetite for Blues-Rock-Jazz, We were able to perfect some of his little 'bluesy' riffs and runs – and we began to swing our way through many of his numbers."

With some disciplined rehearsal behind them, the pair now returned to the lunch break crowd at the Commons room of the college – and their classmates were shocked. What weeks before had been little better than a shaky blues parody had transformed into something much, much better. With Steve's runs on the keyboard exuding confidence and control while Chris fluttered and soared next to him on flute, their classmates not only applauded but wanted more. Gratifying, the reaction was also a crucial stimulus to keep at it, to go further.

A parallel path of partnership, assimilation and growth was also emerging in Chris's artistic life. Among his classmates, an open-faced 'Black Country' youth named Trevor Jones stood out. Possessing an innate gift in figurative drawing and painting, Jones was the best graphic artist at the school at the time. Frequently circling around to watch him work, Chris was soon peppering him with questions and comments. But before long Jones became aware of Chris's own distinctive artistic approach, "I had more of what people would call a 'natural talent', but the thing is, Chris had this other sort of thing which is, in a way, more valuable – which was an incredibly fertile imagination."

Many years later Trevor still treasured a sketchbook Chris left behind, one that reminded him of his friend's distain for pointless orthodoxy. "And I still look at it, with a sort of envy, at the thought of the things he tried to work with. I mean, he was envious of me, but I was envious of the other quality that he had. His paintings – he would paint with anything! (Today) everybody sort of paints with household paints and stuff, but at the school we went to, it wasn't allowed – you would use the traditional oil paints which were properly in tubes. He'd want to know what happened when you used Haversol gloss with it, or paraffin, or whatever. He'd throw it all in – it was that sort of 'breaking the rules', at that simple level, that he enjoyed doing. Of course, they were there to be broken."

Personality-wise, Jones was a study in moderation compared to the wilder Chris – a straight-arrow who neither drank nor smoked. But the differences would soon prove a strength – they drew as close as brothers. As a result Chris came to rely on Trevor's dependable, clear-headed nature; he would be one of the very few that Chris would ever share his inner thoughts with.

But there was another person whose artistic opinion Chris valued above all – a man named John Walker. Only a few years older, Walker had set out, with some struggle, to make a career from teaching. With a family to support, Walker's part-time position at the SCA provided only the most meager living. And yet he taught with a zest and enthusiasm that drew in and infected both Chris and Trevor. His credo was simple – a straightforward question, cutting to the core of artistic expression, "How do you imbue a square with feeling?" Like a Zen Master, he confronted each student, looking for those who had understood. In Chris's case, the connection was there. John Walker recalled, "People have been doing that, since god knows when – and he seemed to know *that* was the challenge." His other nugget of wisdom also hit home because it entwined painting with Chris's musical talent, "I used to say, 'listen to the sound of your brush – don't stick any music on, or in your ear, just listen to the sound of the brush – its music!' He (Chris) was very aware of that. If you can't hear yourself, how can you create these moods?"

Informally at first, Walker took Trevor and Chris on as his charges, showing by example that a career in art could be worthwhile. Especially enticing to Chris were weekend trips to Walker's home in a rural village outside Birmingham. The Lickey Hills, an area of rolling topography, fields, marshes and woods, was quirky enough to have previously served as Tolkien's model for the Shire. Trevor Jones recalled, "We both used to go up there…he had a studio, and he was struggling away. And in fact (in later years) he made it – he's quite famous. But me and Chris used to go visit him on Sundays – just to look at him: *So this is what you do, is it?*" Walker's bucolic lair helped seal the deal for Chris. The lifestyle seemed to have it all: creative work surrounded by friends and family, grounded in the beautiful countryside, but with the excitement of the city not far away.

If Chris was sure of John Walker, the opposite certainly was not true. While appreciating his potential, Walker noticed a rather delicate psyche in Chris; one very much needing support. Emotionally closer to a boy than a man, the artistic skills and ready smile came bundled with an incongruous lack of self-confidence. Walker had a clear recollection, "He was a *kid*. I'll never forget him, because he was such an innocent – and he wasn't very sure of himself, either physically, or in his art. And you had to keep reassuring him that he was okay."

If art was the sun around which Chris's life currently revolved, music was certainly his moon, and the conflict between them, if mostly subconscious, had already emerged.

Culturally, music now proved a force impossible to ignore – a flood of foreign, mostly American groups pouring into England in the past few years had changed everything. A UK ban on foreign bands, started in 1933 (Louis Armstrong was the last through) by the British Musician's Union kept American and other groups out until 1956. While individual artists were allowed (backed by British musicians), foreign groups were deemed to take work from the natives. As a result, many of the great American jazz and R&B bands were heard on record, or radio, but never seen. Lacking the visual, the imagination of youth created a mythological view of American music. *Jazz On A Summer's Day* capped this phase, its sights and sounds captivating many a budding musician, Chris very much included.

With the restrictive ban now at an end, nearly every well-known group that played London also hit Birmingham. Stan Kenton and his Orchestra was the first American ensemble to play there in '56, at Birmingham's Town Hall. Other performers followed – Duke Ellington, Count Basie and his Orchestra, and so on. The pent-up demand proved overwhelming – people were nearly ravenous to see performers previously known only from records. The sudden exposure also encouraged many British musicians to form bands of their own.

It was at the Odeon Cinema that Chris saw his first major jazz show, and it was huge. If the impact of Ray Charles's records had been incalculable, actually seeing him proved almost too much. Having sent away for tickets, and spent weeks in anticipation, Chris's reaction in the actual venue came before Charles even opened his mouth. As the rhythm section vamped and the blind musical genius was led to his place on the arm of one of the band members, the young fan's eyes welled with tears; the frail humanity juxtaposed against a radiant musical soul, hit him like a punch. Hadley recalled the reaction, "Chris nearly fainted with the emotion of it. It was such a powerful image, and Chris just couldn't get his breath – he was really taken with it." The rocking, soulful show that followed merely confirmed everything the two suspected: Charles's preeminent position was unassailable.

Filled with enthusiasm, Chris and Steve met again the next day at 'The Royal Turf', a small pub down an alley off Stourbridge's High Street for a serious talk. After much discussion, they decided it was time to put a real group together. The logical format – a quartet – would allow both Steve and Chris room to solo, while keeping the sound rooted in rhythm. If that was as far as either could envision a musical future, it was enough for now.

The first recruit was Eddie Davis, a local drummer who had already played with several groups, including the local blues legend, Perry Foster. Then came Dave Higginbotham, a friend of Hadley's who played standup double bass. But there was one more instrument Chris decided was absolutely crucial: tenor saxophone. Although he had barely touched one previously, he loved the sound, and rather than bring in another musician, Chris decided to take it on. Besides giving the blues-based jazz band greater musical options, he knew the sax would add power, expression and a wider palate of color to the band.

Steve was there the day he got it, "I went with him. He bought a Conn (an American brand favored by jazz players) with a polished aluminum mouthpiece from George Clay's in Birmingham." Costing around 150 Pounds, more than a month's salary for the average worker of the time, it was surely a major sacrifice, but Chris's excitement often had a way of swaying his parents. Exiting the music store with the instrument in his hands, Steve Hadley laughingly recalled the return trip to Stourbridge, "I remember him, bringing it on the bus and playing it on the top deck as we were traveling home... honking away."

Unlike the flute, Chris never bothered with lessons, which is not to say that he didn't take the saxophone seriously – it became a removable extension of his own body. Going on intuition and what sounded right, he would practice obsessively as well as examining every aspect of the sax's physical structure to unlock its secrets. "I think the flute came out occasionally", Hadley recalled, "but it was the tenor sax that he tended to play more than any other instrument. He very, very quickly mastered it really; because he had the knowledge of the flute...we'd do some lovely blues."

With only minimal practice behind them, the group was ready to proudly deem themselves 'Modern Jazz' players. Drummer, Ed Davies recalled the fledgling musicians quickly adopting an attitude, "As far as jazz is concerned, there was a kind of snobbishness. Modern jazz musicians would feel superior. There was a lot of traditional jazz on the radio – Acker Bilk, Kenny Ball and the Jazz Men, Terry Lightfoot and Chris Barber. All these were national names...and there was a feeling among the traditional followers that they were elitists. But the modern jazz people thought that they were even *more* elite; possibly because the music was much superior in technique and far more difficult to understand." In later years Chris would be less charitable about where the band was really at, telling *DownBeat* (a jazz magazine), "We thought we were playing jazz, but we were really doing 12-bar blues."

Whether truly blues or jazz, by April, the band felt ready for a debut. Unfortunately the available venues were few and far between. Essentially it came down to one – 'The Saracens Head', in nearby Dudley. Like many small music venues in England, it was just a pub with a small stage. But at least this place sided with the 'elitist' jazzers – if only for one night a week. Tuesday evening was set aside for 'Jazz For Modern's', presenting tunes by a local semi-pro band. The second floor held the stage and listening area, and it was here that a group called The Jazz Vendors held a residency of weekly gigs. Studying the situation, Chris and Steve discovered a possible route in. The Jazz Vendors did two sets, with a short break (the 'interval') in between; it was this gap they hoped to fill. As nonchalantly as possible the two approached the proprietor, handing him a newly printed group card before quickly pivoting to the crucial question, "Can we do the interval spot?" To the surprise of both, an audition was granted; the following week, they would play.

A nervous SHQ showed up early. Bringing along both the flute and tenor, Chris fidgeted mightily throughout the Jazz Vendors first set, his foot tapping rapidly enough to vibrate the floor. Once on stage they went for a crowd pleasing set, opening with "Take Five" by Dave Brubeck, then "Movin' On" – Ray Charles's take on Hank Snow, before wrapping up with an exuberant "What'd I Say." With the Jazz Vendors nodding as they sipped pints nearby, the boys would take their leave to applause, if mostly from school friends brought along for support. Having done their best, they could only hope it was good enough. It was – they were asked to return the following week, and the next.

While thrilled, Hadley could only chuckle in recalling the cold reality of their status, "We weren't paid to play; in fact, it was only after a few weeks that they decided not to charge *us* the entrance fee, even though we were playing the interval!" Regardless, the Quartet was soon deemed worthy of their own residency alongside The Jazz Vendors at the Saracens Head, a gig kept for the better part of a year.

The height of the Hadley bands' fame would come the next year. In the fall of '63 they would be written up with a major article in the local newspaper, entitled, "The music of emotion: Modern Jazz, like the original Negro worksongs depends more on feeling than technique." Featuring a photo of the band at the Saracens Head, the article made a serious attempt to understand modern jazz from the perspective of teenage musicians. Articulate and insightful, Chris would strive to explain what the music meant to him, "Jazz of course is a matter of self-expression and I suppose self-tuition. It is a creative thing, like painting. Improvisation is what makes it what it is. It is superior to 'pop' music because it is essentially creative; a genuine art, aside from the techniques. Of course, you must have the technique, but jazz is nothing unless you have something over and above that. The greatest jazz musicians have this feeling, this emotion…"

This would be as close as Chris ever came to laying out his philosophy and approach to making music. With already firm ideas about 'pure versus commercialized' musical paths – his preference was unambiguous and would never waver. But amid the revelations lay a significant downside he failed to mention. As important as playing music had become to him, it came with a cost – stage fright.

Hadley, of course, knew from very near the beginning, "He was a *very* nervous person…particularly when he had to play. He found it quite difficult to come to terms with playing in public until he was there and ready to do it. But once he started, he was okay." Hadley was also aware of a "permanent tremor" in Chris's hands or feet, another indication of discordance with an otherwise easygoing exterior. But, for Chris, having chosen to become intimate with music, from that day forth the paradox would remain – it was a relationship split equally between love and fear.

('Traffic Jam', Hohman and Townley, DownBeat, 1/30/1975)

('Music of Emotion - Modern Jazz like the original Negro worksongs, depends more on feelings than technique', Birmingham Post, 10/23/1963)

A KID NAMED STEVIE

With the school year at an end, Chris launched into his unscheduled summer with semi-planned abandon. His friendship with Hadley was at its height and the two pondered a 'road trip' on Steve's motorcycle. But where? Chris's interests in Britain's history and landscape meant he had a collection of maps already marked with places to explore. Laying one out on the dining room table at Corngreaves Hall the two debated, but ultimately couldn't decide. But the solution proved simple. Lips pulled into a tight smile, Chris stood over the map, pulled a coin out of his pocket and flipped it into the air. Rolling east, it would finally stop at the jagged border between land and sea – fate had decreed Gedney Drove End as their destination – a location about as remote and desolate as could be. And once there, they would be roughing it, their tent pitched only yards from the pounding, misty ocean and flocks of skittered shorebirds.

Steve later mused on the location, and his friend, "To say this place was remote was an understatement. We crossed the fens on the border of Lincolnshire, and with some creative map reading arrived at this god-forsaken part of England. There was a haunting quality about it. Chris had a *very* unusual outlook on life, even at that stage. And he was always prepared to do unusual things, he had a great feeling for the ethereal; he'd pick up an atmosphere…"

Back home in Stourbridge, Steve sometimes took Chris along to the Sunday evening services at Causeway Green Methodist Church, where he'd been the organist for a number of years. Ray Charles made his mark taking gospel hymns out into the secular world, and it was a connection Chris quickly made as well. Hadley recalled, "He enjoyed the non-conformist hymn singing - particularly the old Moody and Sankey type hymns – which had an American flavor and swing to them. The seventh interval chord was used a lot, in a very similar way to the Southern Baptist tradition. Chris would sing blues lines over the melody of the hymn tune. He was a bit like myself really, in that the spiritual thing spoke through music, rather than words." Between music and the ambiance of the church, Chris' emotions were close to the surface, and he was sometimes brought to tears.

Then there were the days when they sought out a spirit of a different sort, which Chris was equally interested in. Hadley recalled, "We had a day out on the motorcycle and ended up at an old cider house called 'Ripperidge'. It was a rough old place – we went in and ordered two pints of the best. The locals looked at each other and seemed to know what the result would be; after some time we staggered out and drove off into the North Worcestershire countryside."

While already acquainted with alcohol, even early on, Chris's suitability for it was questionable. His one non-drinking friend, Trevor Jones, saw how Chris used drink to fit in socially. "I witnessed him getting bought round after round, and not being able to cope with it – and literally going to the loo, sticking his fingers down his throat and bringing it all back up. And on the way back to the table, he'd order another pint." While Trevor was also bought multiple rounds, his would simply accumulate on the table. Wanting to reach out to his friend, he knew that Chris's insecurity sometimes overwhelmed his reason. "I'd think 'you don't have to do that Chris, you really don't have to…', but there was part of him that didn't want to be shamed – to be part of a gang. And he wasn't that sort of bloke – (he was a) middle class lad, very sensitive…"

Musically, by mid-1962, the scene was heating up in the big city of Birmingham. One place that often had something going was a pub called The Chapel. Located in the city center, The Chapel became known for its Saturday afternoon 'jam sessions', attracting some of the better players in the area. One of these was a young jazz drummer named Pete York. While having played enough to pick up a sophisticated 'swing' style, York was still looking to improve his chops, and The Chapel jams had proved fertile ground.

One Saturday, York noticed a kid in 'short trousers', at the pub, accompanied by an older boy. When told that the kid was Stevie Winwood, and his brother Mervyn (known as Muff) and they actually had a musical group – The Muff Woody Jazz Band, he had to restrain a snicker – thinking it perhaps someone's idea of joke. As he recalled, "So Steve (Winwood) came to this Saturday jam session, where all the 'hot' players of Birmingham – as we thought of ourselves then - probably none of us very good, but were all playing in this place. And this kid comes in, with short trousers, and Muff says, 'Can my brother play with you?' And we said: 'We don't know, *can he*?'"

Head down and determined, at thirteen years old, 'Stevie', a local boy from the Handsworth section of Birmingham showed the experienced jazz players that he knew their language – and more. Pounding out a medley of tunes that seemed to contain all of the great jazz influences of the time – Art Tatum, Ray Charles, *and* Oscar Peterson, the young Winwood demonstrated an surprising, if not shocking, technical competency. While he came from a musical family (his father was a semi-professional musician), that alone failed to account for the style and virtuosity on display.

The demonstration proved so powerful that something akin to a religious conversion ensued among the gathered musicians. York still spoke of it with a sense of wonder more than forty years later, "And he sat down and played the piano. At our tender age, we thought we knew something about it all...But he played so far above our expectations. For a young guy, he *swung;* he played all the right notes. To improvise, using the right notes...there was nothing... you couldn't pick any holes in it whatsoever. It was great." From there, the legend spread rapidly. Soon Winwood was *the* talk of the Birmingham jazz/blues scene.

Meanwhile, Chris Wood and Steve Hadley were also making semi-regular visits into Birmingham to keep up with the latest sounds. Hearing about The Chapel sessions, they stopped in to give it a go themselves. Playing their bluesy set in Birmingham for the first time, it went over well, but as they finished, a youth unknown to either appeared. Steve Hadley recalled, "I was with Chris the first time he met Steve Winwood. I'd heard of him before I saw him play – he was the up-and-coming jazz man of the age. So I was on piano, sitting in with the band, and this young chap came along and asked if he could have a sit in, and I said, 'of course, certainly!' It was only later, when he played, that I realized who he was."

But as he stepped aside, Hadley noticed a smiling Chris walk over to confer with the young keyboardist, who then motioned for him to remain. Moments later Chris's flute would soar over Stevie's piano runs as a jazzy tune took flight. Observing the jam between the now recognized Winwood and his musical partner, Hadley couldn't help being impressed, as well as a tad envious, "I have to say that he was better than me. He was more mature in his jazz playing. I was still very blues orientated, but he was beginning to launch out into more melodic stuff. He was obviously some kind of jazz prodigy, you know – there was no one there at the time with the same kind of ability. In fact, he gave me some advice on chord structure..."

While Steve and Chris would excitedly return to see the young 'prodigy' in the near future, Hadley would eventually come to realize that Winwood's musical magnetism held a stronger pull for Chris than for himself, "I went on a few times with him, but then other things happened and Chris was going there on his own and meeting Steve regularly. I think I went for another two or three weeks and I realized that it wasn't my scene, and I bowed out gracefully."

CHAPTER FOUR

'HE JUST BELIEVED IT...'

By the end of their second year at SCA, Chris and Trevor were urged by John Walker to apply to the Birmingham College of Art to finish their degrees. Only an adjunct instructor at SCA, Walker had been shuttling back and forth, working at both colleges. Having seen the potential in both young men, he took it on himself to smooth the way for the move to the bigger (and better) school. Walker's mentorship proved crucial; he alone understood that the Birmingham College was the key to where they really needed to go – graduate school in London.

This was truly strategic, because the last step in this potential chain of events – working as a professional artist – was only likely if Chris and Trevor did their academic work in a nationally acclaimed setting. Three schools provided this opportunity and they were all in London: The Royal College of Art – the most prestigious school, followed by The Royal Academy of Art, then Slade. A degree from any of these held the promise of a real career in art, a status few who remained in Stourbridge would attain. Still, proving themselves in the next year would be critical.

The Birmingham College of Art was England's first municipal Art College. Built in the Victorian Gothic style in 1885, the reddish cast of the bricks stood out among the more utilitarian buildings on Margaret Street, and it remains to this day an impressive building. Upon acceptance to the BCA, Chris's first assignment was to produce art over the summer to present that fall. As usual, Trevor joined him. "All these old buildings and chimneys and stacks, all from that period, he used to love that. We would go hunting for those things, photographing old chain works, mills, things like that. And I know that when I wasn't with him, he did that by himself. He'd become fascinated, read about them, and look into them. He went through a phase where he literally wandered about the country, visiting these old places."

Arising from a mix of intellectual curiosity and his emotions, Chris's interests were expanding. Trevor recalled that mysteries of the past were especially important, "He had a phase where he got totally interested in the American Civil War. I remember him telling me what an awful war it was – civil wars usually are – but that he was troubled by what Americans did to Americans. I can remember him having photographs of that, and talking about it. He was a bit like that – like the ghost hunting – he would focus on it, and get quite intense about it."

It all fed back into the summer's art assignment that Chris and Trevor took quite seriously, "The amount of hours, and times we spent together painting...we'd hide pictures in the woods, and go out the next day and paint them – it was nice. The first time we turned up in Birmingham, I can remember the rest of the students being bewildered: 'where are these two guys coming from, why do they have all this work?'"

Once settled in at school, Chris met another incoming student named Christine Perfect. An outgoing blonde, in later years she would be known as Christine McVie, a member of the mega successful rock group Fleetwood Mac. Even at this point, however, she had played in bands including a blues/folk duo with a guitar player named Spencer Davis. As with Steve Hadley, Chris introduced himself when he heard her play the canteen piano by sitting next to her on the bench. With music again serving as his 'ice breaker', Chris soon had a whole new set of friends.

One of these friends was Paul Medcalf. Thin, pale and possessing a dense shock of black hair, Medcalf was also a painter. Discovering music tastes that overlapped nicely, soon Chris and Paul were tight, roaming the local clubs, pubs and concert halls together. Luckily for them, it was an incredibly fertile period. From 1963, and into '64, scenes were heating up on every front in the bigger cities of England, especially in Birmingham and London. While trad jazz was dying on the vine (though some practitioners didn't know it yet), modern jazz, blues, R&B, and rock 'n roll were all accessible to anyone with an open mind and a few quid in their pocket.

More than forty years later Medcalf remained amazed by the sheer magnitude and eclecticism of the musical tide that swept through Birmingham, "The concerts were incredible then! I can remember going to see people like Muddy Waters, NJQ, Dave Brubeck – 'Take Five' was a number one hit in England. We'd go see people like Segovia, yeah, Ella Fitzgerald, Stan Getz, Booker T and the MG's – we were all over the place! Ray Charles, of course, the Beatles were just coming through…And we got the huge 'package tours', blues package tours usually headed by Sonny Terry and Brownie McGee – Chris would have gone to loads of those. People like Reverend Gary Davis, Rosetta Tharp, Sleepy John Estes – you know, people they found after 'donkey's years' – Lightning Hopkins, B.B. King. We saw Buddy Guy, he was unknown in England – all we knew was that he was a blues player. The 'regulars' would bounce down from London – Georgie Fame and the Blue Flames, Graham Bond – who Chris worked with later on. Of course, he (Bond) had Jack Bruce and Ginger Baker. I can remember seeing John Lee Hooker, backed by John Mayall, at Aston Tech, in 1963… Rod Stewart with the Hoochie Coochie Men, probably with Elton John on keyboards, Inez and Charley Fox, Ike and Tina…"

The art school even had a resident musical group – the Muff Woody Jazz Band. Paul Medcalf recalled, "They played a kind of jazz, and a bit of blues – but mainly jazz. As the art college 'band', they'd play all the 'Hops', as they called them – which were about every month or so, and they played the Art College Ball, which was a big yearly thing. Chris would see a lot of these…" Although they had no records out, Muff Woody did have a powerful draw in their piano player – Steve Winwood.

While it might not seem possible to experience so much nightlife and get any schoolwork done, the system of the day proved quite lax. With the horror and restrictions of the World War II era finally lifted, Art Schools throughout England, particularly in Birmingham and London, responded with a 180 degree philosophical turn. As Medcalf explained, "Art school was an incredible free, free experience at that time – we were (in) the last years, doing our particular (method). We were pretty much left alone. We did lots of drawings of the model, a couple of days a week. For three days of the week we could do what we liked! In fact you know, we were playing Bob Dylan in the studios – records, all the time, and Chris would get his flute out a lot."

The juxtaposition of art and music was in fact having a synergistic effect on the creative bent of youth throughout England – a cultural force that cannot be overstated. Many, many bands of the near future would be populated by ex-art students, including members of the Rolling Stones, Beatles, the Who, the Kinks, Pink Floyd, the Pretty Things, and untold others.

Another aspect of the newly liberalized culture was emerging; the societal subgroup labeled 'Beatniks' were slowly morphing into something as yet un-named – distinguished by longer hair and colorful clothing. A public square with a fountain near the college was a meeting place for the proto-hippies, who would sneak off to covertly smoke a little marijuana. Chris's curiosity naturally required a look. Medcalf explained, "I got on pretty good with Chris, 'cause we both liked blues and jazz – which was a bit unusual at the time. And we both liked to drink, and we both liked a bit of hash and grass – which was also pretty unusual back then, you know, I'm talking about '63."

Whether through exposure to marijuana, academic study, or his own artistic trajectory, Chris's art evolved rapidly. Having drifted from strict figurative work, he now plunged into abstraction. It was quite natural; Expressionism's emphasis on emotion was nothing less than a path to freedom. He, Trevor, Paul and a girl named Julia soon formed an art clique, hanging out, and painting together. Stimulated by each other's passions, furtive wisps of smoke and Dylan's voice of protest echoing down the corridors, the four would claim a whole end of the school's art studio as their own.

Abstract or not, Chris's new work proved quite readable to his friends, especially Trevor Jones, "His paintings were very much about his life. This woman Mary Maise comes into his pictures quite a lot, that he was in love, or falling out of love. The pictures would follow that course. They weren't just straight academic paintings, they were about things he'd done, and what happened to him. Most of the things were sort of narratives – literally silhouettes of him, and silhouettes of this woman. In a way, he didn't want to expose himself, if you like. If you knew him, you'd say 'This is Chris, and this is Maisey', and there'd be little images flying around – whether they'd be flowers or crosses or whatever; very simple things, they were not objectively made at all – they were very much from the observed images of people."

The object of his conflicted affection, Mary Maise (Maisey) was a beautiful Birmingham girl with sparkling eyes and a ready laugh; Chris's first love. But there was a problem – she was the girlfriend of another of his friends, Mike Lewis (Lew or Lewie). Although the attraction grew and became mutual, in the end, Chris would not make an overt play for her. Instead, their relationship, a mixture of love and confusion, would play out barely disguised, as art. "Maisey – that's one of the great tragedies there – they never got it together," Trevor recalled. "He did many pictures of this, we all knew exactly who these people were, and it was sad. It wasn't an organized space, like you'd see in a Uccello (Paolo Uccello, 15th century Italian artist) it was Chris's space, and things would overlap, and things sometimes appeared as shadows."

In later years, Chris would attempt to *play* shadows on his flute, but even here the 'dark side' was recognizable. Chris's slant of investing shadows with emotional qualities impressed Trevor, "The shadows sometimes would be treated in a nafty sort of way – as an ugly shadow, or a cruel shadow, but very simplistically… almost graphic. I mean, this is interesting stuff! I found that, at the time, I couldn't do that. I had to see it to believe it. He just believed it. Color and shape, in certain forms have equivalents, and he was quite conscious of that – that hard and prickly line that describes a person. There was a lot of that language kicking around in his work. One would have liked to have seen what would have happened to it, if he had gone on painting. Where would it have led to?"

The fall of 1963 found the Hadley Quartet still keeping up its gigs at the Saracen's Head, but change was in the air. Drummer Ed Davis somehow snagged the band a slot opening for Acker Bilk at Kidderminster Town Hall. Although Bilk had a huge international pop/jazz hit with "Strangers On The Shore" in the late '50's, he was now on a downward slope. Regardless, in the more rural Black Country he was still quite popular, and the place was packed.

At four hundred seats, Kidderminster Town Hall was by far the largest venue they would ever play, and the band was on pins and needles. But the member best known for his pre-show nerves had now also taken measures to bolster his confidence. Aside from his improved musical chops, being well aware of the image of the 'jazz man', Chris now looked the part – short, well combed hair, dark suit with pointed shoulders, white shirt, and thin tie. Ed Davies recalled, "He was very tasteful, I think that's what set him apart from the rest of us. He bent low with his instrument, particularly the sax – bent forward. He also put his head back when playing the flute – he became very visual. People enjoyed it. After taking a solo, he would stand aside and just hold his instrument – an image that you got from Jazz on A Summer's Day."

Having played their best twenty minutes for the older trad audience, the band would confer and pronounce the effort generally a success. "They didn't boo us or anything," recalled Davies. Steve Hadley thought it went considerably better, "He (Chris) performed well, and we enjoyed it. It was a twenty-minute spot – we filled it, and got a lot of congratulations. And, it was possibly a stepping stone for greater things – particularly for Chris."

Indeed. With Steve soon to graduate and take a full-time teaching job, The Steve Hadley Quartet's days were numbered, something that Chris was quite aware of. But the brush with a bigger audience stirred something inside, consciously or not, and he wanted more. So in the wake of the Town Hall show he edged away. Hadley recalled a soft ending to the band he and Chris built on a common love of Modern Jazz, "We parted company as mates, and not with any animosity. (It happened) casually, as you do when you move to different spheres; we separated, and went our different ways."

Having forged a degree of musical confidence, Chris now sought to broaden his horizons. Taking on the role of itinerant sax player, his self-imposed apprenticeship found him traveling all over both Birmingham and the nether reaches of the Black Country, checking out a wide variety of bands – listening, learning and 'sitting in' whenever possible.

High on his checklist was a slightly older, local legend named Perry Foster. Known for Mississippi delta blues, R&B and rock 'n roll, Foster was a master of the blues harmonica, also playing a distinctive nine string guitar in the fashion of Big Joe Williams. Cultivating a 'wild man' persona, he was either feared or worshipped, and he enjoyed either image. As Foster himself noted, "I had a certain reputation. All the ladies would love me, but they'd never take me home to meet father - 'I've met a wonderful man, his name is Perry Foster!' 'His name *is what*!?' The next thing you know, the old man has got out a hammer and nails, and he's nailing all the doors up. (Laughing) Oh, I loved it!"

Of course with the confluence of the rootsy music and the eccentric personality, Chris was crazy about him – after a set together he would sit transfixed as Foster regaled him with stories such as his initiation into skiffle, "I met Lonnie Donnegan at Dudley Town Hall, a total stranger, I'd never met him before – it was in the bar. I said, 'Hey, I want a word with you'. He said, 'I beg your pardon?' I said 'Listen pal, I've got to tell you – you have *ruined* my life!' And he said, 'I don't know you – what do you mean, I have ruined your life?' I said – 'Ruined! I could have been a High Court judge, I could have been a brain surgeon, I could have been anything I wanted. But what did I do? I went to see you at Dudley Town Hall in 1954 – and you played that fucking rocker! And that was it! I went out the next day and bought a banjo for three quid!' He had a right good laugh over that."

Back among his friends, Chris would repeat Foster's stories, mime his expressions, and garner uproarious laughter. But a serious lesson was also being imparted by the bluesmaster. As the polar opposite to jazz's cerebral cool, Foster offered a lesson in vital, rough-edged music; an approach where attitude and energy counted for nearly everything.

Mostly associated with two pubs - the Seven Stars (colloquially known as the 'Rat Hole'), and the Forester's Arms ('The Ridge Top'), Foster was an open-minded mentor to young players eager to try out their chops; his open-mic policy allowed many would-be performers a chance to test their mettle. Among these was another art student, several years younger than Chris, named Robert Plant. His fame and fortune with Led Zeppelin still years away, 'Planty' was just finding his musical footing. Foster recalled, "He came to me, said: 'Can I do vocals?' His vocals are the main thing, and he brought his washboard along. But of course it was his 'Blind Boy Fuller thing' in those days - he wanted to play Blind Boy Fuller. We used to do things like 'Lost Lover Blues', 'Rattlesnaking Daddy'."

Chris and Robert would jam together on occasion, under conditions Foster recalled as primitive. "We played at the Forester's Arms, which had like a 'scout hut', a shack in the back – with one of them potbellied stoves in it. In the winter, it used to freeze your ass off. Chris played flute and saxophone. He used to take his solos, and Robert would sit and sing."

While Plant's singing held promise back then, Foster was cheerfully blunt about his limitations, "He can't play his guitar, Planty – could never play his guitar at all. But I taught him a little bit on harmonica, and he's quite good at it now."

As for Chris, only ever a semi-regular in Foster's band, he played when he could – typically slipping in the back door and climbing on stage, sax in hand, at the last possible minute. Foster chuckled recalling Chris's eccentric 'rush in and play' technique, "I used to think 'oh my god, here he is, and he's got his saxophone, he's got to play – let him play'. He was more of a jazz musician…didn't rehearse at all, a floating musician, that's how I saw it."

Still, on some nights at the Seven Stars, a band with Chris, Robert, Eddie Davis on drums, Pete 'Gobsy' Groom on bass, and Foster, proved to be quite popular indeed. "It was so successful, that people were queuing up at six in the evening for an eight o'clock start," Foster recalled. Besides Plant's Blind Boy Fuller material, the band tore through a floor-shaking set of blues/rock that gave an indication why people were lining up, even if Perry himself remained nonplussed, "It was all R&B – Muddy Waters, Jimmy Reed, Chuck Berry - the usual sort of thing."

*

Having begun in the early 1950's with a bang that reverberated around the world, the new decade found the American phenomenon called 'rock 'n roll' wounded, staggering, and by all appearances, near death. Plagued with assorted ills, the original stars of the genre faltered one by one: Elvis Presley (drafted into the army), Little Richard (religion), Jerry Lee Lewis (bad publicity from marrying a teenage cousin), Chuck Berry (jail), Buddy Holly (death by plane crash). The bland, manufactured acts which followed, such as the American Pat Boone and his English counterpart Cliff Richard, proved much less inspiring, if not an outright source of derision from hipper kids.

Paralleling the early rock era in England was 'skiffle' – a folk based music that became a craze. Introducing a DIY mindset whose popularity was due in part to its simplicity, skiffle instruments were often homemade, the songs easy to relate to. Youngsters such as Perry Foster listened to Lonnie Donnegan's frantic two or three chord offerings and discovered that they could replicate them with a little practice. In some ways, it was the distant progenitor of what would later be called 'punk'. But by the early 60's skiffle itself was long gone – not so much replaced, as transfigured into other musical forms. Some moved on to 'Trad Jazz', the innocuous 'Dixieland' style which claimed ground somewhere outside of rock and the modern jazz that Chris cut his teeth on.

But many who had so earnestly begun their musical 'careers' with washboards and tea chest basses, now exchanged them for drums and electric guitars. Retooled and injected with new energy, rock 'n roll was suddenly back, poised to tear down the old and again define the character of 'popular' music. Its first victim was Trad Jazz.

The sense that the status quo was losing its grasp was palpable. Roger Bruton pegged his awareness of it to a single event in February of 1964. "Strangely enough, I was working with the jazz band, and it was the night the Beatles played some place in America - it was on English T.V. And the club was fairly empty that night – they'd got a small T.V. on the bar." Having once played on the same bill as the Beatles at a place run by Mary 'Ma' Regan, in Old Hill Plaza, on the border of Birmingham and Stourbridge, Bruton's interest was piqued. Back then, the Beatles were essentially a cover band, and not especially notable. Now, standing stock still in the too quiet pub, Bruton watched with a mixture of fascination and dread as a news report showed the four 'mop tops' belting out an electrifying "She Loves You" on the Ed Sullivan show in New York City. Turning to a friend at the conclusion, he said, "'Oh my god. You know, I can't help feeling that's the end of us.' And it was."

The turning of the tide was as swift as it was unmerciful. Within weeks, trad jazz, like skiffle before it, had dropped dead. All over town, clubs closed. If the Beatles pop-based rock seemed to have single handedly forced a paradigm shift, other bands like the Rolling Stones, the Kinks, and the Animals also found niches in blues, rock and R&B. From there, young listeners were already choosing sides. With little choice, local Trad Jazz bands either faded away or got busy reorganizing (sometimes simply re-branding) themselves into 'beat groups'. Before long, someone dreamed up a catchphrase for the new Birmingham scene – the 'Brum Beat', to distinguish its offerings from others like the 'Mersey Sound' to the north. But, in reality, stuck between Liverpool and London, the Midlands – a little self-consciously – lacked a distinctive 'sound'. Here, a mish mash of Chuck Berry rock, Shadows style instrumental groups, as well as soul and rhythm and blues all had decent followings.

In the Stourbridge area, an energetic, dark-haired young man named David 'Rowdy' Yeats was one of those looking to make a change. Until recently, he'd been giving it a shot as a vocalist with bands such as The Fourstone Jazzmen, and 'Rick Vaughan's Blue Blood Jazz Men'. But stopping in a local pub one night, he found the usual Trad group replaced with the 'Blue Roots', an R&B band with saxophone and organ. Intrigued by the change in sound, and "fueled by alcohol", he asked to sing a number with the band. As if in a scene from a movie, as Rowdy stepped offstage, a self-professed 'Talent Agent' laid an offer on him, "Form a band to back you son, and I'll make you famous!"

Calling the best musician he knew – Andy Silvester, who had previously worked with Rowdy (playing banjo) in the now defunct The Fourstone Jazzmen, he agreed to switch to electric guitar. The two then reviewed their record collections, looking for suitable role models. They came up with only two items – the Rolling Stones' first album, and *Five Live Yardbirds*. With only this much of a theme and no time to waste, the hunt was on for fellow players.

They first picked up a drummer, who happened to be, not surprisingly, the newly ex-Jazz Vendor, Roger Bruton. Ten years older, and considerably wiser, Bruton while still a confirmed 'jazzer', was willing to give the band a try – he needed the work. Bruton's swing style didn't quite fit the bill, but he did make a crucial contribution right off the bat; as the proto-band discussed further instrumentation, Bruton suggested calling Chris Wood.

Finding him at a pub called the 'Spotted Cow', Rowdy pitched his plan, emphasizing his fondness for the organ and sax-based R&B of Georgie Fame and the Blue Flames. Almost immediately Chris agreed to join, but pointing to the pub's back room, would also suggest another possible member. Following the sound of music, Rowdy was led to the source, Chris's Art College classmate Christine Perfect who was playing boogie woogie piano. While Rowdy had already lined up a bass player – an ex-Trad jazzer named Phil Lawless, it turned out that he had a less-than-secure hold on his instrument, which was on loan from a local Woolworths. Christine on the other hand could not only play piano and bass but actually *owned* one – an electric Fender. She was in too.

With that 'The Sounds Of Blue' was born – and almost immediately they were beating the bushes for work. The early repertoire included Slim Harpo, Sonny Boy Williamson ('Help Me'), and Booker T and the MG's – with the odd rock 'n roll numbers slipped in. But even at the outset, format compromises would be required. Paul Medcalf was there at the very beginning, "The first gigs he (Chris) did with The Sounds Of Blue was weddings. They did weddings on a Saturday afternoon at the 'Hen and Chickens', Langley. There was lots of free booze, they got fed – but there wasn't much money. At a wedding you'd get away with what you could, they were playing blues and pop mainly. You'd have to do a waltz, something in ¾ time, so the older lot could dance a bit."

But the on-the-job practice paid off; the band soon got a regular gig – a residency – at the Gladstone Liberal Club, in Dudley. They would play there for the better part of a year – once a week, on Sunday night. Each week everyone, except Chris, would arrive in a paneled delivery van, driven by Andy's father, a Stourport grocer. Chris always came in separately, in his parent's sporty Triumph Herald convertible. The Triumph's speed came in handy because, as Andy remembered it, right from the start – "Chris was always late. He'd turn up when everybody else was already set up. We'd literally just be walking on the stage, or starting the first number – he'd come tearing into the place with his sax case – get the sax out, put the mouthpiece on, and in the middle of the number, he'd just join in. And that was always what he was like."

Neither this band nor Perry Foster's before it ever knew that chronic lateness was one of Chris's methods for dealing with stage fright. Dashing in at the last second and having the other musicians already in place provided a cloak of security, so he tried to make that happen whenever possible.

In the end, Chris's playing would compensate for the late arrivals; the constant wood shedding and one-off gigs had sharpened his craft considerably. But from the start, his interest in reproducing well-worn phrases was minimal. Andy Silvester observed, "He didn't like to be regimented really – he didn't like to play riffs all of the time. He liked to be free. And that was his style I think, that's when he used to excel, when he was allowed to soar around a bit."

Silvester also noted Chris's distinctive sense of humor, "He was actually a very funny guy; he could have made scripts for programs on T.V. He was a great observer of people and characters. He'd been sitting in a pub, listening to lots of guys, just having a beer, you know. He'd come over to Hangman's Gate, where I used to live, and he'd just sort of start imitating these guys he'd seen the previous evening. The one that he sort of started off was 'O.K. Ken?' (in a Black Country accent). That phrase stuck with us, 'cause that's the way guys, spoke to each other in the bar."

While getting regular work, there was still a sense of something lacking in TSOB. Although Andy was a fine guitar player, the driving R&B style they were going for called for more power. Around this time another local blues-oriented band – The Shades Five – had just broken up, freeing up a guitarist named Stan Webb. Rail thin, with a shock of wiry hair and an assertive personality, Webb was approached by Rowdy, and with his acceptance the band was complete.

The stage act became remarkably democratic. By the necessity of pub commerce, the show, stretching over three hours of the Sunday evening, all of the players had a three or four song mini-set of their own. At Rowdy's insistence Chris and the others became singers. Yeats recalled, "Stan would have twenty minutes, Christine would do some, with Andy playing bass guitar. And Chris would do all of the Georgie Fame, Mose Allison numbers – 'Parchman Farm', 'Seventh Son', that kind of thing."

What did Chris Wood's singing sound like? While no one from the band seemed to remember, later recordings make it clear that Chris had a mid-range tenor voice – serviceable, but not distinguished or especially exciting. Regardless, once front and center he began to attract another kind of attention, "The girls loved him, let me tell you!" Rowdy recalled.

With one girl in particular, the feeling was mutual. Mary Maise was often in the audience, dancing in front of stage with boyfriend Lew. Chris of course could do nothing but watch as they twirled around each other night after night. It would only be later, back in the art studio where his feelings emerged – spilling onto canvas as silhouetted figures, close but never quite connecting, surrounded by sad or cruel shadows. But Lew himself would recall only good times at the Liberal Club, "We'd have a bit of rock 'n roll, and a dance…me and Maisey. It was fun – great days – fantastic enthusiasm and joy at being there"

*

In the heart of Birmingham, another band was also working out growing pains. Originally entitled 'The Rhythm and Blues Quartet', the name had recently changed to a more distinctive moniker – the 'Spencer Davis Group'. Having embraced the R&B craze, they now jostled with any number of bands, soliciting gigs where they could. Andy Silvester recalled seeing them for the first time with Chris and Stephanie at a dive in the bad end of town. "I remember that Steph took us to see Spencer Davis at a club called 'The Morgue', (it was) like a cellar. We went down in this cellar, where their gear was all set up, real old amps and stuff."

Surveying the decrepit surroundings, Andy was quite dubious – at first. But as they started to play and the very young guitar/keyboard player opened his mouth, everything changed, "They just absolutely knocked us out, you know. I was hooked immediately." He wasn't alone.

In the intervening time since the Muff Woody band first played their instrumental jazz at The Chapel, something critical had happened: Steve Winwood began to sing. With his voice 'breaking' into an adult tone while in the thrall of Ray Charles, the effect was dramatic. This new quality, combined with already advanced keyboard skills, produced a synergistic effect; seemingly overnight Steve was acclaimed as a musical prodigy, and more – a 'star'. From this point, nearly everyone who saw him for the first time was startled. The skinny kid was blues hollering with a power completely disproportionate to his age, race and frame. The town had never seen anything like it. Of course, it didn't take long for the adults within earshot to realize the potential.

A twenty-two year old teacher, Spencer Davis had been trying to make a way for himself in music for some time with only modest success. In love with the blues, he had done everything from street corner busking to club and pub dates, singing and playing guitar. Having witnessed some of the Chapel jams, he knew that young 'Stevie' Winwood held the keys to a very promising future. Davis was also friends with Pete York, who was already sitting in with the Muff Woody band on drums whenever he could. At Davis's suggestion York was more than eager to form a band with Stevie. The duo approached the Winwood brothers and made an offer. First going by the name 'The Rhythm and Blues Quartet', like many others they wisely played to the R&B craze – heavy on John Lee Hooker ("Dimples"), and Muddy Waters ("I Got My Mojo Working"), and of course, Ray Charles.

At close quarters, York took in the totality of Winwood's talents, "His voice had broken, but he could still sing high – but his ability to pick up on other instruments… he very quickly picked up on guitar. In a very short time, he could play far better than Spencer, which of course didn't help (Spencer's) ego. (Steve) could also play some good licks on the drums, which were fresh to me; he was coming up with things I hadn't heard. His father was a saxophone player; he'd obviously stuck a saxophone in his mouth at some point in his childhood, because he could also play a little bit of saxophone. So, he was quite the multi-instrumentalist."

Of course, with the prospect of popular success looming, a managerial figure claiming to have the artists' best interest at heart is never far away. In this case, it came in the form of a young man named Blackwell. Born in Jamaica to an already wealthy family, Chris Blackwell had been schooled in England. Having recently begun his own record company – 'Island', Blackwell was in Birmingham promoting his first hit artist, Millie Small ("My Boy Lollipop"), the night that The Rhythm and Blues Quartet played the Golden Eagle Pub. A handsome, discerning and by all accounts very 'cool' guy, he wasted no time making a pitch.

And time was of the essence – other potential 'managers' were circling. These included the seemingly omnipresent Giorgio Gomelsky, as well as Mike Vernon from Decca Records – the unfortunate label that had 'passed' on the Beatles after hearing their demo tape. But Blackwell had something in abundance – charm. Pete York recalled, "Blackwell was known in the business as the 'Baby Faced Killer', because he was a very plausible guy, he could be *extremely* charming – all the wives and girlfriends of the band fell for him." He also had a philosophy, wrapped neatly in the metaphor of a game. "I always remember, very, very early on, Blackwell was a poker player," York recalled. "And (he) used to maintain that if you could just keep raising the stakes, everyone would drop out – that's how you play poker." Whether by bluff or a genuinely good hand, Chris Blackwell played his cards perfectly. The competition outwitted, The Rhythm and Blues Quartet (soon rechristened the Spencer Davis Group) would become Island Records' new recording artists.

Aside from all of this, both Chris Wood and his sister Stephanie were now friends with the band. Already a kindred soul with the jazz-loving Steve, Chris could converse about music with him for hours. Steph Wood, less interested in jazz, loved the energy and drive of the Davis Group. But it was soon a two-way street – they and other local bands would be seeking *her* out. In the years that Chris had been developing his creative pursuits, Steph had also been developing into an artist. Like Chris, she took a left turn out of art school, following her own muse. Beginning with a sewing machine set up in the uppermost floor of Corngreaves Hall, she was now producing quirky, sharp and very hip items of clothing for Chris and his friends – ties, shirts, pants – which soon became recognized for what they were – wearable art. Andy Silvester ordered clothes, as did Steve Winwood, and the other members of the Spencer Davis Group. Soon Stephanie Wood designed clothes were all over Birmingham, then London.

Meanwhile, in Chris's own band – problems, small at first, began to mount. Although they had sizable collective talent, TSOB never seemed to get any closer to the pot of gold at the end of the R&B rainbow. The

'Talent Agent' who had spurred Rowdy on with visions of fame, showed up once more, only to stammer excuses of having been swindled by his business partner. For better or worse, there would be no 'Chris Blackwell' waiting in the wings for them. In fact, with seemingly every band around them swept up and signed, they received no other offers at all.

Perhaps the most insurmountable obstacle was a simple lack of emotional maturity. Drummer Roger Bruton, ten years senior to the others, pegged it early on, "They were a bunch of kids! They would waste a lot of time talking things through and getting upset over small things – and there was me thinking 'Oh, come on, let's bloody do it – don't worry about that! It was good fun for a while, but it was also annoying. I got a bit fed up in the end." Begging off that he needed steadier work, Bruton finally resigned, to be replaced by a sixteen-year-old named Rob Elcock who idolized Ringo Starr. It was slightly, but ever so steadily, downhill from there.

Even the choice of songs could lead to irreconcilable conflicts. At one point Rowdy wanted to cover a Kinks song – 'You Really Got Me', as a tribute to Ray Davies who they'd recently met. Andy argued against it, not at all appreciating the "too commercial" tune. Being the 'leader', Rowdy insisted and had his way. But while he 'won' the argument, whenever the song was announced, Andy would put his guitar down and walk off, only returning to continue the set after it was over. It didn't help that occasional forays outside of the Liberal Club didn't always go well. Rowdy noted, "I recall that we did play a couple of gigs in other places, and that we 'died the death', because people didn't know us, (or) knew what we did."

Andy Silvester remembered another, decidedly surreal set, "We had this gig in Stourport, it was right on the river – a pub. The owner was trying to get us to play 'Blue Beat' music – Jamaican stuff; it must have been about '65. Anyway, we were playing away, and this rough guy comes right up to the end of the stage, and says 'Webb, I want to see you after', in the middle of a song. Stan didn't say anything, and at the end the guy just came up and hit Stan – right in the face – flattened him. And actually, Stan started crying. He was supposed to be this sort of big guy that everybody fears, but... all hell seemed to break loose, the atmosphere, you could cut it with a knife. But Chris was wonderful. He went up to this guy, and said something like 'There's no need for that'. He had this quality, which I stood back and watched, and thought 'bloody hell, he's risking a bit saying something to that guy'. He wasn't trying to be aggressive or anything, he just seemed to calm the situation down – and the guy didn't want to hit him – he could see something about him, that he was a peace lover. He saw his angle, and just sort of backed off."

Then one day in March of 1965, it was suddenly over. David Yeats blamed himself for the dissolution of The Sounds Of Blue, but could only recall, "It was probably because I was stupid." Both simple and complicated, the end actually came as the result of festering hurt feelings and the overall immaturity. Andy Silvester remembered it all falling apart on stage, "We had a bit of a... I was making faces behind him (Rowdy) while he was singing, and he turned around and saw me doing it. It happened pretty quickly... like that really." Rowdy walked off, and away. And since he owned the amplifiers, microphones and P.A., the band literally lost the power to play. Andy said, "With him out of it, we couldn't really do anything. We couldn't afford to buy any amplifiers – that was basically it."

Chris's reaction was little more than a shrug. In later years, while listing TSOB on his résumé, he couldn't bring himself to praise the band. In one interview, he referred to it as a "semi-professional group who played... any kind of shit that was going on in the discotheques." He also inferred that the band's long residency at the Liberal Club was an obvious dead end, "You see, Birmingham is one of those places that, unless you get out of it, you're stuck there for life – 'cause there's no output. No way of getting your thing out without going to London." For her part, Christine (Perfect) McVie would be even more concise, referring to the band simply as "Terrible." Rowdy Yeats, the originator of the band, disagreed but wished he'd had the foresight to have taken a different approach. "I should have managed them, 'cause without me they were great – but I was like 19, 20 years old, and just broke up the band."

The Sounds of Blue quickly vanished into local musical lore. With no recordings, press clippings, or a single photograph of the band having ever turned up, faded memories aside, almost nothing at all was left behind. But, in the end, both Rowdy and Chris's concluding thoughts were proved right. Not long after the demise of TSOB, a group called 'Chicken Shack' was formed – without Rowdy or Chris, but including Andy, Christine and Stan Webb. And that band *did* find a measure of fame and success, but only after getting the hell out of Birmingham.

Chris's sanguine attitude to all of the musical drama may have been because the £3 and free beer per gig were all he ever expected out of it. Certainly, as far as anyone knew, his long-stated intention to be a professional artist remained unchanged. But, well-hidden from everyone, his musical plans for the future may have been far grander than anyone imagined.

As the Spencer Davis Group gained momentum with its R&B-powered pop music, Steve Winwood's jazz roots were, if not cut off, at least forcefully suppressed. Instead, the band and management plotted out a more 'commercial' sound as a path to mainstream success. It wasn't just hitting the clubs and hoping; no, the Spencer Davis Group with three singles out already, was well into recording their debut album in the spring of '65. With The Beatles, Stones, Animals, and others having re-written the rules, the SDG was now set to take its own shot at the big time. And with Steve's talent as their foundation, the dream was indeed coming true – the girls were screaming, the records were selling, and the concert venues increasingly packed.

Yet amid this seemingly fated juggernaut to the top, a small seed of a different species had been planted. Having discovered a kindred spirit in one another, Steve and Chris now spent time huddled around record players, smoking cigarettes and listening to Eddie Harris, Ornette Coleman, and Roland Kirk – rebels and musical artists, deliberately on the fringe and willing to risk failure by making sounds true to themselves. And if Winwood was firmly entrenched on a career path whose goal could be best articulated as 'fame and fortune', ever so subtly, tendrils were also growing in an entirely different direction.

And there was more than mere talk; something kept very quiet. According to Chris's childhood friend and neighbor Peter Harris, Chris and Steve had actually made 'secret' music very early on at Corngreaves Hall, "People like Steve (Winwood) were already stopping around. I can remember them putting together a session at the living room of the Hall. It must have been '63 or '64, because I went to college in '65 – I lost contact with the local scene at that time. I can remember, we were sworn to secrecy, Steve was still with Spencer Davis, so this was a move that would have wider implications to the music public - if it had been known that Steve was thinking about moving on at that point. So it was something that was not talked about, they were working out what they might do together at that time."

('Traffic Jam', Ray Townley, DownBeat, 1/30/1975)

('Rock Family Trees', Pete Frame, Omnibus Press, 1993)

THE SPELL OF WITLEY COURT

The 1964/65 school year would be Chris's last year at the Birmingham College of Art. His mentor, John Walker, had been keeping an eye on his progress, as well as that of Trevor Jones. Collecting their best works, Walker showed them around to the major art colleges in London – an informal audition for their future admittance. It worked. Trevor was accepted at the Royal College of Art, while the Royal Academy of Art took Chris. Walker noted, "The Royal Academy wasn't rated as highly, but with some encouragement, we got him there. His work wasn't as flamboyant, so you had to pressure people to notice it – he wasn't out there screaming. He never was. His work reflected him in that sense."

His canvases were now quite subtle, seemingly simplified. As Walker had long emphasized, he was producing squares "filled with feeling." Preparing to face London, Chris made a phase transition, leaping into a deeper, more mysterious level of art. John Walker explained, "He was certainly an abstract painter. And they were rather refined, not a whole lot of color, rather tonal. That's what I remember – large, some of them…"

As for his music, and all the drama associated with it – somehow his teacher and mentor never knew. "He didn't let on to me at all. Maybe he wanted to show me that he was a painter. As everyone knows, I take the whole thing very seriously, and he may have thought that I wouldn't be impressed with him if he started to diversify. So, he probably kept that right away from me." This is certainly the case. Chris's respect for Walker, not to mention his fear of being reproached, meant that he kept that part of his life well hidden. Thinking about Chris and the path he ultimately chose, Walker could only look back with melancholy bemusement, "For Chris to join a rock 'n roll band, character-wise was, you know, crazy! He was much too gentle for the world he went into."

But that was still way off. The opportunity to move on to one of the London art schools was huge, and not something to be treated lightly. So, with The Sounds Of Blue having folded, Chris devoted himself to art once again. As always, a world of mysteries tugged his sleeve, demanding to be explored; and with another summer in front of him, again he would roam in search of inspiration. While always confounded by the sense of a hidden *something* that needed to be uncovered in his life, locating the source was another issue. But intuition always seemed to lead him back to that ephemeral, liminal space between life and death.

What Trevor Jones said of Chris' approach to art – "I had to see it to believe it – he just believed it." – was never truer for his passion for the 'spirit world'. Whether from experience or deep desire, when it came to ghosts, their existence was a given. Trevor recalled that around this time his curiosity intensified. "He liked that side of things, would have loved to prove that the supernatural was all it was cracked up to be. He would have desperately liked to have met a ghost. I'd been with him when he was absolutely shit scared - but he'd overcome *that* to find something out. He'd be a bookworm – he'd find books on it." And seeking evidence now meant that any potentially haunted location within reach would be paid a visit – with anyone brave enough to accompany him.

One less-than-willing participant was Mike Lewis. Returning home from a hitch-hiking trip to Wales to visit Lewis' grandmother, and with dusk approaching, Chris suggested a stop. "We were stuck in the middle of nowhere" Lewis recalled, "Somewhere between Wrexham and Stourbridge, and we were both quite thirsty. He said 'Right, there's a churchyard over there, let's go in…' He started telling me bloody ghost stories – he went on and on, and he completely spooked me. It got worse: 'I can see something, *I can see something!*' I said, 'Christ sake! You're bloody frightening me to death!' I had to run off in the end…"

While, in this case, Chris was likely having fun; getting Lewis back for stealing Maisey's affections, by now his childhood 'ghosty games' were very serious. What he really wanted was a place where he could see, feel and study the phenomena first hand.

Then one day he found it.

Having followed a map directing him through the Worcestershire countryside, Chris poked his head out of a patch of overgrown shrubbery and stopped dead, staring in amazement. A huge one-time mansion, now a modern ruin, stood before him. Gazing in wonder at Witley Court, all of the pieces of the puzzle quickly fell into place; forevermore he would be under her spell.

One of the most elaborate English homes of the nineteenth century, with hundreds of rooms and several hundred acres of grounds, Witley had been a true Victorian-era palace. Evolving over the centuries from previous dwellings that stretched back to medieval times, the structure reached its zenith during the late 1800's, blossoming into utter opulence under the benefaction of the first Earl of Dudley – William Humble Ward. Ward had been fortunate enough to somehow be the sole heir to a distant relative – one John William Ward, a man who single-mindedly amassed a fortune from over 200 coalmines in the Midlands region. Perhaps the knowledge that his Black Country coal miners lived, worked and died in squalor while he was enriched somehow contributed to William's own death – which came after a prolonged period of insanity in which he endlessly talked to himself, alternating between high and low voices. His acquisitive heir, the Earl, unmolested either by conscience or insanity, used the equity siphoned from the miners' labors to build Witley to true magnificence. Besides the mansion, the surrounding grounds were incredible: manicured topiary gardens framed a huge, stunningly ornate fountain depicting a life-sized Perseus rescuing Andromeda from a sea serpent.

But fortunes change, and by the late 1930's the distressed property was sold to a certain Herbert Smith – another wealthy industrialist who had long wished to possess the prestigious Witley for himself. Known, not so lovingly, by the locals as 'Piggy', among his other flaws, he neither fully insured the building nor maintained the hydrant system. When a fire (of unknown origin) began on the seventh of September, 1937 it burned enough of the structure that he could not afford to salvage it. Subsequently stripped of her valuables, Witley would simply be left to rot in the elements. By the 1960's Witley Court was in a state of elegant, even exquisite decay – with vines creeping up the marble steps of the formal entrance of the forecourt and trees growing within the walls of once impeccable rooms. In the formal gardens, now hopelessly overgrown, even the mighty Perseus sitting astride his rearing steed seemed to look down only in sorrow; one of his legs had been hacked off by looters.

To say that Chris loved the place is an understatement – from the first, he felt utterly at home here. At Witley Court, time distorts into a knot, the past blurring into the present even as the shattered infrastructure glimpses the future of all man-made things. An atmosphere of endless intrigue exists here; amid exposed cellars, uncertain passages and sharp debris of every sort. With signs threatening prosecution for trespassers, Chris's car had to be carefully hidden before sneaking in. Over time, he would explore all of it. He also researched her history, uncovering the complexity, contradictions and human toil which made it possible. Reading *Germinal*, Emile Zola's gripping story of the lives of coal miners, Chris developed empathy for the hard working employees of John William Ward – long gone people whose energy he sensed embedded in Witley's skeleton. Tellingly, a stark, slightly foreboding charcoal sketch of Witley Court was the only art of his own that Chris kept throughout his life.

What convinced him that Witley was haunted is unknown, but it soon became his paranormal laboratory. Recruiting friends, he led groups out at night, to better contact the spiritual energy. Before long 'Witley stories' began to filter back to the outside world. Besides the usual ill-defined noises and shifting shadows, tales of pagan and/or witchcraft rituals emerged, as well as the notion of the ghost of a man and his dog, whose howls echoed amid the ruins. Later, a fleeting image of a man was also reported – staring down from a second-storey window in the forecourt, behind which were no floors. Still others reported the sounds of phantom horses galloping across the lawn in the dead of night. All in all, the place became a heady source of fright and inspiration.

One of the people that Chris specifically wanted Witley to inspire was Steve Winwood. While the Spencer Davis Group's success grew on an almost weekly basis, sixteen-year-old 'Stevie' had nonetheless developed a vague sense of dissatisfaction. Surrounded by adults whose own success depended on harvesting *his* creative energy, he now lived a life akin to a young Tibetan Lama – revered as 'special' for his talent, while also a near-captive to it.

On a break from Winwood's touring schedule, a trip was arranged. With Trevor Jones as designated driver, they barreled down the country road at night, Steve rolling a smoke on an album cover. While dumping the debris out an open window, the wind caught the album, sending all of it out into the dark. On hands and knees, using the headlights for illumination they eventually found the joint, laughing as they piled back into the car. But once at Witley Court, humor gave way to a more cautious attitude. Using only moonlight to avoid obstacles, they roamed the massive building, taking tiny steps and holding on to each other. Trevor recalled, "It was quite dangerous – but just *the idea* of the thing, a baroque ruin which was full of extraordinary fantasies – he (Chris) used to love it."

If nothing else, a night at Witley - as a backdrop for Chris' imagination, was nearly incomparable. As for Winwood, it might just as well have been a different universe from the clubs and pubs he'd been immersed in; from here his worldview would never be the same. Be that as it may, the unexplained creaks and seeming whispers finally proved enough – one and all scampered for the car.

Another visitor that summer was art school buddy Paul Medcalf. An avowed realist, he went on the trips, enjoyed the ambience, but gave no credence to the notion that anything other than rampant imagination was at play, "I was just curious; I didn't believe any of it…I'm more worried about being attacked by humans." But that said, there was one strange object found on the overgrown grounds he couldn't explain. Many years later Medcalf recalled the vaguely disturbing sight, "The only description I can give is like a totem pole, a figure. It must have been about ten feet long – a great lump of wood with a *head*, painted garishly. And it was just lying in the grass."

*

By the fall of 1965, the rural adventures were set aside, at least for the moment. Officially notified by post – Christopher Gordon Blandford Wood had been accepted by the Royal Academy of Art. In later years, he would profess to be mystified as to why they had him at all, referring to his acceptance as a mere "fluke." This self-deprecating attitude emphasizes why Chris was fortunate to have John Walker promoting his work. Left on his own, Chris certainly would not have had enough confidence to get himself there.

The move to London coincided with big societal changes just beginning to take shape throughout the Western world. Stimulated by a heady mixture of politics, art and music, many of Birmingham's neo-beatniks now found their way there as well, congregating in underground enclaves throughout the city, puffing weed, talking politics and dreaming of a better world.

Chris's first step into London unwittingly took him into one of those dank caverns. Alone with only a bed and a duffel bag of possessions, he took up residence with boyhood friend Hugh Fraser, who had arrived ahead of him. A newly minted Drama School student, Fraser described the apartment this way, "I was living in a very seedy flat with a couple of other people; smoking a lot of dope, listening to jazz, getting drunk, and paying very little attention to work." Taking it all in, Chris made an atypically decisive act – he backed away. Fraser recalled that, "Chris stayed for a while, but he was far more focused. He left the flat, I remember, and was more focused on his studies than I was at the time."

Luckily a safety net was nearby; his old friend, the reliable 'straight arrow', Trevor Jones. A small flat in the Shepherd's Bush region, Trevor's residence was a one room 'bedsit' he kindly let Chris share. Anything but luxurious, they got by with a single burner gas stove for both heat and cooking, and just enough room for two beds (Trevor's being a double and Chris's a small single, with green painted bedposts).

As humble a beginning as it was, the situation held the seeds of a bright future. Two years at the Royal Academy would land Chris a graduate degree in fine art and tangible career options. But there were others attractions as well. Steve Hadley recalled hearing stories of those first days in London, "while he seemed to tie himself very deeply to his work, and he would work for hours uninterrupted, he enjoyed the *image* of the artist (as well). I think he wanted to live in a garret, and take his models to bed – do a Van Gogh!"

Chris did make an effort to do exactly that, but like many aspects of his life, it was not without humorous complications. Trevor Jones recalled, "I remember we were at a party one night. I left, there was nothing there for me, but he was clearly getting a lot of attention. I went out, and went to bed. At like two in the morning, I'm aware that there are people in the room. He'd brought this very attractive blond woman home, but (having only a single bed) had nowhere to put her. So he just told her to get in bed with me! Not for any reason other than to get a night's sleep – but I just sort of rolled over, and thought 'My god – what on earth is this!' And he was quite happy to say, 'Well look, you know – you understand the circumstances…' And I sort of curled up on my bed, terrified."

Other, similarly uncomfortable experiences led the roommates to seek more private lodgings. Ultimately they would be taken in by John Walker, who had a house in Turnham Green he couldn't quite afford. Trevor and

Chris were each offered rooms on the upper floor, with Chris's rent discounted on the condition that he baby-sit for Walker's children as necessary.

Moving into Walker's home with his green-posted bed, the only issue was which bedroom to take. But Trevor observed that apparently simple decisions could sometimes elude Chris, "He spent about two days deciding which room he wanted - I mean, I didn't care. Then, painting the damn room out – he spent weeks deciding what color it should be, methodically going through mixing the paint, and changing his mind."

Ensconced in the big city, his love of wandering hadn't changed. In fact, with so much electricity around him, Chris was even more easily distracted. In a memory which made him chuckle forty years later, Trevor recalled, "It was in that period, he'd walk out of the house with his laundry under his arm, and he'd come back, two days later with his laundry under his arm! He'd obviously met someone – quite eccentric, and he would be seduced to go off and do something else, ghost hunting or…"

Settled in or not, he was now officially a London art student. But having already made the transition to the abstract style, Chris was immediately distressed to find that the Royal Academy put all incoming students into a three month period of figurative drawing, followed by a graded evaluation. Focusing on images of a pop singer that he had a crush on (Sandy Shaw), he made an effort, but soon grew exasperated. Having been spoiled by the endemic freedom of Birmingham, in the end he would decide to simply ignore further objectionable assignments, return to abstract and hope that no one noticed. Writing to a friend back home Chris fretted and complained, "I took a risk, and didn't send in any academic work – but I think it will be all right. However, I was a bit worried when the Keeper came up and asked me to explain my drawings!" Trevor Jones was sympathetic. "He said 'Sod it, I don't need it', and many, many great artists have not gone that route. He said 'No, no, this is the wrong struggle, I'm not that sort of guy'. So he went straight to making the pictures and struggled with the *ideas* behind making the pictures."

In the end he would go back to where he was most comfortable – the fringe. During this period, Jackson Pollock became a role model of sorts. Having transformed his art in the 1950's, Pollock's complex, abstract drip-based paintings were reviled by some in the art community as random nonsense. But Chris loved them. Buying a book of Pollock's paintings, he carried it everywhere for weeks. Much later on, analysis by a physicist showed that Pollock *was* making deliberate organized imagery, layering his drips and swirls in precise relationships resembling fractals – the repeating patterns seen nearly everywhere in nature from the branching of trees, to the ripples of waves. While never directly emulating the style, Chris clearly got it. More than anything else, it was Pollock's subliminal organization, camouflaged with seeming chaos, that proved deeply appealing.

His own work now shifted from oils to water-based acrylic. Cheaper and easier to work with, the new medium allowed his paintings to become more expansive and expressive. One of his classmates at the Royal Academy, a young woman named Gloria Wheeler noticed both the art and artist, "It was good. I can honestly say that he influenced me. I can remember one that he did of water lily pads… he used to do these quite beautiful, watery things. They were abstract; although they looked like water lily pads, they weren't, they were just an abstract sort of shape. And I think he used spray paint on it – (but) they were quite watery, and dreamlike. I just found them very attractive and I started to work a bit like that myself." Although married at the time, Gloria was also attracted to Chris, and she and another female student used to look forward to his visits to the studio, "He was very striking. He had a pale complexion, blue eyes, he was quite beautiful – there was something ethereal about him. If I hadn't been married…"

Emerging at irregular intervals, Chris's large canvases said something about both his emotions and the worldview he was processing. Years of studying nature now found their outlet – transmuted, refined and distilled to essences. One friend remembered a couple of them displayed on the corridors of the Royal Academy as, "Huge – massive, it (the first) was slightly geometric, yellow and green. The other one rather looked like wallpaper. It was a strange thing…pink and brown, elephant's feet-like shapes, I can remember them being across the canvas."

A professional artist in later years, Trevor Jones was in a position to reflect on Chris' evolution at this point in time, "He was doing some interesting pictures. In fact, I look back and see some of the '70's pictures from Germany – (Julian) Schnabel and (Georg) Baselitz and people like that, and Chris' work is a lot like that. And that was ten years before these guys, and you think 'I wonder, I wonder…' because you can arrive too early, and nobody notices you. He was playing with those formal elements in what he did – and it was good."

John Walker tried to sum up where Chris was at, as his first semester at the Academy came to a close, "He was very aware of the American abstract impressionists. He wasn't prolific; he worried too much to be prolific – he was unsure of himself. But my thing with Chris was, the potential was enormous – it could take him into paintings that were very ambitious in their intention. He (also) did a lot of paper work, monotypes, a lot of work printing on a press. I had a press in my studio, and he used to come there to print." Walker stopped for a moment to consider the promising student that he had shepherded through four years, and three different schools, "He was a very sensitive, gentle guy – almost shy in many ways, and devoted to being a good art student, and that's what I picked up on. I would say that his paintings were in transition. It was interesting to see the evolution but it was not…before he really resolved anything, he'd left."

(Witley Court, English Heritage, 1997)

CHAPTER SIX

PAINTING WITH MUSIC

While seemingly on the cusp of an artistic breakthrough, the absence of music left a gaping hole that Chris had not anticipated. While his instruments came to London with him, they often remained buried under a pile of dirty clothes. Opportunities to play were rare, and mainly consisted of entertaining John Walker's kids with his flute or blowing his saxophone into a wardrobe cabinet full of clothes – necessary to muffle the sound from neighbors. While art offered Chris a full, creative life, a restless feeling was emerging and it was getting harder to ignore.

Meanwhile, Steve Winwood's success was accelerating. The SDG single "Keep On Running" would be #1 in England in December. Having reached the upper echelons of British popular music, they were now called on to do BBC television appearances ("Top of the Pops"), and play huge tours only one down the bill from the Rolling Stones. While all seemed to be going according to plan, the limitations were showing. As the wild 60's vibe had altered the palate of music with sitars, oscillating tapes, backward loops and drug-inspired lyrics, none of that had much effect on the very straight Spencer Davis Group. In some ways they actually seemed to be going backwards, a prime example being the insipid teeny bop movie they'd agreed to star in – a *Help* knock off called *The Ghost Goes Gear*. With few hopeful signs on the horizon, Steve was looking more and more askance at his own band.

But an alternative, at least on paper, was taking shape. With musical dreams invading his sleep, Chris began seeking out Steve whenever schedules overlapped. With each having felt an ill-defined need for change, their conversations and musical ideas now converged toward a single path. Surprisingly like-minded considering the differences in background, they sketched out the makings of an ideal band. If perhaps a bit of an 'escape fantasy' for each at first, before long it would evolve into something quite serious. Intellectually driven, the construction of this 'band' started with a philosophy, a spine of thought from which everything else would grow. At the base was a recognition that the best music came from the heart, *not* from what was simply marketable or 'popular'. Arising out of personal expression, the idea was to convey emotion, share the inner space with others, influence feelings – to create 'mood music'.

The actual structure could be – in fact, had to be – fluid, leaving room for anything that felt *right* – jazz, rock, folk and even classical influences and sounds from 'primitive' cultures. Out of that mix, perhaps they could do something no one else had before; just as jazz was distinctly American, why not transform these influences into a timeless *English* sound? With his art training and eclectic manner of thinking, Chris could envision how the different components could be juxtaposed, layered and balanced. It was ambitious, but Steve and his deep musicality held the key – his deft touch, inerrant facility and self-confidence was essential to pulling the myriad pieces into a unified whole.

Coming away from these discussions, Chris was both excited and shaken up. Having treasured art and music equally for years, a great divide unexpectedly materialized as his way of thinking was transformed. He would later say, "I had this strong feeling that painting wasn't the right kind of communication for the materials and things that were going on around me. I had this idea of painting musically." But while powerful, the dawning understanding of the transferability of his artistic skills to music didn't quite change everything; being Chris, he also vacillated as his insecurity nagged – perhaps it *was* just a dream.

To make it come to life, for the first time he seemed aware that a full-on break from his artistic path might be required; a most difficult task indeed, since it was something he very much loved. And while Chris had always relied on friends, circumstances and even fate, to make changes, this one would be entirely up to him, even if he didn't know it yet. Meanwhile, caught between two worlds, all he could do was fret.

But the most important single question was also the hardest to divine – would Steve *really* give up the highly successful Spencer Davis Group to work with him? However enthusiastic Winwood appeared, the answer remained unknown. Certainly to an outside observer, the notion of Chris – a complete 'nobody', forming a band with a musician of Steve's stature was ridiculous. It went without saying that his musical skills would need to be top rate, and this of course was a problem. Blowing his tenor into a *closet* for the past few months wouldn't cut it with someone whose chops were razor sharp from playing six nights a week. He'd need to get up to speed, and fast – but how?

So despite the grand plans, in the end, talk was cheap, while the forces holding both Chris and Steve where they were remained were strong. For a while, Chris grew quite discouraged. As Christmas approached, he wrote a letter to Steve Hadley, still back in Stourbridge; the weight of his indecision clear. To his old friend he expressed a homesick anguish, yearning for the simpler days of playing jazz and drinking with his mates, "I don't know when I will be back yet, but I am certainly looking forward to a blow – you don't know how I feel, it really is terrible…"

Meanwhile, another musician – Jim Simpson, was desperately trying to keep his group alive. Leader of the Birmingham based The Kansas City Seven jazz band, Simpson's tenor player had quit. To his dismay, there was no replacement in sight; the straight-laced R&B and jazz scene was receding into obscurity in an inverse relationship with rock's ascendancy. With groups like the Beatles and the Rolling Stones having huge hits ('Day Tripper', and 'Get Off My Could' respectively), the writing was on the wall for jazz bands. While willing to refit the band with a hipper sounding name – 'Locomotive', Simpson would stay true to the fading genre, even as others fell around them. Jim Simpson recalled, "It was a seven piece, rough, tough band, playing Kansas City Blues things, Rhythm and Blues – a big swinging band. It was very unusual, 'cause there was a lot of 'Beatle type' bands around at that time – with those stupid jackets and what not. We just wore rather rougher, straightforward things, and we were probably the only band in the land that made a living that didn't have a guitar! We had Hammond organ, bass, drums, trumpet, tenor sax, baritone sax and a lead singer."

Minus a tenor player, the front line had a gaping hole, and someone mentioned Chris Wood. Finding him at home during the Christmas holiday trying to clear his head, the call would prove a near-miracle of serendipity. Pulling his gear together, Chris rushed over to meet the band. And while the first rehearsal was a bit rough, it also revealed a quality that made Simpson press Chris to join, "He sort of sounded like Lester Young in those days, a diffident rather delicate sound I suppose. But he played so well, when he really caught things, he was exceptional."

Locomotive had the potential to both simplify and complicate Chris's dilemma. A professional band, and reasonably popular, they would tour all over England, and possibly on the European continent – so his chops would certainly improve. Fitting jams with Steve on the side, he just might be able to get to the level where the 'dream band' could be possible.

Practically speaking the idea was almost crazy. With the artwork getting deeper by the month, the logical way forward seemed clear enough, whereas music was at best, a highly uncertain move. In addition, having indulged him in so many of his whims and passions, his parents *really* expected him to finish his degree. With mindsets shaped by the shattering events of World War II, for them, safety and stability were the key things worth striving for career-wise. But worse, by far, would be telling the man who had helped Chris in innumerable ways, the one who had seen and nurtured his potential as an artist from the earliest days – John Walker.

As Christmas break ended, a decision still eluded him. Back in London, with possibilities festering in his mind, he made a last desperate attempt to reason his way out. Having done art and music together in Stourbridge, why not again? Minimizing the logistical problems, he tried to make it all fit: with most of Locomotive's gigs in London, Birmingham, or somewhere in-between, he'd do music at night and art in the day, just like before. The call was made to Simpson; he would join the band.

While initially telling no one at school, the changes in his behavior were noticeable anyway. As Trevor recalled, "Eventually he started to stay out longer, on more nights in the clubs… and the impression I got, he was going out on long night binges, jamming, or gigging with people." With Chris living at his house, John Walker also got glimpses of *something* going on, "I vaguely remember meeting Winwood a couple of times, Chris brought him to the house and things. He'd say, 'I've got to get up early, can you give me a call?' And you'd pound on his door, but it took a while to get him out of bed."

Of course, in the end, there would not be enough hours in the day. For that, Chris's remedy was as simple as it was short-sighted; he turned to the old musician's standby – speed. Showing Gloria Wheeler a handful of pills, Chris explained that he was using them to keep sharp. But as always, amphetamines only postponed the inevitable. Increasingly frantic to resolve his dilemma, he sought other perspectives. Of his friends at the Royal Academy he seemed to want someone to convince him to stay.

make their own record, they were curious to see how it was done. Amenable, Haines not only demonstrated the recording equipment, but also showed how he could transfer the tape to disc – producing a demo 'acetate'. While the self-made record only came with a handwritten label and a plain paper sleeve, it played like any other. Ever the technophile, Chris took note.

As 1966 unfolded, it was clear that the musical winds were shifting again. Under the influence of LSD, the hippest musicians now produced music tinged with an as yet undefined change in the frame of reference. While still mostly under the surface of societal awareness, 'acid' now seeped lysergic tendrils in many directions. One of the first Birmingham area bands so affected was an outfit recently dubbed 'Deep Feeling' – a name possibly inspired by an obscure Chuck Berry b-side. Led by dark haired, gregarious young Englishman of Italian descent from nearby Evesham in Worcestershire – Jim Capaldi, the band had mutated with the times. Claiming to be one of the first in England to have taken LSD, Capaldi's visions had a huge impact on both him and his band.

Prior to his drug-fueled revelations, the group had gone by the rough and tough moniker of 'The Hellions'. Having paid their dues on the club circuit – including a stint at the infamous Star Club in Hamburg Germany, for the previous two years the Hellions had pumped out a raw R&B sound laced with soul. The restless yet earnest Capaldi (who once held dreams of becoming a priest) possessed a gravelly voice and was devoted to the success of his band. But with a repertoire including songs like Screaming Jay Hawkins "I Put A Spell On You", the Hellions impact had been minimal – they sounded not dissimilar to a hundred other bands. But having shed the old name and influences for a new, consciousness-centered approach, "Deep Feeling" was now very much in tune with the times. Their recent songs, such as "Pretty Colours", "The Necessitarian" and "Ruin" were complex and strove to impart a sense of space and mystery.

Besides writing lyrics and singing, Capaldi was a drummer. The rest of the band was equally eclectic and flexible. John 'Poli' Palmer drummed when Capaldi sang, otherwise he played vibraphone – which he'd recently electrified, or flute. Gordon Jackson played guitar, and could sing with a range that went to the high end of soprano. Dave Meredith handled bass, and the newest member of the band – Luther Grosvenor, could readily play an energetic and suitably psychedelic-tinged lead guitar.

But Deep Feeling's birth had come only after a troubled labor. Grosvenor's inclusion was a result of the departure of the previous lead player, another local Worcester lad named Dave Mason. Recently fired, Mason's leaving had nothing to do with skill or musical competence – an obsessive practitioner, he quite good and getting better all the time; the real issues were all below the surface. Poli Palmer recalled the guitarist's difficult-to-read motivations as a major concern, "Mainly, Dave – his thoughts – you don't actually know *what* he's thinking, or where he's coming from. There's sort of this deadpan expression that you never quite get behind. I'm sure there is somebody with emotions behind it, but I don't think anybody ever saw it." Gordon Jackson, who knew Mason longer than any of the others, believed he understood the core of it, "We were just kids from Worchester. He was fitting aerials when I met him, putting aerials up on roofs. He's a great guy, I like Dave, but he's Dave, he can't be in partnership with other people. He's got to be in control."

And there lay the nut of the problem – to reorganize a new hipper Deep Feeling from the now passé Hellions, a unified vision was essential to their success; and Jim, not Dave was the band's leader. Poli Palmer recalled, "Jim was very shall we say, 'Italian', so he wanted to give one hundred and ten percent, and Dave sort of does it, but there's no reaction." As for Mason, "He'd sort of make a decision on something and do it, and you'd say 'why didn't you say anything, you know?" With an already long history between them (including many ups and downs), Capaldi could only envision more of the same coming down the road. An ultimatum would finally be delivered. Gordon Jackson recalled the fateful day, "We had to throw Dave out of the Hellions. I can remember sitting in the van and Jim saying 'Dave's gotta go, it's either him or me.' So we said 'O.K – *you* tell him!' And Dave left."

And that was that, or so it seemed. Drifting around London and Birmingham for a bit, Mason's next career move (later viewed as either shrewd or lucky), at first seemed a major demotion – he took a position as 'roadie' for another band. The typically thankless job usually involved humping equipment, keeping guitars in tune as well as setting up and tearing down stage gear. But Dave didn't seem to mind – he was working for Birmingham's most important musical act, and thinking about bigger things.

Mason's hookup with the Spencer Davis Group coincided with the emergence of issues threatening the band's existence. While wildly successful, the bigger gigs and piles of cash couldn't mask the widening cultural divide. Between the dope and extracurricular activities with Chris and others, Steve Winwood was primed to be part of the next musical wave surging in – the rest were not. In hindsight, it was quite clear. Pete York noted, "One of the great rifts between us, and it never should have been – it was indicative of the times – was between those who drank a little beer and wine, and those who were doing drugs."

But the drugs may well have been the least of it. Approaching his musical maturity, Steve had simply surged past them. One direct witness was Dave Mason. Although he'd seen the Davis group many times before, Mason's presence in their midst now provided a penetrating insight into Winwood's importance, "He *was* the band. He was so blessed with a gift, from a very young age." He also noted a burgeoning disenchantment, "Steve was tired of being tagged 'the young Ray Charles', and wanted to try something different."

If Mason had thoughts of capitalizing on the situation, he wisely kept his ambitions to himself – at first. As it was, he was certainly in no position to control *anything* in his current position. But with a guitar always within reach, his intentions surfaced soon enough. It all started at a Davis Group performance where Dave, standing slightly offstage, plugged in and started playing along unbidden on some songs. While Steve merely looked over and smiled, the others, Spencer especially, were peeved at the presumptive move. But it wouldn't be long before Mason's knowledge of the band's repertoire would be better appreciated. With ghost hunts now sometimes taking precedence over gigs, here and there Steve missed a show. Frustrated, on one of these occasions the rest of the group decided to play anyway. Asked by the others to sit in, Mason didn't hesitate. He recalled, "I had to stand in for him one night – which freaked me out, but we pulled it off." While the band's fit of pique might have felt good and gotten them past a tight spot – it was no solution, since neither Mason nor anyone else could come close to filling Winwood's shoes. Still, it was a nice coup, a showcase of Dave's talent and adaptability. And the payoff wasn't long in coming.

(Phillip Knightley, Sunday Express Magazine, May 1999)

('Traffic Jam', Ray Townley, DownBeat, 1/30/1975)

CHAPTER EIGHT

'QUITE COOL, SLIGHTLY HIPPIE'

By the spring of 1966, the once simmering societal and musical stews were beginning to boil. At the center of it all, *Rubber Soul* – released the previous December, still reverberated. Beatles Producer, George Martin described the new universe, "It was the first album to present a new, growing Beatles to the world. For the first time, we began to think of albums as art on their own, as complete entities." Steve Winwood, too, later acknowledged the pervasive influence, saying, "*Rubber Soul* broke everything open. It crossed music into a whole new dimension, and was responsible for kicking off the sixties rock era as we know it." Fueling their minds with pot and psychedelics, the Beatles had uncovered new possibilities for creating music. Besides exotic instruments like the sitar, they were experimenting with studio technology – recording sounds backwards, even trying to go *inside out,* by pushing vocals through Leslie speaker circuitry as they did on "Tomorrow Never Knows".

More important were the ideas behind the songs – a novel mix of introspection and a full embrace of life's experience. And with the model established, the excitement spread to a wider culture awakening to the perception of popular music as art.

The Spencer Davis Group too had reached an apogee, although their positon was more fragile than it looked. While their hit "Keep On Running" knocked the Beatles "Day Tripper" from the number one spot on the British charts in late January, close scrutiny revealed a rather ordinary R&B number energized mostly by Steve's powerful vocals. And in an era defined by groups writing and performing their own material, the SDG still relied on a Jamaican songwriter recruited by Chris Blackwell named Jackie Edwards. The lack of originality didn't bode well for the future.

Unable to keep pace with Steve, by now even their drummer saw trouble brewing, and a weak link in the musical chain. Pete York recalled, "I think one of the reasons that Steve got frustrated with us was that Spencer Davis himself is an extremely limited musician. And I think he just thought 'My god, there must be something more than this', because Steve was *so* far ahead of Spencer, yet it was Spencer's name on the band."

As for Dave Mason, while he may have filled in once for an absent Winwood, a more promising prospect now beckoned. Seeing Steve as *the* talent, and fully aware of his discontent – Mason switched allegiance. Now, whenever Steve wanted to play elsewhere, Dave was there too. For Steve and perhaps Chris, this looked providential. Along with his demonstrable guitar chops, Dave could sing a little and was also willing to play bass, thereby possibly filling two gaps. Meanwhile, fed up with the too-often absent roadie, Spencer Davis finally fired him. But this (once again) merely proved a form of career advancement. Now available 24/7 to play with Steve and Chris, all that was needed to start again was a compatible drummer – hopefully one who could write decent lyrics.

*

Frank Devine isn't quite sure how, or why, he was asked to record with Steve Winwood, but his acceptance was never in question. In recent months, he and the Blueshounds had served as the backing band for Jimmy Cliff. Not yet the reggae star he would be in later years, Cliff's current band was a soul outfit, known for versions of James Brown, Joe Tex and Marvin Gaye songs. While finding success on the road, for Devine the endless covers were beginning to pall – he wanted more. Then from out of the blue, a very promising lead presented itself.

Muscling his drum kit through the door of Birmingham's little Zella Recording Studio, Devine soon came face to face with Winwood, along with Chris Wood and Dave Mason, ready to make music. With the kit arranged and few words exchanged, an effortless jazz-based jam soon flowed as Johnny Haines rolled tape. "I remember it being very jazzy and bluesy, and just saxophone and flute with Chris and Hammond organ with Steve, me on drums and Dave Mason on guitar," said Devine. "It was an informal session, but there *was* a formality about it as well – and it was being recorded. I can remember Muff Winwood standing there, with his great big eyes, and he was sort of tapping his foot, giving encouragement, and I'm sure that he picked up a bass guitar at some point."

Just like that, the 'mystery band' simply came together. Head down, Winwood led while testing his sea legs with a new instrument – a Hammond L100 organ (an 'upgrade' from the classic B3). On this night, he explored the possibilities, pivoting from a Baptist church spiritual feel to the sultry soul shimmer of Memphis as the jams unfolded. Sensing that the sessions, which lasted a day or more, were a big deal – Devine tried to take it in his stride, "He was a giant…And I remember thinking 'That was nice, if something happens, it happens.'"

But what actually *was* happening was anything but clear. Other than asking Devine to keep quiet about the session, Winwood would say little. Secret or not, the excitement was abundant as the Hammond swirled a deep groove while Chris's squealing and crooning tenor sax soared over it. With the commercial constraints removed, the music quite naturally seemed to find a more authentic texture. From Frank's perspective, "They (the Spencer Davis Group) were a rocky, poppy sort of rhythm and blues, and this was absolutely more jazzy. It was really, really nice. I think it was just Steve feeling for a new direction; it was really sort of jamming. I can't remember how long it lasted, but it was an LP's worth."

As dawn broke all got into a van and headed to Corngreaves Hall to relax. Sprawled out under the towering battlement of the Wood's grand home, Devine felt a sense of exuberance as his day wound to a close, "I remember sitting there on the grass, in the sunshine, drinking orange juice, and I thought I'd been transported to another way of life – absolutely gorgeous." He recalled Chris as "An incredibly nice, very quiet, unassuming chap. I remember him standing around in one of those stripy jackets that everyone seemed to have had in the sixties. I think he was quite cool, slightly hippie." But the idyll would prove as brief as it had been magical.

Soon after the date, Frank took ill, and went to Scotland to convalesce. Thinking ahead and hoping for the best, he wrote lyrics he thought might be a good match for Steve's voice. And upon his return the word on the street was encouraging – Winwood had indeed been seeking him. But the lapse in contact proved crucial; by this time Steve had moved on, their paths would not cross again.

Even the tantalizing recordings would lapse into obscurity, neither released nor apparently even preserved. So what was it all about? Was the Zella session only a test of the waters to see if Winwood, Wood and Mason could really make music together? Or perhaps, with the 'Age of Aquarius' looming, the changing times required the jazzer to be replaced by a psychedelic soul drummer. Regardless, an opportunity had slipped by, and Frank knew it. Later he would seek out Zella's owner, Johnny Haines, hoping at least to get his copy of the acetate, but that too had already vanished. If frustrated by the outcome, in later years, with his wife's help, he found a sobering way to look at the road not taken, "(She) said, 'It was a good job you didn't go there – you would have been dead.'"

*

Down South, Jim Capaldi's group Deep Feeling was busy and, in their own fashion, flying high. With no records out of any kind, the band still bustled around the burgeoning underground scene springing up in London. Managed by Giorgio Gomelsky – one of the original suitors of the Spencer Davis Group, they played Blasies in Kensington, and The Scotch of St. James at Mason's Yard in Mayfair. Capaldi's drive for success was the prime mover. "I had all of this mad energy. I had *so* much energy you wouldn't believe, you know?" Capaldi recalled. And that energy was crucial since, "We were unknowns. Professionals, at the time, doing it for a living – but completely unknown." Even so, Deep Feeling's diverse approach kept the increasingly sophisticated audience's attention. "We had a great repertoire in those days. Most bands could do R&B and tasty stuff, we were already writing what would be like 'acid rock'. We had the sound, 'cause we had Poli on flute, and he was trying to 'bug' the flute with a bit of electronics to get strange noises. So we had a real jazz/rock/blues/soul, *and* it was acid!"

Completing the circuit from London back in their home ground, Birmingham, quite naturally they sought out the coolest place in the Midlands – the Elbow Room. The Hellions probably couldn't have played there, but Deep Feeling's sound provided an invitation into that exclusive world. Capaldi had nearly rapturous memories, "It was the classic night club, mainly because of the owner – Don Carless. You couldn't get any cooler than Don, he had a fantastic look, and he was always suited up. He was the magic ingredient there, and he was kind of a tutor to us all musically. He had a wonderful (record) collection."

Capaldi quickly fell under the spell of Carless' carefully arranged ambience. "My experience would be like Bob's (Dylan) in the Village, we had all these fantastic characters. There was a guy named Michael Jones, he was called 'Mick the Twitch', 'Mickey Twitch', his eyes continually flashed left to right, permanently, like a nervous shake – you weren't sure if was looking at you or not." A DJ at the club, the tall, gangly Twitch was often seen wearing slightly ill-fitting suits. Jim was also impressed by the ever-present Royston, who circulated amongst the crowds in a black porkpie hat, "the Jamaican kind of host, wandering around in a very dapper suit, dishing out chili con carne if you wanted any."

But the musical opportunities provided the greatest attraction. Guitarist Gordon Jackson remembered an exciting time when talents and new friendships co-mingled, "When Spencer Davis had finished doing their gigs, they'd head for Birmingham and the nightclub if they were close enough, and there'd be sessions. So Steve would come and sit in with the band. Steve always came with Chris – he was in Locomotive at the time; they'd come in together. And then, obviously from the sessions we got friendly with them. After finishing up at two in the morning we'd end up going back to Don Carless' house, and carrying on, doing various things and listening to music."

Poli Palmer remembered the offhand way that Winwood slipped into their midst. "We'd say, 'the roadie's gonna get up and play a couple of numbers', and he'd either play drums, or he'd just get up and sing. He wouldn't sort of do too much, but he enjoyed it, and we'd hang out together."

But soon it was more than that – the pieces of a very interesting mosaic began falling into place. "Winwood would jam there on the old, upright piano. That was when I first met Chris. I would play vibes all of the time and Chris would play, usually, flute. And we'd just sort of jam – there'd be flute, vibes, piano, guitar, bass and drums. It wasn't sort of jazz at all, it was blues, in the blues idiom", Palmer noted. While seemingly casual, everyone was also playing their best – consciously or not trying to impress Steve, hoping it might lead to more.

The handwriting on the wall for the Spencer Davis Group was now visible to all. In discovering a creative outlet that satisfied him, Steve's enthusiasm for a change was obvious. Even Pete York understood the attraction, "I used to go down and sit in with them at the Elbow Room sometimes, and it was great – much more exciting than it was in the Spencer Davis Group, and I can quite understand why Steve liked to play with them. They were playing their instruments a lot better. Chris played flute and tenor, and the sessions that I sat in with them I really enjoyed it."

Astute and ambitious, Jim Capaldi quickly sized up the situation – with Steve poised to go his own way, he'd need someone to hold down the beat – a slot that wouldn't go unfilled for long. His 'Italian charm' set at full strength, he signaled his availability loud and clear either perched on the drum throne, or joking and rubbing elbows with the young prodigy at every opportunity.

And once behind the kit, Jim put all of his considerable energy into it. While not as technically adept (or precise) as some, he quickly showed an innate ability to follow whatever turns Steve made on piano, organ or guitar. And like Chris, he also had an intangible *feel* that mattered above all else. It probably helped that Capaldi's hero was Al Jackson, the drummer for Booker T and the MG's – also an expert at shadowing a keyboard player. From Jackson, Jim picked up the shuffling, adaptable beat that served as his basic rhythmic pattern. Over that, he could also throw thunderous fills and drum rolls as punctuation, adding his own dynamic to the mix. While both Steve and Chris were impressed, it might have been Jim's ebullient and sometimes raucous personality that actually sealed the deal; with his smiling face behind the drums, jamming became inevitable each time Steve and Chris arrived at the club. With his future suddenly shining much brighter, it seemed that Jim couldn't have been happier.

But Jim's joy in seeing Steve walk through the Elbow Room door was tempered by the sight of the guy he'd recently kicked out of his band only steps behind. Later he could only muse on the fates that had somehow drawn he and Dave Mason back into each other's orbit, "Dave – he was a handful back then. He was an acolyte of Steve, because he had such enormous talent. So… he's kind of hanging out with Steve." Still Capaldi couldn't deny a grudging admiration for the musical growth; in the time away Dave had managed to take his guitar skills up yet another notch. And with his sinuous and stinging guitar lines now punctuating the bluesy jams, the results caught them all off guard; the synergy was off the charts.

With sparks flying, as if by an unspoken signal, the previously wide open rank of players suddenly narrowed to a nucleus of Steve, Chris, Dave and Jim. Based on equal parts musical sympathy and Jim and Dave's strong desire to attach themselves to a rising star, the aggregation seemed to just fall together. And like new lovers they began to seek out a surreptitious location to rendezvous. Luckily, one was nearby.

Having recently moved into London, Chris's Art School buddy Paul Medcalf now worked for Chris Blackwell's Island Records, putting his degree to good use designing record sleeves and advertisements for the Spencer Davis Group. And although the seventeen year old Winwood's official residence was still his parent's Birmingham house, whenever he was in London Medcalf's flat was his crash pad. With Chris's place only a short walk away, Paul's dwelling became the de facto contact site, and ultimately the genesis point of a new musical group. With the four now toe-to-toe, the music would speak for itself. Medcalf recalled, "Steve was living at my place in London. When they'd start jamming together, those guys, it was just ridiculous. There was incredible chemistry between those people. Capaldi had incredible energy – you can imagine somebody's mind constantly dancing."

Jim's energy and enthusiasm was no doubt fueled by the knowledge that with the possibility of forming a band with Steve Winwood, real success in the music business would be tantalizingly close at hand. He was straightforward about the potential, "He was the star of course, he was the name. We were all *thrilled* to be involved with him. We knew it was like an instant step up to stardom once we got it going, you know. So we were thrilled to have such a break."

Already quite tight with Winwood, Dave Mason saw a more nuanced angle to the situation. While Steve was certainly dissatisfied with his old band, the Zella sessions with Frank Devine showed that a few great jams might not be enough to cause him to up and quit. No, a special kind of push would be required, something neither Dave nor Chris were quite suited to do. Whatever else he might have felt about his old band mate, Mason certainly knew that Jim Capaldi was that guy. Only his "mad energy" could catalyze the reaction necessary to separate Steve from the Davis Group. As Mason put it, "We were always just looning around together, and then Jim came."

Dave had no problem visualizing the potential sparkling amongst the four of them, "We sort of started talking about creating a band that was just *different*. Chris was from more of a jazz/art school thing, and Steve, with all his input. Jim and I were sort of, from rock 'n roll and I was, if anything, pop. But of all those elements, creating together, made for something more than the single parts. That's kind of the feeling of the whole thing for me." And from there, a certain sense of inevitability began to crystallize in his mind.

Unbeknownst to Mason, he came perilously close to missing the ride himself. According to Paul Medcalf, early talks between Steve, Chris and Jim singled out Dave Pegg, guitarist for the Blueshounds, as a replacement. The nature of the objection to the obviously talented Mason is unclear, but Chris's perceptivity could have easily foreseen where this particular tangle of personalities might lead. And while Steve hadn't yet experienced Dave's other, more difficult side, Capaldi's previous misgivings about the guitarist almost certainly figured into the mix.

But fate would intervene. Pegg's recent marriage and the perceived lack of freedom that would entail was the deciding factor in not making the offer. Had they done so, rock history would have been quite different, as Pegg, (who would go on to play bass for Fairport Convention) would later say, "I would have loved to have been asked to play..."

Chris had one other candidate in mind. Andy Silvester, his old Sounds Of Blue mate, was also pressed to try out. Andy recalled, "He (Chris) tried to get me to come with him. He said, 'Oh, we're gonna' have a play. I'd like you to have a play with Steve – come and have a jam.' But, I don't know, maybe I was in awe of him (Winwood) too much to relax and enjoy it. I lacked confidence I think, and I declined. But I remember Chris, really trying to get me to go." Having reached another dead end, and with no other compatible prospects in sight, the idea would be dropped; Mason survived the potential ousting none the wiser.

As for Chris, if the thrall of Steve Winwood's presence at first pushed everyone else well into the background, over time the Elbow Room crew finally took stock of the quiet, smiling flute player in their midst. In Jim Capaldi's memory, Chris Wood seemed to just materialize on the scene, "Chris was just *there*. You see, it's hard for me to remember exactly how he came in. We said 'great, let's play together'. I can't remember. All I know is that he was around."

While some would continue to be mystified by his presence – a man seemingly out of place next to a musical giant like Steve – Jim began to get it; slowly waking to the awareness of an extraordinary, yet subtle person who played by his own rules, "He was so...enigmatic, Chris. And he had such a presence – his presence just commanded attention. His musical outlook was so cool – he was never, *ever* putting his foot in the wrong place. He never blew a note that was an obvious, clichéd phrase. He had this gift of putting something in there that made you look in another way, a different direction. He had an angle on things that was different. And he was, to use a cliché, really 'hip'. And when you're really hip, you just know where it should be, and how *not* to be – in the obvious stereotypical kind of stuff. Chris had heaps of that."

Chris's oblique approach was very much a double-edged sword. Certainly his musical expression, especially from the flute, was best when it reflected his inner self. But the source was also delicate. Deep Feeling's Poli Palmer, also a budding flutist, recognized this. "Chris, his nature, in a way, was a very fluttery sort of player – it was his personality… it was very attractive. But he was emotionally aflutter, a fragile person." And this fragility required both proper context and sympathetic musicians for his best expressions to emerge.

Central to his sense of musical security was now Steve Winwood. These days they were like two sides of a coin – diverse in approach, yet utterly compatible. The Elbow Room's proprietor, Don Carless, had insight into the affinity between them, "Chris wasn't technically as good, as in a John Coltrane, but it was what Steve wanted – he came in with his flute at the right time. He could only be natural, Steve would never tell him to play like this, or play like that." In fact, the tight connection served each by compensating for the weaknesses, while amplifying the strengths of the other.

For Chris, music was a reflection of the totality of his life. Having cultivated a wide range of interests, all would be filtered through his artistic perspective – emerging as an eclectic mix of melancholy, humor, pain and outright quirkiness. But the originality came with a tradeoff – playing-wise, traditional technique held little interest. While he could do conventional melody lines when necessary, it was never part of the plan. He would later tell another musician that even when listening to others' music he tried to ignore the solos – preferring to add an improvised spin to the work, even if only in his mind.

And now, released from Locomotive's jazz/R&B bandwidth, he let the last connections to conformity dissolve. Amid the synergy of like-minded players, he went his own way, launching into uncharted territory. The metamorphosis would be as rapid as it was dramatic. Jim Capaldi recalled, "He didn't play sax like a sax player. He was always bringing something *to* the sax, an element of color, of experimentation. He didn't just play it as an instrument to make the sound of a saxophone. He used the saxophone to be *another* instrument, to be a journey into space."

But this disinterest in conventionality meant that some of his fellow musicians didn't get that approach at all, thinking instead that he lacked proficiency. And perhaps jealous of his bond to Steve, some actually regarded him with a measure of contempt. Of course, Chris was often dissatisfied with his own playing, sometimes visibly struggling as he worked himself to the point of frustration in search of a phrase he couldn't quite express. As with his art, second thoughts and self-doubt were all part of the game.

Conversely, Steve seemed to have been born with all of the raw facility and confidence which Chris lacked. Even as a child, his casual aplomb fooled his piano teacher into thinking he could read music when he was actually only reproducing what he'd heard. This talent, combined with the ability to turn his hand to nearly any instrument – not to mention that now titanic soul voice, afforded a unique position in the music scene. Yet Winwood himself suspected that he'd never really earned his so-called 'gift'. In his authorized biography he discussed the talent that brought him such effusive praise as a boy, "But it didn't mean any more than being able to do something like…bend your thumbs back. It just seemed like a trick really."

And while the innate talent had taken him very far, a price would be exacted for the laser focus on music. Having left school at an early age to spend endless days and nights in the company of much older band mates and/or screaming fans, Steve's life, and it seemed his personality, had been channeled into a single dimension. As such, books and the wider world of ideas rarely figured in. Even the emotional connection to the music seemed partly an illusion – an artifact of an ability to mimic. As such, while his vocal inflections on songs like "Georgia On My Mind" could render heartfelt responses from nearly all who listened, the relationship to his actual feelings remained an open question.

So, the partnership between Chris and Steve, as unlikely as it was, started with an interesting symmetry and a kind of equality. Having connected with his generation's version of Ray Charles, Chris understood quite profoundly that Steve's talent was *the* conduit in which his own unconventional musical ideas could be fully realized – there was no other route. And Steve, having befriended a metaphysical wizard, knew he'd located someone capable of filling the spaces between the notes with magic and meaning. As long as the connection between them remained strong, the future of both looked bright indeed.

*

More and more, it was becoming apparent that conjuring magic was what Chris was really about. In an era when many young people were intensely searching, but with only misty notions of a destination, Chris seemed at least to know where to look, and he was on the case. Poli Palmer identified Chris as the low-key leader of their social circle, "It was a spiritual thing at that time, and Chris had it more than anyone else. He was always looking for something, and it was an emotional thing – that he never quite found." Palmer also recalled the confusion of the times, as young musicians tried to reconcile the external goal of 'making it' in the music business from the need for inner spiritual understanding, "That's the reason for all the dope as well. Between the two, you are trying to look for a kind of nirvana, you know?"

If Chris didn't have the answers, any promising angle – internal or external – would be pursued. Of these, his current fascination was with ley lines, quasi-mystical energy traces that supposedly crisscrossed the British landscape. Having found a book on the subject, he was immediately smitten; for Chris, ley lines represented nothing less than a new way of seeing – a hidden world revealed.

It all started in England. By the 1920's Alfred Watkins from Herefordshire had already spent years pondering the odd arrangements of ancient stone circles, burial mounds and churches scattered around the local landscape. One day, while on a trek through the countryside he was struck by a sudden, blinding flash of insight. His vision revealed what he believed to be a complete system of ancient wisdom, lost in modern times. Watkins considered the find so important, he would spend the rest of his life researching and writing about it.

John Michell, who later followed up Watkins' work, described the fateful day, "The revelation took place when Watkins was sixty-five years old. Riding across the hills near Bedwardine, in his native county (Herefordshire), he pulled up his horse to look out over the landscape below. At that moment he became aware of a network of lines, standing out like glowing wires all over the surface of the country, intersecting at the sites of churches, old stones and other spots of traditional sanctity."

The basic idea was that ancient peoples, living in close contact to the land had the sensitivity to perceive patterns of energy emanating from the Earth itself. These linear traces, some of which ran for many miles, could be found all over England, and theoretically, the planet. The lines were a form of power, a connection to the mysterious energies of the Earth; an ideal location to build holy sites. Standing stones, often weighing many tons, were somehow moved great distances to the proper alignments, and arranged in circles and other obscure formations. Even as Christianity spread across the British Isles, these power sites were initially acknowledged and respected. Churches were built on ley lines, not just to wrest control from the pagans, but because strange forces seemed to guide them there. Michell noted, "When Wrexham church was being built on a low meadow, it was found every morning that the work of the previous day had been destroyed. One night a watch was kept. Nothing happened until towards morning, when a voice in the air was heard crying 'Bryn-y-groy,' the name of the field on higher ground. The stones were taken there and the building continued without disturbance."

According to Watkins and Michell, with modernity's encroachment, the co-dominant paradigms of Christianity and science inexorably ground the ancient knowledge away. Over time, only a vague dream-like memory of the Earth's energy lines remained, lingering only Mankind's subconscious, or so it seemed.

Watkins book, *The Old Straight Track*, became Chris's bible. Although a somewhat dry academic tome, there was an exciting angle to it; readers were invited to carry on the work themselves. With Britain covered with ancient sites, undiscovered ley lines awaited, beckoning the ardent student.

His mind inflamed with the possibilities, Chris soon imagined an original angle to pursue – could the energy from those lines be somehow directed into music? While some chuckled at his eccentricity, eventually he would find, if not converts, at least folks willing to share adventures. Before long, Chris, the Watkins book in one hand and a map ruled with lines of ink in the other, would be guiding quests across the countryside. And before the others really knew what was going on, the distinctions between the spiritual and musical landscapes would blur, overlap and eventually, merge.

Well past midnight in the Malvern Hills, Deep Feeling's van bounced in and out of rutted tracks cutting through the semi-wild, windswept Herefordshire night. This was ground zero – Alfred Watkins home ground – a land of craggy outcroppings and deep ravines pulsing with subterranean energy. Following Chris's map, headlights cut through the grey pre-dawn gloom until the van rattled to a halt at Midsummer Hill, adjacent to British Camp, an Iron Age hilltop fort. With that, the disheveled musicians tumbled out into the twilight, unloaded their instruments and prepared to meet the sunrise – a fiery point for the ley line cutting across the landscape. Here they would perform; making a musical offering to Mother Nature, hoping for a rush of inspiration in return.

Poli Palmer recalled the free-form ritual, "We got there about five in the morning, with the sun coming up. There's congas, and I set up my vibes, and Chris had his flute, Winwood had an acoustic guitar, and we just spread over the hills. I remember we were jamming away, and Winwood, as he would, would just wander off away from people. We said, 'where's he gone?', and suddenly twenty feet above us, on a bit of a crag, he sort of sat there – strumming away, singing. If you can imagine, twenty feet away, there's this natural morning acoustic, you know. It was one of those things that obviously was impossible to record, but it would have sounded… just the ethereal quality, of the mist coming off of it. It was lovely you know."

Now able to call the music/ley line conjunction a success, Chris perhaps paused for a moment's satisfaction, but there was much more he wanted to do. In reality, the ethereal times were just beginning, and a wayward American musician on a quest of his own would soon join them.

('The Beatles Recording Sessions', Mark Lewishon, 1988)

('The View Over Atlantis', John Michell, 1969)

('The Beatles, The Biography', Bob Spitz, 2005)

('The Old Straight Track', Alfred Watkins, 1925)

('Roll With It', Chris Welch with Steve Winwood, 1990)

BOB DYLAN'S GHOST

The spring of 1966 found Bob Dylan touring the world with a new, electrified sound – the poetic stanzas loved by millions now accompanied by drums and loud guitars. Fueled on speed and other drugs, Dylan had become a creative blazing ember; his English tour with the group later dubbed 'The Band', found him producing the best music of his career, even as the supercharged lifestyle took him to the end of his tether. On his eventual return to America, he would be waylaid by a mysterious motorcycle accident, which precipitated a seclusion lasting for years.

Having probed the aristocracy of English rock for the past couple of years, Dylan's interest was winding down by the first quarter of '66. He'd smoked pot with the Beatles, played harp with Brian Jones, and jammed with Eric Clapton and John Mayall's Bluesbreakers, and yet something remained unsatisfied. There was one more contact he desired to make – to find the origin of a particular *voice* – the volcanic soul emanation that had been erupting from the radios across England that spring. Like most people who heard Steve Winwood belt out tunes, Dylan was impressed, amazed even.

The opportunity to trace this last musical strand came as his tour rolled into Birmingham. Spencer Davis and Muff Winwood were ushered backstage to meet the poet laureate of the generation before Dylan's Birmingham Town Hall concert on April 12th. While they were thrilled to meet the legend, all Bob wanted to talk about was Steve; his first question the same as nearly any other fan, "How did he learn to sing like that?" The fact that Winwood was absent only enhanced Dylan's interest. When it was revealed that Steve was out ghost hunting with a gaggle of friends at a place called Witley Court, the desire proved irresistible. Muff would later tell of Dylan's eager response, "Oh, where is it? Where do I go? I love those kinds of places." Piling into cabs, Bob Dylan and the others took off in the middle of night for a fifty-mile drive to find the dead mansion and meet 'the voice'.

So far, so good – but beyond here the story becomes as convoluted as the winding road to Witley Court itself. The sudden appearance of Bob Dylan, seemingly out of nowhere, was a shock that no one was prepared for. To the stoned spirit seekers, it was almost as if *Dylan* was some kind of ghost, and the psychic repercussions would be great enough to distort the memory of some of the participants. Jim Capaldi, for example, believed that *only* he and Steve Winwood met Dylan at Witley – arranged when Dylan's road manager called for Steve at the Elbow Room.

Yet Poli Palmer had a very clear recollection of being there too, along with the usual group of explorers. And he was equally sure that Dylan was definitely *not* expected, "We didn't know anything about this – it's sort of three o'clock on a Sunday morning and we were all frightening one another to death, climbing around on the ruins. Suddenly these four black cabs pull up at the entrance – these London Taxi type things, and we're like 'What's this?' We thought it was a raid or something. Suddenly a door opens and Dylan gets out – it's the middle of the night in Worcestershire – not a light anywhere. He gets out with a pair of shades on and looks around. Then someone else gets out with shades on – Dylan and all the guys playing in his band were sort of wandering around this place saying 'wow, wow!' He really just wanted to meet Winwood, basically, then he got into the whole thing, 'cause it was a spooky place."

Anna Westmore worked at the Elbow Room at this time, and remembered it going down this way, "One night we were at the Elbow Room, and we decided to go, we all said, 'Let's go to Witley Court'. It was Chris, Jim, Steve and myself and my girlfriend Cindy. And of course, it was a full moon - all of those kind of calendar things were important. The English countryside is dark – and we were going with a flashlight down the hill, and all of a sudden there was a flashlight coming up. We were freaking out, screaming – and these people were getting closer and closer – and we gradually got next to the people, and it was Bob Dylan and the Band. It was an absolute coincidence – they were doing the same thing – and we were freaking each other out. Bob Dylan was standing there with long fingernails, and I was *screaming*. All I could see were those long fingernails, like 'what the hell is this?'" And this detail checks out – Dylan's right hand (guitar picking) nails were indeed freakishly long at the time.

Stephanie Wood remembered, "We all went after the Elbow Room – I *do* remember being there. I drove Steve in my orange minivan. We decided that it would be great fun to go ghost hunting. Witley had this strange fascination; there had been a fire, things must have gone on, people must have died – there *had* to be a ghost. It was a cool thing to do at three in the morning, after the Elbow Room." Steph was nonplussed by the American visitor, "I remember that no one was fazed that it was Bob Dylan – rather, it was Witley Court! It wasn't the fact that Dylan was there - it was only after you get older…"

In the end, Witley would enrapture Dylan too, and later he would briefly recall the visit in a *Rolling Stone* interview. While hazy on the history, he did recall, "We went out to see a haunted house, where a man and his dog was to have burned up in the 13th century. Boy, that place was spooky."

But was there a ghost appearance for Bob? Muff Winwood – who claimed to have gone with Steve in Dylan's limo, had a very specific memory that jibed (more or less) with Dylan's. Muff recalled, "We told him that the guy that had lived in the house had died with his dog and how if you went there you could see him walking around with his dog. And he was absolutely fascinated… We said, let's all be very quiet, let's see what we can hear… and in the mists were these old statues in the garden that had got ivy growing all over them and they looked really eerie – and somewhere a dog barked! Now this is likely to happen in the countryside in Worcestershire at gone midnight, but Dylan is convinced that he's heard the ghost of the dog! He was like a kid! He amazed me because I looked up to this great man, but he'd just keep running up to you and grabbing you by the arm, saying, 'This is unbelievable! This is fantastic!'"

Their guest satisfied, the party finally decamped back to Birmingham. In Jim's version, he, Steve and Bob returned to Dylan's digs at the Albion Hotel to spend the rest of the night in a one-sided conversation. Slumped against a hotel wall, Bob would rap an elliptical stream-of-consciousness monologue, which ultimately proved a bit too much for Steve, who eventually slipped away. As sunlight finally flooded the room, a dazed Jim would be sent off with a sort of apology, "I'm sorry about that, but if you weren't here, I would have said all of that to the wall anyway", after which he too stumbled out into the street to hitchhike home.

Although this was the story that Jim recalled, others obviously disagreed with the exclusivity of it. Anna remembered the evening concluding this way, "So we ended up going back to their hotel room, and we sat up all night talking about music – Jim, Steve and Chris to Bob Dylan and Robbie Robertson, and all of them."

It is both interesting and kind of odd that Chris, who was nearly always at the epicenter of this type of spirit-seeking goings on – especially at Witley Court, would be entirely left out of Jim's narrative. In later years, he would go so far as to assert that "Chris wasn't there", as well as laughing out loud at Dave Mason's purported recollection of the night. "He (Dave) said to me – you remember when we went out to Witley Court?' I said, 'What do you mean 'you remember', *you* weren't there!"

But Poli Palmer was equally sure of the opposite. "*I know* that Dave Mason was there… *and* Chris, I suspect we all (Deep Feeling and friends) were." Stephanie Wood bluntly placed her brother at the center of it all – the instigator of the adventure, "They wouldn't go if he hadn't told them about it, (and) *I* wouldn't have gone without Chris."

Irrespective of which version of the story happened, Chris would never contradict Jim's account of the evening at Witley Court. In the end, his affection for his friends and family was simply more important than historical detail. As Stephanie always believed she had introduced Chris to Steve Winwood in '65, (although Steve Hadley recalled that they'd met years before) – rightly or wrongly, when it came to people he cared about (and Jim was already in that group), if it was important for them to believe something, their version of events would go uncontested. And while there was a significant downside to this empathetic approach, that would be of no consequence to Chris until much later.

('The Rolling Stone Interview: Bob Dylan', Jann Wenner, Rolling Stone 47, Nov 29 1969)

(Muff Winwood interview, from a Bob Dylan fanzine, 1980's)

THE 'DREAM OF TRAFFIC'

Based on the amount of time Steve spent with his new friends it might seem that the Spencer Davis Group had already died from antipathy, but from outward appearances the opposite was true. With manager Blackwell pushing hard from behind, the band continued its juggernaut to the top. From March and into April of 1966 the song that helped to inflame Bob Dylan, "Somebody Help Me", was a number one hit in the British record charts. Soon after, they would tour with The Who, an up-and-coming band who often ended shows in a manic haze of smashed guitars and drum kits.

By May, the Davis Group was fifth on the bill at the *New Musical Express*' Poll Winner's Concert at the Empire Pool, Wembley, in London. The lineup presented an unmatched pinnacle of 1960's rock talent, including Roy Orbison, the Yardbirds, The Who, the Rolling Stones, and for the last time – the Beatles. Although this would be a high water mark, performance-wise, Winwood's disenchantment had become an open secret to many British musicians. With the scent of blood now in the air, hopeful suitors now circled to see if they could lure the talented Mr. Winwood their way.

Still sharing his London Flat with Steve, Paul Medcalf saw the offers roll in. "I've got to go off and see Alexis," he announced to Medcalf one day while heading out the door. Perhaps *the* elder statesmen of the London blues scene, Alexis Korner's early 60's band, Blues Incorporated had at one point included Jack Bruce, Charlie Watts and Mick Jagger. Always a widely respected figure, over the years Korner had been involved with almost everyone associated with British R&B. Many of the young players that he nurtured would go on to form successful bands of their own.

Upon his return, Winwood announced, "Alexis wants me to join with him and do something." Although given a quizzical look by Paul, Steve seemed to be seriously considering it: "Well, I could learn an awful lot from Alexis, he knows more about blues and jazz than anybody I know." A short time later, Medcalf watched the other shoe drop. "And of course, there was a bit of bad feeling with Jim and Dave, 'Ugh, what's he want to go with Alexis Korner for? An old, fuckin' has-been like Alexis Korner'. Here was the young bloods looking at someone who was middle-aged to them. And I didn't say anything to them at the time, but I'd (also) been 'round to see John Mayall...'"

Like Korner, Mayall was a slightly older musician and bandleader who helped incubate young talent. His band, the Bluesbreakers, had just recently lost the services of their guitar player, Eric Clapton, who left to form his own band with Ginger Baker and Jack Bruce – something they called 'Cream'. In Mayall's apartment with Medcalf, just a week after his visit with Korner, Steve sat impassively as Mayall hinted at his motives while playing demos from a tape player. Fretting that he was losing Winwood's attention, and lacking a spare take-up reel, Mayall finally let the master tape just unspool into a wastepaper basket as they listened. But again there would be no sale.

As for the newly formed Cream, they too were thinking about popping the question. Clapton had known Winwood as far back as early 1964, when the two shared a stage backing Sonny Boy Williamson at the Birmingham Town Hall. Friends ever since, they had even recorded tracks with the ad hoc, one-off 'Powerhouse' band that included Jack Bruce, Ben Palmer and Pete York in March '66. In the early stages of Cream, Clapton floated the idea of adding Steve as the keyboard player and another vocalist. But meeting resistance in a band that could already agree on little, Clapton wisely chose to bide his time.

Imagining Steve's next move became a preoccupation for many. According to Paul Medcalf, Chris Blackwell thought that sending Winwood out as a solo artist was the best plan. "How Blackwell saw it when Steve wanted to leave was 'Oh well, what about Las Vegas? We can probably set you up with Ray Charles in Las Vegas!' He wanted to groom him like Tony Bennett, as a singer. That was the first thing that Blackwell came up with – 'You can do big shows, we can put orchestras behind you' and god knows what." And the manager's opinion of Winwood's jamming buddies from the Elbow Room? "Blackwell had all these big ideas for Steve, and he wasn't too happy for him to go off with three total unknowns," Medcalf recalled.

CHAPTER TEN

So the tug of war for Winwood's future was on. The only ones unconcerned were Steve, and surprisingly, Chris Wood. From Medcalf's perspective, "Chris was not a big ego… it sort of explains a lot. Chris didn't bother with all of this (tumult), he just kind of went along… he was easy going in that way." One thing that set him apart was his commercial ambition, which was minimal. While others heads' may have danced with visions of chart position, money and fame, Chris's long held disdain for the financial definition of 'success' allowed a certain clarity and detachment. He also had something else the others lacked – a deep sense of security about his relationship with Steve. Having taken the time to develop a true friendship that included intellectual seeds, humor and musical sympathy, Chris had only a casual confidence about where things were heading in the fall of '66. As he would say later, "All this time Steve and I had this dream of Traffic and after another three to six months, it happened."

Meanwhile, his days with Locomotive sputtered to an end. While the band was still popular, even scoring a televised appearance on the BBC, the once hidden agenda was finally exposed. Jim Simpson saw the change when Chris and his new clique showed up at a rehearsal one day, stoned and giggling, "I remember once, Steve Winwood had a fast little Triumph car, a Vitesse, and they'd just come back from London, all together, and they were really high. They rushed me into the corner and said, 'Listen to this man!', and they played me a tape recording with the microphone taped next to the exhaust of the car. I don't know who was behind it, but you know, they weren't exactly center field." It was true. With months of jamming behind them, by now Chris, Steve, Dave and Jim had drawn so close as to have evolved into a kind of four-headed entity. The combination of music, friendship and drugs cemented a sense of inevitability as to what was coming. Chris turned in his notice.

While unhappy with the loss of his sax player, Simpson couldn't find it in him to begrudge his departure. Having also known Winwood from the very early days, he was aware that Chris would have been crazy to pass up this chance, "When Steve was going to form another band, we all felt it was going to be important. Steve was a strange, introverted guy. And I think the 'family' thing beckoned to Chris. I think Chris felt very much at home with him as a person."

And yet, as he watched him go, Simpson's last thoughts (like those of John Walker) were to wonder how well the shy horn player would fare in the rock 'n roll world. "He was an exceptionally nice, gentle man. I don't know anyone who disliked him; I never heard a bad word against him. He was sensitive, he was easily hurt. Maybe it was the age difference; I know that I felt protective toward him. He was faintly bewildered by life. In a way, we jazzers felt it was a shame that he went into that sort of music. We lost a good player like him…"

*

With the musical approach evolving, an equally dramatic shift in lifestyle, very much centered on hashish, accompanied it. While illegal drug use is often ascribed as a unique aspect of the 1960's rock scene, among jazz musicians in America the tradition stretched back to the '20's and before. Even earlier, it could be traced to the 19th century intellectuals of Europe. French Psychiatrist Jacques Joseph Moreau wrote an article titled "Hashish and Insanity" in 1845. While initially intending to show a connection between the drug and mental illness, in the end Moreau's less-than-scientific study made hashish sound more like a portal to enlightenment than a road to madness. Noting the bliss exhibited by the participants, Moreau himself would soon join in, handing out hashish paste to the others with the knowing comment: "This will be deducted from your share in Paradise."

The drug of mirth and visions would prove the glue that bound the not-yet-named group of four together. Jim Capaldi recalled friendships incubated in wreaths of smoke, "We had this energy that immediately clicked, and before we knew it we were going around Birmingham from the club, scoring. I was scoring the hash; I loved hash then – from this Jamaican woman on Pershore Road in Birmingham. Her name was Maria. You'd go in, for ten bob…and you'd get a little block of hash that was the size of a gambling dice, and we'd cook it up in the car – roll up a smoke and we'd be as snug as a bug in a rug. And it quickly formed into jamming and playing together."

As they planned their future, this drug became their touchstone. The preferred method of ingestion, also picked up from the Jamaicans, was to mix the hash with tobacco, joining two rolling papers and a third one for the end and using matchbook cardboard as a mouthpiece. Besides the social bond and creative insight, for Chris, hashish also provided another cushion against anxiety and general insecurity. Henceforth, the loaded cigs became the required ritual prefacing playing music, especially in public.

And so the endgame to extract Winwood from his band played out. Released from his roadie duties with the Spencer Davis Group, Mason was set. But while Capaldi professed to be ready, he also hedged his bets doing recording sessions with Deep Feeling (funded by Giorgio Gomelsky). He also kept his mouth shut. With half of their debut album in the can, as far as the rest of his group knew, things were only moving forward. Certainly the members of Deep Feeling needed no reminding about the unpredictability of the winds of change that shaped rock music – trends were changing monthly, if not weekly. Still, as September waned, the band's eclectic and electric approach fit in quite well with the burgeoning underground scene; gigs were offered in both Birmingham and increasingly in the place where it mattered most – London. Jim's moonlighting aside, things never looked better.

But none were prepared for the hurricane of change – incarnated in the form of a skinny American guitar player – that blew into London that fall. One night in October, as Deep Feeling prepared to play a rather important show at a club called 'Knuckles', Gordon Jackson recalled a backstage request, "Viv Prince took us down there, 'cause he was trying to manage us, and McCartney was there. Then Chas Chandler walked in and said 'Can this guy play?' And we said '*Well…*' you know." Chandler, the former bass player from the Animals was now trying to break into artist management. The clout from his days as an Animal was enough to convince the band to give his client a shot.

Poli Palmer was playing drums and Jim Capaldi was up front singing when Jimi Hendrix joined them. Although he stood near the back, Hendrix proved a visual magnet even before he played a note. "He was dressed all in black, with a black polo neck sweater, black jeans, with his 'Dylan hair', which is now an 'afro'", recalled Palmer. As for preparation, he asked only, "What key is it?" before the band kicked off a blues-based number. But within seconds, the walls of the club shook as the unknown guitarist unleashed a barrage of sound. Without any preconceptions of what to expect, the band staggered under the onslaught which bled from the amplifiers. Uttering a disbelieving *"Jesus Christ!"* Palmer nearly jumped out of his skin as the vibrato and feedback emanating from Hendrix's guitar roiled around him. Gordon Jackson, realizing it was hopeless to try to add anything, simply dropped his hands from his guitar and backed away. He recalled, "To start with, he just got up on stage and started jamming. And one by one everybody left the stage apart from Poli, who was drumming and Meredith on bass – there was just the three of them. I can distinctly remember Hendrix being there, playing guitar with his teeth." Poli Palmer added, "It's easy to say, 'Oh, I knew he was going to be famous', but I don't think we actually thought that. We were just blown away… it was just so uniquely different."

Hendrix' arrival shattered the smug complacency that had developed in the wake of the overwhelming success of bands like the Beatles and the Rolling Stones. Chandler's plan to expose Hendrix to the scene by letting him blow away the bands he sat in with was both shrewd and devastating. Like a startling apparition he appeared, seemingly everywhere, in his first few days in London; first in Zoot Money's apartment, and then on stage with Brian Auger and the Trinity, before ducking into a small club to play with Alexis Korner's blues band. All who visited were left in a state of shock. Even Cream, a band with huge talent and egos to match, were left humbled after Jimi's visit.

At only twenty-four, Hendrix's arrival heralded a rare rewriting of the rules, and the impact was profound. Within a week, he was putting his own band together – not surprisingly a trio, with Mitch Mitchell on drums and Noel Redding on bass. Known as 'The Jimi Hendrix Experience', the band was instantaneously famous, at least in the U.K., and soon found success on every level.

In the audience for that Deep Feeling gig, Chris was immediately smitten with the guitarist. Thereafter, wherever Hendrix played, he made a point to be there, once even dragging his old Birmingham friend Mike Lewis along to see a show – raving the whole time. Upon their backstage meeting, Chris was impressed but not intimidated, discovering a shy off-stage demeanor in Jimi not unlike his own, as well as an artistic kinship similar to that shared with Steve; a rare situation indeed. The relationship would grow from there.

While Hendrix's trajectory was straight up, Deep Feeling suddenly faced its demise. After one last jam session at a club back on the home turf of Evesham, a remorseful Capaldi pulled the plug. While taking responsibility, he also cast the break up into the hands of fate, saying: "Guys, I'm sorry, I know this is terrible, I'm abandoning you all, but this thing is like destiny – It's not like something I can turn down. It's the direction I'm going in now, and I can't miss it you know."

CHAPTER TEN

The time was ripe. As Frank Devine found only too late, just because Winwood hadn't yet summoned the will to separate from the Spencer Davis Group didn't mean that others shouldn't show their intent. With Chris free and Dave more than ready, for Jim, it was none too soon.

From here the intentions were overt – wherever Winwood went, Mason, Wood and Capaldi were there as well. The end of the original Spencer Davis Group played out over several months; a slow motion crash that everyone should have seen coming. Having just released another album, *Autumn '66*, the rest of the band found themselves increasingly estranged from Steve even as his creativity took a quantum leap forward. Months of jamming with Deep Feeling and Chris had done something astounding. Fueled by hashish and new influences, his vocals had gotten even stronger and more self-assured, while the musicianship suddenly matured.

The last two singles that the Spencer Davis group did were their most powerful and original; "Gimme Some Lovin" was written around a throbbing riff Muff Winwood had heard on a recent Homer Banks record – "A Lot of Love". Opening with Muff's four note bass prelude, the tune jumped to life as the Hammond blasted a loud chord followed by four descending notes, a shout of 'Hey!', and finally Steve's startlingly powerful vocals. The lyrics, written at Medcalf's London flat, were sung with a gusto that belied their simplicity. Released in Britain, it went to number 2 on the charts in early November.

Even more importantly, the song was scheduled to be released in America. Spencer had long dreamed of a huge U.S. tour – the path to true superstardom. And now, with their best ever work about to float across the American airwaves, his band stood poised on the brink of that precious threshold.

But there would be no American trip. Unbeknownst to the others, as 1967 dawned, a crucial shift had occurred. Manager Blackwell finally understood that – hit records or not – Winwood was departing. His own Vegas plans abandoned, Blackwell accepted that the band of "unknowns" would be the ones taking Steve to the next phase of his career.

In retrospect, the warning signs were impossible to miss. In the rock press, Winwood had already stated that all of the hit records in the world couldn't make him stay. "I feel that I have done all that I can with the group, and now I must get out or be swallowed up into the oblivion of just another hit making machine. I must do more with my life than that." The original Spencer Davis Group was already dead; the others just didn't know it yet.

Blackwell covertly facilitated the transition, allowing the as-yet-unnamed new group to test their legs by making overdubs on the already completed Spencer Davis Group single. Medcalf recalled the secrecy as "Steve and his Gypsies" (as the proto-group was known with some derision) met up at Pye Studios in the Marble Arch district of London to do overdubs on "Gimme Some Lovin". "They were asked to come in and pepper it up. Blackwell snuck 'em in. Spencer really wasn't seeing it. Steve would clear off with me, and we'd meet up with them." Jimmy Miller, an American drummer turned arranger/producer that Chris Blackwell had recently begun to work with was brought in to oversee the process. In Miller's hands a new dimension emerged as Capaldi played an African drum, changing the feel and adding power. Then even more percussion was added. Balancing this, a backing chorus was topped by, of all people, Chris Wood, who pulled out a surprisingly high falsetto.

Arrangements were made to add a similar zest to "I'm A Man", the last major contribution Steve Winwood would make to the Davis Group. For this track, Winwood's tune borrowed a bit from "Coming Home Baby", a Mel Tormé number from 1962, which in turn had been influenced by Ray Charles's version of "Hit The Road Jack". The American version of "I'm A Man" again saw added production, with Miller squeezing the potential with more backing vocals and several layers of percussion. The overdubs added a flavor of Latin exotica that had an impact in the United States, creating a sense of anticipation in this exciting 'new' group.

By now, the press was finally waking to the understanding that all was not well. Two weeks after "Gimme Some Lovin" had nearly reached the top of the charts in England, the *New Musical Express*, the country's foremost popular music paper reported that: "Steve Winwood and Spencer Davis are no longer on speaking terms." The vibes were obvious in the promotional video for "Gimme Some Lovin". Filmed in a closed London department store, the mostly grim faced band lip-synced a series of silly scenes including Winwood singing under a woman's hair dryer. Another shot of the store escalators captured a prophetic, if unintentional indicator of the near future – on one a smiling Winwood ascending, while Spencer Davis and Pete York were on the other, gliding downwards on an unstoppable track.

As Spencer Davis watched his dream crumble, Jim Capaldi couldn't help feeling overjoyed to see his own being fulfilled. In early 1967 a final set of tours took the Davis Group to the northwest coast of England, and then to Scandinavia. For Capaldi it was a heady time, somehow both carefree and rolling forward full tilt. Solidifying the relationship with Winwood, they wrote their first song together – "Paper Sun", at a bed and breakfast in Newcastle.

Jim drew closer to Chris as well – recalling a sense of indefinable destiny when he appeared seemingly out of nowhere, from the foliage of London's biggest park. "I remember meeting Chris in London. He was wandering across Hyde Park, I was coming across the street and we ran into each other! That was a warm moment. It was wonderful, a great buzz to see him – just to run into him, you know." And in these intoxicating times, chance and fate now seemed fully intertwined.

Chris was there at Newcastle too, then on to Blackpool , as the 'Gypsies' shadowed the Spencer Davis Group's last commitments. Having hitchhiked to the coast with the Elbow Room's 'Mickey Twitch', Jim recalled a crazy, joyful time, as they slept on the beach, and played like children: "Chris would be there, and we'd be hanging out – just hanging out. And we'd go to the 'Fun Fair', (ride) on the Helter Skelters, the Big Dippers. I remember Chris was so sensitive, so finely tuned and artistic. But his whole presence, his whole spirit, was so beautiful – he was such a beautiful person, I can't tell you. He was also nervous'y. Not nervous, but he was very… like we'd get in the car on the 'Big Dipper', and he'd be crushing me up against the bar, on top of me. And I was laughing, 'cause I couldn't catch my breath. I'd be going, *'Chris!'*, and he'd be hanging on for dear life, squashing me up in the corner! But it was wonderful, just a wonderful brotherhood that we'd got going."

And that in a nutshell *was* Chris; finely tuned, artistic and in his core, vulnerable. How well this combination of traits would work in a landscape of egos, cash and fleeting fame remained very much to be seen.

At Chris's insistence, all had their astrological charts read. More than just a lark, the result seemed to confirm the personalities, and to some extent the roles, each would play for years to come. Born in the early morning hours of June 24, Chris was a Cancer. He had been checking into astrology for years, and by now he was a true believer. And it made sense; the aligning of human personalities into the context of the planets and stars was almost like a cosmic extension of the ley lines; perhaps it was *all* interconnected. Looking at a modern day description of his star sign, it is easy to see Chris's character reflected in the words of Astrologer Stephanie Norris:

"The symbol for Cancer is the crab, which retires into its shell if threatened.

'I FEEL' is the motto for Cancer. You are emotional, sensitive and easily hurt. You need to be needed and are very caring. Children, plants and artistic projects all thrive under your protection.

Home and family are very important to you and you can remember things from your childhood as clearly as if they happened yesterday. There is a part of you that doesn't want to grow up and you make a ready playmate.

You are imaginative and empathetic and will mirror other people's feelings back to them. They trust you and will confide in you, although you yourself are a very private person and keep your own feelings to yourself.

Your sensitivity can make you touchy and you can also be very moody. Your reluctance to let go of the past can make you clingy.

You are the nurturer of the zodiac."

Capaldi also saw an extroverted side, attributed to Chris's 'rising' sign, "He was so funny, he'd suddenly get up, in a field, on a rock or something, and he'd start doing a Black Country preacher. Where he comes from, is on the outskirts of Birmingham, Cradley Heath – 'Black Country', and the accent is *so* strong. And he'd do a 'preacher' – fire and brimstone – going on about 'fornication', you know, and he would crack us all up. You see, he was Leo rising, Cancer, and I'm Leo, Cancer rising, so we're like the opposite. But because I'm Leo, I have all this outward – my energy is Leo, you can't escape that you know. I was much more the spokesman, the madman… it was my energy in the beginning. Steve was quite quiet, and Dave was quiet too – both Taurus. Chris was also sensitive and quiet, but the Leo rising – he could suddenly be outrageous you see. And he could be more extrovert than me sometimes, so it was a good combination, it could be very nice."

But while the Taurus personality is well known for its fabled stubbornness, Winwood's chart actually showed him to be a 'double Taurus'. But if he and Mason were sometimes akin to bulls with locked horns, each needing to have their own way, any selfish tendencies would be pushed aside by the first blush of musical love. And now all that was needed was the right title to bind the individuals into one.

Not surprisingly it was Jim's 'constantly dancing mind' that came up with it. "I said, to my mates, 'I've got a great name for the band – 'Traffic'." Capaldi recalled. Around the time that he had run into Chris in Hyde Park, the word had popped into his head, born out of the frustration of having his path literally blocked by rushing cars. He instantly knew he was on to something, "because it's one of those names that's absolutely right there, in your consciousness, the whole time. It's so obvious, but you don't think of it that way. So 'Traffic', you know. I had so many crazy ideas – that the drums would be covered in lights, with things flashing – traffic things, on and off."

If some of the wilder ideas never came off, his label proved solid. Even so, the name wasn't accepted without some scrutiny. While Chris apparently loved it right off, the group skeptic, Paul Medcalf, was dubious, saying, "I don't know, it sounds druggy to me", to which Jim countered, "Oh, I love it, honk, honk, beep, beep!" followed by Winwood's laugh and suggestion, "We might as well call ourselves 'Roadworks'!" But without any other serious contenders, the name stuck. They were *Traffic*.

Having long brewed in the minds of Steve and Chris, the "dream" had finally been realized. While coming together through a combination of planning, chance, chemistry and conniving, they would go forward with the best of intentions – a sort of collective, utopian ideal, in tune with, and even a little ahead of the times. From the Beatles, they accepted the notion that fluidity and growth were essential to harmonize with an ever changing world. But Traffic's identity was also based around being wide open to all influences, any muse, for the final product. And with each member bringing something to the table, an interesting symmetry had already emerged – the jazzy side favored by Chris and Steve was balanced by Jim's 'acid' soul and Mason's blues and rock leanings.

It also was agreed that serious preparation was required before any product would be issued, "Six months of writing and studying," as Winwood had told *Rave* in early '67. Heavily influenced by the art school perspective, the idea was to let the group grow organically to a natural maturity, so as to not let the rush to marketplace ruin the work. They made another step forward from the Beatles template – songwriting was to be a group product. It was to be all for one and one for all – a band of brothers.

There was one more area to nail down; although here the unity wasn't as solid it appeared. Since their earliest philosophical meetings, Steve and Chris had agreed that the 'pop' approach was out. With money at its core, it was crass cynical approach to music, the enemy. Of course, Chris had always felt that way, but Winwood's experience with the teeny-bop world had opened his eyes as well. He again told *Rave* (a decidedly 'pop' music rag): "I don't like pop. It has done nothing for me… I'm not flattered when kids scream at me." And yet, in adopting this view, both had apparently willed away a nasty little fact – popular music is what it is for a reason – it sells. And with 45's and LP records being the wares peddled in the modern musician's trade, an inherent conflict of interest was already in place – one which would forcefully reassert itself in the not-too-distant future.

Typically the first question asked by the press of the day when encountering a new band was: 'Who is the leader?' In this case, nearly all assumed it was Steve. Certainly it would be reasonable to conclude that the other 'unknowns' were simply side men, hired to assist the boy genius. But Medcalf, the ultimate insider, flatly refuted the notion, "I don't think there was a leader in Traffic. It was a melting pot, they all just contributed. With Steve and Jim and Mason there was too much (conflicting) ego to be a leader." But with egos submerged for the time being, the intentions were initially all good.

The brotherhood was sealed with a symbol of identity. Carol Russell, a London artist familiar to Chris Blackwell and Penny Massot met and talked philosophy with the band. Inspired, she returned with a painting that showed something that looked vaguely like a swastika or a wheel with a square axel point and four arrows projecting from it and folding in on each other. The symmetry implied both separate parts and unity, and with a little imagination, a sense of motion – rolling forward. They loved it – like the name 'Traffic', it was somehow familiar and mysterious at the same time. The original artwork would be kept and treasured by the band, and from that day forward the 'Traffic Symbol' served as a mark of identity on all of their records, the group van, and really anything associated with them.

Even before the Spencer Davis Group had played its last show, Chris Blackwell heard Winwood loud and clear when he said that a long 'study time' would be needed. From a manager's point of view, the idea of a 'star' taking half a year 'off' only to begin again from scratch was likely hard to swallow. It was, in fact, unprecedented. But in a world where 'cashing in' as quickly as possible was the default management position, Blackwell was smarter. Having observed the growth in young Winwood these last few years, he made a reasonably safe bet that given the investment, something damn good would come out at the far end. Besides, the way it penciled out, the whole thing wouldn't really be *that* expensive. Wood, Capaldi and Mason were only too happy to sign contracts giving each a stipend of twenty English Pounds a week (bumped up to 50 after the first record was released).

With details settled, Steve relied on his brother to break the news to York and Davis. Amazingly, despite warning signs being flashed for months, it still somehow came as a shock. Pete York recalled, "I never spotted it, that's why it came as an awful surprise when suddenly Muff said to Spencer and me, 'By the way, I have to tell you that Steve is leaving.'" It also confirmed his suspicions that their manager had chosen sides, "a great connivance of Chris Blackwell, because I think Chris had *always* wanted to get Steve on his own – to be solo."

But the real 'solo' act could wait. For now, making Steve happy meant letting Traffic do its thing. Ever the high stakes poker player, Blackwell was in for the long game, and as Steve's manager, he won either way. As for the new band of mostly unknowns, the contract drawn up gave *him* the rights to the name 'Traffic' as well – just in case it might prove valuable.

Finally, it all came down to an issue not of what, but where – the place where the promised six months of 'getting it together' would happen. Having jammed in clubs, studios, apartments and open fields, Chris Wood knew what he preferred, and Steve was in the same groove. A communal band required a communal space, one that would incubate and inspire as they developed. With cities full of distraction, the country was where they belonged – a place on a ley line being ideal. Reportedly, their first attempt was a rundown house in Worcestershire known as the 'Dog Kennel'. While this was abruptly aborted due to inaccessibility and an undesirable interest shown by the local constable, another, far superior location would soon present itself…

(1960's Rock and Pop Chronology, 1966)

('Go Wild In The Country', Q, 4/1994)

('Siegel', Intoxication, 1989)

(Stephanie Norris Astrology: http://www.psychicsconnect.com/astrology/traits_cancer.asp)

(Rave, 5/1/1967)

('Traffic Jam', Ray Townley, DownBeat, 1/30/1975)

MELODIES OF A HAUNTED COTTAGE

Chris Blackwell's tendrils went out in many directions. One of his friends, a young aristocrat named William Pigott-Brown, had recently inherited a huge landholding. Included in it, were a couple of isolated houses outside the village of Aston Tirrold in Berkshire County, about an hour's drive from London. When asked, Sir William was surprisingly amenable to having a rock band as tenants, suggesting the larger dwelling, a half mile down a backcountry dirt road, might fit the bill. And the rent was certainly hard to beat – for his old friend, the going rate was £5 a week.

Trouping out to have a look in March of '67, the young band was confronted with a stark, seemingly abandoned house in the middle of nowhere – with no indoor toilet, or electricity, and plaster falling off the walls. But the physical conditions were superseded by the vibes, which were apparently very, very strong. There would be no hesitation. As if by instinct, the original art for the 'Traffic Symbol' would be nailed to the living room wall as a claim, after which everyone went home to gather their belongings. Officially known as 'The Sheepcote Farmhouse', among Traffic insiders hereafter the place would simply be called *The Cottage*.

And while Chris Blackwell deserved credit for the band ending up at this specific location, the idea of a country house as a creative haven had been germinating in the mind of Chris Wood for a long time – John Walker's artist hideaway in the Lickey Hills outside Birmingham being the model. That quirky place, where the landscape, play, and family co-mingled to inspire art had sparked the arc of choices ultimately leading here. But, as was the norm for Chris, little evidence of that chain of events would remain; to the others 'getting it together in the country' merely seemed the natural thing to do. And with everyone's energies focused, the guiding path no longer mattered; in a very real sense, they were home.

And what a home it would be. While other groups like the Grateful Dead and The Band would collectively move into houses that year to make music, none quite had the same ambience as the Berkshire Cottage. Over time, the stories filtering out would contribute to a near-mythology – a swirl of strange goings on ranging from tales of past suicides, séances, midnight rides across the countryside, and dream-inspired songs written by candle light. In the press, it would later be portrayed as a near-cosmic nexus where Traffic and friends dropped acid, picked up their instruments and played around the clock. Last but not least, it was also said to contain a ghostly presence which stimulated and frightened the occupants in equal measure.

Oddly enough, all of that was to some extent, true.

The origins of this special dwelling owned by Pigott-Brown can be traced with a hand-drawn map of "The Hamlet of Aston Upthorpe" from 1794. This shows a 143 acre boot-shaped 'Tithe Free' parcel owned by a "Mr. Slade", and references a structure identified as the 'Sheepcot Barn', with a stable and finally the house to follow.

From outward appearances, the dwelling was typical for the period, with two storeys, a slate roof and a wooden skeleton protected with a 'wattle and daub' exterior – a mixture of the local clay and limestone. Inside, the front door led into a dining area, to the right a kitchen and to the left a living room with a large coal or wood burning fireplace. It was upstairs that the house showed its quirkiness. While having four bedrooms – two on the left and two on the right, the top floor was literally divided. With no connecting hallway, separate external sets of stairs served the upper floor.

In the early 1900's, mechanized agriculture allowed both efficient production of 'the corn' (barley wheat) and consolidation of parcels by a succession of landowners. Now all that remained of the feudal past were fanciful names – the 'Grumble Barn' to the east, 'Riddle Hill' to the north, and the forty-four acre 'Sheepcot Wood' to the west of what was now referred to as the Sheepcote Farmhouse.

By the 1940's, the house was used by owners of a nearby stable. The 'Fair Mile', which ran across the property to the east allowed the landed gentry a place to train and run horses. Serving as a residence for the stable master and stable boys, eventually the house was leased to the Maxwell-Hislop family who raised their children there until asked to vacate before Traffic's arrival in early 1967.

CHAPTER ELEVEN

The Cottage that Traffic moved into was very much of an earlier time, even by the standards of the 1960's. Quite derelict in appearance, the external walls had numerous holes. While repairs and modifications would have to be made, they were surprisingly minimal. Electricity would of course be required, but the small cable installed allowed at most a few lights and a refrigerator. Power for instruments would instead come from a portable 100 watt generator behind the house. And although the outhouse was replaced with a small bathroom tacked on to the back, keeping warm could be a challenge; with the fireplace as the sole source of heat and the floor's unvarnished planks sitting just above the bare earth, the chill regularly crept in. The water in the house remained unheated as well. Even contact with the outside was dicey; the nearest telephone was half a mile away in the small cottage down the lane.

Perhaps strangest of all was the old well, still projecting its bricked lip from the ground outside. While having been partially filled in, supposedly due to having turned poisonous, rumors of an even darker reason for its disuse would soon emerge.

Just getting to the cottage could be a test of will. The road, really just two tire tracks, was rutted and often full of water and mud, making anything other than midsummer driving an ordeal. Most people with decent cars would park back at the barn near the main road and walk. Wisely, Winwood and Medcalf would soon purchase a World War II American Willys Jeep (later replaced with a Land Rover), providing a reliable mode of transport, and for trips to the village and excursions into the countryside.

Even before they moved in, a concrete slab was poured directly in front of the house as a place to park that would not be a muddy mess. But once they got settled, a more important function would organically emerge; whenever the weather was good, the slab facing an undulating farm field became their first stage.

Within the house, the four upstairs bedrooms provided each member with a private room. Naturally, the main space downstairs was set up for music, with Steve's organ in a corner facing Jim's drums, while saxes, guitars and amplifiers were strewn around the periphery. With the low ceiling, wattle and daub walls and underlying timbers, the house absorbed the vibrations and added back some of its own – something that Chris recognized and valued right away.

To keep things together, Traffic was given an assistant, Albert Heaton. A road-hardened 'tough guy' from Carlisle, Albert would fit in surprisingly well with this "band of introverts." Having earned a name for himself as a no-nonsense, get-it-done roadie for the VIP's, Heaton's legend would also loom large in the early days of Traffic. Tall and thin with a prominent nose and long dark hair, 'Count Albert' made his living driving the boys around, scoring dope and generally 'entertaining the troops'. His mode of transport was a large van, painted pink, with Traffic's rolling arrowed symbol stenciled on the sides. As such the locals always knew when Traffic was in town; eventually it would be dubbed *Big Pink*, after The Band's first album.

*

The official move-in was on April 1st, 1967 – April Fool's Day. And if the furnishings were straightforward – beds and musical equipment – so were the decorations. Besides the Traffic symbol, the walls would display only one other item (in the kitchen) – an Ordnance Survey map of Berkshire and nearby Oxfordshire, marked with ley lines, including one crossing the nearby Chalk Horse of Uffington (a huge abstract figure wrought into a hillside thousands of years ago). If the map signaled Chris's intention to confront the local Berkshire mysteries head on, he wouldn't have long to wait – the house itself would prove to be ground zero.

Settling in, they came with cans of paint to color their environment. Downstairs would remain a neutral white (except for the bathroom's dark red), while each member was responsible for their respective rooms. An old hand at this, Chris chose his pigment carefully; his psychic comfort depended on it. Before putting his bed in, he did the walls and ceiling, and then opened another can for the floor. Old Deep Feeling mate and now a friend of Traffic, Gordon Jackson related how this simple act led to the first (of many) confrontations with the inexplicable. "They painted or varnished the floor. It was probably painted purple or something, knowing Chris. They painted the floor, shut the door, and put a notice outside saying 'Do Not Enter – Wet Paint!' The next day, when they went back there were footprints all across it. But the footprints went from the door to the far corner, and didn't come back again."

None had trouble interpreting *that* sign. All of his life Chris had sought evidence for the existence of ghosts, and it seemed the trail ended here, in his bedroom. The entity would be given a whimsical name – Harry Tibbits – and over the next few years would prove an active, eccentric and inspirational force bearing an eerie resemblance to Chris himself, perhaps his doppelganger.

Rarely at a loss for words, Jim Capaldi could initially only shake his head at this memory. While the mental images remained vivid nearly forty years later, articulating his thoughts was another matter. Clearing his throat, Jim finally stated emphatically, "That Cottage had some fuckin' ridiculous vibes. There were some *heavy* vibes in that fuckin' place – Jesus!" And while he recalled that initial incident – and others to follow – he sometimes wished he hadn't: "We saw the footprints across the wet paint, and there was none coming back. I don't even want to *think* about that period of the Cottage… I don't want to think about that side… I don't want to think about it!"

While some visitors took no stock in supernatural explanations for the house's squeaks and unknown rustlings, few who spent much time there took the activity as a joke. Gordon Jackson recalled, "It was *very* serious… there *was* a ghost at the Cottage. Things did happen, and noises were heard." The divided nature of the house itself contributed to uneasy situations that couldn't be resolved. The strange floorplan of the upper floor – a set of stairs on either side of the house, meant that there was no way for the human occupants to walk all the way across. Even so, Jackson noted, "There were incidents – of people hearing noises in the next bedroom, running up to the rooms, finding nothing there, and then hearing noises on the other side. It moved from one room to the other where there was no door." The experienced varied. Besides the sounds, Chris and Steve reported objects moving by themselves, especially near the fireplace. Sandra Jackson, Gordon's wife at the time saw and heard doors, drawers and cupboards open and then slam closed again. Winwood too would tell the press that he "heard unexplained footsteps and the opening and closing of doors in the middle of the night." When fed up with the goings on, Albert would sometimes shout abusive epithets into the mouth of the fireplace, where it was thought Tibbets resided.

It would be around this time that the village girl, Rosie Roper, would walk down from the village pub with Chris and fill in the back story; giving the unexplained happenings a plausible, if dark, context.

Rosie recalled the discussion going like this (Chris): "You know there's ghosts up here don't you?" (Rosie) "Yeah…" (Chris) "How do *you* know?" (Rosie) "Because my Dad used to live up here." (Chris) "What do you mean?" (Rosie) "He was a stable lad. The lady that used to live up here, he used to lodge with her… he was about seventeen. Dad couldn't wait for a place to come open in the village. He said, 'We used to lay in bed at night, and you could hear someone coming up the stairs – it sounded as if they were chained.' I said, 'Dad, stop lying to us, you're just trying to frighten us'. He said, 'No, we were petrified. She used to put a lot of the stable lads up, and a couple of them had their beds on the (second floor) landing – so you can imagine being the one who had to sleep on the landing! And there's this *thing*, coming up the stairs.'"

The locals ascribed the source of the haunting to the spirit of an earlier stable boy, a lonely lad who'd hung himself in the well outside after an undefined period of depression. Based on sounds heard outside, it was said that his spirit was linked with his dog's, killed soon after the suicide because of its non-stop howling. Right or wrong, the tale was as close as any of them would get to understanding the odd phenomena which ebbed and flowed over the years.

In a way, the belief in the haunting of the Cottage became the first test of the solidarity of the group. The otherworldly presence drew Jim, Chris and Steve together with a slight sense of fear but also overwhelming wonder; a combination which very much drove them on musically. Jim, in particular, began having dreams so compelling and vivid that he would write down the details as soon as he awoke in the hope of making them into song lyrics. And, for all, the jamming was more and more purposeful, and intense.

But even in these early days, Dave Mason stood slightly apart; like the divided second floor, three stood on one side, one on the other, with no apparent way across. A major stumbling block seemed to be that despite the inspiration provided by those 'heavy vibes', Mason didn't quite buy into it. On the subject of the Cottage ghost, he was terse, "Let's put it this way – I didn't see all of the things that they saw. I mean, my point about it was that it wasn't that different from the place I'd grown up. All I did was play over the fields like that, all my childhood."

This divergence in point of view manifested itself almost immediately in the music. Dave Mason recalled, "The problem was, from the beginning… I had my musical sensibilities, being whatever they were at the time. But it developed that it got split a little bit, in the sense that Chris, Jim and Steve would work very closely together on creating a song. And at the time, my stuff, I wrote it alone. I wanted to find out what it was like to do – I didn't know. Basically, other than a song Jim and I wrote together called 'Shades Of Blue' when we were like, 17, 18, I'd never really written anything. So you had all of these divergent styles…"

CHAPTER ELEVEN

Mason's solo-oriented perspective also meant that he didn't hang around quite as much either. Just as likely to dart off to London alone, the privacy gave him space to write his own way.

If Dave was content with the rural childhood he'd already had, Steve's experience had been quite different. Having been a working musician prior to puberty, he'd missed a good bit of the carefree days that typically accompany adolescence. But with Chris and Jim more than happy to help make up lost time, untold hours were now spent skittering across the landscape in the Jeep or hiking for miles. As always, Chris was in it for more than mere entertainment. Winwood would later tell a journalist how his band mate pushed the concept of purposeful exploration hard in the early days, "We'd visit ancient places like beacons, lakes and wells, to try and drink in something, learn something, understand something. A lot of this came from Chris; he was a very big influence on us. He was interested in geological formations. He was a keen ornithologist and an amateur cartographer, not the sort of things you'd normally associate with rock 'n' roll."

Jim had similar recollections of a life both wondrous and impossibly concentrated, "It was crammed, crammed full. In those days, Chris was magic; he would have the birds, all the birds, down in his book. He would have the stone circles, the burial mounds, he'd have the Ordnance Survey maps where you could go and find detailed things, like the site of a Roman Villa, or a megalithic monolith, or a tomb, or a long barrow. He had his binoculars, and his maps. We had this fuckin' incredible Willys American WWII Jeep that we would ride up and down the tracks of the Cottage – fantastic! Investigating some old farmhouse and some bloke would come chase us off! It would be brilliant man. We were so country, when everybody else was in the city – everybody else was in some studio or back room, knocking out their stuff – we were in this incredible fuckin' Berkshire Downs, in the middle of nowhere, with the 'corn blowing in the breeze, and the crows overhead, and the birds. Nothing but nature…'"

Surrounded by a world of wonders, Chris simply embraced it. After a night of loud jamming, after the others staggered off to bed or just collapsed, he would sometimes take his flute outside and join the morning chorus of the local birds. Sitting cross-legged under a nearby tree, man and bird would exchange comments and phrases until, hours later, he would be found in the same spot, curled up and asleep.

Anna Westmore, the Birmingham girl who knew the band from the Elbow Room days, and the romp with Dylan at Witley Court, was also a frequent visitor. She remembered that Chris's knowledge of the language of the birds was extraordinary, "I used to go for walks with Chris in the woods, and he could replicate (the song of) any English bird. He must have grown up with that ear to tune into bird song, and it came out very much in his flute playing. I mean *any bird*, and he could get it perfect – the pitch and everything. He just whistled; this was without a flute. I just used to be in awe, I would say, 'Okay, do some more, do some more – do a blackbird, do a thrush.' And it would be *so beautiful*; it would be just like listening to the bird. It was remarkable."

In fact, the Cottage environment seemed to generate a metamorphosis in the others as well. Even Jim, the very urban Leo always overflowing with mad extrovert energy, found himself changed; for the time being at least, tamed and strangely subdued. As he explained it, "We were all kind of hiding in the Cottage. Total introverts really; but that was kind of the magic of the band. We couldn't help but do what we did, we couldn't have done it any other way."

Now submerged in a sort of modern Garden of Eden, the play and exploration would soon merge with a higher purpose, the reason they were there. Having nudged the others onto the same psychic wavelength, in his low key way Chris had done what he set out to do, to harmonize the diverse perspectives with this place and time. What looked random and even chaotic from the outside was actually a rough plan – and it was working. The music was flowing.

Awakening to the methodology, Jim in particular began to view Chris with a sense of awe, "He wanted to play music and be organic. He loved to be able to capture something on tape. He had loads of stuff in his pockets, sax straps hanging off his neck. He'd always have a cassette somewhere, and he'd have a microphone, and he'd say, 'Ahh, just let me…', and he'd spend hours in this menagerie of this, bits and pieces and cassettes and shit, you know? And you knew that it was all part of him – it was wonderful – it was like a work of art! *He* was art, himself. You'd be an hour or two in his messin' about, but you just accepted it, because it was just wonderful, a world of strangeness going on with him, with all of his bits and pieces. Then he'd say something really good, and we'd actually do something…"

Often present during the early days, Gordon Jackson also had insight as to how the musical patterns were settling. Regarding the genesis of the sounds which would shape the future of the band, he noted: "Obviously, Steve was of major importance in Traffic. But behind it all; the ideas, the mood of the band and everything, a lot of it came from Chris you know. Magic, Chris – a lovely guy. You couldn't help but like him, he was just so *human*."

Dave Mason too mused on Chris's unusual place in the musical mix that was emerging. "He was just a sweet guy. I don't know – there's a lot of sax and flute players that musically, you could say were way better than him – there are a lot of guitar players more adept than I am – but the thing was, it all worked together, helped to create that sort of sound. Most certainly, I think the flute added that overall – especially at the days in the Cottage – sort of 'country vibe' kind of thing. And then there would be a lot of things he'd do that weren't really featured or solo stuff, but it would be something *within* the sound of what we were doing; probably, if you took it out, you'd miss it. Yeah, art, art college and stuff; he'd approach it like that."

And as their energies unified, Traffic's music did indeed surge; the preferred form, paradoxically, formlessness. Starting in any key or tempo, with any combination of instruments – the direction never fixed – the music was defined only by the moment. Jackson recalled, "It's true, jamming was the rule of the day, when you were with Traffic you had to jam. Sometimes it would go on for days. You'd go to bed, and someone would be playing, then someone else would go to bed, and some else would sit in. It would just be like people changing places, but the thing had a life of its own. Crazy times – plus the fact that if you'd taken enough speed, you'd have to stay up."

Trevor Burton visited in the early days too and had similar experiences. A fellow 'Brummie', he and Chris met backstage at a Spencer Davis Group show in '66, where they shared a joint. He was also the bass player for The Move, which had recently joined the pop/psych bandwagon with a single called "I Can Hear the Grass Grow". Like Jackson, he recalled the mad energy swirling around the Cottage, "Experiments were going on with the music – it just seemed to flow out. It was a magical place you know, it brought out the best in everybody. And the music never stopped, somebody would be jamming somewhere. The gear was permanently set up, and you could just pick it up and play, jam with whoever was there. It was wonderful for me, it was like 'Yeah, this is it; this is what I want to do!' I spent a lot of time with them… and as Steve would put it, 'we experimented with a lot of different substances'. We were all kids really, experimenting with the music and the drugs."

So if the mysteries of the countryside were the source of inspiration, drugs had to be credited with lubricating the creative process. Paul Medcalf noted that while the band did "loads of acid", hashish was the touchstone. "The amount of hash we went through, I hate to even estimate! An ounce would go in an evening without even thinking about it…"

When the supply was low, they did what they had to do. There certainly wasn't much besides beer and hard cider to be had in the village, so road trips to London and Maria's flat in Birmingham were frequent. And once back at the Cottage with the stash, surprisingly, the local police left them alone. It seemed that Sir William Pigott-Brown had clout, and his lodgers were not harassed. This was not an insignificant advantage, since in London the cops were nailing rock stars with a vengeance. The Rolling Stones were busted that year, and an air of paranoia and harassment hung over the whole scene in England – *except* at the Berkshire Cottage. Here, Traffic enjoyed a state of utter freedom, puffing away and having the time of their lives.

Of course, management found cause for concern. Spiraling off on a trajectory to the unknown, at times it looked like the band and the house itself might simply disappear in a cloud of smoke. Especially when under the influence of acid, the aura around the Cottage took on a mystical sheen more real than anything in the outside world. And the concern was not entirely misplaced; while the music was critically important to them, it was only part of a much bigger but less obvious picture.

The existential state reinforced the need to look as deeply as possible into this new 'reality'. As many of the generation questioned of the meaning of things, Traffic's communal, rural experiment served as sort of a role model for their peers. Mike Kellie, Chris's old Locomotive band mate, was getting together his own band, something they were calling 'Spooky Tooth'. Seeing what Traffic was connecting to, they got their own 'country cottage', as would other groups. Kellie noticed a common theme: "You see, we were spiritual people then, it was a spiritual searching – the music of Spooky Tooth and Traffic. And I'm not comparing standards or success; I'm talking about the roots. It was spiritual music, that's a fact. The colors were not tied to the mast at that time." Considering Chris, his friend and ex-bandmate, Kellie said, "Do you remember that Pete

CHAPTER ELEVEN

Townshend song, 'The Seeker'? In the context of always searching, spiritually searching; with maps, searching, searching, searching. He was always searching for that – that consciousness."

Anna Westmore agreed, "We were all searching. Chris was very interested in Aleister Crowley, the occult, but on a pagan level, not on the dark side but the other side, the spiritual side. (Finding out) what was going on was always, always, part of everyone's thought. When Steve and Chris would play, sometimes you would absolutely get transported to those other places. We would go on (LSD) trips sometimes, and when we came down, we would say, 'Where the hell did we go?' Those private moments were definitely an incredible experience."

Once again, the connections between the physical and mental landscapes proved crucial to the music. Westmore elaborated, "It would probably be when we went out someplace, checking out ley lines, or the Rollright Stones (an ancient Oxfordshire stone circle), or being in a full moon. You could feel the energy and come back and have an amazing jam session that would take you to other places. It had nothing to do with, 'we need an album done by October 8th', or 'we've got to make money'. It had *nothing* to do with it. At that time it was just for the experience, the spiritual connection. All time and the material world just disappeared."

('Go Wild In The Country', Go, 4/1994)

(Hit Parader, 1/1968)

'STUDYING MUSIC'

On the other side of the hazy veil, the accountants were never really that far off. Increasingly jittery, either Blackwell or a designee from 'the office' began popping into the Cottage on a frequent basis to check things out, their presence an unspoken reminder of obligations. The fear was misplaced; beneath seeming disorder, the plan was intact and the building blocks of songs already emerging. Jim Capaldi recognized the process, "We'd jam all day long, or all night long, whenever we felt like it. And out of that jamming came a lot of riffs, a lot of stuff. Then, in the early days, I would write something down." A circuitous route to songwriting perhaps, but it worked for them – words and music were finding their way together.

It helped tremendously that Blackwell had wisely equipped the Cottage with a recording system including two Bang & Olufsen reel-to-reels. With microphones hung from the ceiling, sounds could be effectively captured as they were made, even overdubs. Right off, Chris Wood appreciated the aural qualities the Cottage itself gave to the tapes – some combination of low ceiling, wattle and daub walls, even the birds and other ambient sounds coming through the open windows. All added an intangible *something* to the recordings, not to mention the underlying vibe emanating from the house's non-corporeal inhabitant. As the tape boxes began to pile up (most labeled simply "Traffic Jam"), he began talking up the idea of recording their whole first album right there – pure and undiluted from outside influences.

Besides the ideas skimmed off to tape, the non-stop playing improved everyone's chops. Not only was each musician progressing on their usual instruments, but they constantly swapped, sometimes just to cover as people dropped out of the jam; it moved things to a whole new level. Consequently, Dave Mason played a lot of bass, before coming back to the Cottage one day with an Indian sitar given to him by George Harrison. Whenever Jim got up, Steve readily moved to drums, while Chris took Winwood's seat at the Hammond. When in the mood, Jim played acoustic guitar, enthusiastically strumming Richie Haven's style to variations of the chords he knew. Of course Winwood often grabbed his white Fender Stratocaster, playing fiery, spiraling figures, as Chris or Dave backed him on bass. Just as he'd told the press, it all boiled down to one thing: 'studying music'.

When the jams died away the phonograph was always spinning. Completing the cycle, diverse sounds emanated from the stereo. Jazz of course was the benchmark, with John Coltrane a critical touchstone, especially the newer spiritual works like *Ascension*, which only had one song, split over each side of the album, and *Meditations*, his free-form stab at musically encompassing the human heart. Miles Davis was never far away from the turntable either. Like Coltrane, he was admired for his musical truthfulness and unwillingness to go along with convention. Miles Davis would prove an enduring influence; his mood-sustaining emphasis on single notes and the critical silences between them was a revelation for Chris. The all-important third leg was Eddie Harris. Like Roland Kirk before him, Harris was an innovator on the saxophone, using homemade devices to alter the sound and break new ground.

They delved into a lot of the older jazz stuff too, Charles Lloyd, Cannonball Adderly, the B-3 magic of 'Brother' Jack McDuff. The mystical and sometimes kitschy Sun Ra was often played, as well as the hypnotic drones of Indian music, especially Ravi Shankar. And from there, it was literally all over the map with everything from African drum records to traditional Chinese folk. The classical masters were heard and discussed as well, with Beethoven's Piano Concertos and Symphonies, and Ravel's Bolero being favorites. As for the others, Jim was mad about soul and blues: Otis Redding, Sam and Dave, Junior Walker, and then more contemporary heroes – Van Morrison and Bob Dylan. Dave held a bluesy perspective, especially appreciating Albert King, but also following Eric Clapton's evolution into the psychedelic path of Cream. All in all, the mix was very good, with everybody taking in something new, every day.

Unafraid to upset the cart if he felt things were getting too comfortable, Chris might play Igor Stravinsky's dissonant, initially panic-inducing "Rite of Spring", or go further out if necessary. Gordon Jackson was at the Cottage the day "Threnody to the victims of Hiroshima" by the Polish composer Krysztof Pendereki leapt out of the phonograph. "It was a classical record, but it was written about Hiroshima. It was one of the scariest things I've ever heard – you know, with a hundred violins, all doing this manic, sort of fast tremolo thing... He was always turning up with obscurities."

When the mood, weather, and spirit was just right they sometimes played a special recording that served as *the* soundtrack to the Cottage, the Downs, and the entirety of the experience. Of all the music in the world, a Spanish-themed classical guitar piece scored with a swelling dramatic string section apparently moved the collective soul of Traffic more than anything. Composer Joaquin Rodrigo who, like Ray Charles, had gone blind at a young age, would develop a powerful musical insight – a conduit to melodic, majestic sweeps of emotion uniquely his own. Indeed, his "Concerto de Aranjuez" (as played by guitarist Narciso Yepes) was deemed so special it couldn't be contained within the walls of the Cottage.

Poli Palmer, old friend and visitor to the Cottage recalled how the natural echo chamber from the surrounding hillsides was exploited to enhance Rodrigo's masterpiece, "I remember their big thing – they used to put the P.A. system, pointing across to the next hill. They used to get their roadie there, then they used to go all the way up to the next hill, which was maybe three quarters, maybe half a mile away. They all traipsed over there, and waved at the roadie who put on the "Guitar Concerto" by Rodrigo. It was the P.A., flat out, playing right across the valley – and they were up on the next hill, kind of matchstick figures! But you've got *that* music, which is very evocative – that was one of their very favorite tunes."

On beautiful summer days, with the deep blue sky above and the spirit-freeing music rolling over them like an invisible tide, the inspiring and mesmerizing times seemed endless. Trevor Burton's wistful impression of those idyllic early days in the Berkshire countryside got right to the heart of it all – "It seemed like paradise at times, you know..."

But even as the last Spanish guitar strains faded into the ether, the day of reckoning was at hand. Months before and seemingly a lifetime ago, Winwood had agreed to do soundtrack recording for a film called "Here We Go Round The Mulberry Bush", a teen-oriented movie involving the Spencer Davis Group. With the title track finally required and Traffic now his going concern, their first proper recording would go towards fulfilling that contract. Keeping to the plan, they created as a unified entity, the track called "Here We Go Round The Mulberry Bush"; it was credited to Winwood/Capaldi/Mason/Wood.

Fresh from the open countryside, the recording session flowed smoothly, producing a powerful instrumental that all were satisfied with. The opening organ notes swelled up like the morning mist from the Downs, lending an initial air of mystery. From there, frequent dynamic shifts punctuated with flute, guitar and a touch of sitar added interesting textures. Complex yet compact, the piece sounded like a day of jamming compressed into two minutes and thirty eight seconds. Had they been allowed to stop there, the artistic accomplishment would have been complete.

The problem was that the tune was actually supposed to be a *song*, one with an unfortunately daft title. Sent back to finish it, Capaldi wrote feverishly but the product, while serviceable was, by nature, a bit of an artistic compromise. Called in to get things to completion, Jimmy Miller tried to reprise the magic from "Gimme Some Lovin'" by arranging the backing to again feature full falsetto mode to top the chorus. But this time it was all just a little off the mark with the lead and backing vocals merging into a murky 'sing along'. In the end a strange hybrid would emerge – a vaguely ominous sounding pop/rock tune.

The movie's Director, Clive Donner, claimed to love the track, but also noted that, "It was so unlike Stevie Winwood, which is of course due to him being in a pretty morose mood, not sure what he was going to do next." While Donner's comments were ill-informed, the band was also somewhat conflicted with the final product. *But* with the movie not scheduled for release for many months, the rarest of opportunities emerged – they could actually scoop themselves by recording a new single to beat "Mulberry Bush" to the punch with an earlier release date.

Motivated, they reconvened at Olympic Studios in London with the song Jim and Steve had hacked out at the Newcastle Bed and Breakfast some months before – "Paper Sun". The goal was simple – make it everything "Mulberry Bush" was not. Opening with a blast of tabla drums, a ringing sitar figure played by Dave provided an electric jolt. Steve's clear, powerful vocals followed, playfully inhabiting Jim's enigmatic yet still accessible lyrics of a surreal day the beach. Clean flute and sax lines laid over a punchy bass kept the sound firmly in the rock idiom, while the exotic flourishes (and Miller's crisp production) let the song soar. Somehow bridging a pair of opposites, "Paper Sun" would prove both psychedelic and in the best of all ways, poppy.

Acknowledging everyone's significant creative input, the writing credit would be given to all four. While reducing the cash flow to Steve and Jim, the show of unity helped cement the brotherhood, and that was worth a lot.

What would become the flip side was a shuffling number called "Giving to You" (actually the first song recorded after "Mulberry Bush"). With only a single verse of vocals, the words served merely as an accessible prelude to the freewheeling jam that followed. Within that, a breezy melody hung on Chris's flute line, but left space for all to improvise – another nod to the band's communal character. A very deliberate counterbalance to "Paper Sun", "Giving To You" demonstrated clearly that below the 'pop/rock' surface, Traffic's blood was actually jazz.

In preparation for the release, Island authorized a small budget to produce a promotional film. While not a brand new phenomenon, rock promo films were only very recently being treated as artistic statements in themselves. Once again, the Beatles broke the ground with a film for "Strawberry Fields Forever". Shot at dusk in a farm field, it portrayed the four interacting with an otherworldly tableau – constructing and then destroying an enigmatic object as twilight merged into night. Beautiful and compelling, the "Strawberry Fields" film would prove a triumph of the budding genre.

Traffic's film seemed less a reaction to the Beatles than the Spencer Davis Group. While the "Gimme Some Lovin" video portrayed the SDG mindlessly cavorting in a shrine to commerce – a London Department Store – Traffic would travel to Belgium to the Royal Museum for Central Africa, in Tervuren. Set amongst exhibits of art and culture of the Congo, the 'action' in this film consisted entirely of the four meandering and discussing the displays while the song played.

Like "Giving To You"'s jazzy counterpoint to "Paper Sun", the incongruity of the pop/rock song within a totally unrelated setting reiterated that Traffic's interests ran deep to the superficial culture. But as a means of hooking a teen audience the footage was an almost provocative nonstarter. With more than half of the scenes showing only close-ups of skeletons, totems or stuffed animal heads, the sex appeal was all cerebral. And the overt rejection of the teeny bopper worldview would come at a cost – if the strange "Paper Sun" video was ever shown on the BBC, no one remembered it; promotion-wise, its impact was quite close to zero.

Even so, the stakes riding on the "Paper Sun" single itself couldn't have been higher. While Winwood clearly had a lot on the line, it was actually the others – the band of 'unknowns' who had everything to prove – and lose. If this record didn't chart, the pressures to jettison them would have been enormous. But, amid the nail-biting, the time for second guessing had passed – record presses were already pumping out thousands of black vinyl 45's.

Released on May 27th, "Paper Sun"/ "Giving To You" would be unqualifiedly praised by the rock press as it raced up the British Charts to the #5 position by the first of June. Although kept from very top by a huge Procul Harum hit ("A Whiter Shade of Pale" which held the #1 spot for thirteen weeks), they came close enough –Traffic's first record was a smash, and a palpable relief. Afforded some vital breathing room, it seemed that the Traffic experiment would continue.

Celebration commenced. Renting out a London club, the band members invited their friends, and partied until dawn. Staggering out in the morning, someone noticed a message scrawled on a dusty mirror in the lobby. One by one, the still laughing group came over to see. Standing in a semi-circle, silence suddenly fell as the short note was read: "Congratulations on your success! Paul McCartney." Heads would swivel, but the apparition-like Beatle was long gone. Chris would tell a friend later, "We didn't see him, but the message was on the mirror."

The acceptance as a peer from someone like McCartney – seeking *them* out, only days after the release of the Beatles' greatest artistic triumph, *Sergeant Pepper's Lonely Hearts Club Band*, meant more than any critic's commentary. It was no hollow gesture; McCartney along with the other Beatles would be keeping an interested eye on Traffic during this 'Summer of Love'. While the Beatles defined the 60's for many music fans, decades later Paul would give Traffic perhaps the ultimate compliment when he told Jim, "If me and Linda ever just want to capture the sixties, have a little trip down memory lane to bring that period back, we just put Traffic on."

But back at the Cottage, the realization that they still had a long way to go was dawning. Linda Eastman (not yet 'Mrs. McCartney') would pay another visit, her camera in one hand and the new Beatles album in the other. Sitting around the phonograph as the needle dropped, *Sgt. Pepper's Lonely Hearts Club Band*, induced a sensation of awe as well as a vague, sickening feeling. Listening to one sparkling track after the other, all were jolted by how high the creative bar had just been re-set. "A Day In The Life" especially, seemed to capture the essence of the times in a way that no one else had, or maybe, ever could. As the album's massive final chord faded to silence, they found themselves in equal parts enthralled and intimidated, able for the moment only to stare into the mouth of the cold fireplace.

Whatever the alternate reality established back at the Cottage, having officially entered the marketplace, Traffic now had to face the facts of the disposable pop music world. The first was perhaps the harshest – "Paper Sun" was already yesterday's news. To stay fresh, a new single would be needed every six weeks to two months from here out. Arguments as to whether this was humane or conducive to the art were in the end irrelevant; at its deepest level the industry's objective was cash, with music merely the medium to attain it. And while no one at the more artist-centered Island wanted Traffic to burn out, even there the ledger books would ultimately have the last word.

So the 'vacation' was officially over – two more songs and hopefully another hit were needed by August. After that, the debut album was expected in the stores by Christmas. Jim recalled Chris Blackwell as strategic, knowing exactly who to lean on to keep the wheel turning, "*I was the one that he would put the pressure on, to say 'what's happening? Where's the next record, where's the material, what's going on? Are you just goofing off at the Cottage?' It was me he could talk to like that.*" If Steve and Chris were content to let things unfold at a slower, more organic pace, Jim's combination of pride and ambition helped push the others forward, to get things done.

Despite the external pressures, back at the Cottage the work went on as before, the methodology seemingly unaffected: smoke, jam, dream, explore, write, edit, smoke, record. As such, a songwriting team based around Steve, Jim and Chris was coalescing. With minds and intentions aligned, the three were now working very, very closely. Jams, while seemingly free-form, involved a lot of eye contact and other non-verbal gestures guiding the musical path in a way that all understood. The process was incredibly powerful, almost telepathic and utterly walled off against corrupting commercial expectations – just as Chris envisioned it.

But that left Dave where? As much as the passion to play had drawn them together, something was already amiss, and all knew it. Certainly, his 'psychic' connection to the others was tenuous, at best. So while Dave worked furiously at songwriting, he preferred to do it alone, even surreptitiously. The trends might have been troubling, but with the rush for material suddenly on and little time for self-reflection, sleeping dogs would be left where they lay.

With jams gradually being winnowed into songs, another important dynamic emerged: if Jim was the wordsmith, and Steve the music's main generative engine, Chris was the filter keeping the product true and cliché free. Jim Capaldi recalled, "Chris had a huge influence on the sound – the flute and how he would phrase the sound. His attitude – he kept us on the straight and narrow. He was almost like Jim Morrison, where it had to be pure; it had to be, you know, no bullshit – that kind of attitude. Making sure, even like a 'Bob Dylan' kind of vibe, where he would do something and you would almost think, 'What the fuck, you're messing it all up', you know? But then you'd realize, it would kind of dawn on you, what he was doing. You didn't get it at first, 'cause it was coming from another angle. But it reminded you not to be… to watch the obvious."

He could also stop the music cold if he thought it was going wrong. Jim noted, "We'd go – 'how about…' – normal suggestion – you know? (Chris): 'Fuck it, *fuck it*'. It made you not want to be too cute, twee and 'nice' around him. He represented like, 'let's have no fuckin' stupid bullshit…'"

With music built on a foundation of close relationships, Jim also pondered the link between Chris and Steve, "He had a great empathy with Steve, 'cause Steve was already in that direction too. They really complemented each other." But while Winwood would later be acclaimed as the major talent, Jim emphasized how, in the early stages, Chris was heavily influencing Steve, and thus Traffic. "Yeah, of course he did, 'cause he had it even more, more of that kind of personality, that would really manifest itself, stronger than Steve's. You know, Steve could go anywhere musically, but Chris's personality was in there too. He was an influence on us all."

More than anything, it was that personality – his luminous presence of being, that Jim held in a kind of awe, "I don't know what it was. We were all in a room, and Chris would come in, and his spirit would be so… it was such a pure kind of thing, I can't describe it. People loved him, just loved him, instantly. You knew exactly; the sort of compassion, and sensitivity was immediately present."

('Here We Go Round The Mulberry Bush', CD notes, 1997)

CHAPTER THIRTEEN

'THE EGO WENT MAD'

As the summer of '67 unfolded, a regrettable paradox was slowly being revealed – Traffic's best music was unfit for mass consumption. Penny Massot was a high-level Island staff member, as well as Steve Winwood's new girlfriend (and a huge Traffic fan). As such she had a unique insight into the not entirely unexpected confrontation brewing between art and commerce. She recalled, "They were a proper outfit – they were doing music that nobody else was. It was difficult to put that into a 'pop' context – because you had to make music that somebody wanted to buy, slightly kind of poppy. And that was difficult, because they were a kind of jazz outfit in a lot of ways. Chris was very much a jazz player, and R&B, and so was Steve. I know that Steve would have actually wanted to play only small venues, and gone out as a sort of jazz outfit. But in those days, it wasn't a going thing. I can remember saying, 'You don't need to have lyrics to put something out, you can have music!', but that wasn't accepted. The jam sessions that they did down at the Cottage were *out of this world*, and somebody's got those, because they were all taped. It was unbelievable. Traffic's best work was done just jamming. And I always used to say: 'Can't you put these things out? Just put this out!', and it was 'No, no, it has to be a song.'"

So the trick was to see if the contradictions could somehow be resolved – to distill the best of the jamming into a more conventional structure. With June waning, the clock was definitely ticking. For a band barely seen in public, much less having played a single concert, their chance to impact the summer rock scene was slipping away. After much discussion, the task would be pursued with renewed intent.

Suddenly (and much to Island's relief) the prize seemed in hand. During the first week in July, word was sent to book Olympic Studios again, the next single was ready – the suitably lysergic sounding "Coloured Rain".

A product of a growing confidence and the ability to marshal the influences amassed so far, "Coloured Rain" was yet another hopeful mutation in Traffic's musical evolution. With authoritative aplomb, Steve's powerful voice alone opened the song. The lyrics, expressing the sound of a youth culture discovering itself, were a paean to personal growth via sensory experience. From there, a pulsating spectrum of sound radiated, with Chris's tenor tearing furiously into the musical fabric while Dave's rubbery guitar line vibrated to its own frequency and Steve's B-3 shimmered and made abrupt turns. Below it all, Jim's web of rhythm wove the separate elements into an organic whole. Full, yet uncluttered, "Coloured Rain" simultaneously packed a punch, and grabbed the mind.

With the air of a driving jam that could have gone on into infinity, Jimmy Miller's crucial fade at 2:42 made the song compact enough for the radio too. Listening back in the control room, the circle of smiles confirmed that they'd done it; "Coloured Rain" was boundary stretching but not *too* far in front of the public. With their unique imprint on something that could still be a hit, the logical follow-up to "Paper Sun" was in perfect alignment. Or so it seemed.

Before celebrations could commence, Dave let it be known he'd written a song too – something called "Hole In My Shoe". Surprised at the announcement, the others fidgeted in silence as he played for them – a sing-songy tune with lyrics recalling a children's fairy tale. Afterward he would make it clear that the song was indeed finished, requiring only the help of the band to get it recorded – something he very much wanted to do. Chris, Steve and Jim were, to say the least, dumbfounded.

Mason would later explain, "The problem for them was that I tended to create on my own. In other words, 'Here's the song, it's done – it's written'. With all of the other stuff… they would create together. Mine – I'd have the song, it would be done, it would be finished." Did Mason think "Hole In My Shoe" would lead to a rift? "No, no…" But for a band founded on collective music-making, the ramifications were profound. Still, in Dave's mind it made sense – being the first song he'd written by himself, he simply wanted to see "Hole In My Shoe" through to completion – his own way.

Broken rules aside, there was another issue: once they'd had a good listen, Chris and Steve decided that they really didn't care for it – at all; the song's overtly pop qualities were exactly the approach they'd sworn to avoid. But feeling strongly that he was on to something, Dave dug in his heels. Amid arguments leading nowhere, it seemed that an impasse loomed. Hoping to avoid more conflict, the others finally agreed to record it. Starting with a demo done at the Cottage (along with a new Winwood/Capaldi/Wood tune, "Smiling Phases"), time would be booked at Olympic to get a master.

Faced with the prospect of making it official, however, things suddenly faltered. With a sitar as lead instrument and a rhyme scheme pairing "sky" with "elephant's eye", several partial takes later, the band ground to a halt – it wasn't working. With looks of disgust openly exchanged, a full-on train wreck seemed in progress. Trying to rescue the situation, Jimmy Miller lightened the mood by cajoling and suggesting changes, smoothing the path a bit. After much talk, work resumed and by the sixth run through things suddenly fell together. Augmented with a melodic flute line and an organ part from Steve, Dave then overdubbed bass, before adding a nice Mellotron track to fill in the gaps – an end was in sight.

But one more little problem would surface. Somewhere along the line, Dave decided to have a *child* recite the middle stanza of lyrics. It was an interesting retrofit – suitable in some sense to the nature of the song, but also one with possible political motivations – Chris Blackwell's seven-year-old stepdaughter had been selected for the part. One way or the other, the lisping voice of a little girl would be recorded and inserted.

It was a step too far. Having struggled to bring Traffic's music into the market with as few compromises as possible, to Chris this took them perilously close to surrender. While he might not have been as blunt to Dave's face, to friends he held nothing back, calling the song "horrendous" and "dreadful" among other things. Jim too would later complain about what he called Mason's "toy town" lyrics.

Having seen the song slip past some kind of artistic point of no return, Chris, Steve and Jim could now envision only one solution to the "Hole In My Shoe" problem – scrap it entirely. But as much as they might have desired it, the story wasn't over.

Not long afterward, the group found themselves sitting around a table in one of Island's offices in London with Jim, Steve and Chris on one side, Dave and some of the Island marketing staff on the other. Interestingly, in the intervening time, the top brass had somehow gotten the idea that Traffic had now decided on "Hole In My Shoe" as the next single. Having just sweated bullets to produce a nearly perfect 'Traffic' song – "Coloured Rain", this news came (to say the least) as quite a surprise. In fact, Chris would later tell a friend that he, Steve and Jim were now boiling mad at Dave: "We were gonna' chase him around the table and hit him."

But as the anger subsided, 'voices of reason' began to weigh in. Dave Betteridge was Island's Records Managing Director, and his opinion carried weight. According to Penny Massot, Betteridge very much saw the potential for a hit and agreed that 'Hole' *should* be the next single. This view met resistance head on, "Chris never wavered – didn't want it out, neither did Steve. It just wasn't indicative of what they did." Penny recalled. The pushback would continue until the others noticed that Jim had fallen silent.

Something had shifted. Having heard Betteridge out, he now moved (symbolically at least) to the other side of the table. Penny recalled Capaldi responding to the office's position of "This will make money", by changing his tune: "Jim went along with that, (saying) 'Well, if it's going to be a hit, let's have a hit.'" Motivated by an over-riding desire for Traffic's success, for Jim the complicating factors could be worked out later. Paul Medcalf noted the distinction between the egos that drove Mason and Capaldi on issues such as this: "He (Mason) was very much like Jim in some ways; whereas Jim was sort of out for the group, Dave was sort of out for himself."

But with Jim's defection, the balance of power suddenly tipped – the argument was over. "Hole In My Shoe" (with "Smiling Phases" as the B-side) would indeed be Traffic's next single. Coming so early in the game as it did, for Chris and Steve the outcome was the bitterest of pills; having honored the democratic approach, neither anticipated it to come at the cost of their artistic integrity. In the end, the decision would be pivotal for all in one way or another.

Either a testament to Mason's ability to see into the market's heart, or a crazy fluke, when released that August, "Hole In My Shoe" would race up the British charts to #2 – three steps past where "Paper Sun" had landed. "Hole" would, in fact, secure the highest position the band would ever attain in the U.K. becoming *the* song forever associated with Traffic there.

Talking to the press, Mason provided a much less contentious version of how "Hole In My Shoe" came to be the new single, first telling *Rave*: "I didn't even know until the last minute that my song would be the 'A' side!" Later he elaborated, "We all have something to say. It just happened that my song suited my voice better than Stevie's. I had no idea that it was to be the single, until the others all agreed on it."

There was one more reason for pride. Just before the Beatles left England to visit an island (Leslo) in the Aegean Sea they were thinking of purchasing, Dave slipped Paul McCartney a demo copy of his song. He recalled, "I gave it to Paul, he took it to Greece. About a week later, I get this telegram from all of them going, 'Man, this is a fucking great record.'" Validated by the Beatles and the record-buying public in a way utterly denied by his own group, perhaps not coincidentally, from here things would be different.

While carefully crafted comments from the band would make sure the fans never knew of the divisive struggles behind Traffic's new hit, for the insiders the reverberations were profound, and lingering. Paul Medcalf's metaphor for "Hole" was dark: "The nail in the coffin." Penny Massot uttered the same phrase and emphasized the transformation that came with it, "Dave thought he was the 'bee's knees'; he thought he was *really* good. Already, there was a problem with Dave. From now on, the ego went mad."

*

For Chris, this particular saga was more than an intra-band squabble. As hadn't happened since he contemplated leaving college, serious doubts resurfaced. Despite all the play and adventures, when it came to the work his intentions had always been serious – it had to be *right*. Now, with the prospect of a future holding even more compromises (such as a frenetic jingle recorded for Pepsi Cola, ultimately discarded), the old question rebounded: 'Have I made the right choice?'.

Even in this new, free, 'hippie era', some things hadn't really changed – 'English reserve' still dictated that he not share his innermost feelings with Steve or the others. But he really needed *somebody* to talk to. As in his last days at art school, the psychic turmoil was manifesting physically; his hair was falling out again.

Rosie Roper, the girl from Aston Tirrold, became a substitute sister. In a roundabout way she also became one of the few to understand what he was going through. "I used to get the impression that Chris had just left his Mum. I used to think 'He keeps going on about home cooking, and somebody doing his housekeeping, what was he thinking?'" The two developed a good natured, give and take relationship. "I used to say, 'When you're rich and famous, you can pay me to come and do your housework', and he'd say: 'Can't you do it on your day off?' I would set him straight – 'I ain't doing your bloody work on *my* day off.' Maybe, because I'd argue and be cross with him like his sister would have done it was like 'my sister isn't here, but *she* is.'" Close enough to sometimes wash his hair on lazy summer days at the Cottage, that's when she noticed it: "He was very thin at the crown of his head; it was very, very thin. I can remember when I was washing his hair he said: 'Aagh, don't rub there hard'. I said, 'Oh, but you're meant to', and he said 'No, that hurts!' Unwilling to let him get away with any nonsense, 'Sister Rosie', would insist on the last word: 'No, it *doesn't!*'"

During these reflective times, Chris kept returning to the need for the girl to protect her future; to not give it up her academic ambitions even though her family life was in some turmoil. On that point, he was uncharacteristically insistent; his vehemence betraying an impression that he knew what he was talking about. Rosie recalled, "He kept on saying to me, 'Don't throw your life away.'"

If Chris found a surrogate sister in Rosie, an unlikely chain of events starting in a pub called "The Red Lion" would soon lead him to be 'adopted' into a whole other family.

Requested to locate a quick a meal and a pint on the way home from London after a Traffic studio session, Albert would steer the band to an inviting brick pub on Chapel Lane in the village of Blewbury, not far from Aston Tirrold. But once inside, the colorfully dressed musicians would find themselves cut off from the bar by a gaggle of friendly teenagers, full of curiosity and questions. There to replenish beer for a nearby party, the kids would soon invite Traffic back to that gathering. With the alternative being a sleepy pub populated by a few farmers, the decision wasn't difficult.

Around the corner, the scene at the thatched cottage known as 'Barn Hall Close' was more complex than expected – the parents were home. It was in fact the dwelling of a middle aged couple – Helen and Patrick Hamilton, their eight-year-old son Giles, and their eight-month-old baby. Also, there was a pretty eighteen-year-old American girl named Christie Nichols, boarding with the Hamilton's while attending college in nearby Reading. As for Traffic's unexpected appearance amid an already full house, Helen and Patrick would prove casually welcoming; the party continued.

CHAPTER THIRTEEN

Surprisingly, the rock band and the rural family quickly discovered an easygoing, comfortable vibe. But it would go much deeper than that, starting with Chris's attraction to the playful but sensitive Christie Nichols; feelings which were unexpectedly strong and mutual.

The adults were interesting as well. A graduate of Divinity school with a degree in Theology, Patrick worked in publishing and was sympathetic to the hard knocks of the music business. But Helen was simply unique. Fair-skinned and raven-haired, she possessed eyes both inviting and knowing. She was also spellbindingly articulate, able to make connections across a wide spectrum of thought as she drew others in to listen and converse.

After that night, Traffic would return regularly, to relax and enjoy the company. Far removed from the swirling rock 'n roll cauldron – a world of great excitement but little actual substance – the time spent here always proved worthwhile; Helen's insight into the questions they were all asking, together with the jazz on the stereo, food to be shared, and (when the kids were in bed), the freedom to smoke a little hash was difficult to beat. In fact, Traffic had lucked into something they all subconsciously needed: a hipper version of their own families, close enough to visit whenever they wanted.

Looking back at those days with great fondness, Helen said, "It was all very musically oriented, atmospheric. They tended to come and relax, enjoy the countryside, and some good food. And play – music, improvising. And the children loved it." She also recalled the energy that passed between Chris and Christie on that first day, "The attraction – she and Chris had an initial, spiritual experience with each other. They (Traffic) came as a group, and left as a group, but he wanted a little extra time with Christie, because they had sparks, and it was endearing…" Christie knew something special was happening too, "It was a beautiful time, very interesting, everybody was very real. I know that I had a very deep connection with Chris. We'd just get together and 'crcch, crcch!', all this electricity, I'd never felt that before with anyone. You could say that it was a sexual attraction, but it was more, it was just really lovely." The house with these two amazing women became a magnet that Chris couldn't resist.

After Traffic's early visits, tales of the amazing Helen got around. Soon, Barn Hall Close became a must-stop for other questing musicians, typically arriving in the middle of the night, after a gig. Christie recalled, "A lot of people would end up at our house, like Eric Clapton and Ginger Baker, people from The Move, Jeff Beck. They'd just come to our house, because she's a great talker; the spiritualist, the philosopher. She'd be in bed at 11 or 12 o'clock, and they would come at 2 or 3 in the morning. They would all lay around her bed and discuss philosophy, and spiritual stuff and psychology." Reveling in Helen's thoughts and word play, the road-weary musicians let the ideas she presented tunnel into their brains and ultimately, perhaps the music. She knew when to slip the humor in too. "I remember once", Christie said, "it was so funny, she was telling Chris something, and he said 'I can't stop pointing my finger', maybe being judgmental or something. And she said: 'Well then, put it in your pocket!' We were hysterical, we just lost it. Things like that would happen all the time."

Even ordinary activities took surreal turns around Helen who, seemingly by the force of her personality, could whimsically alter the consciousness of others. Christie recalled, "One night Eric Clapton and Ginger Baker came. Helen was a great chess player. She and Eric were playing, and we all got involved in this amazing chess game. For hours, we just watched. Ginger Baker's a very big man, very impressive, his whole stature – big, wild red hair, he wore a white sheepskin jacket, like everyone wore at that time. After a really long time, he was hovering over the board, standing up, and we were standing around it. Then we noticed that they, somehow…it went from playing across the board, to playing sideways! We all went crazy, and started laughing again."

Before long, Christie and Helen began visiting Traffic's own dwelling, each developing a keen insight into the personal and musical dynamics. Right off, Christie noticed the group operating on a very sensitive frequency which allowed them to bank their energy and then at some unspoken signal, spring into action: "I was kind of young, and I was observant. Things kind of flowed or they didn't flow. When we were at the Cottage, Chris would be cleaning his instruments, putting new reeds on them." In the rarified atmosphere of the Cottage's music room, even simple tasks seemed significant, a ritualized prelude to jams never far away, "Chris would often clean his sax, oboe or flute with all the pieces carefully dismantled, and placed around him on the floor. I loved watching him as he prepared a new reed – it always astounded me because it seemed like such as skill. He had to lick it and suck on it a lot to soften it and mold it to his lips and mouth. He would polish his sax and flute diligently and peacefully while Steve would be doing something else across the room. It was a small room, but it seemed big to me at the time. We never talked, it was all silent. It was really weird, everything was silence. There was a definite, non-verbal communication going on with everyone. And then, all of a sudden, they'd all be in the other room, jamming! It was like, jamming, jamming, jamming. And all of a sudden, it would be over, and we'd all go for a ride in the Land Rover, over the Downs, in the middle of the night. It was all very flowing, non-verbal communication."

As for Helen, she first noticed Jim's selfless approach to the seemingly non-stop jamming and playing; a stubborn willingness to give his all even though he feared he might pay the ultimate price. "Jim said, 'I'm terrified sometimes when I'm drumming that my heart's going to burst.' That was one of the things that was a great worry in the group, that Jim's drumming might cause him to have heart failure. But he certainly didn't stop!"

As for Chris and Steve, Helen noted that the two were inextricably entangled in their musical relationship. She observed, "He (Chris) was very, very creative. In fact, he was the instrument of the music that was created at that time, even though Steve wrote it down, and put the words to it with Jim. But mostly, the sounds that were being made, the melodies, were *all* out of Chris. They would jam together, and Chris would produce a riff, and Steve would take it over, and make it his own. And Chris, time and time again would say, 'It's not right, but it's okay', or 'It's okay, but it's not right (laughing).' And *that* was Chris; that was his creativity. He would end up laughing, and they would all end up laughing. And that was how it worked. Without Chris, Steve wasn't able to get off on his play. Once he had the input, he could then use it as a grinding stone for everything that he wanted to put in."

But the near constant tight-rope walk between creativity, work and other factors was already becoming quite precarious. In his own way Chris tried to keep it all balanced for his friends. Jim recalled the lateral humor of their off-beat 'master of ceremonies', "He could be very comical. He wore this long trench coat – pink. See, militaristic, but *pink!* (We) would walk into a pub, Chris with his long pink trench coat – with one hand on the lapel like a barrister. Before the bar man could breathe he'd have ordered – had seven or eight drinks on the bar. He drank anything – he was doing anything."

Christie also recalled how alcohol interlaced with humor as Chris and Albert swigged Southern Comfort and Coke and entertained by mimicking U.S. Southern and Black Country accents. But the things could tip sideways when, in a darker mood, Chris would skip the jokes and just drink until he was "totally wiped out drunk." She witnessed him passing out several times, once at Roger Daltrey's house, where he came in, staggered to a bed and collapsed.

Helen was concerned as well, "Going down was not an option. They had to keep Chris from going down – it was 'come on Chris, snap out of it.'" Like Jim, Helen observed the play of radiance and vulnerability behind Chris's enigmatic smile, "He was the darling bud of May, the little buddy, the friend, the sympathizer – he was the will. And loved by Jim, who was down to earth, but going with it. Not holding on to Chris, but supporting him, letting Chris get very close to him. I think Chris probably wanted to get back to Mum and Dad, in a way."

And yet, for his real family and old friends, the whirlwind of Traffic had already carried him far enough away as to sometimes make them seem like characters from another life. His art school mate and stalwart defender Trevor Jones tried to keep a relationship going, but it wasn't easy. "I saw him every year at Christmas, but he became very difficult to see. He'd say, 'Give me a ring any time', but I could never get past the people, the groupies who'd move in. They'd say, 'Hold on, who's this? Oh I'm afraid he's…', and I could never talk to him." But Jones persisted, and on the rare times that they did get together, was pleased to find his quirky, creative friend hadn't changed, "I do remember going over to this flat of his, it was on Cromwell Road… there was a garage, and there was this flat right on the top, it overlooked the whole of that road. He said, 'You've got to come and listen to this record!' I thought, 'Oh, he's trying to get me to listen to some new Traffic bit', and it wasn't. It was that record of the 'Jungle Book'. You know that bear in the *Jungle Book*? (Baloo, singing "Bare Necessities"), he played me that! He said, 'Isn't that fantastic, it's great!'"

Despite, or perhaps because of, all the ups and downs, the creative current flowed strongly throughout the summer – recording sessions were frequent. But with fall approaching, major loose ends remained. A tour of Scandinavia already booked, not to mention their U.K. stage debut, and the record company was getting anxious for the big product. Chris would later recall a distinct sense of being "pushed" to finish the as yet untitled album whose form was just emerging from the haze.

Encouraged by the success of "Hole In My Shoe", Dave had been writing furiously and by now several similarly flavored songs were recorded. Jim came in with the Spanish flavored "Dealer", (supposedly inspired by the card playing Chris Blackwell) that he took lead vocals and sole writing credit for. Another Winwood/Capaldi/Wood tune appeared as well. "Heaven Is In Your Mind", inspired by a phrase Gordon Jackson used in a letter to Jim, was built around a marching beat and a fat sax riff, and was a strong contender to serve as the opening track. Sounding like an old time music hall number, "Berkshire Poppies" had lyrics playfully contrasting the madness of city life with the beauty and freedom of the country. In the background Steve Marriot and the Small Faces laughed and belched, egged on by Chris, who added his own apropos Black Country exclamation: "Pint of bitter!" to what amounted to a raucous pub singalong caught on tape.

While the diversity of material produced so far was good, it was also becoming apparent that something important was missing. If *Sgt. Pepper's Lonely Hearts Club Band* taught anything, it was that a great album could accommodate a few weaker numbers as long as it held a sparkling diamond at its center. "A Day In The Life" had so much vitality and spirit that any talk of Pepper invariably mentioned it. And despite all of their thought and effort, Traffic didn't have a song anything like that. Yet.

('Rave's whether Chart', Rave, 9/1967)

(M. Grant, Rave, 11/1967)

DEAR MR FANTASY

With the summer solstice long past, the nearly mature barley in the fields now reflected gold in the late morning sun. But amid nature's bounty, a vague restlessness had settled into the Cottage; the harvest Traffic still hoped to reap hadn't ripened yet, and no one was quite sure why. Awaiting inspiration, Chris, Steve and Jim had already lit the first cigarettes of the day and were fiddling with the instruments when a car drove up the tracks and stopped; things were about to change.

Syd and Brenda Bryan were a married couple, friends of Chris since the art school days who had kept in touch. Driving down from the Black Country to hang out and enjoy the day, they'd brought two items along – a camera and a little vial. As they got out of the car, Brenda held up the glass tube and smiled as the light refracted through – it was liquid LSD. "Polaroids…tripping. Every time we went there we took acid, and had wonderful weekends, me, Chris and Syd," was her recollection. Welcoming the distraction, that day they all got "quite out of it", as Brenda put it.

With the day turning dream-like, the musicians went outside and played waves of music to their guests, who sat facing them in the open field. Later, all would wander out into the undulating hillside, smiling, outstretched arms and fingers feeling the still growing plants, taking pictures of each other. As evening closed in, the Cottage spirit seemed awake as well; Brenda recalled hearing "a few squeaky things" emanating from somewhere in the house – but nothing too scary.

Jim recalled the day as magical, "It was alright, jamming, summer of '67. We had Syd and Brenda from Birmingham – tripping in the cornfields, the wind blowing the corn. When you've got a massive cornfield and it blows in the breeze, right in front of you, you know? The whole fucking thing was great. We were so young, and up for it and all that."

Years later, he still recalled the song they'd jammed on – "Feeling Good" – a cover of a Newley/Bricusse number which somehow encapsulated the musical/cosmic nexus of the Berkshire countryside. Jim added, "The organ at the end of 'Feeling Good' is like a Bach fugue – and with Chris's flute, *that's* the Cottage, right there. If you shut your eyes, you could be standing at the front door of the Cottage, on the stage, looking out across the slowly rising hill, with all of the corn blowing and all the land around us. This just incredible…"

Later, with Chris and Steve having taken yet another midnight mystery drive, Jim sat alone in front of the fireplace holding a pen as he stared at a blank piece of paper. Thinking about a possible cover for the not-yet-completed album, he finally sketched a crude figure wearing a spiky hat, with puppet strings from somewhere above connecting to hands dangling in front of a guitar. Next to it he scribbled a short, bittersweet letter to 'Mr. Fantasy', a character who gave mirth to others at the cost of his own grief – a sort of psychic echo to Smoky Robinson's "Tears of a Clown" (written about the same time). With just four lines of verse accomplished and the creative urge satisfied for the moment, he stumbled upstairs to bed.

Back from their drive across the Downs, Steve and Chris would discover the paper. While having no idea what Jim had been up to, the drawing and words set something off. Staring at it for a long moment, Chris then walked over and picked up a bass guitar and plugged it in. Soon after, with Jim still snoring away in his bed, a musical figure began to form in the room below. As the rhythmic thumping continued, he finally roused, later recalling, "I was asleep upstairs, and all of a sudden I heard it: 'dum dum, da dum dum, da dum, da da da dum da dum,' I heard it going on. And Chris was playing bass, quietly on an amp, and I'm hearing it for quite a while. I'm half awake, and I'm 'huh, hmm – that's good! That's really good, what they're doing.' I went down… and they were writing "Dear Mr. Fantasy" – magical, right there. I knew it was good, I could hear it in the riff, in all that. And it was very much Chris in all that. I mean, I'll never know, it was just him and Winwood, but I remember, from the very first, what was said then, and it was that Chris was very powerful in that bass part, which probably led to it being that shape you see. Bass! He was a horn player, a flute player, but he had *music* – where things would be original, an original idea." Aware they were on to something, from there the three worked through the dark hours amid shadows dancing around candle light.

With the bass riff serving as the melodic skeleton, the rest of the song coalesced around it; a hanging guitar figure played by Steve coming first, over which he slung a series of solos. Moving to the Hammond, Chris would add an atmospheric organ part which hovered and darted away like Harry Tibbits. As for Jim's minimalistic lyrics, they would turn out to be nearly perfect as is, having just enough substance to create an aura of mystery while leaving the rest to the listener's imagination. Sung in a hollow cadence that could have been channeled from a Middle Ages chant, Steve's vocals would provide the glue that held it all together. Running the song through once more as sunlight filtered in, they knew they'd found it; the missing heart of the album had finally materialized.

A sense of urgency to capture "Dear Mr. Fantasy" on tape pervaded the Cottage. Heading to the other cottage down the lane to use the phone, they called Dave, then Jimmy Miller to book Olympic Studios for the night. From there, Albert would hustle them into 'Big Pink' for a mad dash to London; a rush less about finishing the album than in fear that the song's otherworldly essence might somehow fade away like a dream in the dawn.

By evening one and all were settled into the bowels of the studio. Assembling the crew was merely the first step. From there, certain elements had to be arranged to get the 'feel' – a nebulous but very real state critical to making the music flow. Phill Brown, a studio engineer at Olympic, recalled the ambience being of primary importance: "Traffic liked to recreate the atmosphere of their rented Berkshire cottage and, while working in the studio, they would burn incense and work in almost total darkness."

Of course a good smoke didn't hurt either, and unlike more straight-laced studios such as Abbey Road, Olympic had no problem with a little of that other 'incense' while a band worked. Indeed, Paul Medcalf recalled that his primary job that night was to "roll joints, roll joints."

With Jimmy Miller onboard to Produce, and Eddie Kramer as the head engineer at the recording console, they sorted out the instrumentation: Chris on Hammond, Steve on guitar, Dave on bass, and Jim on drums – easy enough.

But a seemingly minor detail – again related to the feel, threatened to derail everything at the start. Essentially one big room, Olympic used large dampening screens to keep instruments from 'bleeding' sound from one channel to the other – normal practice in a professional studio. But in this case, preventing one problem created another. Walled off from each other and wearing 'cans' (earphones feeding the mix) the musicians lost their primal connection to each other – and soon their way, with take after take petering out or simply collapsing. With "Dear Mr. Fantasy" seemingly dying in front of them, a demoralizing vibe had crept in; something had to give.

Ripping off their headphones, the musicians scowled as they talked before gesturing for Miller. The changes required were simple but crucial – the 'cans' had to go, as well as the baffles; the band had to be set up as it was done at the Cottage – with full eye contact, almost nose-to-nose. And with the physical and psychic proximity restored the payoff was unambiguous; whatever the sacrifice in separation, a collective musical force suddenly surged.

The pent-up frustration pouring out, Winwood tore off solo after solo, bending strings to produce powerful curling figures with a vaguely Middle Eastern flavor. Behind him, Chris's Hammond shimmered while Jim's sticks cartwheeled in a mad dance around the drums. Dave was right in there too, adding the crucial bass lick and then elaborating on it. Having been inches from despair, Traffic now seethed with an energy they'd never known before. The song now even had a unique *sound*, seemingly embraced with a strange, breathing presence.

Observing from behind the glass of the control room, Jimmy Miller's eyes widened as his excitement grew. Fidgeting as the song chugged toward its conclusion, he suddenly bolted from his seat. Engineer Kramer saw it all, "I look around and Jimmy Miller's not in the control room. The next thing I see out of the corner of my eye is Jimmy hauling ass across the room, running full tilt. He jumps up on the riser, picks up a pair of maracas and gets them to double the tempo! That, to me, was the most remarkable piece of production assistance I'd ever seen. They were shocked to see him out there, exhorting them to double the tempo. Their eyes kind of lit up. It was amazing."

With a last pass at vocals and a wailing harmonica track by Dave on top, it was done. Listening back in the control room, the glances exchanged as the last note faded would say it all. They'd done it. Conjured out of a typically unique day in the Berkshire countryside, the ambience of the Cottage had been captured – preserved forever in the form of a song. Oh, and without any debate they also had the title of their debut album: *Mr. Fantasy*.

*

With no trace visible, the high water mark for Traffic had, in a way, just been reached. A conspiracy of events – some related, some random – were already threatening the life they'd established. While keeping their bedrooms in Berkshire, all were drawn like moths to the lights of London. With the hippest phase of the 'swinging sixties' in full flower, the action-packed scene proved irresistible. Steve had a place with Penny in Notting Hill, Jim would live with Chris at Millie Small's old flat on Cromwell Road, a place sometimes shared with Dave, although he also had a room elsewhere.

The drift had multiple causes. Certainly the drama surrounding "Hole In My Shoe" didn't help. That aside, the intensity that flowed between them created a sense that they'd almost lived a lifetime together already, bringing out what Chris later called "petty jealousies." Or as a friend put it, "They were really close – almost too close. They were inward looking guys… but they couldn't see the forest for the trees occasionally."

Jim Capaldi specifically blamed the introduction of females (Penny Massot in particular) onto the scene for breaking up the 'boys club'. Seeing Steve with Penny a bit too often for his liking, Jim began derisively calling her "Queen Bee" behind her back. Complaining to the others about her influence he would rail, "What the fuck's he doing with her? We can't stand this!" Failing to raise much enthusiasm in Chris or Dave, Jim would finally give Steve an ultimatum himself: "Either the Queen Bee goes, or I go." While a similar line had worked out well in the Deep Feeling Days, this time he'd overplayed his hand; Penny herself recalled Steve's terse checkmate: "Well then, I'll break up the group."

The ill-advised confrontation sent another chill through the already fragile psyche of the band. While sworn to democracy, everyone understood that Steve could veto the entire enterprise by simply walking away. It wasn't as if he didn't have other options. And now, having needlessly challenged him, the steely substrate beneath Winwood's seemingly easygoing exterior had been exposed.

Another swing in the dynamic was the continuing tussle over songwriting. While the partnership with Dave was obviously deceased, as the 'Fantasy' sessions concluded the trio's writing arrangement would soon falter as well. Looking ahead to the next disc, Jim began writing lyrics and presenting them directly to Steve. With the sheets of words and an implied obligation in front of him, Winwood could often be inspired to shape out a tune to go with it. And therein lay the change – with words and chord structure put together, the writing job was considered 'complete' credit-wise. Interestingly, the new dynamic became retroactive; recently someone had gone back and changed the credits on "Paper Sun" (written pre-Traffic by Jim and Steve in Newcastle) from the whole group to simply "Winwood/Capaldi".

From Jim's latter-day perspective, as the communal life splintered, and feeling pressure to get the product out, keeping things on track required the change in method. But he would also acknowledge a cost, "That was the only way we ever got any work done – any material got produced or any albums got made, 'cause I would write something on paper and give it to Winwood, and he would write some music. That's basically how it continued, and became the 'formula' after the Cottage days. And Chris felt very left out."

Having witnessed the band's rapid evolution up close, Paul Medcalf found similar words to describe the outcome, "Jim… he'd come up with lyrics – all the time. Every morning he'd dream up something, and try to make it into a lyric! Of course, there was Dave writing. Steve would just concentrate on writing all the music. So, Chris was left in the cold a bit on all of this."

It was on his mind. With fewer 'jam/songs' progressing to a final product, Chris would fret that his usual instruments made solo composition difficult. By early '68 he would tell a reporter, "You can *think* more on a piano for composition. If you can play chords you can construct. The saxophone has no chords."

('We Still Rolling?', Phill Brown, 1997)

('Traffic's "Dear Mr. Fantasy"', Blair Jackson, Mix, 2/1/2003)

('Player of the Month – Chris Woods' (sic), Beat Instrumental, 1/1968)

CHAPTER FIFTEEN

POINTS OF DEPARTURE

As the first week of September 1967 rolled around, the often discussed but never seen band 'Traffic' was finally exposed to the world, sort of. Many British bands followed the tradition of testing their sea legs in Scandinavia before debuting on their home turf. With a culture similar enough to appreciate the art, but far enough away so that any issues could be kept quiet back at home, Traffic's first shows were booked for Norway and Sweden. As it turned out there was nothing to worry about – having rehearsed their asses off, they were on fire from day one.

Getting there was a bit traumatic though. While excited by the prospect of seeing more of the world, Chris's initial experience with air travel proved less than positive. As often as he fantasized about flying with the birds, in real life, actually hurtling through the sky in a metal tube at hundreds of miles an hour didn't appeal at all. And when the day came, it was no better: the ultimate 'Big Dipper' ride – his only consolation being alcohol and, once again, Jim Capaldi's arm to cling to.

Once back on solid ground, the first show (at the Samfundssalen in Oslo, Norway) found them *all* nervous as hell. To compensate, each tried to look sharp, and distinctive. A blurry photo taken by a fan showed Steve wearing a bright Middle Eastern striped shirt, which caught the light as he hunched over the Hammond. At the back, Jim projected his presence with huge silver buttons running up his shirt to his shoulders. The picture of a psychedelic jazzman, Chris stood center stage in a paisley jacket, a bright cravat adorning his neck. But at the far right, literally outshining them all was Dave. Wearing a full-length sequined cloak, he was a human mirror ball, reflecting streaks of light in all directions.

Musically, they needn't have worried – Traffic proved a smash. Amazingly, the show in Stockholm – the second concert that Traffic *ever* did, was recorded and broadcast on the radio. A tape of that show documents a confident, if somewhat set-limited group. With audience expectations ruling out free-form jamming and having zero desire to delve into Spencer Davis material, only a handful of originals were left to work with – so they played them all.

Opening with a shot of jazz – "Giving To You" – Winwood set out the Cottage vibe right from the outset, singing the only verse before giving way to the solos. Chris took the first on flute, but each would have a turn – all confident and surefooted. Next up, a powerful "Smiling Phases", followed by the 'lost' single "Coloured Rain" – as good as ever, with Mason's bent-string rhythm lines and Chris's sax punctuating and propelling the song forward.

Then came "Hole In My Shoe". In later years, Jim would adamantly claim they never played the song live. While perhaps willing it out of his memory, play it they did, most likely at every gig for the first couple of tours. After all, it was their hit single. Beginning alone mid-stage, Dave sat cross-legged and unleashed a long sitar solo, with Jim tapping out a simple beat in the dark behind him until the others joined in. At the conclusion, Winwood could only manage a weak, "Thank you... (Pause)... Dave."

"Feeling Good", originally a Broadway musical number, was the only non-original song played, but it was possibly the purest Traffic ever. First played into the golden waving corn at the Cottage, it translated perfectly to the stage – incarnating the spiritual power of nature with poignant references to birds, sun and sky. Although influenced by Nina Simone's 1965 interpretation, Traffic's "Feeling Good" possessed qualities held by no other. Treated like a living organism needing to breathe and move, a critically arranged quiet passage tapered all to silence before a surge of music ended the song on an incredibly powerful note. And it was appreciated as intended; the audience response was loud and sustained.

Two strong punches wrapped up the show: "Paper Sun", shining in all its pop/rock glory, and a song nobody had yet heard: "Dear Mr. Fantasy". Here Steve somehow managed to outdo his original solos – yelling out with uncharacteristic bravado, "Watch me now!" before scorching the fret board to the song's crashing conclusion. Whatever their personal squabbles, on stage the unit of four embodied their fiery wheel symbol – spinning, burning, and throwing sparks into the night. With even Chris's nerves conversely calmed by the overload of stimuli, for a while at least, all were happy and fulfilled.

CHAPTER FIFTEEN

The rest of that first tour was a mad dash from Stockholm to Gothenburg, and on to Copenhagen, Denmark. It was chronicled in a similarly breathless fashion by Traffic's newly minted Fan Club secretary, Sally Meyers, in a newsletter sent out to the faithful:

"Absolute and complete sold out success! The grooviest tour on record. All the theatres packed—all the reviews full of enthusiasm and praises. At every town receiving such fantastic receptions. Looning in between shows added a touch of humour to all the glory, and on several occasions' total chaos completely took over. One night, Jim and Chris, who were starving at the time, were forced to trail practically all over Sweden in search of something to eat. The big drag being that they were not wearing ties at the time, and so politely but firmly they were put off at every stop. Eventually they ended up in a Swedish Beer Garden, enjoying a huge rave-up and leaping about in a mad drunken stupor."

"In Landsdrona one night there was not enough room on stage to take all their massive equipment, so they decided to set up on the floor amongst the kids. The kids went mad and started rioting and loads of police had to be rushed in at the double before the place was torn apart." With shades of *A Hard Day's Night*, so went Traffic's first appearances.

And once back in the homeland, there was little time to recover; the all-important first British tour was upon them.

The first show was scheduled for the Saville Theatre in London on September 24th. One of the hippest venues in town, until recently it had been run by Brian Epstein, the Beatles manager, who had died (likely by accidental drug overdose), only the month before. For Traffic, the stakes were considerable higher here. Having heard the singles, and the 'getting it together in the country' hype, the critics as well as many of the band's peers were anxious to see what Traffic really had to say. The packed house included Brian Jones, standing abreast of Jimi Hendrix, Noel Redding and Eric Burdon. Cat Stevens and the Hollies were there too. Behind a balcony curtain discreetly stood one more curious fan – Paul McCartney.

Playing essentially the same set as in Sweden, the unexpected "Feelin' Good" again proved the showstopper, and "Dear Mr. Fantasy" – dedicated by Chris to Frank Zappa – the rocking closer. Fans and critics alike loved it, and more importantly, so did their fellow musicians. Despite the fact that the crucial first album was, as yet, unfinished, in a single stroke Traffic shot straight to the elite level of British rock.

From there things happened fast. While lauded in the press, the critical praise paled in comparison to McCartney's reaction. Immediately after the London debut, he was on the phone to Island, telling Muff Winwood that "Traffic was the most interesting new group around", and offering the band a scene in something he called "The Beatles new mystery film." And it wasn't simply talk; soon afterward he made a personal visit to discuss plans with the group. Christie Nichols heard the tale of Paul's trip out to the Cottage with sheepdog Martha in tow. She recalled, "Paul came walking up with his dog, this big shaggy dog, and she said that their jaws dropped… they were beside themselves… just *so* thrilled." If further details of the Beatle's visit are lost to the mists of time, the results were not – Traffic got a collective ego boost which would never be equaled.

The Beatles' film crew were duly dispatched to the Cottage, and the scene (filmed in one day), was set to the title song from the still unreleased film "Here We Go Round The Mulberry Bush". As "Hole In My Shoe" fell in the charts, "Mulberry" was the next single, and with the Beatle's film due for Christmas, the cross-promotion was ideal. But problems ensued. Asked about it not long after, Chris drily replied, "One shot includes this huge globe of the World, which rolled down a hill. Unfortunately, it broke. We are awaiting the bill." Technical issues aside, Traffic did their part, turning in footage that was low key but sweetly whimsical. Shot in part with a violet lens filter, the clip centered on the above-mentioned globe precariously perched on a Berkshire hilltop – the four musicians marching around a twenty-foot diameter 'Earth', each carrying a personal totem. While there was little 'acting' as such, Winwood was given the most screen time. But one of the last shots featured Chris – smiling as he stumbled forward across the crest of a ridge, one hand vainly grasping for flowers dangling from a string on a stick, held by the other hand.

Unfortunately, whether the result of the broken globe or Beatles film editing squabbles (which were frequent), when *The Magical Mystery Tour* was shown on British television, the day after Christmas, 1967, Traffic's scene was inexplicably absent.

*

With the excitement of their U.K. debut behind them, Traffic now faced the life of a British band with a hit record: BBC radio and T.V. appearances, then a tour. The first homeland trip had them topping the bill as part of a 'package tour' with Keith West, Tomorrow, The Flower Pot Men, and Art. They got a good workout – starting in London, then Chesterfield, Newcastle, Liverpool, Croydon, and back home to Birmingham, followed by Bristol, Wolverhampton, Leicester and finally Ipswich.

With less than a week's break (including recording another BBC radio show), they returned to the road, on yet another package tour across England with The Who, the Tremeloes, and The Herd. This one took in fifteen more dates (two shows a night) concluding with yet another BBC session.

Even prior to the first night, Chris had concerns. He anticipated (correctly) problems with a sizable percentage of the audience – mostly girls – who would be "screaming" rather than listening. Wanting Traffic to be taken seriously, in his first major press interview, he sought to distinguish his band from the teeny bop set, "It will be good working on the same bill as the Who. They certainly get the girls screaming. We have had them scream for us too, but we feel that we aim for the musical side of audiences rather than the screamers."

To some extent it worked that way; Traffic would prove the most 'listened to' of all the bands on the bill. Regardless, the whole thing would never be more than semi-controlled chaos, right from start. The Who's leader, Pete Townshend wasted no time setting the agenda, "For this tour we are going to blow your bloody head off…" But even off-stage, their already infamous drummer, Keith Moon, made each day memorable. The master of many guises, including playing the perfect innocent, 'Moonie' breathlessly told the press, "Before we go on, I have groups lined up, and make sure they've brushed their teeth and they all have nice ties on. We run a clean show!" Of course, underlying reality was closer to pure mayhem. Jim Capaldi shook his head recalling a typical situation, "One night he went completely berserk and kicked the drums all around the stage and then stabbed each skin with his stick."

The Herd's keyboard player, Andy Bown, pronounced the tour as "intense but fun"; with the most extreme 'fun' traceable back to Moon. While he tried to keep "reasonably straight" by drinking only miniature bottles of Courvoisier between shows (two shows a night being standard practice), any other time, all bets were off. Bown recalled that any attempt to get a good night's rest afterward was typically rewarded with, "A few firecrackers rolled under your hotel door." He also experienced a ride in Moon's specially outfitted lilac Bentley, "He had a microphone set up, and amplifier, and a speaker in the grill. He'd stop at a zebra crossing for instance, and some old lady would go across. She'd be halfway across, in front of the car, and he'd go (screaming) 'Get off it!' He'd leave a string of heart attacks behind him."

Bown also noticed that another Who member, known for his reserve, was not always what he seemed, "But it was John you see, John Entwhistle (bass player), and he would say (in a low voice), 'C'mon Keith, c'mon, you can do that'. Then he'd stand back and pretend it wasn't him – the 'Quiet One'! He was egging him on all the time. It was mad."

Even Townshend sometimes seemed quite off his rocker. The *NME* reported that when the tour manager once cut the power due to The Who's excessively long set, Pete reacted by "tipping amplifiers on top of him, and attempting to throttle him in full view of the audience."

Amidst the testosterone and drug-fueled madness, the music was good, but as would become the norm when members of Traffic were around, some of the best sounds were never heard by the audience. Reporter Keith Altham was lucky enough to witness some of the off-stage jams, "Perhaps the greatest performance on Friday was missed by the first house. I spent an enjoyable hour at rehearsals listening to a modern jazz session including Peter Frampton on guitar, Jim Capaldi and Andrew Steel on drums, Chris Wood on sax, and Stevie Winwood and Andy Bown on organ. Shades of Jimmy Smith…" The jazzy after-show jams helped to restore a little musical integrity, smooth the rough edges, and return a touch of sanity to the three ring circus.

The continuously crazed atmosphere affected Chris. Andy Bown recalled him as "a quiet, gentle guy, he was lovely, (but) he looked nervous. He had a permanent air of nervousness, or shyness." Concerned that Traffic be taken seriously, it didn't help when he read that his own attempts at singing sometimes came off unintentionally comical. Reporter Keith Altham noted, "His expression going for a falsetto note is akin to someone shot in the posterior with an arrow." Perhaps not coincidentally, soon after, he would quit singing on stage altogether. And as the mad caravan rolled on, Chris would find himself in the orbit of the devil himself – 'Moon the Loon', and doing whatever it took to keep up.

And, of course, the ubiquitous hash smoke touched all, like it or not. Andy Bown's first ever experience in getting high came on the tour – when he found himself packed into a car with Traffic after a gig. Without ever touching the joint, he breathed in enough to get thoroughly stoned, "After about twenty minutes in the car, I thought, 'Cor, I feel a bit *funny…*'" Following a lengthy drive, he would find himself at Traffic's Cottage, completely out of his head, jamming by candlelight on organ, with Winwood supporting on drums. An undeterminable time later, both finally fell over from exhaustion in front of the fireplace; a suitable enough metaphor for the tour itself.

*

With autumn sliding into winter, and the tour finally at an end, they settled once again into the womb of the Cottage to rest, and explore a little more. And, oh yes, they still needed to finish the album. With one more song to record, the pastoral "No Face, No Name, No Number", the basic track was recorded right there at their rural abode, validating – at least in principle – that it could be done from home. And with that in the can, they were done.

The time had come to bring Mr. Fantasy to life. Jim's original sketch inspired the photograph made for the album cover: an oddly dressed character with a funny hat sitting in the living room of the Cottage, lifting puppet strings connected to disembodied hands playing an old acoustic guitar. With the fireplace roaring, the band was photographed as they sat, watching with rapt attention. So who embodied Mr. Fantasy? None other than their old Birmingham pal, Paul Medcalf, who recalled, "I was the mug who happened to be there. Jim got the costume, we went to Monty Berman's, and he had all this wonderful stuff. I had these (manikin) hands, we spray painted an old guitar, and we just sort of set it up. To get the glow from the fire, you'd throw the odd candle on and it would roar up." Photographer John Benton Harris, used a lens filter on the camera to achieve the reddish cast, something Medcalf thought a bit over the top; comparing it to a film scene adapted from the Edgar Allan Poe story, "The Fall of the House of Usher".

Unintentionally, Benton Harris also captured something else. To the far right, on the fireplace wall, emerged the image of a coarse, vaguely evil looking head – staring directly at Traffic. More disturbingly, the 'neck' of the figure appeared encircled by a loop of rope. While likely a coincidental smudge of chimney soot; it was close enough to a human shape to allow imagination to fill in the details. Chris noticed right away, and neither Steve nor Jim had any trouble interpreting it. Found at the exact place where roadie Albert often could be heard yelling and calling his name, to them the image was no less than the manifestation of their ghost: the distorted apparition of the young man who'd hanged himself in the well many years before.

Inspired, Chris designed the inside sleeve himself, cutting photos of the band members, some into squares, some circular, to resemble an old photo album. In the inner photo spread, he also wrote the album dedication in his own sloppy scrawl, "In memory of Len Tibbits, Brother of Harry Tibbits, he died shuvling ? . Gravel," And with that cryptic comment, their ghost was official; exposed, if only obliquely, to the world.

With the album wrapped up, the old/new "Mulberry Bush" single ready to go, and Christmas on the way, a most remarkable year wound down. On top of it, they had something big to look forward to. The office had already made arrangements for the New Year to come – Traffic would be heading to America. Breaking through there was absolutely critical to 'success' as first defined by The Beatles back in '64. Aiming for the bull's eye, Traffic's initial point of contact, San Francisco, was the epicenter of the hip world in '67. The tone of the times had been shaped that summer by the nearby Monterey Pop Festival; more than any single event, the prototype for a new way of looking at music. Melding styles from Indian ragas to R&B, folk to acid, and hard rock, the glorious patchwork somehow added up to a unified whole. Accompanied by Brian Jones, Hendrix had been there, and from a distance The Beatles had blessed it. Yes, 'Frisco was where Traffic belonged, and they were excited to slip into the burgeoning west coast scene to check it all out.

Then Dave quit.

It has been said that Dave Mason was 'fired' from Traffic. Considering the strife and hard feelings spread around the band, the assumption is reasonable, but *this time*, it wasn't the case. Instead, like any employee with better opportunities elsewhere, Mason simply gave notice; agreeing to play out concerts scheduled for the rest of the year before departing. The reason remains, to this day, elusive. To his mystified band-mates he mentioned an opportunity to do some record producing. But years later, Mason would indicate that it really came down to one thing: nerves. "I left the first time, because of that. That's why I left. It's like, 'I can't deal with this'. It was all too much for me. Not the music – (but) the success, all the crap, all the stuff – how you are perceived. So for me, at that time in my life, being very young, it just freaked me out, so I elected to leave."

After his last gig with Traffic, Dave did produce Family, a British band making their debut album, *Music From A Doll's House*. From there he was a free agent and a blur of action, playing with Jimi Hendrix (to whom Dave signaled his willingness to play bass if the job came open), Eric Clapton, and others. Then, as the New Year dawned, he was gone – jetting off to California, where he hung out and jammed with people like Gram Parsons, Delaney and Bonnie, the Mammas and the Pappas. But with his "Hole In My Shoe" not a hit in the United States and Traffic's first album not yet released there, there was a problem. Few Americans had any idea who Dave Mason was. His path now uncertain, he would subsequently pack a bag and an acoustic guitar and jet to Greece, alone, in the hope of clearing his head.

Within Traffic, the official reaction to the departure was muted. While Chris said nothing at all in public, Steve, on the night of their last concert together, was nonchalant, "Unfortunately, Dave decided to leave us. Well, sure it hurts, but that's the way it is. It's kind of wild in a sad sort of way, but we've had some nice blows together." Jim too seemed only mildly perturbed. Having had many ups and downs with Dave over many years; basically he'd seen it all before.

But behind the scenes, feelings were definitely bruised. Winwood's girlfriend and confidant, Penny held nothing back, "Having said 'Traffic's not nearly as good as Family', he dropped them in the shit (before) we got to the States. He's out for himself, Dave. He had no concept of a band, working together."

In the end, a punishment of sorts would be meted out. As Traffic's album was prepared for release in America, last minute alterations were made. First, some of Dave's songs were dropped (although interestingly *not* "Hole In My Shoe"). Then a new cover was shot showing only a serious-faced trio of Steve, Chris and Jim. For all the average record buyer in America would know, Dave was perhaps a session musician with some songwriting credit. Founding member or not, at the time when some name recognition in the U.S.A. would have been a help, Dave Mason had been more or less erased from Traffic.

As for the remains of Traffic, the U.S. tour was neither cancelled nor delayed. Interestingly, with all of the prior talk of replacing Mason before the band was ever really formed, now that he was gone, there seemed no interest whatsoever. Perhaps there just wasn't time to think about it. With Christmas come and gone, they had about six weeks to get themselves together before the first scheduled concert, at Bill Graham's Fillmore Auditorium, in San Francisco. They would play as a trio.

There was a lot to live up to. *Rolling Stone* magazine, still young and trying hard to both follow and define 'hip culture' of the 60's, had already heard tales of the crazy goings on in the British countryside. Photographer/reporter David Dalton was sent to check it out. Conducted to the Cottage in the Land Rover he quickly fell under its spell. Hearing an unclassifiable sound from somewhere inside, Chris casually attributed it to their ghost. A surprised Dalton asked, "Do you *really* believe in the supernatural?" Chris replied, "It's more natural you know – it's a natural thing really: *super* natural, more real…" Realizing he was on to something, Dalton knew this story would require more time to tell properly. Ultimately, his piece would not be published for a year, but when it was, that article, more than any other would capture the essence of the band and the unique ambience of the Cottage.

While the loss of Dave should have been daunting, instead a quiet confidence pervaded. With months of mad jamming and roadwork behind them, the trio's capabilities, individually and collectively were considerable. Besides Steve's ability to switch from guitar to organ at any time, the Hammond's foot pedals allowed him to play bass notes with his feet, leaving hands free to cover the melody and solos. The fact that Winwood could do all that, *and sing* at the same time – a precarious musical balancing act few others could manage – was the key to how they could manage.

With Chris able to play multiple instruments as well, the trick was for Jim to keep a steady pulse whenever Steve and Chris needed to switch places. This subtle little dance was the only real show they had to offer, but there was a kind of beauty in it, and many viewed 'the trio' as the band's best incarnation. Paul Medcalf definitely thought so, laughing as he recalled Chris's musical appendages, "When Steve went onto guitar, Chris had to play bass. At other times, he had to play the piano or organ. Of course, he was filling in on sax as well. So he had a bass around his neck and a sax around his neck! And he was at the keyboards!"

One more leap of faith followed. With the Americans having no preconceptions about what Traffic was supposed to sound like, they were free to bring some of what they did best – jamming – to the stage. Minus

Mason, a new approach had suddenly opened up. Returning by instinct to their original jazz-form intentions, they would play as they felt; Traffic was reborn.

Just to make sure, they played a few gigs on their home ground, the last being an unscheduled appearance at London's always hip Speakeasy club. Anxious about how they'd be received by the sophisticated London audience, the new trio was a bundle of nerves. But once on stage, everything clicked and the praise was effusive. Palpably relieved, there was no further time to fret – the New World awaited.

('Danger: Who At Work!', NME, 11/1967)

('Rock and Other Four Letter Words', Bantam Books, 1968)

('They're Off!', Disc and Echo, October 28 1967)

('Traffic's British stage debut is well worth waiting for', Keith Altham, N.M.E. 9/30/1967)

(Traffic Timeline, J. Sommerseth)

(Traffic Newsletters, 1967)

('Who Know What Tomorrow Might Bring', David Dalton, Rolling Stone, May 3 1969)

CHAPTER SIXTEEN

THE TRAIL OF THE HEADLESS HORSEMEN

The trip to San Francisco, California, might as well have been a rocket ride to another world. Flying non-stop from a very chilly London to Los Angeles, the subsequent flight dropped them into a sunny, warm 'Frisco day. Steve came with Penny, and Jim with his new French girlfriend Danielle. Only Chris was unpaired. Fidgety and dazed from the trip, like the others he was excited to see what America held in store. Having only known the place through the prism of film, jazz records and his vivid imagination, he worried that reality would prove a letdown.

But shuffling off the plane into the fading afternoon sun, he would stop dead in his tracks after only a few steps. With a rocky coastline, a seemingly boundless intersection of ocean and sky, *and* a vivid late afternoon sun displayed before him, the long dormant painter inside suddenly awakened. Turning to Penny he tried to speak, but seemed in shock. Smiling and shaking his head, he finally muttered: "The light, the colors…" before once again staring into the horizon. The hazy filter of England was suddenly removed from his eyes, Chris's own *Jazz On A Summer's Day* had suddenly come to life: another dream come true.

If the reality of America was blowing his mind, the breeze would quickly turn surreal. Sensing Traffic to be a band of kindred spirits, the Grateful Dead had sent Augustus Owsley Stanley III to meet them at the airport. Aside from the technical work he did for the Dead, the self-crowned Acid King's mission was to produce the highest quality LSD and proselytize its use as far and wide as possible. Traffic was no exception; the acid was in their systems even before they ever got to town.

The day after the kaleidoscopic introduction to America (March 14th), they would play their first gig at Bill Graham's Fillmore Auditorium. This part too had been arranged very deliberately. Graham put Traffic at the top of a bill also holding a psychedelic band (HP Lovecraft) and the proto-punk Blue Cheer. Unmatched at mixing musical styles in ways that would educate if not always satisfy the preconceived notions of the audience, Graham also went out of his way to create a respectful vibe for the artists by paying attention to details like sound and lighting. Returning the favor, Traffic would give their all.

Opening with an improvised jam featuring a long, fanciful flute solo, midstream Chris would switch to sax and emit honking car/traffic sounds – his way of saying hello from the band. In a clever split-second pivot, Winwood's organ then riffed a lead into the psych-blast of "Coloured Rain", bringing the band to a boil before backing off for the pastoral "No Face, No Name, No Number". The big windup of "Dear Mr. Fantasy" with Chris on bass guitar followed, with the devastating closer – "Feeling Good", bringing the house down. "Blind Man", an obscure Bobby 'Blue' Bland cover sung by Winwood (in his best Ray Charles voice) ended the show. Having spooned out a near-perfect combination of talent, taste and wild abandon, the proof of success was in the pudding – the Americans ate it up.

Naturally, the debut was not without complications. Chris managed to kick his box of sax reeds off stage, leading him to have to ask the first row to help look for it. And somehow the band never understood Graham's policy for headliners to play two sets per show. In England, two *shows* an evening was standard procedure, so the second time on stage they would play the same songs again – to the same audience. As they finished the repeat performance Bill Graham ran up to Winwood, sputtering, "Listen you…*it's the same people!*" But he was soon smiling again; both Graham and the audience forgave any sins. "They loved it. The boys were fantastic without Dave; they were great as a trio," Penny recalled.

With the next concerts not scheduled until the following weekend, they settled in to enjoy the San Francisco scene, catching shows by the Jefferson Airplane and the Electric Flag. But that was only the beginning; music and adventure seemed to be in the air itself, calling for them to join in.

On the 17th, the Grateful Dead agreed to play a gig supporting DJs at a local radio station (KMPX FM) who had gone on strike. It was to be a free show, performed outdoors that night on a flatbed truck parked on the street near the station. Asked by Jerry Garcia to contribute a set, Traffic agreed – but before they could, interference by the police first delayed, and then required, the whole operation be moved to another location.

CHAPTER SIXTEEN

Morning had broken by the time it was all sorted out, but the show would go on. Although the audience was by now equal parts tired as hell or not yet fully awake, surprisingly the vibes were great and the music compelling. Still high and smiling, Traffic beamed positive energy back and forth with the crowd, also impressing the Dead – especially Jerry, who reportedly joined in for a high flying "Dear Mr. Fantasy".

Observing it all from up close, drummer Mickey Hart appreciated the metaphysics of the band right from the start, "Traffic was heading into 'sacred dimension land' – playing from the heart, from the gut… so many doors you could go through musically, in Traffic. They left a lot to the imagination, that's what made it a great band."

Afterward, all went separate ways. Stoked by the reception, Jim and Danielle stayed in town and hung out with musicians and hippies, taking in the sights. Steve and Penny were whisked off by Hart and Garcia for a few days in the mountains at a place near Lake Tahoe, playing ping pong, doing a little hiking, and "just enjoying great hang time", according to Mickey Hart.

Not surprisingly, Chris went off on an entirely different tangent. While the others chilled with the local musicians and peace freaks, *he* made friends with the infamous Frisco Hell's Angels, who often served as the Dead's security. With their dirty jean jackets and elaborate 'colors' defining their tribe, the Angels were larger than life – real outlaws, known to beat the hell out of anyone slighting them, intentionally or not.

Either ignorant or blithely unconcerned Chris simply hung out, asking questions as he examined their bikes. And when they revved their motors and left the scene, he was with them. Last seen heading down the road on the back of a Harley, Chris's further adventures with the Angels remain a tantalizing mystery. Penny recalled only the need to physically retrieve him once they caught up again, "Chris got involved with a lot of bikers. You had to watch Chris. He was so wonderful, he wanted to experience *everything* – he was artistic in that way. He wasn't afraid; he'd just get out there. You'd have to sort of grab him, and get him back."

Finally returning to Traffic's base of operations – the Seal Rock Inn, a hotel facing the Pacific Ocean – Chris would find time for a couple of short-term relationships. First, he and a girl named Marsha shared an evening together which ended with Chris praising her honesty, slipping a ring off his finger and onto hers as a gift. Later, based on that encounter, Marsha would move to England, seeking (unsuccessfully) to develop a relationship with him.

Soon after, he met Dian Melzer, who lived near another Bill Graham venue that Traffic would play called 'Winterland'. Dian had worked for Graham back in '65 when he was just getting started and was well connected on the local scene. Between sets at Traffic's gig on March 21st, a housemate brought the whole bunch home. Dian recalled, "We had this Victorian flat, you know, long hallways and all the rooms. We had a music room with a bay window and a piano. I met Chris in the kitchen, and looked at him and it was like 'Whoa!' We went off to the music room and he started playing a little piano, and we started to talk. I went back for the second set at Winterland, and then we came back to my house for the evening." The attraction was equal parts physical and intellectual interests. With a house full of maps, books about the history of the Earth and various sized globes, Chris was impressed. Possessing a pilot's license, she even offered to take him up for a ride, which he laughingly declined.

In their few days together, a lot was shared. "We would watch the sun go down, the ocean was right across the road, and you could look out at the colors – purple, red, oranges – of the sunset. And he would talk about when they landed, how he had never seen a sky like that, it reminded him of the fireplace on the first Traffic album, *Mr. Fantasy*. He was like a kid, overwhelmed with the sights and sounds, just everything. We started talking about ancient maps, going to sea in ships, their images about the world – how they might fall off the world and dragons would eat you. We talked about the way the world evolved, we talked about Pangaea. I said, 'Oh, it's just like a puzzle', and we looked at one of the maps, and I actually cut one of them apart, and we put the puzzle back together again. We had so much fun, doing childish things like that."

Dian had another intriguing skill. "One of my friends told him that I read fortunes, so he said, 'Oh, let's read my palm!'" Hesitant to give him a reading, although not quite sure why, Chris proved insistent. "We smoked a lot, sitting on my bed in candle light, and he said, 'Read my palm, read my palm', and he turns his palms over. And I saw, like… both of his lifelines sort of ended in the early forties. And I sort of went (sharp intake of breath). Usually if someday you see something that is not really pleasant, you dissemble, you try to keep your poker face as much as possible. And he said, 'What is it? What is it?' And I said, 'Oh no, I was just wondering if we needed rum again'. I don't know if he believed me. But what I did tell him was 'You have to be very careful about your health… and certain places he shouldn't go."

Just like that, everything would change, "We were getting along so well, it was like a cloud came over when I looked at his palm. He wanted to know where the local liquor store was. I said, 'we're hippies, we don't drink, we smoke. I like to get high.' He said, *I like to get obliviated.* I think he was so sensitive and felt so much that it scared him. It made him feel better to 'obliviate' his awareness, to sleep or be out of it. But he didn't sleep that much! Very mysterious…"

*

At a party the next night at Buddy Miles's house (drummer for the Electric Flag), Chris was already looking to the future. He and Buddy spent much of the evening discussing how Traffic and a mutual friend – Jimi Hendrix – could meet up when their paths crossed the next month in New York. Hendrix was anticipating it too. Not long before Traffic arrived in San Francisco, Jimi (along with Buddy Miles) had played a fiery version of "Dear Mr. Fantasy" at the Fillmore Auditorium. One of only a couple of times that he would ever play the song live, it was his way of preparing America to welcome his friends.

Up next for Traffic was Los Angeles and Hollywood. The fabled town of celluloid heroes now had some new gods in residence – an aristocracy of rock musicians taking advantage of their recent financial success. Flocking to a wooded patch just outside of town called Laurel Canyon, members of groups like the Doors, the Byrds, the Mamas and the Papas, and Buffalo Springfield had rented huge houses with gated entrances to live undisturbed as Traffic did, albeit in a luxury far removed from the primitive life in the Berkshire Downs.

They played a warm-up gig at the tiny Whiskey a Go Go, then a couple at their largest venue yet – the Shrine Exhibition Hall. It was a big step up, but to be fair, while the place had a capacity of fifteen thousand – the Friday show drew a paltry three hundred and fifty (fifteen hundred for Saturday). Regardless, the reviews were glowing, with the *Los Angeles Times* hailing Steve for his bluesy approach and his "magnificently harsh voice", and then Chris, "Wood's horn work lifts the group out of comparison with the droves of contemporary blues units." The highlight came when Buddy Miles joined them on the Saturday for a half hour encore jam which *The Times* termed: "an incredible performance."

So America was working out very well indeed – perhaps a little too good – music aside, the drugs flowed much faster than could be consumed. Penny remembered that in L.A. Chris was the target of many 'gifts' from fans, "People used to pull him off stage and just throw pills at him – they'd put them down his sax. So after the gig I would have these pills out of Chris's sax; I'd take one pill and divide it in four, and everybody would get a piece to see what this pill was like."

Feted once again by the local rock elite, the gathering place was Peter Tork's place, a mansion in the Studio City portion of Laurel Canyon. Having made a bundle from the Monkees', records, tours and T.V. show, he clearly enjoyed the perks, although in a way utterly foreign to his guests. Penny Massot recalled, "It was Peter Torks' (place), where there was a lot of cocaine, huge amounts, and he was *naked*. It was the most extraordinary thing, and we were quite shocked, being sort of rather virginal English people. He (Tork) was sitting in a chair, naked, and he had all of these handmaidens – it was very bizarre. There were about five women, the eldest one was waited on by the younger, by the younger, by the younger – it was all that kind of carrying on. One of them fell in love with Woody, Karen she was called."

With too much of everything at their disposal, the non-stop L.A. scene would culminate with Chris passing out face up on a Malibu beach where he lay unattended for hours – the sunburn would be severe. As Penny remembered, "It was boiling hot, the sun was fierce; he was in a terrible state." But, by then, the vibes were deteriorating anyway – Traffic's roadie had crashed their van and soon after, Jim's drum kit was stolen. With all signs pointing elsewhere, they were ready to move on.

If L.A. had proved a little rough-edged in the end, their next stop couldn't have painted a starker contrast to the west coast psychedelic idyll. The Traffic fan club labeled this leg of the tour: "Bad land – draggy country", and made note of the scary surroundings, "Detroit police and machine guns all over the place." While San Francisco had produced a 'Summer of Love' in 1967, Detroit's claim to fame that year had been a race riot resulting in death and massive destruction. One year later, the local baseball team (Tigers) were doing great but otherwise the city was still a mess. Despite or perhaps partly because of the chaos, the music scene was alive and kicking serious ass.

CHAPTER SIXTEEN

Patterned after Bill Graham's Fillmore, The Grande Ballroom on 8952 Grand River Avenue was the premiere venue in town, snaring all of the up-and-coming British acts like Savoy Brown, the Who and Cream – as well as menacing homegrown bands like the MC5 and the Stooges. The impresario was a high school teacher, part-time D.J. and concert promoter named Russ Gibb. Riding to meet Traffic at the airport on a motorcycle with his black helmet and a leopard skin jacket, Gibb tried to make the band feel at home, fulfilling their wish to see the 'Hit Factory' – Motown Studios on West Grand Boulevard. He would also arrange a meeting with South African jazzer Hugh Masakela, who loved Traffic and later recorded a cover version of "No Face, No Name, No Number".

Of course, the burned out buildings and people openly walking around with shotguns only enticed Chris to check things out. On the day of their show, as the others huddled safely inside the Grande after the sound check, he casually strolled out the back door to explore the neighborhood – a slight, eccentrically dressed Englishman, wandering alone. Soaking in Detroit's damaged ambience, he was back in time for the show, but just barely, nonchalantly walking past the kids lined up and waiting for the night's concert.

In that line was fifteen year old Doug Fieger. A fan since the days of the Spencer Davis Group, he'd bought that early Mason-annulling pressing of *Mr. Fantasy* and was even knowledgeable about the Berkshire Cottage. As such he was primed to see Traffic, and wasn't disappointed. "They weren't flashy – the music was just good – it was just about the music. And yet, I loved the look. To me, they were everything." In the roughest town in America, the gauntlet was always waiting for unproven acts. With Detroit audiences notorious for loudly rejecting bands that somehow rang false, how did Traffic go over? Fieger recalled, "They were remarkable, it was astonishing – everybody was listening. They weren't tall guys, but they had a commanding presence, they had unbelievable amounts of charisma." For Fieger, the influence was profound. Not long afterwards, he would form a band of his own (Sky), and the next time Traffic came to town they would be the opening act.

Watching from the wings, promoter Gibb also fell for Traffic, seeing them as a counterbalance to the heaviness of the times, "I loved them. Traffic is still one of my favorite bands. Chris was very quiet, and always a gentleman. I had a lot of respect for him. Even though he didn't come forward a lot – he was there, and you had a feeling that there was a great influence in him at that point. I still love their music because there's a melodic and gentleness with some of their things, if you listen very closely."

As for Chris, he later told friends that he actually felt quite comfortable in old Detroit – it reminded him a lot of the Black Country.

Next up was Cleveland, where once again, things went beautifully. A fan in the audience described Chris as "magnetic", recalling that he even got some laughs – waiting for a spotlight to shine nearby he would suddenly jump into it from the shadows, a playful grin on his face. In Chicago, Traffic again took on the hip clubs – The Cheetah and The Electric Theater, finding more success with fans, critics and fellow musicians. With the Midwest leg now complete, the biggest stop of all loomed – New York City.

Checking into their hotel in Manhattan, an important call came in before they'd even unpacked: Jimi Hendrix was on the line. Penny Massot recalled how the plans changed as a result, "The thing with Hendrix really comes from Chris. He was close to Hendrix. We were on tour, and when we hit New York, I remember Hendrix ringing up. He must have rung up Chris, and said: 'Look, I'm staying at the Lincoln Square Motor Inn, why don't you guys come and stay here?' And we did."

By now, Jimi and Traffic already had a long association. Since that first jam with Deep Feeling there had been numerous encounters, with the guitarist sometimes crashing at Jim and Chris's apartment on Cromwell Road in London; once even having to be dragged in when he'd partied too hard. The musical situation was tight as well. According to Jim Capaldi and Paul Medcalf, in December of '67, Jimi had actually written the song, "Crosstown Traffic" about the band. Medcalf recalled, "You know how Hendrix worked, he made stuff up as he went along – the lyrics, he could make them up on the spot. Chris and Steve were stuck in a taxi, trying to get to the studio. And I think they must have phoned or something, 'cause Hendrix was doing "Crosstown Traffic" when they walked in!" And, of course, the final twist of irony – Dave Mason had somehow beaten them to it – he was singing background vocals when they arrived.

The Experience had just come off a long tour, following a route similar to Traffic's. Now they were recording tracks for their second album at the Record Plant studio. Unlike San Francisco's beaches and awe inspiring sunsets, New York provided a nocturnal experience – the sunrise a mere reminder of another inverted 'day' come to an end. Chris hung out with Jimi and his entourage at the hotel and at clubs, especially Steve Paul's The Scene, where numerous mad jam sessions took place. Music aside, they also partied hard. Penny noted, "Of course the minute we got to wherever it was that Hendrix was staying, it was absolute chaos – with all of those girls – Chris was gone! You know, we had to go find him...Woody hadn't been to bed for a couple of days."

An American who became a star in England, Hendrix had finally returned to conquer his homeland. One of the perks of his success was women and Hendrix's personal magnetism meant he had more around than anyone else. Yet from Penny's point of view, the hangers-on were distractions, or worse: "There were hundreds of groupies around; there was Devon (Wilson), loads of these girls that were around Hendrix – wonderful guy, fabulous guy, but surrounded by dreadful people."

But amid the throng, Chris would make an unexpectedly strong connection. Waif-like and olive skinned with dark almond-shaped eyes, Jeanette Jacobs was a singer and songwriter for a moderately successful band called The Cake. Having known Jimi Hendrix even before he was famous, she often told people that they were a couple, and in love. But in a relationship best described as 'fluid', when something clicked between her and Chris, exploring the situation was never a problem. The courtship began with deep conversation. Although only nineteen, her band had been together since '66, and Jeanette had as many, or more, stories from the road as he did. But even more interesting was her family history. Explaining her exotic looks, Jeanette wove a captivating tale: she was actually royalty, albeit of an unknowledgeable sort – her father being King Farouk of Egypt, her mother a highly paid prostitute he'd met while visiting America. Of course, her upbringing would be anything but easy or conventional.

Chris likely never bought the story, but he *was* deeply intrigued by the fact that she told it so convincingly. In fact, Jeanette's need to conceal her background made her even more attractive. Amongst all of the girls and women he'd met on the tour she alone presented a real enigma, and he was smitten. Besides her beauty, Jeanette's apparent vulnerability showed him someone in need of protection.

In contrast to Chris's open embrace of the freedom and intensity of the American experience, Steve had begun backing away. Confronted with strange people and sensory overload at every turn, by the time the New York craziness kicked in he was seeking some insulation. Penny became his gate-keeper, making sure that he stayed clear of the mayhem that Chris seemed to thrive on. "Steve and I extricated ourselves from that whole scene. At night we would be in the room, because he wasn't a party animal. I needed to be there to protect him...'keep them away' he used to say. He smoked dope, but that was it. A lot of people (thought) because he was so laid back and couldn't communicate very well... I heard rumors that he was a junkie and stuff, and that's absolutely ridiculous – total rubbish," Penny asserted.

Out of the semi-wilderness of New York City, order finally emerged and work was getting done. First, on April 22nd, Chris added a gentle flute part to Hendrix's long, dreamy "1983(A Merman I Should Turn To Be)"; about ten days later Steve, Jimi, Mitch Mitchell and Jefferson Airplane bassist Jack Casady would furiously jam a blues workout called "Voodoo Chile". Both tracks found their way onto *Electric Ladyland*, the Hendrix double album released that October. A couple of days after "Voodoo" Chris also recorded a track with Noel Redding on which Hendrix played bass ("Walking Through the Garden").

They also got it on in the local clubs, especially at Steve Paul's, The Scene. A labyrinth of dim corridors, side rooms and a tiny stage, The Scene was the premiere place to play in New York City and the closest thing to the Elbow Room Traffic would ever find in America. Like Don Carless, Steve Paul sometimes met people at the door himself. As a result, the place was inhabited mostly by musicians and the hip set (and of course a fair number of groupies). Traffic would make an immediate splash in this innermost sanctum, welcomed with open arms even by the jaded New Yorkers.

A reporter for the ultra-hip rock magazine, *Crawdaddy* attended one of the gigs and was blown away by the dexterity of the trio, taking special note of Chris's contribution, "So, at Traffic's promo party, just a week's old memory, held at Steve Pauls' "fabulous" Scene, I saw Chris Wood (complete with body motions making it look as if he might be fat and easily exhausted) play the organ, the flute, the saxophone (with the flute inside it, like Roland Kirk), once more the flute, and the bass." Summing up the band's importance on the rock scene, writer Sandy Pearlman nailed Traffic's unique approach in one sentence: "Metaphorically, the sound's been *woven* into sonic tapestries."

CHAPTER SIXTEEN

With the music flowing so freely, and spurred on by Hendrix's progress, Traffic was ready to get their own thing going. Although some new songs and ideas had come with them to America – continually high, distracted by strange people and/or scattered to the winds – as of yet, little had been finished. But the pieces on hand were strong, and the pause in New York allowed time to assess and move forward, starting with a Winwood/Capaldi/Wood composition filled with not-so-sly drug references, "Who Knows What Tomorrow May Bring." The other on hand was called "Roamin' Thru' the Gloamin' With 40,000 Headmen". Both had been previously recorded at Olympic but still needed overdubs. Others included the panoramic ballad, "No Time To Live", and a Biblically inspired parable of betrayal, "Means to An End".

Having flown over from England with the tapes, Jimmy Miller and engineer Eddie Kramer, (both already working on the Hendrix sessions), were ready to go at the Record Plant. Musically, everyone understood that the psychedelic pop and gimmicky songs were a thing of the past. But it would soon be clear that a more profound change was at hand. After gestating at the Cottage with all of its attending influences, the sound now emerging was a primal flux arising out of the personalities of Chris, Steve and Jim; something they were calling (for lack of a more precise term), 'Headless Horseman Music.'

The song that most encapsulated what they were going for was "No Time To Live". Opening with an eerie soprano sax figure, the body of the tune swelling up from behind, the initial mood was pure foreboding. A stark piano followed, and then a shimmering organ leading into the body of the song. Propelled by rolling and galloping drums, Winwood's vocals proved the perfect instrument to take Jim's meditative lyrics on the approach of death to the desolate place they were supposed to go. Hovering above it all, Chris's sax cried like a departing spirit. It was truly fantastic, a huge step forward from anything on *Mr. Fantasy*.

While rightly proud of his lyrics and Steve's arrangement, Jim credited Chris's mysterious touch as crucial to the final product, "Oh yeah, Chris would try to conjure up all those magical elements – trying to conjure that up into the music. He would almost paint that for you. That intro to 'No Time to Live' was wonderful you know. You can't really say what it is – he just kind of comes up with this strange howling cry – this shriek. You could get Wayne Shorter some fucking monster player; I don't think they could come up with anything better than that intro. You just kind of went, 'Wow!' It stopped you in your tracks, because he's listening to the song, he's *breathing* with it. He's making a statement there. The minute you put the brush on the canvas, that's the important thing – that moment."

Winwood too was impressed, telling a reporter: "It was like a hunting horn, very distant. It was like a mood that was created, rather than a piece of music." When asked directly about his role by the same journalist, Chris's off-hand reply was classic art school cryptic-speak, "*Everything* has a mood. A song has a mood, but it has to be strengthened by what goes on around it."

"Roamin' Thru' The Gloamin' With 40,000 Headmen", later mercifully shortened to "Forty Thousand Headmen", was built around Capaldi's hash-inspired wordplay. The rather slight lyrics would be rescued by Winwood's vocal dynamics and moody acoustic guitar motif which seemed to suspend time. But the overall feel was again set up and elaborated by Chris – a simple two note invocation of the alto flute, followed by spooky lines weaving supportive strands of sound throughout. The conclusion, too, belonged entirely to the bird-like flute's luminous, echoing trills which resolved into a mad flutter before tapering off into silence.

With each of the new songs greater than the sum of their parts, Traffic had arrived in a wild, wide open territory ready to be explored and built on.

As for Chris's part in all of this, one intimate observer – Penny – was finally able to connect the crazy side-adventures to his musical approach: "He was doing it for art! He was the artistic one in the band. He was different from the others. Chris had this thing – to be an artist you had to suffer. And he did have that. I can see him thinking of all of those writers who starved in garrets and took to drinking absinthe, and produced this amazing work. All of that was swimming around in his head a bit. Money and things like that were not on his mind – at all."

But in the end, a price would be paid for the laissez faire attitude. Despite the crucial moods and amendments given to "No Time To Live" and "Forty Thousand Headmen", Chris would receive no composing credit for either. It's not as if he wouldn't notice. In later years, he would hold up albums, point to song titles and say things like: "I had a lot more to do with that than it (the writing credits) makes out." But at this point in time, advocating for himself just wasn't in the cards.

This invisible-to-everyone-else problem aside, the band had never been so together. With some great songs in the pocket, the freewheeling, wide open trip across the United States had paid off in ways no one had anticipated. With the musicianship of each maturing in remarkable ways, the vision of Traffic they searched for had now focused into a unified, if hard to define theme. But before they could get any further, the winds of change swirled in an unexpected yet familiar pattern – Dave Mason was back.

The details of exactly how Mason came to rejoin Traffic are as usual, conflicting. The oft-repeated version is that Jim just happened to run into Dave on the street in New York – a city of millions. This random meeting supposedly rekindled a spark, which in turn led to a happy reunion. Penny Massot, however, believed that there was nothing random about it whatsoever. "He (Dave) *knew*. I think it was all connived. Traffic was great as a trio – really good. Which is why they started picking up lots of word of mouth, and by the time we hit New York – everybody – the buzz word was *Traffic*. Then, in walks Dave again."

She was aghast. "I said, '*No!*' I remember sitting on the bed when he's trying to worm his way back in. And I'm telling Steve after he leaves, 'No Steve, don't have him back.'" Remembering too well the interpersonal traumas from the last time around, she actually cried, begging Winwood to reconsider. But the decision had apparently already been made: Dave would be part of Traffic again.

From Mason's perspective, however, rejoining was a straightforward, rational and entirely practical deal. "I wasn't looking for any 'stardom' shit. I'd spent about ten days in Greece, with a bag and a guitar. And over there, I wrote "Feelin' Alright?", and "All Join In", and I'd started some other things; so I had like, five songs. I came over to the United States, I got to know the people in Delaney and Bonnie, and I was in New York at the Record Plant. And the three of them were there, cutting a new album. And they had five songs, five tracks. And it was like, 'Okay, we've got five, you got five, that's the next album.' So that's what happened with that."

In retrospect, the initial break was starting to look more like a necessary sabbatical rather than a conclusion. Mason recalled, "At the time, I consciously, because of the stuff I'd written on the first album – it was very sort of, 'of the time', and very naïve in a way – I just realized, that if I was gonna write songs, I needed to have some experience in life. So that's what I set out on the path to do. And I felt that my (new) songs had a little more depth to them. So we did the five things and we did the album."

Undeniably, Dave's offerings were a major step up from the material he'd written for the first album – no "bubblegum tree" references or twanging sitars were anywhere to be found. And "Feelin' Alright?" was the glittering jewel, something that Traffic could easily get behind – simultaneously relaxed and intense, unhurried yet driven. Lyrically, it hit home as well, since it seemed to be about *them* – expressing both Mason's initial alienation from Traffic, and his apparent willingness to let bygones be bygones. Amazingly, in the few months away even Dave's singing voice had greatly improved, having picked up a world-weary tone which lent the new songs an air of authenticity.

"Feelin' Alright?" was so good, great even, that on its strength alone he might have been invited back. But with his return, the others could only hope that it was worth it, because the same dynamics, tensions and issues remained. It was still 'three plus one', and always would be.

With Dave on hand they finished off one more Winwood/Capaldi tune – the mid-tempo rocker – "Pearly Queen" – to which Mason played bass, and another song that Dave had music, and Jim had words for: "Vagabond Virgin", which Chris overdubbed two flute tracks to. Perhaps inspired by the eclectic sprawl of "Electric Ladyland", plans were made to make the album a double as well. But for now, having done what they could, it was time to go home.

*

A special device came back to England with Chris. An amplification and effects system designed to alter the sound of the saxophone, the Gibson 'Maestro' resolved several issues, especially in concert. With feedback, overload, and other sound inconsistencies being frequent problems, Chris was often frustrated that his parts weren't getting through. Having previously experimented with something called "The Bug" that amplified his sax with a small mic and an unreliable lead, Chris (and the long-suffering roadies) found the Maestro much more stable – the microphone screwed right into the mouthpiece with a heavy coiled cord leading out to an amp, just like an electric guitar. The idea came from jazz saxophonist Eddie Harris, who had been experimenting with amplification and effects since the 50's. A true innovator, Harris shared the idea that the sax shouldn't be limited by tradition.

The Maestro came with a demonstration record on which jazz saxophonist Sonny Stitt played and explained the effects. With only that much to go on, the investigation began. Later Chris would excitedly share what he'd learned with a reporter: "There are seven stops on the bass channel, whereby you can obtain the tonal effects of bassoon, bass sax, tuba, cello, and also a fuzz tone. There's also an octave switch which either plays one or even two octaves below. The other channel has four stops, which give a natural sax sound, or the effects of a muted trumpet, oboe or English horn. I can get a tremendous variety of tone colors, and the stereo system also gives a second sound if I wish. And with the greater variety of sounds at your disposal, the more ambitious the experiments you can carry out."

While clearly loving the palate provided by technology, in parallel he was also seeking the path of simplicity. In a remark to the MIT college newspaper in Boston in early '68, Chris mentioned that he "used to admire a lot of jazz people", but was now more into folk music, mentioning Janis Ian, and The Young Tradition, in particular. Even before the U.S. tour, Chris had been talking up some of the more "primitive" influences – Leadbelly, Woody Guthrie, the Clancy Brothers and especially a British acapella group called the Watersons and their 1965 album *Frost and Fire: A Calendar of Ceremonial Folk Songs*. Playing the record at the Cottage, Chris had fixated on one tune, "John Barleycorn", which he referred to as "the Killing of the Corn." In it, he heard a classic tale of the life cycle and death, transformation and rebirth. Just as important, the Waterson's natural, acappella sound held much more appeal than the over-hyped psychedelic path, which had rapidly played itself out.

But before the various influences could be assimilated and reconciled, the road beckoned again. Traffic was scheduled to play a big rock festival known as the 'Monsterkonzert' that spring in Zurich, Switzerland with The Animals, The Move, John Mayall, and Jimi Hendrix.

The Zurich show was an odd affair, like an old-fashioned 'package tour', but with only a single stop. Traveling together on the same plane, a great time ensued as the musicians socialized, drank and smoked. Still, tension would emerge. Warned mid-flight that they would be searched on landing, pockets and bags were hurriedly emptied of all available drugs, which were then consumed, ready or not. At Zurich airport, a bleary-eyed Jim Hendrix would be singled out, taken aside and intensely searched, including the indignity of having his hat removed as a security guard ran fingers through his hair.

The actual concert – a two day outdoor show – often teetered on the edge of chaos. The venue – the huge Hallenstadion – had a pit at the foot of the stage, but kept most of the fans sequestered in stands a good distance away. Those who tried to get closer ran into problems. Between a nearly hysterically heavy-handed Swiss police and a local brand of drug-crazed Hell's Angels who'd decided to attend, an air of tension permeated the event.

Keith Altham, a reporter for the *New Musical Express*, witnessed some of the surreal goings on, "I remember watching Hendrix playing, and the Hells Angels arrived at one point in the gig – with their bikes and everything – managed to barge their way in. We were watching from a box. The lead Hells Angel – sort of bare-chested and tattooed, started to climb into the orchestra pit. The security guard was remonstrating with him. All this I could only see in slow motion and silent movie aspects. And the security guys had these kinds of 'pass pins' in the lapels of their jackets, and he kept pointing to his security guard tag, indicating 'No, only people with security guard tags could be in the orchestra pit with the photographers'. The Hells Angel took the tag out of his lapel – which had the pin in it – and stuck it into his bare chest. At which point the security guard waved him hastily into the orchestra pit."

If the Angels were scary, the police proved worse. From his report to *NME* of the concert, Altham noted: "I have seen some rough stuff handed out by British police at some of our bigger events, but nothing compared with the nastiness of these Swiss police. A good clubbing with a drawn truncheon was their answer to any sign of disturbance."

As for Traffic and their music, being that it was Mason's first show back, many were curious to see how the 'new' (or was it the old?) group would function. But despite the rough conditions Steve assured the press that the band was in fact "Together, together" and a few tentative moments aside, he was right. Richard Green reported, "Traffic were, once again, quite superb. Complete again with Dave Mason, they wove magic spells which kept even the stewards still. Chris Wood's flute playing was nothing short of amazing, and Steve confirmed what everyone thought – he is a genius!"

Hendrix was also well received, although in retrospect, Keith Altham thought perhaps too much respect was paid for a rather undisciplined performance: "Hendrix is out there, going into mad, extravagant guitar solos that everybody thought was fantastic, and everybody kind of hung onto every note. But a point of fact – what he was actually doing was practicing. There was an awful lot of, I don't want to call it nonsense, 'cause he was a genius, but it didn't mean very much. The extended jams were really very self-indulgent…"

But, as so often happened, the audience missed the best of it. Away from the heavy vibes, bands huddled together inside in small enclaves and played for themselves. Backstage over the two days, the jamming – often centered on Hendrix – was feverish, and sometimes off the chart. Richard Green witnessed it and raved, "On Friday afternoon, a most amazing jam session took place at the concert hall. The participants were Jimi, Chris Wood, Stevie, Trevor Burton on drums, Carl Wayne on conga drums, and Vic Briggs. Let it be said that if ever the record companies concerned could be persuaded to do so, they should let that sextet loose in a studio and release the ensuing LP! It would be a lesson in harmony, freedom of expression and a sock in the eye for the pundits that say that pop stars can't play jazz."

Trevor Burton, a bass player by trade, recalled, "That session, I'll never forget it, because I played drums. Zurich is where Zildjian cymbals come from. At that time, they were the newest thing on the scene, so all of the drummers were taken to the Zildjian factory to have anything they wanted, any cymbal they liked to take away. So the rest of us decided to go down and have a jam. It was like a sports stadium, holds about twelve thousand people… it was on stage at the gig, but it was before the show. It was literally jamming – you'd start something up and everybody would join in – have a break and a joint and start again. Chris played flute and sax – he would never miss a jam."

Supposedly it all began with a long, loose version of the traditional tune "Danny Boy", which included the perfect line for Chris to melodically mirror: "The pipes, the pipes are calling…" Playing until near-exhaustion, a photograph would capture him in full flight, standing amid Jimi and Albert Heaton, flute pressed to his lips, eyes wide, hair sweat-plastered to his head. While Chris also recorded this and other sessions on his portable cassette recorder (as did Jimi), to date no tape has ever turned up among collectors. Perhaps left behind to be thrown away by an indifferent maid, Chris's misplacement of precious music was unfortunate but not infrequent.

With the jams now popping up like mushrooms in a farm field, Altham witnessed one involving Jimi, Chris on flute and Dave Mason on bass, that was loud enough that the police burst in to quell the disturbance, truncheons drawn. Later, Roy Wood from The Move found himself playing bass at yet another, alongside Jimi, Chris and Steve, with Jim Capaldi (possibly) on drums.

On and on it went for two days and nights, after which the exhausted musicians dragged themselves back to the plane that would carry them home. In the wake of the 'Monsterkonzert' a sense that things were changing hung in the air, and it was true; this was to be the last 'package' type show for this cluster of bands. But while the external conditions had been crazed, the friendships and camaraderie were rock solid, and that was enough to get them all through. Keith Altham wistfully recalled, "Those days did disappear…you didn't get that kind of thing happening again. They all knew each other. It was all silliness really, with some good music thrown in now and again, into the mix. It was a bit more friendly in those days, like everything else was."

('Steve Winwood, English Soul', BBC 4, 2010)

('Traffic', J. Cott, Rolling Stone, 5/3/1969)

('Great Show: Except For Battle', R. Green, NME, 6/8/1968)

(http://www.mickeyhart.net/site2003_dev/0617.html)

(Pete Johnson, Los Angeles Times, April 2 1968)

('Versatility is Traffic's Meat', Sandy Pearlman, Crawdaddy, Issue 18, September 1968)

('Roy Wood: The Wizard of Rock', K. Sharp, Goldmine, 9/30/1994)

(Traffic fan Club notes, 1968)

('Weird But Wonderful, That's Amplified Sax', Melody Maker, 2/8/1969)

(http://www-tech.mit.edu/archives/VOL_088/TECH_V088_S0255_P009.pdf)

Trees of Corngreaves Hall, painted by Chris, circa 1962.
Brenda Harris collection (Photograph © Dan Ropek)

Chris's charcoal drawing of Witley Court, date unknown.
Stephanie Wood collection (Photograph © Dan Ropek)

Steve Hadley Quartet, performing at the Saracens Head,
18 Stone Street, Dudley, 1963. (© Ed Davis collection)

A reflective moment at the Cottage (Sheepcote Farmhouse),
circa 1968. (© Gordon Jackson)

Traffic, outside Chris's home (Corngreaves Hall), Cradley Heath,
West Midlands, summer, 1968. (© Stephanie Wood)

Ready to rock at the Cottage, Berkshire, 1968.
Jimmy Miller, out of focus at right. (© Gordon Jackson)

One of Traffic's first 'comeback' shows – at the Roundhouse,
London, April, 1970. (© Gordon Jackson)

Double exposed photo of Paul Medcalf, taken by Chris Wood while both were on acid at Steve Winwood's house, circa 1971. (© Paul Medcalf collection)

Chris at the wheel, Steve's property, circa 1971. (© Paul Medcalf)

Relaxing at Jim Capaldi's house, Marlow, Buckinghamshire, 1973.
(© Chistopher 'Noggie' Nolan)

Traffic in full flight at the Academy of Music, New York City,
February 9th, 1973. (© Dan Ropek collection)

From last ever Traffic gig, Chicago, October, 1974.
(© J. Summaria)

Jeanette Jacobs Wood at Great Cumberland Mews flat,
London, 1976. (© Pete Bonas)

Pete Bonas and Chris at Great Cumberland Mews flat,
circa 1976. (© Pete Bonas collection)

London, 1976. (© Pete Bonas)

Visiting Witley Court, Worcestershire, circa 1981.
(© Stephanie Wood)

Performing with Stuart Carr at Pastoral Center, St. Laurence's Church,
Northfield, Birmingham, circa 1982. (© Stuart Carr collection)

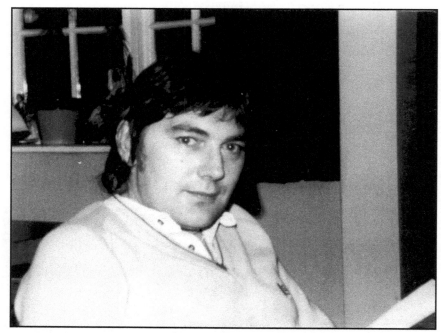

Chris relaxing at home, Spindle Cottage, Romsley, circa 1982.
(© Stephanie Wood)

CHAPTER SEVENTEEN

THE END OF THE BEGINNING

Back at the Cottage, everyone seemed to need a dose of normalcy. Steve, Penny and Chris decided to get even further away, taking a ten-day vacation in Cornwall, but doing it on their own terms. With Chris's dog-eared books and well-marked maps serving as guides once again, they were off to see where the ley lines would lead.

Running straight through Cornwall to the ocean is one of the longest leys in England – connecting everything from the Christian era back to the mists of pre-history. Churches, many named for St. Michael, an archangel said to have slain the dragon (sometimes interpreted as a manifestation of Satan) formed the spine. Interspersed were ancient, scary places like a haunted field supposed to contain a classic chain-rattling ghost, and 'Men-An-Tol' – featuring a large circular stone with a hole in the middle said to cure the sick which pass through it.

One important stop near the southern coast was the 'Merry Maidens' – a circle of standing stones, and the nearby 'Dawn's Men', two larger stones. The legend said that the Dawn's Men had once been human musicians: flute players. The pipers, desperate to impress the local girls, played for the maidens to dance, but their timing was off – being a holy day, music and frolic were forbidden. As warning to others, a sorcerer turned them both into the rock figures now visible.

Through the mist and fog, these ancient tableaus reached across time, whispering a message Chris strained to hear. By physically re-tracing the lines on his map, Penny recalled that Chris was definitely still on a quest, searching for an understanding seemingly close at hand, "We would drive around (to) the Stone Circles, going all over the place. We went to Tintagel. Anywhere that was said to be magical – we were there. Chris was very much into that. He'd just get out and walk around, sit in the middle; get the vibe, that sort of thing. The ley lines were supposed to give you energy. I suppose he was trying to connect to the old ways, the gods, the giants. He was very much into all of that, Chris. He was very spiritual, sort of into England, the Earth."

If nothing else, places like the ruins of King Arthur's Castle and the energetic nodes of the planet would serve as a muse for future Traffic music. Paradoxically, they also provided some solace from an otherwise frantic life that more and more threatened to drain Chris's soul, or perhaps turn it to stone.

There was time to squeeze in one more adventure. One night, Anna Westmore and Chris took off to a place called the Hell-Fire Caves. An eccentric, underground labyrinth carved out of solid rock in West Wycombe, Buckinghamshire in the 1740's by one Sir Francis Dashwood, the place was arranged with angled passages, grottos, an underground stream and even a pond. Used as a meeting place for a secret pagan society, some of the leading (supposedly solidly Christian) aristocrats of the day – and even the odd American, such as Benjamin Franklin, participated in now unknown rituals. Whatever transpired was far outside the boundaries of the day and scrupulously guarded; but just to be sure, as the aging members approached their deaths all records were meticulously destroyed.

In the intervening centuries, the Caves fell to a dank vacancy, while still holding the power to draw the curious with reports of moans, whisper-like sounds and inexplicable lights emanating from deep inside. As for what it was all about, by the 1960's the only clues were some vaguely disturbing faces carved into the walls, beckoning the brave into the receding darkness.

Anna remembered the research that led them there, "Chris was very much into like, Wycombe. It was a very important place to him – the caves. He took me down there one time; it was the place where Aleister Crowley used to do a lot of his rituals. That hooked up to some kind of ley line too, so it was all very important. We would just follow each other and go with it. It was a full moon, three o'clock in the morning. We lived in the night; we didn't live in the day."

Slowly creeping into the bowels of the complex with only candle flame holding back the darkness, they went as far as they could. With the strange energy hanging in the dank air and time seemingly suspended, they strained for signs of whatever else might be there with them.

Once back in fresh air, the sunrise would be met in a meditative reverie, "I can remember standing by this river or lake. And we would just sit, and listen and look – for hours. There were no words that needed to be said. At that point, it was Chris's time away from the rock 'n roll world, away from the craziness, where he could just sit, and throw a pebble into the water on a full moon, and just listen and watch... We would both come away feeling more peaceful and more serene." In the coming months, it was that sense of serenity, more than anything else, which would be in the shortest supply.

With summer rolling around again, the work schedule was crammed full – recording sessions, concerts, BBC dates, and of course necessary work and play at the Cottage. Having heard the mad tales, more and more musicians were making a point to stop in. Gordon and Poli and Trevor Burton were regulars of course, but any number of others now braved the ruts: Pete Townshend and Keith Moon, Jeff Beck, American folk singers Tim Hardin and Shawn Phillips, Chris's old band mate Christine Perfect, African drummers Remi Kabaka, Reebop Kwaku Baah and Lofty Amal, Steven Stills and Dewey Martin from Buffalo Springfield, Sly Stone, Noel Redding. Even Hendrix was said to have popped in. Eric Burdon also came by with his wife Angie. Ginger Baker was there too, and more and more frequently his band mate from Cream, Eric Clapton. Most came specifically to play with Steve, often harboring desires to woo him into a new venture.

The most serious, perhaps desperate suitor was Clapton. Cream, while always volatile, rolled into the summer of '68 a band of raging and combative egos. In a last ditch effort to save the group, Eric once again had thoughts of asking Steve to join, but ultimately lacked the nerve. But having known Winwood for years, Clapton's respect and affection for him was considerable; something revealed the time he showed up at the Cottage with his young girlfriend, Alice Ormsby Gore. Flying on acid, they arrived in the middle of a jam where Winwood was singing and playing the organ. In his state of heightened awareness, Clapton suddenly saw Steve in another light. Eyes widened, he leaned over and whispered into Alice's ear, "He's an *angel!*"

Of course, Ginger Baker also enjoyed a good jam. With his wild red hair and brusque demeanor, he was known for roaring around the back roads of Berkshire in his Jensen Interceptor at death-defying speeds – scaring both locals and hapless passengers. Musically, he intimidated his peers as well but was also respected for his thunderous, African-inspired playing. Trevor Burton was there when Eric and Ginger came by one day. From his perspective, Clapton and Baker's skills combined with Winwood's boosted things to a new level, "That was a magical part of it all; one of the best times I had. I knew Eric anyway, but to be suddenly stuck in the middle between Eric and Steve and Ginger on the drums, was just mind blowing. It made me grow, and taught me a hell of a lot."

Aware of other players angling to make something more out of it as well, Burton would tersely note, "A few applicants were there." While Steve gave no hint that he was anything but happy with his current band, those hoping to separate him from Traffic were never far away.

One of the highlights of the summer was an appearance in London's Hyde Park on the 28th of July. Topping the bill over the Pretty Things and The Nice at only the second major rock event held in the huge city park, it was a lovely day before a relaxed and entirely mellow audience. The band's 'togetherness' was evinced by an intense jam at the end of "Heaven Is In Your Mind" where Chris's tenor sax, and Winwood's guitar meshed in a mad swirl, each driving the other on and on. Below, Mason's bass and Capaldi's drums matched the dance step-for-step until a sharp descending figure brought the song to an abrupt yet deft halt. With four wheels once again, Traffic was rolling smoothly – a band that couldn't be denied. Having seen an impressive lineup of bands in the park that day, a fan in the audience was able to sum up Traffic's performance in one word: "Sublime."

Traffic's Hyde Park chops were the product of the musical high they were still riding from their previous gig. In contact with the Hungarian Minister of Culture, Chris Blackwell somehow got them a pass to cross Eastern Europe's 'Iron Curtain' for a gig at the Kisstadion in Budapest on July 7th. With bullet holes from the 1956 uprising still pockmarking downtown buildings, the city exuded a repressed energy ready to be released, one way or another. Needless to say, nerves were on edge. To make matters worse, the band couldn't risk bringing the accustomed load of hashish to sooth the pre-show anxiety. About to face a huge outdoor stadium filled with a restless audience, the angst was running high.

Backstage, they first paced before going into what must have looked like a mad dance. In a last frantic effort to locate a buzz, everything in sight was searched – instrument cases, then every fold of stage clothing. And like a gift from above, suddenly there it was – a small, lint covered chunk of hash fell out onto the floor. By Traffic's standards it wasn't much – a puff or two each, but the psychological boost was just right. Grabbing their gear, they hit the stage beaming to an audience of 16,000 which immediately reciprocated. Jim recalled, "And there was a great roar from the crowd, and a flash of electricity from the people. It was like an arc... we all saw it clearly."

That night, repressed youth and a foreign rock band commingled. Their energies went back and forth, song after song. Even equipment failure – usually a concert killer, was turned into art. Mick Weaver, a keyboard player whose band, Wynder K. Frog was backing the show opener Jimmy Cliff, saw it happen, "We were watching Traffic do their set – 'Who Knows What Tomorrow May Bring?', they started that song off, Steve was playing it on the Hammond organ. Suddenly the Hammond breaks down, and you see Albert crawling on the stage, messing about with wires and things – it wouldn't work. Meanwhile Capaldi is still there, chugging away, and Steve just picks up the bass, plugs it in and carries on with the song – and it was just as if it had been with the Hammond... incredible."

They concluded with the usual powerhouse – "Dear Mr. Fantasy". While the earliest versions ended in any number of ways, often simply grinding to a crashing halt, a nearly perfect coda would be found. Borrowing the rhythmic beat of Ravel's "Bolero", they sped up the outré, with Winwood's loudest guitar chords crunching on top of marching drums and bass. The stunning 'rock Bolero' created a sense of heightened tension – a stuttering beat which drove on and on before the final crashing chord supplied resolution. With the audience exploding with an almost sexual release – Traffic had found the ideal closer.

With time to relax afterward, Jim, Dave and Albert took off to a lake resort while Chris and Steve stayed in town. Before going home, they roamed the city, taking in the sights and listening to gypsy musicians play ancient melodies on street corners.

Once all were safely home again, Chris would smile and pull a souvenir out of his pocket – a tape of Traffic's Budapest concert. Playing the cassette for friends at the Cottage, once again the energy would arc, lighting smiles around the room. And having heard it again, a consensus would soon emerge: that hectic, electric night in Hungary had been Traffic's best show, ever.

*

However well the music was going, for Chris, another facet of his life remained unfulfilled. In the area of women, he was still unattached – unhappily so. While thoughts of New York's Jeanette Jacobs kept reoccurring – time, space and various entanglements stood in the way of a resolution. With a sense of emptiness gnawing at him, that summer would see a string of short affairs, some with married women that he knew held no future. Although surprised by his long lost, never-quite girlfriend from Birmingham, Mary Maise, who stopped by the Cottage just to see him with Twitch from the Elbow Room, by now his feelings for her had melted away.

And then there was Christie Nichols. While the attraction between them was genuine and strong, their relationship never quite made it to the deeper level where it once seemed heading. She recalled that Chris could be "very moody", and sometimes seemed to need refuge more than anything else, "Once he came in, in the middle of the night. I don't know what I did with it, but he wrote a poem on the typewriter in my room. It came out of nothing, because he was typing sort of 'junk typing', letters and things then all of a sudden came this poem. It was like; 'A place where I can lay my head, be myself, write poems and rest...' then he went back to (junk) typing." While their proximity was a plus, in reality the rock star and the college student probably never had much of a chance. Nichols recalled, "I know that I had a very deep connection with Chris, although we couldn't expand on it much really, for our own personality reasons, or development or whatever."

While that relationship would fade, her insight into Chris's bond with Steve remained. "I think astrology is kind of funny, it sometimes reflects the character in real life. He (Winwood) was very ambitious, persevering, and stubborn – moving forward, forward, forward – a Taurus. And Chris (Cancer) was very 'out there', sensitive and more psychic – dreaming. He really needed a partnership to keep him in line." And as long as this partnership was strong, the music and the magical times would stay entwined in an inseparable knot.

But astrology was only the tip of the iceberg. For Chris, literal magic was becoming part of the lifestyle as well. Back home on a visit to Birmingham, he took part in a séance that literally shook things up. Brenda Bryan recalled the night, "I remember doing that when I was married to Syd, and I was pregnant with my daughter – Me, Syd, Trevor Burton, Chris." The group first held hands, and then started in with a Ouija board. The results were not ambiguous, "It spelled out all these things, and glasses were moving, and the table flipped over – and everybody stopped then. I was quite freaked out 'cause I was pregnant – like 'what are they doing? What are they doing?' I would say that Chris was in tune with the other side, whether he knew it or not. He was intrigued with it, it didn't scare him."

But fear *was* part of the equation at times; a fear oddly mixed with music and friendship. At the center was Graham Bond, a musician Chris may have met as early as 1963 in Birmingham when his band – the Graham Bond Organization came to town. A master of the Hammond organ and any number of instruments, Bond was acclaimed by his peers as a master of R&B and jazz; an eccentric capable of startling originality. But over time his music would evolve into more esoteric forms, part of an overall transformation of his self-perception.

Adopted as a child by working class parents, Graham was convinced that he was actually the son of Aleister Crowley – the prolific, if often self-published writer and practitioner of *Magick* – a school of thought enfolding white and black magic. More than a mere eccentric, Crowley's experimentations with drugs, sex and the occult were so shocking to a staid Victorian society as to earn the moniker 'the wickedest man in the world'. While clearly hyperbole, Crowley's credo: "Do what thou wilt shall be the whole of the law", and his willingness to try anything made him a vivid symbol of the chaos lurking beneath the supposedly moral, ruling class.

As for Bond, while his birth did overlap with the last part of Crowley's life, he never offered any real proof of being the wizard's progeny. Still, he was convinced of the relationship, and as the years rolled on, his life, music and thinking would be more and more based around Crowley's works; repelling some, and drawing others into a shadowy, turbulent world. For Chris, the musical/magickal combination was irresistible.

Brenda Bryan on the other hand was not impressed. Running into Graham with Chris not long after the séance, she recalled, "My daughter had just been born, so it was 1968 when I first saw them together. I got back from the hospital and they were sitting in the house, and I can remember Graham Bond – 'cause at the time I had a lot of 'slimming pills', they were legal then if you got them off a doctor. They were like pure amphetamines, and I'd gotten a bottle of them, and this bloody Graham Bond had taken most of them. I said, 'Who are *you*?' And he said, 'Ohh!' – He was very rude – 'I'm the son of Aleister Crowley!', and I said 'I don't give a fuck who you are, how dare you take my pills. And what are you doing Chris, bringing people like *that* around here!' And I can remember being very upset."

The two of them were indeed sometimes a less-than-healthy combination. While Bond sincerely believed and loved to teach others about the ways music intertwined with mysterious forces, he also lacked self-discipline. Even his close friend, and fellow occult practitioner Long John Baldry noted that Bond tended to "get his spells all mixed up." Others would later speculate that Bond suffered from an undiagnosed mental illness, perhaps bi-polar disorder. Regardless, with Graham and Chris each having their own particular insecurities, the drugs added to the confusion even as the music cemented the friendship. But for Chris, almost any door was worth opening for a quick look inside.

*

During the hot summer of '68, *Rolling Stone's* David Dalton returned to the Cottage, quickly zeroing in on the mystical thread running through the heart of Traffic. Either lucky in his timing or good at prompting the band, all were soon in the Land Rover, confronting the countryside's strangeness head on. He later wrote, "Chris is checking out our position on an Ordnance Survey map. 'Look over there, The Devil's Claw-marks' – Chris points to a bank across the valley. I look out the window and on a steep hill there are several long gouges about a hundred yards long where the chalk has been exposed on the grassy green slope. It looks like some slimy Paleozoic monster lost his grip here..."

They finally parked at the base of White Horse Hill, walking up to the beautiful and enigmatic Chalk Horse of Uffington. Located just below the eroded remnants of Uffington Castle on a 30 degree slope, the Horse is an enormous flowing figure created in the Iron Age when surface plants were cut to expose the white calcium carbonate layer below. The beast's allure is such that it has been kept 'alive' for more than two millennia by villagers holding 'sweeping parties' every couple of years to remove encroaching plants. This is no small task – she is three hundred and seventy four feet in length.

While ultimately belonging to the ages, at that time the Horse was very much Traffic's place – a node of energy connected to the Cottage and in a way, everything they were about. Smoking joints as the sun arched over a deep blue sky, here the past and present overlapped, blurred and lost distinction.

Chris suddenly jumped up and began a slow walk around the form – part shaman, part historian, leading the others in a human chain. Trailed by Dalton, he narrated as they walked, "They don't actually know what it is, some people say it's a dragon others think it's a horse. Down there is where they are supposed to have killed the dragon, he's buried in that mound down there. That's the eye of the dragon up there at the top of the hill." Upon reaching the eye, he first circled and then jumped in – stamping his feet, spinning, and gyrating to his own internal rhythm. Witnessing the playful ritual, Dalton would later report, "Chris dances on the eye of the dragon like a witch doctor."

When finally published in 1969, Dalton's article would inflame the imaginations of many Americans regarding the nature of this band. In the context of the ancient sites and the haunted Cottage, Traffic was portrayed as a modern link to an Earth-centered pagan past; a peerless band of musical alchemists living out a near-mythic experience.

Decades later, Dalton recalled that energies of the countryside did indeed seem to be taking them all to the verge of some kind of breakthrough, "We were all into these mystical emanations from the land. It was all there for us – it was right beneath your feet – the White Horse, the Giant with the huge erection (Cerne Abbas Giant) – all that stuff in the clay there. And it was mind-blowing to us, all these sort of fantasies come true. It was sort of like Blake's vision of England – that we were all sort of going to bring back this wonderful organic, mystical kingdom. In a certain way it was sort of rediscovering it, and it *really was there* in England."

Observing the group dynamics, Dalton noted that Chris was the risk taker, while Steve imposed strict limits on how far he would follow, "The thing about Chris, he always seemed very impulsive, and kind of reckless. We got into this Land Rover, it was this big, big estate and we'd drive all over the place. The way they renewed the fields was to set them on fire. So they would burn these fields, it was kind of an amazing thing because they were huge. And Chris wanted to drive down into these fields – not into the flames, but the hill was *very* steep. Steve said, 'No', you know, and got out, and told me to get out. I don't know if Chris continued or not…"

So there it was in a nutshell. If this really was a time of quest and adventure, were not the risks and the rewards inextricably bound? With the lifestyle bleeding so deeply into the music, perhaps it *was* necessary to dare the steeper slope, to sometimes get a little closer to the flames than the flesh would prefer. In return for the gifts bestowed, Chris naturally had no problem offering himself – metaphorically if not literally – to the sleeping Gods of England's living soil.

*

The activities of the summer of '68 were so numerous as to eventually merge into an inseparable haze. Besides the Traffic concert dates, BBC and recording sessions at Olympic (including one for an American singer, Ann Bird featuring Luther Grosvenor, and Ric Grech), Chris did a session with Chicken Shack – the group made up of remnants of his old The Sounds Of Blue mates. In return, they would name their new album, *O.K. Ken?* after an old Black Country catchphrase of his. He also did a poetry session for an intended album of readings by rock musicians (never finished) and a spoken word band promo for an American radio station. Surprisingly, a track ("After Tea") was recorded with the Spencer Davis Group as well, for whom Chris added flute, and Dave – guitar.

Traffic also helped Gordon Jackson make recordings for a solo album (produced by Dave) that would be released in 1969. Remembering how Chris could quickly get to the essence of something when asked, Jackson said, "Yeah, Chris was great. On the last track ('Snakes and Ladders'), I said to Chris, 'Just imagine a procession, a grand procession, walking very slowly up the isle of a church', and so he came out with – 'da, da, downnn…'(on soprano sax), and it was just so… just a few notes, and he got it, captured exactly what was wanted."

To top it off, a session with Mick Jagger took place at Olympic studios in September. Traffic added their distinctive sound to a track recently written by Jagger called "Memo From Turner" for a movie called 'Performance' by Donald Cammell and Nicholas Roeg. While only Steve and Jim have been credited on this, Chris later listed a session with Jagger on his resume of extracurricular work as well. While quite good, the 'Traffic version' would never be released. Music aside, Chris knew Jagger and his girlfriend, Marianne Faithfull, both of whom shared some of his esoteric interests. In fact, the ley line vibe had already soaked into Rolling Stones' lyrics in songs such as "Child of the Moon".

The frenetic pace exacted a toll. Driven to the point of exhaustion, Chris had to get away from it all now and then. Sometimes he went to Helen's cottage in Blewbury, and other times Gordon Jackson's place – just to hide out and recover a little. Jackson recalled, "It was a bit of a refuge in a way; he'd come and stay with me, mostly overnight – where he could get a bit of rest, and get away from things sometimes. I usually used to just let him be, and not push him a lot." Back at the Cottage, Albert Heaton bought a dog, a white Alsatian named 'Fantasy' that became the cottage pet for a while. Long walks with Fantasy in the nearby fields gave Chris a chance to relax; it was almost like being home.

But, the intervals of rest were shrinking. Traffic was scheduled to play a string of concert dates in England, then fly to North America – first Canada, then New York, and on from there.

As for the album, plans were made to record the whole second disc at the Cottage. Jim discussed what they were going for, "We want it to show exactly what the group are capable of. We're doing this by having a contrast between amplified and acoustic sounds, using a lot of other things besides just organ, guitars and drums." Optimistic that all of the travails with Mason had finally been worked out, Jim predicted only good things to come, "The group seems to be progressing well… We're making sense of all we do, but still incorporating various levels. It's all moving on, though not so fast we can't keep hold of it. And on stage, at least we're all coming across, with a happy medium being struck between all of us…"

In a final flurry of activity before flying to America, they played dates in England, Sweden, then back to London (a BBC session) before shows in Albert's hometown of Carlisle, then Dartford. The next night in Middlesbrough, North Yorkshire, Chris reeled off the stage coughing and unable to catch his breath. He was taken to the hospital with "bronchial pneumonia and exhaustion." While these particular symptoms were often used as a euphemism for a drug overdose, it seemed that Chris really was exhausted and ill. Even so, there was little time allowed for recovery.

While Blackwell cancelled the Canadian dates, he kept the two scheduled for New York City, as well as a two-month U.S. tour to follow. About that time Traffic's next single was also released – "Feelin' Alright?" Once again, Dave had come up with the song deemed to hold the most commercial potential. Soon after, their second album (*Traffic*) would also be released. Comprised just of the tracks done in New York (and London before that), in the end, vague artistic intentions for an acoustic and electric double would bow to the more practical need to get product on the shelves.

Still, the record represented a huge step forward. Artistic growth and the resulting self-assurance showed Traffic coming into its own – creating, rather than following trends. Jim would later assess the special niche they'd carved out, "Even though Traffic wasn't out and out Latin, you'll hear some sort of cowbell or percussion going on – we were very aware of that Latin groove. And we were the only English band that had that 'American vibe' where, through Chris, Steve and all of us – we could go from jazz, rock, blues, to whatever you wanted – to folk. The Who couldn't do that. The Stones couldn't do that. The Beatles didn't do that. The Animals didn't do that. Hendrix didn't really do that, although he had some wonderful variety in his stuff. But we could go through *all* of that."

Dave too seemed to have made an effort to acknowledge and even write in the style Jim, Chris and Steve had forged. One of his new songs, "Don't Be Sad" included lines for Steve to sing, as did "Crying To Be Heard" – a tune very consciously going for the 'Traffic sound'. As he would later say, "That second album, that's when it started to get some focus. Yeah, that's what I tried to do with that song."

The confidence seemed to extend in every direction. The album cover, shot by photographer Gered Mankowitz, showed all four looking older and infinitely wiser, with Chris mischievously pointing to the Traffic symbol which appeared to hang in the air in front of them. Honoring their muse, the inner fold pictures would be taken on a windblown day at the Chalk Horse by Richard (Dick) Polak, a longtime friend to the band.

Later, Polak would recall how his photographs could sometimes capture Chris's sly take on life. "When we did a photo session, he would all of a sudden have the most unexpected props in his hand, I don't know – like books or a trumpet – no, not even a trumpet, that would be too close; things that made you say, 'Hey Chris, why are you carrying that – what?' And he would never tell you. He would never say, 'Oh, I thought…' No, he would just smile."

To push the album, and stir up interest for impending arrival in America, a promo campaign was launched by the U.S. distributor, United Artists, on underground FM radio. A typical ad intoned in a knowing, hipster voice: "Traffic is different, it defines itself – *Traffic*, it drives…" How much that helped was debatable, youth-oriented radio was playing it anyway and the record sold well right off the bat. From all indicators, this was a band ready to move up to the next level of success – rubbing shoulders with the Beatles and the Stones. But, as had become oddly the norm for Traffic, confounding factors were already bubbling to the surface.

On the ground in New York City, Chris was fine again, but now Dave was having problems. What exactly transpired to bring on the next stage of conflict is, once again, maddeningly vague. Things started off okay – a couple of successful shows were played in the city (though one reviewer did note an ill-defined 'lack of togetherness' in the group) – but from there *something* happened, and things quickly went to shit. Of all of them, Mason had the most to say about this mysterious time, and he wasn't especially illuminating, "We did two shows in New York, one at the Fillmore East with the Staple Singers opening and I think we did one in Central Park. And the same thing happened again. I'd never been in New York, and after five days, it just freaked me out. I wasn't used to looking out a window and seeing nothing but buildings – building after building… I grew up on a farm. Yeah, so things happened, and for whatever reason."

Leaving aside the fact that this was actually Dave's *second* trip to New York (they had recorded there in the spring), the things that happened proved serious enough to literally debilitate the group. The stress affected Winwood to the point that his voice fell into a state of laryngitis – leaving him unable to sing. That was the official excuse, at least. And just like that, the U.S. tour was cancelled; one and all simply went home. Asked later to explain the aborted trip, Steve was cryptic, saying only: "It was getting ridiculous. We just had to come back. There was a bad vibration in the group."

The vibrations had in fact become intolerable – emanating from a readily identifiable source. Back in London, Dave Mason had a clear enough memory of what came next, "We went back to England, and I got a call to meet everybody at Chris Blackwell's house. Basically, I'm sitting on the couch, and the other guys are sitting across, and Steve says: 'I don't really like how you write, sing, play and I don't want you in the band anymore.' And that's how it ended. And for me actually, it was like having the rug pulled out from underneath your feet. Because that second album was, I thought, one of the better albums Traffic ever did. Everything started to come together in a way that was really cool, you know? And then, after that meeting – that was that."

So Dave was out – cast into exile despite (or perhaps partly due to) having penned the band's latest single. But for those left behind, the future suddenly seemed nearly as bleak. As much as the wild spirit of the Downs had been flowing in past months – seemingly leading them on to a wondrous breakthrough of some kind, the tide was now in unmistakable retreat. In later years, Chris would brood about the whole tangled affair. A latter-day friend (Graham Broadbent) would say, "I remember him slagging off Dave Mason – in a strange sort of way going on about him; (that) he caused the downfall of Traffic… basically it all started to go wrong when Mason left."

Days after his departure, *Rolling Stone* sent another reporter to the Cottage. This time around, the tone was quite subdued. A perfunctory trip out into the countryside in the Land Rover was followed by time mostly spent at the Cottage, smoking and a jamming, but mostly talking. Jim, Chris and Steve covered a range of topics – from the way moods affect music, to a not very expansive explanation of the last trip to New York ("a disaster"). Much of the discussion focused on the past, giving the impression of a band that had been together for decades, though it had barely been a year and a half since the fateful move to the country. But while the reliable trio still remained, reverberations of Mason's departure filled the space of the Cottage and their unity of purpose, previously unshakable, was now quite tentative.

Steve was in an analytical mood, "Music is a science, in many ways it's mathematical. For instance, a lot of Bach's things were just mathematical exercises, patterns, but in doing that he turned out beautiful pieces of music…" Jim talked about songwriting and fans reading too much into the songs, "It loses its natural beauty. But it can't help being pushed that way because the kids expect it." Striving to conjure a plausible vision for the future, Chris emphasized the work still to be done, musing on new angles Traffic could explore, "There are stacks of tapes, which aren't completed things, but things we've never done on record. There are lots of sides to us which haven't come out." So the promise of was still in there somewhere, but was the will?

The talk settled for a time on the longevity of musical groups. In a band used to having 'telepathic communication', the subsequent conversation read like a coded airing of feelings about the future of Traffic itself. Jim enthusiastically emphasized that The Band had been together and quite successful for nine years. Steve seemed to agree; pointing out that the Stax Records house studio band had enjoyed fifteen good years together. Suspecting that Steve was poised to leave, Chris again took a flexible view, reminding the others that it didn't have to be all or nothing. Noting that it was common for members of jazz bands to branch out with solo albums, Chris closed with a thought aimed straight his band mate: "And this is good that it is now happening in pop – *as long as you try to keep the group together.*"

With November closing, the grey autumn clouds hung close to the ground and the band went back to doing what they knew best – playing gigs. But the clock seemed to tick ever louder. Regaining a sense of normalcy and enthusiasm became the goal, at least for Chris. A few ideas to shake things up emerged. The top of the list involved outfitting 'Big Pink', the band's van, with an electrical generator. With the power and mobility they could play where and when they saw fit. Slipping into places unnoticed and performing for the sheer hell of it would likely have done them all a world of good, returning to the quixotic visions of '66. But like any number of concepts emerging from a glowing ember at midnight, the light of day would dispel the notion as impractical.

More sensible was to do what they had set out to do that spring in New York – finally get a full album of 'Headless Horseman Music' onto vinyl. Doing so would redefine the group as a trio, demarking a new, hopefully fertile field to till. This would have been great, especially for Chris, since jamming and working things out among the three could put him back into the songwriting game. As noted in the *Rolling Stone* interview, with all the 'stacks of tapes' already recorded it couldn't have been that difficult to pull something together – if the commitment was there.

This goal at least seemed within reach. Steve talked up the idea of an album in the press in October, and they actually had two tracks ready to go as the next single: "Medicated Goo", a druggy yet soulful rocker, backed with "Shanghai Noodle Factory", an airy track with a powerful Winwood vocal, recorded at the Cottage. And just maybe the co-op process was returning too, Chris was credited as a writer on 'Noodle'. But the promo picture taken for the single was interesting, and perhaps telling. It showed the three huddled close – Jim gesticulating and apparently pleading, Steve with arched brows and wide eyes, and Chris, hunched over between them, lips curled up in a smile and yet appearing to cry at the same time.

As usual, Jim was ready to give his all, still optimistic about the future. Asked by a reporter about how things were going in the wake of Mason's departure, he said, "The sound is great, it's going quite well. It sounds better to me, but I suppose people will all say it sounds better with three. It's much freer, but it always was free…"

Of course, things weren't quite that rosy. Record-wise, they hadn't gotten any further than the two songs for the single and on a day when they could have been working, Chris had gone home to Birmingham, and Steve was absent as well. Not long after, a shadow seemed to drift over the whole enterprise and even Jim couldn't ignore it – though he couldn't quite put his finger on the cause.

In later years, Capaldi would recall that amid all the swirling turbulence, even the spiritual vibe of the Cottage had somehow changed. Whereas in the early days, Chris had referred to the otherworldly presence in the Cottage as "mischievous", lately it seemed dark, foreboding, and even sinister. Jim noticed it especially on those brisk fall days when he was there alone, "It didn't seem too apparent until the kind of first euphoria of being there (wore off), and all of that. Then it kind of *came on* – you know, as things got splintered, towards the end of that little period, where it kind of got… heavier and heavier, that place. Ain't it funny, places do have atmospheres. It was alright (at first)… but it kind of gradually came on. There was something *evil* in that Cottage – a feeling of evil, you know. It's freaky, isn't it? There was something there man."

Having spent time there in those later, colder days, The Move's disaffected bassist Trevor Burton could relate, "I don't know if I believe in ghosts. But there was definitely… I think there *was* something there – what it was, I don't know. You were always glad when somebody turned up… you didn't want to be alone there for too long."

Whatever the reason, the safe, enveloping atmosphere they'd always counted on to get them through was evaporating fast. Then a portentous omen – the band played a late November gig that ended (as in New York) with Steve complaining about his throat. Retreating to the Cottage, by the first week of December he had packed his bags to leave for Amsterdam with Penny and photographer Dick Polak for a "vacation." But it was more than that. On the very day their new single had been released, and with the album still rising in the charts – 125,000 copies of *Traffic* were sold in the U.S. that week, Steve Winwood decided to leave; Traffic was finished.

He left it to Blackwell to tell the others.

In no time, the press was calling around, looking for explanations. While all seemed to speak freely, having been taken by surprise with the news, Jim and Chris's public comments were essentially the reverse of how they really felt. *Melody Maker* spoke to both. Jim said, "This is the best thing we could do – all make a clean break… I feel less frustrated than I have in a long time and I feel that I am on my feet again." To that, Chris added, "The decision to disband came as rather a shock to me… (However) this isn't a setback, but a step in a new direction."

Outright stunned by the news, Traffic producer Jimmy Miller realized more than most what had been lost. Unlike the others, he chose to speak from the heart, saying, "I'm absolutely bewildered by the breakup. I'd always felt that Traffic was just coming and coming, getting into it more all of the time. Each session was shedding restrictions. Traffic was a group experimenting with form, pushing musical expansion… I still haven't been able to completely accept the split mentally."

In interviews soon after, Steve's reasoning regarding his departure was vague and contradictory. He told *Melody Maker*, "All of a sudden it felt like here was nothing anybody could say. I was going to Amsterdam anyway to see some friends, so I just walked out… Traffic wasn't going wrong except it was always producing internal problems… The breakup wasn't to do with music – yet in a way it was."

He even implied that the group simply played too loud. He also justified his decision from a kind of sociological angle, referencing Chris's *Rolling Stone* comments on side projects, but inverting the conclusion, "We feel that today's scene is moving very much away from permanent groups, and more toward recognition of the individual musicians. The trend is going more in the direction of the jazz scene where musicians just jam together as they please."

Away from the press, Jim and Chris's actual confidence about the future was a different story – they'd been shaken to the core. Even decades later, Jim found livid emotions arising from the memory, "That was a shock really, 'cause we were *so* sure of what we were doing, and suddenly you had *nothing*. We were thrown into, like, the fucking ocean with no life jacket. We didn't know what the fuck was happening, you know. And what was *gonna* happen, what the future was gonna be. We were like totally… I mean it was really awful the way Steve abandoned us, and left it to Chris Blackwell to tell us. He (Blackwell) just turned around one day and said: 'It's over.' We said: '*What are you talking about?*' And there we were, boom – dumped."

Dick Polak, who traveled to Amsterdam with Steve and Penny, was also caught off guard at Steve's casual approach to the momentous change. "I remember driving with him on the way to Holland, and he said, 'Yeah, I think I'm finishing off Traffic… I'm disbanding the band.' I said '*Really?*' He said, 'Yeah, yeah…', and I said, 'Have you told them?' He said, 'No.' And I said, 'Don't you think you *should?*' …and I said, 'Let's stop the car and call…'" (laughs) It was that fucking loose."

But perhaps he'd given it more thought than it seemed. It *was* interesting that he quit almost on the day that Cream also broke up, leaving both Steve and Eric free to combine their talents. Planned or not, rumors already swirled regarding a musical pairing. Music aside, the two represented something else as well: a potential 'money machine'.

The pseudo-Darwinian philosophy of breaking up good groups, skimming off and then recombining the best players to make an even better or 'Super Group' was an idea just starting to take hold in the rock world. While the practice was often initiated by the players themselves, in Jim's view there might also have been a deeper layer at work, "You don't see that in the chronology, where they just dangled that in front of him – the Super Group – and probably a big fucking payday: 'Goodbye!', and off he went without even telling me and Chris."

Even if true, should it have come as a surprise? Steve's willingness to leave a good thing for the next opportunity was the way that Traffic itself had begun. Perhaps the real difference was that Traffic's formation actually came in defiance of the conventional business model. From a 'show-biz' point of view, leaving the still rising star of the Spencer Davis Group to go with a 'band of unknowns' was commercially uncertain, hence foolish; something Winwood had no doubt been told. No such admonitions would be forthcoming this time.

In regard to their fabled Cottage, it would be made clear that Chris and Jim needed to vacate. *Melody Maker* quoted an anonymous spokesman from Island who appreciated the poignancy – the end of the magical Berkshire adventure had come: "Jim Capaldi and Chris Wood have locked the door of the cottage and walked out. It's all very sad." That part, at least, was accurate.

CHAPTER SEVENTEEN

So that was that. The sudden divorce also meant a goodbye to the lifestyle they had come to know and love. After the totality of what they'd experienced, departing that place was perhaps the bitterest pill to swallow. Passing through the village of Aston Tirrold, Jim and Chris made a nostalgic stop in at The Boot. Chris's young confidant, Rosie Roper noticed the strange mood, "They were in the pub, and we were going out to a dance somewhere. James said, 'I've never known anyone like you – you run in and you run out – you're never still!' And I said, 'Oh, I know – there's too much going on. Anyway, I'll see you later!' He caught hold of me, and he said: 'I'll see *you* on the other side, where the grass is greener.'"

Later, Chris would make a stop at the other magical cottage – the Hamilton's Barn Hall Close in Blewbury. Always attuned to children, he approached Helen and Patrick's son Giles with a casual smile and something hidden behind his back. Loving Chris's flute playing, the boy was typically obliged with a performance. This time however the instrument would simply be handed over, with the insistence that he keep it and learn to play. Helen recalled, "Chris gave my son Giles a very expensive flute, and Giles loved that flute. That showed a wonderful sweetness on the part of Chris."

The gift of the precious instrument was an interesting, poignant act by Chris. Was it a symbolic act of passing on music to the next generation? Or did he perhaps, on that particular day, feel that he wouldn't need it anymore?

(http://www.ukrockfestivals.com/hyde-park-7-28-68.html)

('Traffic Plan It For Free', Melody Maker, 10/19/1968)

('Groups must play much softer', Chris Welch, 1/1969)

('Traffic Split Shock', Melody Maker, 12/7/1968)

('Traffic Single set…', NME, 9/7/1968)

('Traffic', D. Dalton, Rolling Stone, 5/3/1969)

('Traffic's Happy Medium', Beat Instrumental, 8/1968)

('No More Traffic; Winwood-Clapton Rumors', Ritchie Yorke, Rolling Stone, 1/1969)

('Traffic Go For Mobile Music', Richard Green, NME, 11/2/1968)

('Traffic', Johnathon Cott, Rolling Stone, 5/3/1969).

('Roll With It', Welch, Winwood, 1990)

BLIND FAITH AND A WOODEN FROG

So Steve was gone. More than simply a missing band member, the chasm that opened in the wake of Winwood's departure seemed utterly unbridgeable. But if Chris contemplated quitting the business, events conspired to keep him around.

Back in London, out of a sense of obligation, and perhaps spying another opportunity, Chris Blackwell called him and Jim into his office. His suggestion was straightforward: swallow their pride, call Dave Mason and put the rest of the pieces back together. Form a band with Dave? After all they had been through with Mason, perhaps the best measure of the pair's state of mind was that they would even consider it. But with backs against the wall – and lacking a better idea, they didn't mull it long. Blackwell made the call.

Subsequent to his bitter termination that October, Mason wasted little time in hopping on a plane back to America. But while southern California's climate and laid back vibe suited him just fine – he still hadn't managed to get anything together there musically. Offered another chance to grab the brass ring, he didn't hesitate to return to a cold, grey London. "Chris Blackwell phoned me in Los Angles and told me about it. He wanted me to come back, so I flew home." For Mason, the unexpected offer to rewrite an old script proved irresistible. What if *he*, rather than Winwood had been in charge? It was worth trying to find out.

Blackwell also suggested another player – Mick Weaver, a.k.a., 'Wynder K. Frog', a young guy with an already impressive background in rock, R&B and jazz. That Weaver was highly proficient on the Hammond B-3 organ was likely a key consideration. Equally important, the energetic Jimmy Miller was recruited to help guide and eventually produce. In fact, Miller's positive attitude would prove crucial to lifting the mood and getting the guys on their feet again. Even so, the sense of limitless possibilities when Traffic came together was conspicuously absent.

To see if the new arrangement would even work, a session was hurriedly booked at 'Morgan' – a small recording studio in North West London. A couple of day's effort revealed the common ground: straightforward blues/rock. The only real product to end up on tape was a jam in 'G' led off by Chris's tenor. Huddled in the control room afterward for a listen, the sound – while unremarkable – at least proved discernable from Traffic's. And for the time being it would have to do. As for a name, Miller likely came up the first (whimsical) moniker, 'Wooden Frog', but this too was merely a placeholder. Ultimately, the more conventional (and clearly hierarchical) 'Mason, Capaldi, Wood and Frog' would emerge, and stick. And with that, a band was born.

By December 13th, they had signed a contract to play a gig at the Marquee Club in London on January 30th – so preparing for the stage became their first priority. Island appointed a roadie and a manager of sorts – their old friend, Gordon Jackson. Perhaps hoping to strike gold a second time, they again situated themselves in the country, but further north, renting out an old school house to rehearse at Stoke Lacey in Herefordshire, not far from Capaldi and Mason's home ground of Worcester.

Like most 'new' bands, they shook off the rust by jamming and reworking songs of others. Jim pulled out a Leadbelly tune – "Leavin' Blues" that Deep Feeling used to do. Mason, in a full-on Albert King mood, worked out an arrangement of "Crosscut Saw", and an instrumental of "Born Under A Bad Sign" that showed off his chops. Chris contributed "Long Black Veil" – a country tune first done by Lefty Frizzell in 1959, but more recently by The Band. Sung from the perspective of the ghost of a man who had chosen the gallows for a murder he didn't commit rather than disgrace a married woman he'd had an affair with, the song was a natural for Chris. For their version, Jim and Dave traded off vocals, with Chris adding tenor and flute while Mick's Hammond supplied an earthy vibe.

With all of the covers, it might seem that they were aiming a little low to have a real impact on the music scene. But Mason had a slew of songs, including two new ones; "World In Changes", and "Waiting On You". He also wanted to perform cuts from the *Traffic* album – "Feelin' Alright?", "You Can All Join In", and "Cryin' To Be Heard".

CHAPTER EIGHTEEN

Their first contact with the press was with Richard Green from the *NME*. Although Chris was nowhere to be seen, and Jim seemed still in shock from the changes, Dave was enthused, "We want to go out on stage and have a happy time." But like Winwood before the breakup, he also kept his options open, "There should be more freedom for people to play with each other, the restrictions shouldn't matter. It's valid to play with other people, because it helps you find your scene." While not exactly a ringing endorsement of loyalty, Mason was upfront about it.

In fact, from the start the overall level of commitment to the venture was nebulous. Consequently, only vague memories could be excavated from those involved. While present throughout, Gordon Jackson could only sketch in the period – "There's no reason why it shouldn't have been fantastic. Dave did most of the singing, Jim would have sung from the drums. Who played bass? They did quite a few gigs and it was a proper tour."

Indeed. Birmingham and London aside, they were booked for Kidderminster, Sheffield, Newcastle, Liverpool, Plymouth and Brunel University – taking the whole thing into March. As for bass, it was done mostly as it had been in Traffic; Mick Weaver used foot pedals on the Hammond organ. Chris was experimenting too – playing bass from his tenor sax. Using the Gibson Maestro system that he'd bought back in New York, any notes he hit on the horn were also duplicated an octave or two lower – effectively playing two parts at once. So that hole was filled.

But were they 'fantastic?' With the only real evidence left being the Morgan jam and a couple of BBC radio sessions, the tapes reveal a sound that was indeed tight, but compared to Traffic also dense, and even a little manic. Chris especially seemed to be working too hard, playing a lot of fast-paced rhythmic parts to simply keep up. On "Cryin' To Be Heard", one of Mason's better songs from the *Traffic* album, he reprised his sax work, and even added a new flute part. But where he might have freely soared, he now seemed less sure how to shape the mood. Already, the hard won confidence gained from Traffic seemed strained, ebbing back a little. When they did get on stage in front of an audience, it didn't help that his effects system didn't always work. Dave Mason chuckled at the memory, "I just have visions of Chris, just constantly on stage – everything going wrong – kicking shit."

The first real gig was held back in their old stomping group of Birmingham – at a place called Mother's, on January 25th. Chris thought it went well, later telling a reporter that the audience was "a lot better these days", willing to sit and listen to the music. Perhaps, but Yvonne Haynes, a local girl who went to that show, came home a little confused about what band she'd actually seen. Afterward she wrote in her diary: "Went to Mother's to see the new line up from Traffic (sic) – rather disappointing." Others likely felt the same. Subsequent gigs fared better however – the date in Sheffield was chalked as a success, and they rocked the hipper crowd at the Marquee Club in London. Still, without a record to distinguish a new identity, M,C,W&F might have looked more like a really good club band rather than the next up and coming superstars.

Like it or not, the specter of Traffic cast an unavoidable shadow. The absence of their original keyboard player and vocalist turned out to be a very high hurdle to overcome, if not a fatal flaw. Weaver's musicianship was not the problem, he was excellent – but in having made the decision to hire a Hammond B-3 organist, comparisons were inevitable and Weaver simply wasn't Winwood.

Chris understood that if this band was to have any chance of making it, the implicit 'question' had to be put away. It was on his mind when he talked to a reporter about the new group. "Our main problem was to make it quite clear to people that we were something quite apart from Traffic. Really we don't mind much what people choose to call us just so long as it is clear that it is not the old Traffic with just one change in personnel." But, of course there was no escaping the issue, and unwanted expectations lingered.

The real problem was more subtle, and below the surface – that multidimensional bond intrinsic to Traffic simply wasn't there. Mason, who never had the deep connection with Chris, couldn't hope to fill the void, while Capaldi, who'd lapsed into a quieter, less assertive state these days, wasn't much help either. To top it off, his natural songwriting role – feeding lyrics to Winwood, was also absent – and Mason didn't require a partner.

With no grounded center to work from, an odd lassitude took hold. Weaver recalled the band's work ethic lacking right from the start, "It probably could have worked, but I don't know, we seemed to have difficulty even making gigs. A couple of times, we just didn't do a gig. One day, I remember it was raining, and I think it was decided on the basis of the nasty weather that we weren't really up for going up the motorway and doing the gig. I would think, 'How can we do that? How can we just not turn up at gigs?' It didn't seem to bother the rest of the boys too much."

Amid the mixed feelings, Chris did his best to promote the band and in his own way, lead. He did at least two major interviews for the music press by himself – something he'd never done before. While the group was clearly important to him, an air of hesitancy was also noticeable, especially concerning Dave's involvement, "We sometimes could be just a trio – that's an idea. But the group as such remains the same. Dave is a composer and doesn't really like playing all that much. I'm not saying this is something that will happen but…" Making this work was going to be tricky indeed.

Lingering doubts aside, they forged on, hoping to somehow stumble upon a unifying plan for the future. Mason, missing his favored climate, pushed the others to move, lock, stock and barrel back to L.A. Failing to find any enthusiasm for that idea, he did get them to agree to do a U.S. tour, and they prepared to get started on an album. Jimmy Miller was the designated spark plug, with whom it was hoped the group would discover their muse. Chris in particular held the cheerful American with a mindful of ideas in high regard. In turn, Miller understood that Chris had music inside him, even if he was reticent to come out with it.

But even Miller's goodwill couldn't save Mason, Capaldi, Wood and Frog. What actually precipitated their downfall is unclear, but one popular story suggests a specific incident: having ingested too many hashish cakes, the band failed to show for their critical first recording session. Supposedly, Chris Blackwell took this as a sign of the band lacking a sufficient work ethic, and took the offer off the table for the time being.

Mick Weaver didn't recall that happening, but did confirm that hashish was utterly endemic to the band, its use sometimes leading to a mixture of confusion and humor. A road trip he and Chris made typified the situation. "We were doing a gig somewhere up north, we had to go up the A1, it's not a freeway, but a road full of roundabouts… it took hours and hours to get anywhere. Before we got to the A1, we were still driving through London, Chris was asking me if I had any hash on me, and I said, 'No, actually I've got nothing.' He said, 'Have a look in that glove compartment, you might find some scraps.' And sure enough, I found this little ball of hash, and we rolled it up and smoked it. We got to the A1 and Chris said 'Have another look in that glove box – you'll probably find more.' And I kept doing that at Chris's request, and I kept finding these little lumps, and I kept rolling them up; we were getting very, very stoned. Next thing I knew, we were looking out the car window, and I said to Chris, 'Where the hell are we?' And he said, 'I don't know… we were on the A1 weren't we?' It turned out that we were just on this big flat field with concrete running down the middle of it – we'd somehow managed to get onto a disused World War I airstrip! I have no idea how we got there."

Whether from the hash or simple lack of motivation, by spring, the group's prospects suddenly darkened. Not seeing the future unfold the way he'd imagined, Dave wasted no time announcing his imminent departure. *NME* covered the break up, taking a somewhat incredulous tone, "Mason, Capaldi, Wood and Frog – the group which emerged following Stevie Winwood's decision to disband Traffic – have themselves decided to split up on March 8, after being in existence for only 60 days!"

In retrospect, Dave had little to say, good or otherwise about his time with the group, except to dismiss the underlying validity of the entire venture. In later years, he seemed to barely remember having done it at all, saying, "It was a reaction to Steve leaving, and trying to create something. I did it for a minute, and I went, 'You know what? This is stupid, you can't replace Winwood. It was like 'ugh', you know. So I was out – I don't want to do this." Jim Capaldi essentially blanked it too, able to come up with little more than a sentence to cover the whole experience, "Yeah, we had to do *something*." He did however recall a silver lining, "But the great thing about that was that we got to do that last gig at the Albert Hall with Jimi Hendrix – *that* was wonderful."

For the rock world, the latter part of the 1960's was a time of personnel changes, break ups and abrupt transitions. Besides the recent demise of Cream and Traffic, the Yardbirds too had finished in late '68, as well as some of the best American groups like the Buffalo Springfield. Since leaving England in '66, Bob Dylan had remained in hiding, making music, but – with only a couple of exceptions – staying as far away from the public eye as possible. By the end of 1969, the Beatles would be finished as well, while the Rolling Stones would fire Brian Jones only to learn of his death soon after by drowning as they prepared to play a free concert in Hyde Park with new guitarist Mick Taylor.

CHAPTER EIGHTEEN

The Jimi Hendrix Experience was staggering as well. While immensely successful, an enormous toll had been exacted. Between the relentless touring, the recording dates crammed in on the rare 'open' days, and the wild, excessive lifestyle, Hendrix and band were often unhappy, fighting, and teetering on the edge of collapse.

As if knowing time was short, Jimi spent the middle of February recording a slew of songs in London's Olympic Studios. Always interested in Hendrix's activities, and having a day off the road himself, Chris was there too on the 22nd to check things out. He found Jimi working alone in a recording booth, sketching a tune that could be read as a message to his band – "Go My Own Way". Once accomplished, he shifted back to re-plowing a very old field. Hurriedly calling for the group to assemble (Chris included), Jimi called out, "What did you say? What's the name of it? It's called 'Hound Dog Blues' – 'Hound Dog Blues.'…" With only that much preparation, all would launch into the old Big Mama Thornton tune which soon whirled like a dust devil on the Mississippi delta. With Chris wailing behind him on tenor, Jimi seemed intent on exorcizing frustration and clearing his head. And it seemed to work, or at least lift the mood for what was yet to come: two nights hence the Experience would play a concert across town, with Mason, Capaldi, Wood and Frog as opening act.

Since 1871, the Royal Albert Hall had held every kind of British performance on its stage. Artistically it was hallowed ground, a place most rockers only aspired to perform at. On the day, surveying the packed seats from behind stage curtains Chris was, not surprisingly, nervous. Besides being by far the biggest room MCW&F would ever play, it was also Jimi's audience, and expectations would be sky high. Sensing trouble brewing, Jim Capaldi kept a close eye on his skittish band mate and sure enough, when signaled to play, Chris's expression darkened. Catching sight of it, Capaldi's own anxiety skyrocketed – what was Woody going to do? But, years later, he could only laugh recalling Chris's apparently spontaneous method to relieve his angst. Coming to a dead stop just short of the stage he would knit his brow and draw back his head before dramatically spitting onto Albert Hall's fabled floorboards. Only then would he walk on, a slight smile now set on his face. The mildly vulgar act broke the tension for everyone – all were chuckling as they found their places. From there Mason, Capaldi, Wood and Frog rose to the occasion and played one of their best shows.

The Experience too would blaze through a great set, finally overcoming their recent string of subpar concerts. Near the end, having begun "Room Full Of Mirrors", a tune never played live before – Hendrix went up to the microphone and said, "Does anyone else want to play?" before sticking his head behind the amps and gesturing. Ghanaian hand drummer Kwasi 'Rocky' Dzidzornu came out, followed by Dave Mason, who plugged in and stood next to bassist Noel Redding. Chris was backstage too, but once again he wasn't quite ready. Sweating and clutching his flute, he instead hunched behind the amps, listening as the rhythm fell into a groove.

But as the music swelled to a roar he summoned his courage once more, briskly walking out to the vocal mike while Jimi's back was turned. With no room for subtlety, he blew hard-edged, bluesy notes and runs, trilling in a manic huff to be heard above the stacks. Swinging around and signaling the rest of the band to take it down, Hendrix gave Chris a chance to get his playing across. With the intensity written on his face he continued, before Jimi walked up and spoke in his ear, encouraging him to keep going – which he did, before easing out with some descending riffs that Hendrix picked up on and took over. Signaled by a few notes of the "Star Spangled Banner" on Hendrix's guitar, "Room Full of Mirrors" finally crashed to its conclusion. In the end, they had put on a hell of a show, all captured on film and sound reels destined to languish in legal limbo and never be released.

Two days later, Chris would again join Jimi and band back at Olympic Studios. Playing first tenor and then a mellow soprano sax amid a full horn section, he helped lay down a most unusual piece – a long afro-jazz funk exploration titled (much later) "12 Bar Blues Jam with Horns". Yet another glimpse into Jimi's musical trajectory, this session would hold some of the last recordings done with the Experience, but again none but the participants would know – it too remained locked in the vaults for decades.

As for Mason, Capaldi, Wood and Frog – a band born in a state of loss and confusion, and from whom almost no recorded legacy at all would exist, at least their last chapter would hold a page all could recall with a smile.

*

During the two months that Chris's new group tried to make a go of it, Steve Winwood did what everyone expected and formed a band with Eric Clapton. Although created out of mutual respect, the new 'super group' would involve a series of compromises and contradictions from the start. Perhaps the most significant was Winwood's proposal to have Ginger Baker as their drummer. Almost certainly the last thing Clapton had in mind… the two tumultuous years they'd already shared in Cream had been more than enough.

But Ginger had been strategic. During the Cream days, when Clapton edged toward Winwood, he was rarely far away. Baker, in fact, made it a point to stop at the Cottage with or without Eric. In turn, Steve had grown to love that thunderous but always tasteful sound that only Baker could produce. He'd also seen less of the 'other side' that Clapton knew too well. So with Eric wanting to please Steve, and Steve wanting Ginger, pride would be swallowed and better judgment discarded – he was in.

That settled, the three rehearsed at Clapton's house in Surrey. While a good sound developed right off, there was still an obvious hole. Having already jammed successfully with the three at the Cottage, Trevor Burton felt tantalizingly close to being tapped to fill it, "I nearly got the job on bass – Steve wanted me, I think, and Ginger wanted Ric Grech. So Ginger won the day, 'cause he was the drummer.'" Being the bass player for Family, the band whose debut album Dave Mason had produced, (and someone Steve had previously played with as well) Grech was a known entity, and could also contribute violin if need be.

If expectations for Mason, Capaldi, Wood and Frog never rose above modest, the same couldn't be said of Winwood's new band. The melding of three of rock's musical giants was seen by many as having potential to redefine the rock scene of 1969. That the music would be great was simply a given and from the business side of things, the sooner it was produced, the better. Indeed, leisurely country jaunts to standing stones for inspiration were now out of the question; a quick hustle into the studio for an album was the paramount concern. Artistic intentions aside, this was essential to set up phase two of the grand scheme – the tour. And so it was that even before the bass position was settled, a full-on excursion of America had been mapped out. *Rolling Stone* was blunt, "The plan is for the band… to play only stadium sized dates – because in the words of their agency, Creative Management Associates, 'They've got to go into super-big houses because it's a super-group.'"

Away from the managers, in a rare moment of reflection (and self-deprecation), Eric Clapton came up with the only rational title for such a band – an overt protest against their own hype – 'Blind Faith'.

As for Chris, hurt feelings aside, he'd never really fallen out with Winwood, so around this time he began stopping in to see what they were up to. Interestingly, he later made a few cryptic comments, interpretable that he too might have been considered for the band, "Steve joined up with Blind Faith, though the lineup, as it happens, wasn't as intended – the exact intentions, I don't know. So then you suddenly realize that you're on your own." But instead of retreating as Jim had, Chris simply hung out and watched them rehearse. And with that, whatever bitterness remained from Traffic's breakup and whatever else did or didn't happen just slipped away. For the time being, he found some contentment as a Blind Faith fan, perhaps the first.

Not surprisingly, the band struggled to come up with material worthy of the sky-high expectations. Not previously known for his lyric writing prowess, Steve somehow brought in several songs, the best of which, "Can't Find My Way Home" was nearly transcendental, an acoustic masterpiece. Eric Clapton could only manage one original, but it too was excellent: "Presence of the Lord", while Ginger's contribution "Do What You Like", was a lively but self-indulgently long jazzy jam.

Realizing that they might have trouble filling an album, they turned to covers. Early on, a stab was made at "Hey Joe", patterned after Hendrix's definitive version – but it didn't click. Mike Kellie recalled seeing Chris with Steve back at the Cottage with an acetate of an alternative that worked better. "I can remember Chris saying, 'Play Kel' that track you brought back', which was the Buddy Holly song." Chris dug "Well… All Right" for a good reason – it was an unpretentious, joyful romp marrying rock with jazzy piano chords as Ginger's drums swung like mad from below. The three sat around the stereo, smiling and nodding. If it wasn't as satisfying as being in the band, at least Chris could enjoy a taste of the life he'd loved – hanging out at the Cottage, smoking hashish cigarettes and listening to good music.

Jim Capaldi wasn't faring nearly as well. Having taken Traffic's break up as a personal rejection, he spent countless hours stewing over thoughts that Steve's unhappiness with his drumming had precipitated it. One incident in particular stood out. Back in the summer of '68, he and Steve had been invited to a Joe Cocker recording session for his cover version of the Beatles "With A Little Help From My Friends". The rhythm required was a waltz-like 3/4 time, for which Jim struggled mightily but ultimately, in vain. Thirty-five takes later, the producer, Danny Cordell gave up and actually wept in frustration. Canceling the session, he later brought in another drummer (BJ Wilson) to finish the song, leaving Jim dejected and feeling insecure. It didn't help that Ginger Baker, a great, supremely confident drummer, subsequently began showing up to jam at the Cottage, on *Jim's* kit – as he watched. Knowing that Winwood actually went on to form a band with Baker only confirmed Jim's suspicions and proved the final straw to an already bruised psyche. The resulting tailspin took him to a place that was quite dark.

Comparing himself to Chris in those days, Jim found that words failed to describe his condition, "He just had the guts to hang out and do shit. Where me – I was just like hanging on to myself in Birmingham, like 'Arrgh!' I went through a terrible… I didn't know up from fucking down – (it) was that big. Walking into the abyss, poking my head into the void, finding out who you are – which came out very badly – failed the test miserably!" To compound matters, Jim had since broken off his relationship with Danielle, an always psychologically fragile girl, now even more unstable than he was. Left behind in London when Jim moved back to Birmingham, Danielle too was brooding, never accepting the finality of the break up.

The one bright spot was that in hanging out in Birmingham with Don Carless again, Capaldi eventually found solace in a new relationship with Anna Westmore, the beautiful girl who had worked at the Elbow Room back in '66. Having had many adventures with Traffic, Anna could relate to what Jim was going through. Appearing just at the right time, Jim was succinct as to her role: "she saved my life."

Chris too was hoping to be transformed by love. Amongst all of the women he had encountered after his rise to fame, it was Jeanette Jacobs who was firmly stuck in his mind. The lithe, pretty, dark-eyed singer from New York held a fascinating mixture of qualities and contradictions. Unlike the throng that hung around Jimi Hendrix, Jeanette wasn't a groupie. Her band, The Cake, had toured America, opening up for groups like Buffalo Springfield, and had even appeared on the 'Smothers Brothers' show. But her insecurities weren't too far under the surface – while the other singers swayed and danced to the music on their television debut, Jeanette stood strangely still, supposedly in protest against the more commercial R&B material being forced on them by the management. Amid the confusion of conflicting motivations, the band would break up in L.A. not long after.

Chris also recalled Jeanette's interesting but fanciful story about her 'father', King Farouk. What drove her to embellish or fabricate this elaborate fiction about her family and history? Her love life was equally convoluted. While she had many short-lived relationships, the one with Jimi Hendrix was special. She professed to love him deeply and flew to him when he called. Even so, Jeanette had given Chris strong signals that she wanted him too. And while some described her as having the classic New York toughness in her personality, Chris saw only a vulnerable, sweet soul that he very much wanted to protect and nurture.

With their album not scheduled for release for another month, Blind Faith was already booked for tours taking them from Hyde Park, London, to Scandinavia, and then to huge venues across the United States. Whereas most bands might do their first show in a bar or an obscure club to check out the response and get the nerves under control, Blind Faith's assumed greatness apparently justified a mass presentation right from the start.

Standing on a platform barely big enough for their equipment and surrounded by a sea of faces at their Hyde Park debut, the reality of the situation suddenly slammed with enough force to nearly un-nerve the lot of them. Eric Clapton seemed the most affected. His face grim, he kept his head down, concentrating on simply getting through each number. Steve, the visual focal point and de facto bandleader tried to remain cool, but some anxiety showed as his voice cracked reaching for high notes. Like Clapton, Grech was merely coping, averting his eyes from the crowd. Only Ginger seemed confident, thundering as usual behind his psychedelic kick drum in the afternoon sun.

And Chris witnessed it all – standing in the press zone with a clear view of Steve. He had plenty of company; over a hundred thousand people stood behind him.

While the as yet unreleased songs from the album went over well, the distance and the lack of stage presence helped mute the reaction. About half the songs were covers, including a tepid version of the Rolling Stone's "Under My Thumb" which Winwood forgot some of the lyrics to. It didn't help that, playing under the London sky, airplanes heading to Heathrow periodically drowned out the music. On the day of their unveiling, it seemed that Blind Faith had gone a little too far, and much too fast.

The shaky start behind them, the band departed for Norway and Sweden to recover their confidence away from overly critical eyes.

By now, Chris had hatched plans of his own. Although he'd recently added a beautiful flute track to a song called "Mourning Sad Morning" by the band Free, he wasn't looking to be a 'session man' or to jump into another band. Instead, he would soon leave England for New York City, alone. Why? In the U.S., he could witness another huge spectacle – Blind Faith's upcoming appearance at Madison Square Garden. But more important was his growing sense of desperation to see Jeanette Jacobs – and New York was her town. Having recently reconnected with her via telephone, by now he was counting down the days.

Still licking his wounds in Birmingham, Jim Capaldi found out about Chris's scheme. "I thought it was incredibly ballsy of him to go off to America. I thought, 'what the fuck is he gonna do there?' That would have absolutely freaked me out. There's no way, I could have gone off and done something like that." But where Jim had looked into the 'void' with dread, Chris had always been willing to leap in if he thought it might somehow help the cause. The difference this time was that he would be doing it without a safety net. Without Jim, Penny, or a roadie to pull him out of a bad situation, anything could and likely would happen. At the very least, it wasn't going to be boring.

*

Upon arrival in New York, he headed straight to Manhattan. Expecting Jeanette to be there to greet him, for some reason, she wasn't. In the wake of his longstanding anticipation, this was a blow. From there he sought out an old haunt – the Record Plant, and if he was looking for a distraction he found it here – the place was hopping. In fact, the same studio where Traffic had recorded their last album was having a promotional event and looking for players. Earl Doud, previously known for comedy albums, decided to remake himself as an Executive Producer in the 'rock business'. Having heard of a recent album by Mike Bloomfield, Al Kooper and Steven Stills (*Super Session*) that had cost little to make and sold well, he decided to see about putting one of these 'super-groups' together himself. Pitching the idea to the Record Plant management that the publicity would be good for their profile, they agreed; Doud was given free use of the facilities.

But when the hoped-for 'cream of the crop' musicians actually started walking in the door, Doud, realizing that he was in over his head, pushed a young assistant forward with orders to 'Produce'. At age nineteen, Mark "Moogy" Klingman was a Long Island musician who had played keyboards in several bands – and had even jammed with Jimi Hendrix in Greenwich Village back in '66, but production-wise his experience was essentially zero. Mortified but excited, he decided to see if he could fake it.

He recalled seeing Chris at the opening night. "He came down to that first session, the one with Mitch Mitchell on drums and Keith Emerson on organ, Buzzy Feiton on guitar, and me on piano. I'm not sure who played bass. It was amazing to see him with that crowd – here's the guy from ELP, here's the guy from the Butterfield Blues Band, the guy from Traffic – and here's the guy from the Jimi Hendrix Experience! So I was lucky, and I was trying to figure out how to blend in with all of these people, and not get kicked out of the room. Because all they had to do was wink, and I'd be gone."

Like Moogy, Chris would start the session with reservations and even dread. While he'd happily recorded here last year with Traffic – now nakedly on his own, he was further outside his comfort zone than he'd ever imagined. And although he knew Emerson, and was friends with Mitchell, his recent experiences with put-together bands based merely on 'names' seemed to have sickened him. Was there no end to this 'Super Group' bullshit?

And so it was that this toxic combination – Jeanette's absence, so soon followed by this musical travesty, festered in his mind. But instead of simply heading to the nearest bar, he made a serious mistake – he opened his sax case.

On paper, it should have worked. Starting the session with a cover of Eddie Harris's "Freedom Jazz Dance" (a song Chris knew well), Feiton and Emerson, both fans of Traffic, called Chris and his tenor over to work out an arrangement. Although he'd heard Chris play fantastically in this very studio during sessions for Traffic, Klingman's initial excitement soon turned to concern, "Chris was a really nice guy, but he couldn't get it together. He would be in the background and he would be playing some of the melody lines, and sometimes he wouldn't; he would start to solo, and then he would stop. I know that he recorded a bunch of stuff with Keith Emerson, and none of it was usable… he was playing and stopping, soloing and stopping."

The session aborted, Chris came back on another day. This time they were working on a cover of Bob Dylan's 'Lay, Lady, Lay'. Assigned the melody and a solo with the flute, again a dark cloud descended. It was clear to Klingman that Chris was confused by his own inability to perform. "I wanted to hang out with the guy a little. He seemed really troubled, like he was acting something out; he'd stop playing and look at his flute. He was very nervous about the whole thing – he couldn't get a sound, he couldn't do the solos, and he couldn't copy the lines. He was very, very nervous about it." After tremendous effort, Chris did manage a spare melody line that ended up on the final track, but the solo proved a bridge too far; it would later be dubbed in by Joe Farrell.

Determined to overcome whatever held him back, he would return the next day, but virtually nothing emerged. In a panic, he began making excuses and leaving, then coming back in to try again. Each time his confidence plummeted further. "He was doing stuff like saying, 'I've got to go get my sax', and wiggling out, coming back the next day… I don't know. He was beating himself up, you know." From there, Klingman watched Chris fall apart. "He was just kind of flying around, but we couldn't get anything out of the guy. He was probably having some kind of mental breakdown. He didn't appear to me to be drunk… he just seemed really nervous, and unable to get his stuff together. And it really bothered him; he was very fidgety about it. So you felt sorry for the guy, you didn't want to yell at him, or say 'come on Chris!' You just wanted to leave him alone." But by now it was too late. Having reached the point of despair, Chris would finally withdraw from the project for good.

Interestingly, the intended record would prove jinxed as well. Despite the involvement of numerous artists and uncounted hours spent, with no plan or theme, little more than mediocre music would ever emerge. With no end in sight, the management finally pulled the plug. Doud would release the sessions anyway as *Music from Free Creek*, but despite the stars involved, the album received little attention and few sales. Ironically, *Free Creek*'s greatest contribution to rock 'n roll would be as a demarcation of the death (symbolically at least) of the ill-fated 'super-session' concept.

His worst fears realized it seemed that Chris had crashed and burned in his first attempt to go it alone in New York City. Yet it was here, at his abysmal low that the wind suddenly shifted to reveal the silver lining he'd hoped for – Jeanette suddenly appeared, turning up one night with her closest friend and former band-mate, Eleanor Barooshian at Unganos where Chris was hanging out. Here they would spend the night talking, laughing and smoking Marlboros. As the sun peaked through the skyscrapers, the couple walked, hand in hand up West 70th street, back to Chris's hotel.

There, Jeanette revealed the reason that she'd been away – her father had recently died. As it turned out, he didn't live in a palace in some far off land, but rather in a subsidized housing project here in New York. In her moment of sorrow, Jeanette revealed an unvarnished truth otherwise known only to Jimi, Eleanor and a few others. Rather than the offspring of a prostitute and Egypt's King Farouk, Jeanette was actually the daughter of a Greek immigrant mother named Tina, and a local man named Samuel 'Buster' Jacobs. After her arrival in the big city of New York, Tina met and married Buster, a working class black man who lived in the Ravenswood Houses project in Queens, Long Island in 1949. On September 27th 1950, their child, Jeanette Jacobs was born. Tina and Buster would eventually separate, leaving Jeanette a conflicted life in which she kept contact with her mother (and was able to speak Greek herself), but resided with her father in the projects. There she would plan an escape into the magical world of musical stardom. Buster would continue to support and encourage her dreams until his death from heart problems in the early summer of '69.

Beside the heartbreak, she was also effectively homeless. Now an adult, the lease on the Ravenswood apartment could not be maintained and Jeanette had to give it up. All that remained now was a nostalgic song about her life there ("Rainbow Wood") written for The Cake's first album.

The truth finally revealed, Chris better understood this restless girl who coped with life by spinning amazing tales and flitting from man to man. Believing that Jeanette needed him, more than ever, Chris desired to take care of her while still giving her the freedom to be herself.

His confidence stoked, he would spend nearly the last of his money on a new instrument – a beautiful Selmer alto saxophone. Having a range mirroring the human female voice, the alto complemented his deeper (male) tenor, and perhaps provided a means to express the dynamics of his new relationship. One thing was certain, with the alto in one hand and Jeanette's fingers curled around the other; his sense of optimism had suddenly revived. Coming in the wake of the dark place he'd been recently, this would change nearly everything.

('Cl'pt'n-W'w'd-B'k'r Coming To Town', Rolling Stone, 5/3/1969)

('Clashes That Led To The Traffic's End', Richard Green, NME, 12/1968)

('After Only 60 Days…', NME, 2/1969)

('Mason Capaldi, Wood & Frog', Sounds, 3/1969)

('Chris Wood…', Sounds, 5/5/1973)

('Joe Cocker, With A Little Help From My Friends', J.P. Bean, Omnibus, 1990)

CHAPTER NINETEEN

DR. JOHN'S TRAVELING MEDICINE SHOW

If I ain't back at half past fo',

You know I done gone to the corner sto',

To git my junk, to satisfy my mind,

I just got to satisfy my mind

Junkerman's Blues (pre-1900's traditional New Orleans blues song)

*

Chris and Jeanette returned to the Record Plant, still the best place in town for musicians to hang out. Before long, a figure familiar to both walked through the door. Surveying the room with a sly smile was Malcolm John Rebennack Jr. – known to his friends as Mac.

New Orleans born, Mac had moved to Los Angeles in recent years. A talented guitar and keyboard player, he had found more than enough work to make a living and could have been financially comfortable as an L.A. 'session man.' In fact, Jeanette's old band, The Cake had used him on their album, on which he played, arranged and contributed music. But a long-term heroin habit also kept him on the hustle, and stability always seemed just beyond reach. And with Mac still deeply immersed in the Cajun culture and voodoo ceremonies of his youth, a conventional career never seemed to be on the cards anyway – his spectrum of special candles, jars of herbs and a prominently displayed grave-robbed human skull tended to limit options.

In the end, this eccentric approach would serve him well as beneath it all lay a prodigious musical talent with wildly original ideas. By the time he broke out from California in early '68, Mac had formed a super-rare racially mixed group, made an utterly unique record of his own (*Gris-Gris*), and invented a Medicine Man persona to sell the whole package. These days, most knew him simply as 'Dr. John.'

Chris, Jeanette and Eleanor were all invited to Mac's show that night at Ungano's with an offer to sit in. After what he'd just been through, the thought of getting on stage with yet another unfamiliar band must have been intimidating. But the confluence of New Orleans voodoo music flowing under the towering spires of Manhattan would evoke a feeling starkly in contrast to his prior train wreck.

Performing in full Mardi-Gras regalia at Ungano's, Dr. John was scarily resplendent with his snakeskin jacket, painted face, feathered head-dress, and colored candles burning around him to ward off evil spirits. For good measure his mummified human head ('Patrick') was set up on stage like one of the band. The living members were nearly as exotic. James Booker, a black, gay, one-eyed keyboard genius, could play any style of music with an astounding fluidity but like others, coexisted with a bad drug habit. Richard 'Didimus' Washington, an Ethiopian percussionist, was credited by Mac with bringing a unique vibe that mixed Afro-Cuban with every shade of jazz. Rounding out the group was a Native American guitar player, and a white rock drummer. While they also usually had three female backup singers – two had recently quit for various reasons. All in all, the unclassifiable gumbo of cultural influences gave the band a feel unlike any other.

Watching for a while from side-stage, it wasn't long before Chris joined in. Right away the new alto sax proved a good choice – it cut nicely through the band's swampy sound, answering the piano phrases and subtly re-balancing the tonal range. Mac's eyebrows rose as he evaluated the dynamic. The band's drummer, Richard 'Richie' Crooks recalled the moment, "All of a sudden Chris was there. We came into town and got up, started playing and bang, that was it. Mac knew about him and knew about Jeanette and Eleanor, and wanted to have some background singers. He hired the whole crew, all three of them. After that first gig it was just obvious that the guy belonged there." While back on his feet and moving forward again, where the hand of fate would guide Chris from here was anybody's guess.

By then Blind Faith had blown into town for their American debut at Madison Square Garden on July 12th. Delaney and Bonnie (Bramlett), a husband/wife team supported by a crack band of players was the opening act. As it turned out, their guitar player was a self-exiled Englishman named Dave Mason. In the insular world of rock 'n roll, perhaps it wasn't that odd a coincidence, but New York City seemed to possess a peculiar magnetism to draw Steve, Chris and Dave near each other again. This time the stratas were well defined – Blind Faith, which quickly sold out the twenty thousand seats in the huge cavern of Madison Square Garden was well above anything that Delaney and Bonnie could draw on their own, while Dr. John was more or less a cult figure, often lucky to attract hundreds. Of course, Chris was at the show. Dressed in jeans with a white tee-shirt adorned with a striped scarf and black jacket, he watched Blind Faith walk on from side-stage, a smile pressed thinly on his lips.

The Scandinavian shows having done wonders for their chops, Clapton's guitar rang with authority as Winwood's vocals pierced the echo of the cavernous arena. "Had To Cry Today" was a highlight – with Eric and Steve dueling each other on guitar; a great jam ensued that brought the crowd to its feet. But downsides remained and they were huge. In a show that Steve Winwood later referred to as "vulgar, crude, disgusting", the audience already wanted more than the band could offer, calling out for Cream and Traffic songs. Contributing to the spectacle, the band played in 'the round'. While the revolving stage gave everybody a look, the band resembled human ornaments in a giant music box. As in Hyde Park, the sense of connection to the audience was strained and distant. And while Ginger managed to get embroiled in a heated fracas with a rude fan near the end of the show, within the band the feelings were already quite cold.

Blind Faith's fracture had begun. From that first U.S. gig, Eric Clapton was disenchanted. Standing in the wings watching Delaney and Bonnie's band have a rollicking good time, it became obvious that top-notch musical chops were no compensation for a lack of sympathy and feel. Sickened by his own situation, afterward Clapton would head to Ungano's and then to the Record Plant to jam with Dr. John. Conversely, Steve would retreat to his hotel room with Penny.

The most serious threat to the band was also the least visible. While Ginger Baker's long status as a UK-registered heroin addict gave him access to a legal maintenance supply and thus a semblance of stability, here in the US, outright illegality and sketchy access were both problematic. To make matters worse, of late Ric Grech had also slipped into a dependency, and even Eric had dabbled. Although Steve's inner discipline meant he would have nothing to do with heavy drugs, the issue was impossible to ignore.

Herded forward by the managers, the group kept their commitments, raking in the cash as they took the tour to the bitter end... but it wasn't pretty. Penny Massot was there every step of the way, "There were so many drugs, all over the place. (It) started falling apart. Eric decided that he wasn't traveling with us; he wanted to go with Delaney and Bonnie in their bus. And Ginger was always needing to get heroin, so he was always in a state, and he would be flying first class. In the end, Blackwell picked up Steve and I and said, 'That's it, I'm taking you two and driving everywhere.' And Chris drove Steve and I from one gig to another. No wonder it didn't last."

Even the music couldn't save the day. Although many fans were pleased, few fond memories were held by the insiders, "It wasn't very satisfying, I don't think any of them were satisfied," was Penny's recollection. "Ginger just took over... he does a half an hour, his solos went on and on. And Eric was just tired by the whole thing. It just fell apart. Steve couldn't cope with all of that. It was hopeless; it wasn't very good at all."

In a parallel universe, Dr. John's Medicine Show began its own mad adventure. Planned as it happened, the band would play gigs from the east coast to the Midwest; small clubs one night and huge festivals the next. Traveling light, the haphazard 'tour' hit big cities as well as backwaters which Blind Faith would never glimpse. Naturally, problems were endemic, the first of which arose as they simply tried to get out of New York. "Basically we had two Volkswagen busses, and everybody piled into them, the whole band," Richie Crooks recalled. "It was pretty wild – we were sleeping on top of amplifiers in the back. But we were young and energetic, and wanted to do it. When Booker hooked up with us – we finished that gig at Unganos, and we got out of there at like four in the morning, and we were driving south (to Virginia). Everybody was wasted and Booker says, 'Oh, hey, I'm fine, I'm wide awake, I'm ready to drive.' So everybody fell asleep. All of a sudden the sun's coming up and we look out the window and see the New York skyline! He'd pulled over for gas, and took the wrong exit, and was on his way back to New York, when we were three quarters of the way to Virginia! And of course, we had to turn around and go back the way we came." Waking up to see they they'd driven all night to end up where they started, a dumbfounded Mac finally managed a frustrated croak in his classic Louisiana drawl: "You should'a nevva' let Booka' drive!"

Incredibly, amid the opportunities, the gig that could have catapulted them all to the big time slipped through their hands. On August 1st, The Dr. John 'Night Tripper' band played the Atlantic City Pop Festival, wowing a daytime audience of 110,000 unprepared for the undiluted Cajun brew. But while the Atlantic City event would end up a nearly forgotten footnote in rock history, another, offered in upstate New York would prove pivotal – the 'Woodstock Music and Art Fair'. Initially, Mac would accept, squeezing the band into the Volkswagens and heading north. But always suspicious when it came to finances, he made one last inquiry just to make sure they would be getting paid. Drummer Crooks recalled why they never made it, "We were, like ten miles from Woodstock – exit 21 on the New York throughway, and he pulls into a gas station and calls the manager. Mac says: 'Did you get the deposit?' He said, 'No, man, it's a zoo up there. Michael (Lang, festival organizer) said that if you show up, he's got cash for you.' And Mac said, 'Aah, fuck 'em. We ain't goin' up there, the guy's gonna rip us off!' And we turned around and went to West Virginia!"

Rebennack had his own version of the incident and didn't particularly want to take the rap for missing the legendary festival, "I had a call to Joe Glaser on the way there – he was the ABC booking agent. I said, 'Mr. Joe, what's happening?' He said, 'Well look, the check didn't clear', and *he said*, 'fuck the gig.' And he was always good. He managed Louis Armstrong, Dizzy Gillespie – he wasn't no lightweight in the bid'ness…" But either Rebennack's memory played tricks or the connection had been *really* long distance; by the time of Woodstock, Glaser had actually been dead for about a month.

Regardless of who was to blame, miss it they did, and it was only much later that anyone cared – much more craziness and aggravation lay ahead. Backtracking yet again, they followed the coastline south, finally landing a paying gig. On Friday, August 15th, the night they could have been playing to half a million people, the V.W.'s pulled up to the back door of 'The Portsmouth Lighthouse' in Portsmouth Virginia, maximum capacity: three hundred. The opening act was a regional blues/rock band known as 'Headstone Circus'.

Michael Johnstone played guitar for that band, and after their performance he stuck around to check out Dr. John. He'd heard *Gris Gris* and dug it, but like Chris, the record didn't prepare him for the show, "The band started playing – the rhythm section, half the band was on stage vamping – and then he (Dr. John) came out of the back, snaked through the club, a conga line with him and the girls, and a little entourage. He came out in a slow, almost like a funeral march, working his way through the crowd. So, he came out on stage with his robe and his Witch Doctor shit and all that – with the feathers, which was all Mardi-Gras stuff, and they went into 'Mama Roux', one of my favorite Dr. John songs. I remember the girls singing it just right, 'Mama roooo…'"

Besides *Gris Gris*, the band worked with material from a not-yet-recorded album, *Babylon*, which would take the themes even further, infusing recent cultural references and political statements. But the concerts were an entity unto themselves. Crooks explained, "It was a wonderful, musical experience. It was that snaky, hoodoo vibe kind of stuff going on – Medicine Man kind of thing. It was very slippery and slidey, almost jazz in a way – R&B and jazz stuff, really great to play. It was very, very, very cool… there was nothing out there like it happening."

A seasoned musician, Johnstone concurred, "When I saw them, I didn't quite put it together, where it came from. I know now, basically, that Mac was doing a sort of take-off on the Mardi-Gras parade, which kind of comes out of that 'Carnivale' in Rio – where everybody's dressed up in masks, and there's something about it that's kind of spooky; there's something about it that seems sort of naughty or weird, or evil, or maybe there's some voodoo involved. You can never quite put your finger on what they are saying, because they had this lingo. It was like, kinda, 'they know something I don't know.'"

Richie Crooks was emphatic, "Mac was the real deal. The Zulu parade, where all the tribes come together… that was where all that was stemming from. And Mac really believed in voodoo – good voodoo and bad voodoo. Oh yeah, the dressing room was always loaded up with candles and incense – he was steeped in it." The rituals were not just about the music either, Mac was also interested in using magic to try to influence events, and when necessary, certain people.

By now, Chris was aware that Mac was also associated with another magical practitioner who happened to be an old friend – Graham Bond. Back in Los Angeles the year before, Mac and Graham had actually tried to combine New Orleans hoodoo and Aleister Crowley's black magic to put the hurt on a malignant record company executive that had ominously held Mac's hand above a piranha tank as a threat. The explicit threat to ruin his means of livelihood was not taken lightly. Working up a full-on magical attack, Bond and Mac retaliated, but for all of their spells, chants and colored candles, the target remained unaffected. As Mac would later say, their energies had been "misdirected."

Bond's time in L.A. left other traces. While some saw in him only a sweet and giving man, others, such as songwriter Harry Nillson would walk away from an encounter with a strong desire never to be in Graham's presence again. For Chris, stories like these produced only a knowing smirk and a quiet chuckle.

Mystical aspects aside, the Night Tripper's music stood on its own merits. "They were received well and the music was so compelling that I can't imagine them *not* being received well – anywhere they would play in the world, it was just that good," was Johnstone's verdict. Looking back on it, Mac himself had to agree; with the band he'd put together, the musical synergy was simply there in spades. "Yeah, Chris, James Booker was in it. Oh yeah. Listen… Richie Crooks was in the band, Didimus was on the road then; the band was kickin'!"

Crooks recalled Chris as adding something integral to the sound, "It was just his approach, his looseness, his inventiveness. The basic arrangements were already there… but the great thing about that band was, if you caught a vibe, you could vary from night to night what you played. He was like *constantly* inventing stuff. And Mac was the same way. Whatever moved you on whatever night, you could expand a little on it, venture out. Chris was always way, way outside with everything." So it was that half a world away from home, Chris would find himself amidst a band of musical renegades and pirates, and the fit was perfect. His sympathy with Mac was not unlike what he'd had with Winwood or Hendrix, a rare match indeed. So with the psychic connection again in place, the door was open for his best music to flow – which was not to say that the sailing ahead would be smooth; quite the opposite.

*

Having brought his Maestro sound system on the road, Chris was experimenting with it – switching between that, straight tenor and flute to help shape the mood. Unfortunately, his prized new alto sax never made it out of New York, an early victim of James Booker's drug habit. Mac recalled how Chris's lack of street savvy brought on the loss of his horn, "One of the things I always remember from that, Chris bought an alto saxophone and Booker asked him, could he see it? And all of a sudden – he didn't even know that Booker could play an alto sax – Booker started playing, it sounded killer. So while Booker's playing, Chris says, 'If you want to play it, use it.' Booker says, 'Sure I'll use it.' A day or two later, he (Chris) says, 'Well, I need the horn.' And Booker says 'Well, I pawned it, and I sold the ticket.' And Chris says (dejected tone), 'That was a Selmer alto; I just lucked out finding it…' He hadn't been in the game as long as Booker and us. It was like a shock to his knees because it was such a good horn."

At least he went forward without any illusions. Now neck deep in the heroin culture of the late '60's – unlike more affluent groups with drug problems, Chris's bedraggled band required deception, theft or whatever it took to keep the habit together. By the time they got down to Virginia, it was all quite out in the open, and not surprisingly, Chris seemed to have fallen into it as well. After the show in Portsmouth, Mac and some of the others made a beeline to Johnstone, thinking he knew where to score, "Dr. John comes up to me and says, 'That girl over there says you know where to get some dope.' I might have, but on this particular night, I didn't. And he said, 'Do you know anybody that can?' He was looking for heroin. It never happened, but he was schmoozing me for that and I think in the background, Chris and a couple of other people in the band were also looking." Richie Crooks recalled, "It's not like it's an avenue I didn't go down – there was a lot of other stuff to partake in. There was always like a gaggle of people around, dealing a variety of things – and Chris was privy to a lot of avenues. Whatever his thing was, whatever he ingested, he would get on that stage and just play his heart out, every single time."

Michael Johnstone ended up spending the evening with Dr. John's band, in a motel room, hanging out and smoking until he crashed on the floor. Seeing them off in the morning, Johnstone told Mac about recordings planned with Headstone Circus, which prompted some unsolicited but hard-learned advice: "Right before he shut the door to the van he said, 'Hang on to your publishin', don't let them motherfuckas beat you outta your tunes.'"

The road less traveled proved to be long, torturous, and quite unforgiving. Going wherever a gig could be hustled meant a lot of inefficient zigzagging and backtracking. Mac was, to put it mildly, frustrated. "We had this crazy-assed booking agent; he was just fucking up royal. He was like, booking us one gig, like in the U.S., and one in Canada and the band mostly couldn't get in. We had guys on the gig like Didimus, who had an Ethiopian passport, and a Cuban passport. You can't get out of this country if you're here with two passports!" So as great as the music was going, the living proved hard as nails. Packed in the vans, the band was cramped, dirty and sometimes dope-sick.

It was already obvious to Chris that Jeanette was a restless free spirit; she stayed with who she wanted, whenever she wanted. Even in Portsmouth they partied separately. Although never happy about it, Chris already knew that her gypsy-like ways could only be accepted. In an odd way, he even admired her for it, since Chris's own life was based on having the freedom to roam as circumstances and mood moved him.

Having been away for months, Chris finally wrote home to let his family know how he was doing. Trying to reassure them, he said that he would be sending some money and told Stephanie, "I bought you something very pretty, you will like it." He also addressed his mother's concerns, saying: "Dear Mom, please don't worry about me, because I know you always worry…" But he didn't paint an altogether rosy picture either, letting them know about problems in New York. While he never mentioned the sax, he did tell them that someone had taken his stage clothes and money. He also described his travels across America as hot and dusty, and his homesickness for "the green pastures of England." As it was, he felt compelled to stay with the tour awhile longer to regain enough cash to cover the losses. It would take a while – he was making exactly $100 a week.

Between the thieves and drug habits, the chance of Chris getting home with *any* money in his pocket looked less and less likely. The roads through the southern U.S. carried them to receptive crowds, but were not the best or safest for finding heroin or other drugs. By the time the band hit Chicago, there was some desperation to score. Mac, Booker and Chris headed to a likely section of town and had a look around. Mac recalled some complications, "Oh, that thing in Chicago? Me and Booker went to cop at somebody's pad in Chicago, under the L-Train. And the cops said, 'You all can't be in this neighborhood.' Man, there was gang kids on all of the corners, with these yellow berets and shit. We didn't give a fuck, we was on our way to do some goodies. So we go, 'fuck that shit!' So the police said, 'Get out of there'. The next thing, they throw us in the paddy wagon and drove us – they didn't take us to jail or nothin' – they just told us to get the hell out of the neighborhood."

Shoved out of the police van, the cops gave a last incentive not to return. As the trio turned to walk away, one of the cops lunged forward swinging a nightstick that nailed Chris, hard, across the back of the head. Falling face-first on the street, he was knocked nearly unconscious. While unsure of the reason for the attack, Mac theorized it was simply the Chicago cop's version of a strong suggestion, "I think they clocked him as a warning." Helped back to his feet by Mac and Booker, all he could do was hobble back to the van, dizzy, dopeless and bleeding. At this bleak nadir, Chris no doubt wished he'd heeded Jim Capaldi's warnings, and stayed home. For better or worse the tour continued, but for the rest of his life a jagged scar creased the top of his scalp, a perpetual reminder of that rough night in Chicago.

Whatever good times the music offered, the tour proved to be a chaotic ramble that wore them all down. Mac, having survived every kind of scrape in his day, had some sympathy for the sensitive, homesick Englishman that had fallen into their company in the crazy summer of '69. "Back then, it was just like – it was just one thing on top of another thing that had nothing to do with him per se, but it was just (like that) when he came on the set. Problems? We had *strings* of them. I mean, even Jeanette and them were subbing for the regular girls – we had like, one girl was in the psych ward, the other was dealing with her children, the other was a dancer, on and on…"

By the time they limped into Mac's adopted hometown of L.A., the Medicine Show had clearly lost its mojo. Although he'd assembled one of the best (albeit nearly unknown) bands in the world, with too little money and too much of everything else, all were quite unhealthy and ready for a rest. Mac wasted no time in cutting the strings, making sure the band knew that it was time to look elsewhere for employment: "It was like, well, I fired them all…"

*

Blind Faith quietly expired as well, although a little further to the west. Having cashed in their last mega-show (apparently in Honolulu Hawaii), the band – such as it was – simply ceased to exist. While Winwood headed home, Eric Clapton flew back to California, deciding to pursue the good times he'd experienced on the bus with Delaney and Bonnie. Hanging with them in L.A., he almost immediately joined the group outright, contented for the time being to take on the role of sideman.

Musing on the ill-fated Blind Faith experiment, Eric would later come to understand that the communal/family vibe he'd vainly sought had actually been present in Traffic all along. What had at first looked like time wasting – the running around the countryside, hanging out, and just being friends turned out to be integral to the band's appeal and music. Clapton would say, "At first I hadn't understood that. I think I even had contempt for what they were doing. But later, I realized that Traffic were the English version of The Band."

As for Chris and Jeanette, after all that had transpired, there didn't seem much left to do in America. Los Angeles was hot, temperature-wise, but culturally rather flat. While staying on for a few weeks, the exciting vibes of '68 had dried up, at least for Chris. Instead, L.A. led him to the contradictory feelings of being both, "laid back and…rather panicky." So it was time to depart, but even that wasn't going to be easy. Having crisscrossed the country chasing one shitty gig after another, Chris finished the tour as he started it – broke. In the end, he had to wire home for money, which got him a three day train trip to New York, and then a jet back to England. Soon after, he would round up a little more cash and send for Jeanette.

With his love in tow, they went back to the Midlands and Corngreaves Hall. Home at last, he finally found real relaxation visiting with his family and catching up with old friends. But in showing Jeanette the sights, it didn't take long to realize that she would never be content with a rural cottage, nor the industrial drabness of Birmingham. Bustling London however proved a different story; she loved it. And with Chris very much in love with *her*, keeping his dear Jeanette happy – whatever (and wherever) that might take, would become his primary mission.

*

Jim Capaldi was living once again at the apartment on Cromwell Road in London that he and Chris had shared in the early Traffic days. Having spent many months at loose ends back in Birmingham, hanging out with Anna and soothing his nerves with endless spins of Van Morrison's *Astral Weeks* on the stereo, Jim was finally rebuilding some psychic strength, emerging slowly but steadily from his low. With Chris's old room in the apartment vacant, Jim offered it back to him and Jeanette. While cramped, it was close to where the action was and would be their first place together.

('Blues, Booze and Rivers of Blood', Nigel Williamson, Uncut, 5/2004)

('Steve Winwood, Rock's Elder Aristocrat', Timothy White, Musician, No. 48, October 1982)

('Traffic…', Ray Townley, DownBeat, 1/1975)

('Under a Hoodoo Moon', Mac Rebennack, St Martin's Press, 1995)

CHAPTER TWENTY

JOHN BARLEYCORN MUST DIE!

Having walked away from the wreckage of Blind Faith, Steve Winwood returned to the Cottage, apparently to recover and ponder his future. But unbeknownst to most, the groundwork for his new path had already been quietly laid. Matching Steve with Guy Stevens – an energetic Record Producer with wild afro-style hair – Chris Blackwell had given the two carte blanche at Island's recently completed London studio. If not quite top secret, the project was still huge – they were about to embark on sessions for Steve's first solo album. While possessing little technical experience, Stevens' ace in the hole was a great feel, and he was often able to draw the best work out of artists.

Work would begin with some covers, the first being Bob Dylan's "Visions of Johanna", which looked great on paper but found Steve struggling to keep up with all the wordy verses. Next came a more compact (and energetic) "Great Balls of Fire"; but even on this safe ground, before long it was clear something wasn't clicking. A lack of external input was part of it. Having taken the concept of 'solo' to heart, Winwood was doing all of the instrumental parts himself. While the process could be tightly controlled, momentum and inspiration became issues. While Steve had a couple of original pieces to work with, Mad Shadows, as Stevens was calling the project, clearly needed more assistance than he could give it.

Splitting his time between the Cottage, where he was trying to write, and London when he needed to record, Steve was in Berkshire one fine fall afternoon when Chris and Jeanette stopped in. They were neither the first or last to do so. With the word of Blind Faith's demise circulating, musicians of all stripes descended, eager to see if they could get in on whatever was next for the newly available superstar. But as the visits increased, the creative vibe dissipated in an inverse relationship. Penny Massot recalled, "Toward the end, the Cottage got quite mad; it was getting too silly out there. A lot of musicians from town would go down there and get out of their heads and career around the Downs, causing chaos in the area around there. Not too much work was getting done."

Ginger Baker certainly knew his way around the back roads of Berkshire. Despite Blind Faith's crash landing, he too would soon make a beeline back to ground zero. With a new musical plan already in mind, he arrived to find Steve swarmed by musicians yet seemingly unattached. So opportunity beckoned; could the Cottage hold the nucleus of the band to rise from Blind Faith's ashes? Taking a gamble, he started at the top. Hearing him out, Steve would indeed agree to join Ginger's project, at least for a couple of gigs. From there, the other pickings simply fell off the tree.

Arms flailing, Nigerian born Remi Kabaka looked up from his conga drums to notice Ginger's assessing gaze, "I used to go there a lot. One night I went up there, I'm kicking ass on drums, Steve playing the bass with his feet, the organ with his hands… and everybody started walking in, Roger Daltry, Pete Townshend, Joe Cocker... by two a.m. the house is packed with incredible musicians, everybody just coming down to play! So, I'm doing this and Ginger Baker walks in, he says, 'Steve, this guy's something else man! Are you that crazy African drummer?' I said, 'Yeah, but I can't play like you!' He told me that Blind Faith had just folded up so he wanted to form his own group, 'Ginger Baker's Air Force', and that's why he came to Steve's cottage. He came to ask Steve, saw me there, and Denny Laine was hanging with me – Moody Blues. Chris was playing tenor and flute; he came with Steve to join the band. It was a gas man!"

By the time he finished making the rounds, Ginger's modern 'Big Band' would include ten. Besides Steve, Chris and Remi, ex-Moody Blues man Denny Laine would play guitar while Ric Grech was back on bass. Respected British woodwind player Harold McNair would double Chris on flute/sax while Ginger's teacher and mentor Phil Seamen would add more drums. Then there was Graham Bond. Having given Ginger his first big shot in the business in the early 60's, he would be invited to play alto sax and more keyboards. To top things off Jeanette and Eleanor Barooshian would do backing vocals, adding spice to the otherwise all male crew.

If the project looked like a potential mess – it was, right from the start. But Air Force did manage to fly, if not straight, at least high. While some fans might have hoped to hear something like Blind Faith (with horns), what emerged was more of an Africanized jazz band with Jimmy Smith and Roland Kirk accents.

CHAPTER TWENTY

The first show in Birmingham was ragged, although some reviewers liked it quite a lot. The second, at the old Royal Albert Hall was by all accounts much better and a recording made by Jimmy Miller captured it – with members of the Rolling Stones and Georgie Fame in the audience cheering them on, they all played well above the rehearsals.

Amid the free-flying outfit, Chris traded flute solos with the legendary Harold McNair and wailed on electrified tenor, where he alternately vamped as part of the horn section or soloed with intensity. And as much as the hyper-creative nights with Dr. John had done wonders for his confidence, sharing the stage again with Steve Winwood must have felt as comfortable as slipping into an old shoe.

Singing in tandem with Eleanor, Jeanette was a hit too; the two female voices balanced the instrumental heaviness like a pair of sympathetic angels. Visually she was fantastic as well – with her hair dyed coal black, cut in bangs across her eyes, and wearing a body length see-through gown Jeanette finally embodied the image of the ethereal Egyptian Princess that she had long portrayed herself to be.

With only two shows behind them, the original Air Force finished when Steve checked out, although by then Ginger was pushing for more. As for Chris – having turned up for a rehearsal drunk and subsequently messing up a horn part – Baker's blood would come to a rapid boil. Rising from his seat he flung a drumstick hitting Chris in the back of the head with enough force to cut his scalp. The sense of déjà vu from the all too similar incident in Chicago being unmistakable, he would walk away bleeding – and didn't come back. He had a better place to be anyway.

*

If Chris had somehow adapted to a life of 'take things as they come', Jim Capaldi was still struggling with the cards he'd been dealt. Lonely and bewildered since the demise of Mason, Capaldi, Wood and Frog, that summer he wandered in a fog of loss and self-recrimination. But as the fall of '69 rolled around, the sky seemed to brighten all at once. Recalling a sense of magic in the air at a rock festival that took place on August 31st, Jim witnessed a performance that did wonders for his state of mind, "I went to the Isle of Wight to see Dylan; it was like a pilgrimage you know. The feeling of Dylan, suddenly being back from this long spell – the motorcycle accident – he hadn't been around. He was with The Band, and people would go there like they were going to see some 'holy man' on top of a mountain."

With more than one hundred and fifty thousand attendees, the Isle of Wight Festival was something like England's 'Woodstock' and the vibes were similar. With The Beatles' John, George and Ringo in the audience, and only months before the Stones' Altamont debacle would cast a shadow over the rock scene, the Isle of Wight carried an optimism that youth culture was still on the right track. As great as it was for Jim to see Dylan again (dressed in white like a visiting deity), someone even more important to him was only a few steps away.

Standing with Steve Winwood near the backstage entrance as Dylan wrapped his set up, Penny Massot made some quick mental calculations as she watched Jim and Anna coming through the crowd. Having lived through the Blind Faith experiment and Steve's struggle to make his album, she believed she had the perspective to see what needed to happen next. As she recalled, "I was always promoting them (Chris and Jim) – all the time, *all the time*, with Steve. I was madly in love with Traffic. I was their biggest fan. To me they were the best band that had ever been. I'm older than they are, and I come from a jazz background – I sort of come from Jimmy McGriff, and Jack McDuff, and all that lot. It's not like I was some 'rock chick'. So I knew they were an amazing band, they were truly fabulous."

Moments later, Jim was before them. Hoping to remind Dylan of their Witley Court ghost adventure – instead he was face to face with his former band mate. Residual bitterness quickly swallowed, he smiled as they made small talk. While cordial, the conversation ended with no clue as to whether Steve had anything more on his mind. But as Jim turned to leave, Penny caught his eye. As he recalled, "I was with Anna, we were near the back stage door. I ran into Penny and Steve, and she just makes some cryptic expression to me, 'It's time to come back to the Cottage', you know, with a look she was giving me: 'Time to do it again, another go.' So I said, 'Okay.'"

So while never directly asked to return, Jim was suddenly back. And from the first meeting up at Island's studio it was clear to him that Mad Shadows needed help. Jim noted, "Steve had a few tracks – he had 'Glad' going, and I came up with the rest, 'Freedom Rider', and so on. He had 'Empty Pages', and I stuck the last verse on there." As for finished tracks, he really only had one – "Stranger To Himself", although "Every

Mother's Son" was nearly there. And while excellent songs were growing, the product was also still lacking in some ill-defined way. Then as if preordained, the missing piece of the puzzle walked through the door.

Chris's return shook things up. Jim noted, "We've got these few bits of ideas going and all that. We didn't have any real intention about a shape or a concept or anything… and then Chris rolls up." True to form, his presence seemed to change the character of the music. With little discussion, the three simply got back to work, and the results were immediate and noticeable; the previously uncertain album was now a lively, viable entity – Traffic had been reborn.

What did it feel like to be back together? Jim was quick to answer, "It felt great, quite natural. We're all introverts, the three of us. Even though I was more outward and would be the one with all of the energy and making statements – it was all out of nerves. We were all very, very introverted. So we could be together without even thinking about it, like it was a second skin, you know. We didn't have to explain, talk or do anything. We melded together, like three people out in a storm hanging onto a life raft."

The reunion couldn't have come at a better time, certainly for Jim, who'd recently been reminded how far his star had fallen. Around this time, he'd peeked into a rehearsal space in a London studio to see Eric Clapton working with John Lennon and Yoko Ono. Excited by the assemblage of talent, Jim gestured for Clapton to meet him at the door and inquired in a low voice if it would be okay if he could come in and hang out for a bit. Going back to the others, Eric conveyed the request to Lennon while pointing toward Capaldi. Glancing over his granny glasses to see Jim's hopeful smile, Lennon – whose own expression never changed – blithely replied: "Who? Never heard of him…"

As for Chris, while never wanting the break from Traffic either, musically, the time away hadn't been wasted. His experimentation with the Gibson Maestro effects system having paid off, now he added another layer – a guitar player's 'wah wah' pedal, also fed through the control box. The combination proved crucial, producing a raspy, gurgling tone unique to Chris. And he wasn't shy in using it. On "Glad", the sprightly Floyd Kramer-styled instrumental track Steve had written, Chris would take the first solo, spinning textural contrasts as his foot went up and down on the pedal.

Grafted onto the end of "Glad", "Freedom Rider" would find itself part of a mini-suite. The pairing would prove inspired; as the former's upbeat instrumental romp balanced the latter's darker lyrical tone. But "Freedom Rider's" dynamic swing still needed work. At about midpoint the chords ascend, leaving a gap where an undefined but crucial solo was needed to incarnate the message of the song – the sense of rising above life's sometimes paralyzing fears. Chris filled it by releasing a stream of long, easy notes that built into a fluttering torrent. Knowing he was on to something, he doubled and then triple-tracked his parts, evoking the image of a lone bird merging with others, intertwining their voices as they soared together.

"Glad/Freedom Rider" would prove a triumph of the art of the trio – a near perfect complement of Jim's lyrical beauty, Steve's deep musicality and Chris's intuitive grasp of the emotional path. Combined with the positive energy which poured out after the break from each other, this was one of the most powerful statements Traffic would ever make. Even so, the best was yet to come.

Having struggled for years to contribute music that would be reflected in the credits, Chris now took another approach. One thing he was the acknowledged master of was finding music that inspired others. "Feeling Good" had almost certainly been his idea during the first Traffic-go-round, and "Long Black Veil" had worked out quite well for MCW&F. Now he was ready to try again.

"John Barleycorn" was a British folk song that Chris had fallen in love with years before. And, in fact, he'd already introduced it to Jim and Steve back in '68, although it seemed that neither remembered. But time had not dimmed his affection for the song he'd first heard on the Waterson's "Frost and Fire: A Calendar of Ceremonial Folk Songs". Even before the Traffic album, Chris had tried to guide them all in this direction – merging the contemporary with the ancient. Now that they had reformed, he would sit Jim and Steve down to listen to the deceptively simple song again.

This appreciation for the primordial was the key to Chris's attachment to "John Barleycorn". While some read 'Barleycorn' simply as a rendering of country folks' appreciation for alcohol, Chris understood the real story lay below the surface. More than mere folk-tale, the myths and songs of the early Britons honored plants as sentient beings inextricably tied to themselves. As he had told *Rolling Stone* back in '68, "The Killing of the Corn" – as he called it, was, if anything a pagan version of the crucifixion story – life's renewal tied to the sacrifice of one for the good of all. And at one time the myth may have actually been made flesh. Legends persist that some country folk selected an actual 'Corn King' whose every whim was indulged for an entire year. On the anniversary of his crowning, the 'King' would have his throat slit and body dragged across the farm fields so the blood would bless and fertilize the coming year's crop. In that context, Barleycorn's emphasis of sacrifice and transformation plowed deeply into the human condition and retained the power to reach out across the centuries. And with Traffic's Cottage literally surrounded the plant, the connection was also as personal as could be:

> There were three men come out of the west
>
> Their fortunes for to try,
> And these three men made a solemn vow:
> John Barleycorn should die.
> They've ploughed, they've sown, they've harrowed him in,
> Throwed clods on his head.
> And these three men made a solemn vow:
> John Barleycorn was dead.
>
> They've let him lie for a very long time
> Till the rain from hea'en did fall,
> And little Sir John sprung up his head
> And soon amazed them all.
> They've let him stand till midsummer day
> Till he looked both pale and wan.
> And little Sir John's grown a long, long beard
> And so become a man.
>
> They've hired men with the scythes so sharp
> To cut him off at the knee.
> They've rolled him and tied him by the waist,
> Serving him most barbarously.
> They've hired men with the sharp pitchforks
> Who pricked him to the heart.
> And the loader, he served him worse than that
> For he's bound him to the cart.
>
> They've wheeled him round and around the field
> Till they came into the barn
> And there they've made a solemn mow
> Of poor John Barleycorn.
> They've hired men with the crab tree sticks
> To cut him skin from bone,
> And the miller, he has served him worse than that
> For he's ground him between two stones.
>
> Here's little Sir John in the nutbrown bowl
> And here's brandy in the glass
> And little Sir John in the nutbrown bowl
> Proved the strongest man at last.
> For the huntsman, he can't hunt the fox
> Nor so loudly to blow his horn,
> And the tinker, he can't mend kettles nor pots
> Without a little barley corn.

Even years later, Jim Capaldi remained dumbfounded at the bounty Chris had laid on their table, "He shows up with the greatest thing, which gives us our first hit – and really put us on the map – 'John Barleycorn'. We would have never come up with that, we would never have really had the insight, never have recognized and grasped what a brilliant little piece it was. He found it, dug it up on an album by the Waterson's, who were just cousins and brothers in this vocal group doing ancient British folk songs. And he had the album… Chris recognized it straight away – that was wonderful, what a gift! He played it for us, and we went, 'Wow, incredible!' So we went and cut it with acoustic and flute, and it became our first big hit – it went gold, the album. And of course, it became like an anthem in America. It's all down to Chris, and his awareness."

Traffic's rendering wrought magnificence from simplicity. Whereas the Waterson's version (based loosely on Robert Burns' interpretation, published in 1782) had stripped the song to a purely vocal core, Traffic's, while still sparse, held even more emotional depth. Following the Waterson's melody with a textured overlap of Steve and Jim's voices, they added acoustic guitar, flute, a few chimes of the triangle, quiet piano and a dash of percussion. The restraint paid off – the ancient soul of the song remained undiluted. Winwood's vocals, joined by Capaldi's were much softer in tone than the Waterson's but even more compelling. And with the opening line, "There were three men…" 'Barleycorn' could also be read as a personal reference to them as well.

As the 'Barleycorn' session tapes rolled it was all sounding great, but with the final take approaching Chris modified his approach. In the place of brief accents and a traditional solo, he instead wove expressive lines around each verse, altering and intensifying the feeling as the stages of Barleycorn's life unfolded. While making the song a little longer, the extra minute and a half was worth it – a deep, subliminal sympathy for the song's protagonist could then sprout in the mind of the listener. Of the myriad versions handed down over the centuries, this interpretation would stand alone – only here is John Barleycorn's *voice* actually heard.

Chris's contribution was in fact a small stroke of genius – the last, essential piece of acoustic architecture. Recorded in an era that would increasingly tilt toward bombast and overstatement, the contrast couldn't have been clearer – "John Barleycorn" beckoned to the path less traveled. Luminous, full of emotion, and tinged with a drop of the Corn King's blood at its heart, Traffic now possessed a quiet masterpiece.

The last song now in the bag, there was now enough material for the album. Prior to this, there had been some thought to calling the LP *Freedom Rider*, but the proper name now stared them all in the face – *John Barleycorn Must Die*. And so it was that the long awaited 'trio album' was born, though in another parallel to the title song, it took the death and reincarnation of Traffic to make it happen.

With the once skeletal album now fleshed out, the excitement proved contagious. Rehearsals for a tour began immediately – with the unspoken agreement that Traffic would function as the trio; Dave Mason's exclusion was apparently implicit. That aside, there would be one non-negotiable condition of restarting Traffic. Steve made it clear that from here out, the band's leadership would lie in his hands alone. At least, now, it was out in the open – the pretension of democracy at long last cleared from the books. Certainly, for Chris, a musical partnership with Steve was all he desired, and once again that was in hand.

The real concern was murkier and well below the surface. In the wake of his previous unexpected departure, from here the others trust of Steve's commitment would remain uncertain. Penny Massot recalled, "Nobody really spoke to Steve – nobody really opened up. He had an aura about him that wasn't really welcoming, very remote." With their leader's intentions less knowable, the confidence of purpose once so vital to Traffic's being also slipped away. And by now the others knew the drill – changes could come at any time.

When asked if he felt any insecurity about the new Traffic that seemed to be working out so well, Jim was unequivocal and emphatic, "*Always!* From then on, I never felt secure about anything. I never felt sure that anything was definite."

There was one last, very personal issue for Chris. As their new record was prepared for release, he would discover that "John Barleycorn" – the song that he had uncovered and added so much to – had been attributed simply as "Trad., arrangement/Winwood". With those few words printed on the back cover of the album, the credit for arranging the (otherwise 'authorless') traditional song had been assigned solely to Steve. Whatever other emotions Chris felt on learning this, he was certainly hurt.

Jim questioned the situation as well, although he too only spoke of it years later, "He (Chris) didn't even get a fucking credit. All you see is: 'Arranged – Winwood' on the album. So Winwood probably gets the royalties! It's a fucking travesty. He (Chris) created it. Not creating the song, but created us doing it." But in 1970, confronting the issue would have likely introduced tension, and even instability, so any negative thoughts were first rationalized and then buried; keeping the fragile 'dream of Traffic' alive was more important. But for Chris the memory of the exclusion would linger like a prickly burr stuck to his mind – a nagging, low-level irritant that years later could sometimes flare into outrage.

*

Word began to filter out to the rock world of Traffic's reconstitution. The anticipation of their return by both fans and critics was genuine and surprisingly deep. In early spring, *Rolling Stone* sent a reporter over to check things out. They found a band confident and supremely adept in what they could do with just three musicians: "Traffic's new music has been pared down to the most basic structure. Rhythm, bass and melody functions have been meted out among the three. In a new song suite, 'Freedom Rider', for example, Jim starts out with an orgy of drums, accompanied by Chris on bongos. Chris then begins a bass riff on sax, Stevie entering on organ with melodic patterns spinning out and back into bass riffs while Chris solos. Stevie takes over with lonesome, crafty, wrong note blues and floating suspensions backed by Chris on bass organ. Then Stevie sings, 'Like a hurricane around your heart', as Chris goes from flute to sax and back again, Jim's rhythms binding everything."

Clearly the enthusiasm was there, but as before, the intricate dance required to make the trio work was precarious. With Steve and Chris shifting places and instruments throughout the set, sometimes within a single song, the sound was much richer and fuller than seemed possible for three. But there was also risk; if any were off, the whole thing threatened utter collapse. On the threshold of a new beginning, none of these scary possibilities mattered however – Traffic was back – with loads of energy and a nearly clean slate to do things the way they should have been done in the first place.

With the exciting but draining road stretching out in front of them again what Chris really wanted was to get back to the source of their muse – the now legendary Berkshire Cottage. In early March, as the album was being given the final touches, he reaffirmed where he thought they all ought to be, "We can't get the same atmosphere in the studio as we get at the cottage. There is a timeless atmosphere there and we like to work at our own pace." Even after all that they'd been through, that place always held the promise of revealing a little more. But an insurmountable obstacle suddenly emerged – they were being cast out. William Pigott-Brown was selling off his land in the Downs, including the Sheepcote Farmhouse. As the incubator for so much of their creativity, the loss would be incalculable – especially for Chris. With all of the turmoil that life had sent his way, even the *thought* that he could go there had always comforted him. Now he would have to find other ways to recharge and soothe his soul.

According to Penny, Steve's share of the profits from the massive Blind Faith tour had given Steve enough money to buy his own place in Gloucestershire. A very old stone farmhouse with significant acreage. In some ways it would become a replacement – with a 'music room' set up and equipped to play and later to record in. But it wasn't really. First and foremost it was Steve's dwelling – a place to visit for a while. Things splintered even more when Jim later bought his own manor house, a beautiful place in Marlow in Buckinghamshire, removed from the bustle of London.

So the communal days of the enigmatic Berkshire Cottage were gone for good. And maybe it was for the best. Certainly the times had changed, but it seemed that the negative energy Jim had noticed there in late '68 was about to discharge again, this time with tragic results.

Not long after Traffic cleared out, a new tenant, a woman in her early twenties named Francis Taylor moved in. A Berkshire native, Taylor was a friend to the family that lived in the Cottage prior to Traffic – the Maxwell-Hislops. Pat Boyd knew her and described Francis as "a pretty girl, with long blond hair, a bit of a beatnik." The Cottage was a natural place for Taylor, since she had a large dapple grey horse called "King", which she took for regular jaunts in the countryside. It seemed that the bucolic lifestyle so treasured by Chris and Traffic had been passed along for Francis to enjoy. But before long something would darken the young woman's disposition.

There were divergent opinions as to what actually altered Francis's state of mind. Some believed that she was depressed over a tangled affair with a married man; others thought it had something to do with Traffic. Regardless, living alone at the farmhouse her mood slowly veered off kilter. Returning from the village one day with gallons of paint, she furiously painted the living room walls and all of the furniture black. Surrounding herself in darkness, not long after, the body of Francis Taylor would be found hanging at the end of a rope in the upstairs' bedroom previously belonging to Steve Winwood.

As tragic and inexplicable as it was, there was a little more to the story – a postscript – and perhaps the final word on the ghostly status of Traffic's Cottage. The next tenant was a recently divorced mother named Shirley Sheldon who, undeterred by tales of spirits or suicide, moved in after Francis's untimely death.

Arriving with her children in tow, in no-nonsense fashion she repainted and settled in to raise her family. Now a grey-haired English grandmother, Shirley still lived in the house more than thirty-five years later. She is quick to assure that there is nothing supernatural in the Sheepcote Farmhouse, *now*. "I've never felt anything spooky, except when the floorboards creak. If you're not prepared to hear that – it's not ghosts; it's floorboards – because this house has to 'breathe'. This house was built straight on bricks or soil. The main walls, the outer walls, there's wood in them, and they are filled with this 'wattle and daub' – well, it all sort of creaks. It's just sort of expanding and contracting. I think you'll find, truly that it's all the creaking. It happens at night, when everybody's quiet and in bed. I hear it still, and it doesn't worry me."

As rational and reassuring as Shirley is about the non-supernatural origin of the sounds that the dwelling makes even today, she presents one major caveat – based on an incident occurring when she first crossed the house's threshold: "When I came, and this is without a word of lie, when I opened that front door, I felt something… *unimaginable* pass through me. It was just as if a spirit had gone – pffft – and out the door. And I felt that."

Whether there ever really was a ghost or other presence at the Sheepcote Farmhouse is, of course, open to interpretation. But if it *was* Traffic's 'Tibbets', perhaps he'd finally had his fill of 'mischief', and had simply gone back to that old brick-lined well where the teenage boy hanged himself so many years ago. Surrounded by a copse of trees near the house, the well is today as it was then; a dank tunnel into the earth surrounded by fallen leaves and stinging nettles – as dark and foreboding as ever.

There would be other unsettling news. Around the time that Traffic was getting started up again, their faithful roadie, Albert Heaton was injured in a horrible automobile accident. In the interval between the first and second incarnations of Traffic, Albert had gone with Spooky Tooth – evolved from the VIP's – the band he originally worked for. One night Albert was been sent to pick up a car for Spooky Tooth member Mike Harrison that had recently been repaired. Driving an American model he wasn't used to, Albert lost control and crashed as he veered to the wrong side of the road. While surviving, his brain was badly injured and he went into a deep, non-responsive coma.

Christie Nichols, still living with the Hamilton family in Blewbury, recalled that Helen visited Albert nearly daily in the hospital, using all of her energies to try to help him. "Helen has this magical way of communicating… she's just extremely gentle. Her personality, her energy would just permeate the whole situation. Helen said that he communicated via feeling and movement and was immersed in a higher plane of understanding. And she got him to come out of the coma, to respond." Helen even considered taking Albert back to her own house, where he could get more attention, and hopefully recover fully. Perhaps threatened by this, Albert's mother subsequently moved him to a care facility to the north in Carlisle.

Sometime later Chris, Steve, Helen and Christie all drove up to see him. While finding Albert only semi-conscious, in the midst of what sounded like gibberish he began to excitedly tell the group about a "huge package of hashish" he had hidden for them – buried under a tree somewhere. Leaning in for the rest of the story, the glimmer would twinkle out as he reverted to silence. Looking at each other and smiling, it seemed that Albert had found one more joke to share. Unfortunately, he never got any better; continuing his existence in a twilight state, Albert Heaton died in the same facility about three years later.

As for Chris, while he may have instinctively desired to retreat back to the country to recharge the muse and recover his energy, that door was closed. Starting over in a new decade, from here on nearly everything would be different.

*

The first concert scheduled for the return of Traffic was in London, at the Roundhouse. But before that, they did a warm up gig at a club in April (the 18th) at Mothers in Erdington, Birmingham – the place where Mason, Capaldi, Wood and Frog had baffled an audience the year before. The still dapper Don Carless, his DJ Twitch (now a kaftan wearing hippie), and a lot of the old Elbow Room crowd was there. Secure among their friends, the return of the 'real' Traffic went over very well indeed. With a rare chance to start again in an intimate club of three hundred, the trio was a natural – the music flowed freely with no stress at all.

The Roundhouse was a different matter. The large, domed, former railway terminal would be the real first exposure of a reformed band that had only rarely played as a trio in England. If that wasn't pressure enough, the bulk of the show was built around music no one had yet heard (the album would not be released until

July), so it was anybody's guess how it might go over. If things weren't quite at the level of Blind Faith's hysteria, the legitimacy of Traffic's revival was indeed an open question.

Steve Hyams was in the audience on April 20th for that show. While he would later do guitar and vocals for the last incarnation of Mott the Hoople, at this point he was just a young musician anxious to see what the reconstituted Traffic had to offer, "The first two or three numbers it was a bit scruffy – Chris playing sax and Steve playing bass with his feet – bass pedals. I'm watching this band in this huge – it was an old railway shed – and suddenly on the third track, something clicked. It was one of the greatest nights of music I've ever had in my life. Capaldi stayed on the drums, Chris switched from sax to flute, and Winwood switches from keyboards to piano. And when he switches to a number where he plays guitar, Chris goes and sits at the organ, and plays the bass with his feet. Absolutely magical…"

Their confidence boosted, an even bigger gig now loomed – the outdoor 'Hollywood Music Festival' at Leycett, near Newcastle-under-Lyme. Headlining the two-day event over Ginger Baker's Air Force – which had powered on in Steve and Chris's absence – Traffic had no trouble justifying their place at the top of the bill.

Amid a reconfigured set, acoustic music now filled the heart of the show. And just as they hoped, "John Barleycorn" quietly commanded attention, with the crowd listening, seeming to hang on every word. The spell was enhanced by the presentation, which began with Steve alone center stage, his acoustic guitar reflecting light in the spotlight. Joined after the first verse by Jim, the vocal harmony and tapping tambourine completed a framework for Chris's flute to spin the tale of Barleycorn's life, step by step. Taken together it was timeless, enchanting and very human. The rock audiences may not have been prepared for the new dimension Traffic was offering, but they clearly loved it. After the contemplative interlude, the electrified instruments packed an even stronger punch, sending nearly everyone away in a contented daze.

The reporter from the *New Musical Express* was no exception. While noting the lack of Mason's "heaviness", Richard Green went on to say: "The sound is pure and exciting and still swings away, as in the days of old. Chris Wood drives along on tenor sax and flute, capturing some delightful phrases. And Steve roars about on organ in fine style. Jim's drumming sounded even better than the last time I heard Traffic…" So the chancy experiment to reignite the lost spark of Traffic worked. But as usual, tests and questions lay in wait around every corner.

As the band set up for a gig at a university in Oxford, Eric Clapton unexpectedly appeared backstage. Having had an epiphany regarding Traffic's organic nature, this time he wasn't there to lure Steve off, but rather to see if he could fit into the group as it was. With little discussion and no rehearsal at all, he joined in midway through the set just after the trio finished "John Barleycorn". Steve announced, "Welcome to the reunion (sic)", as they started right in with "Dear Mr. Fantasy". On Traffic's signature tune Eric and Steve traded solos, and it was clear the electricity was still there. The lesson of Cream and Blind Faith learned – dynamics rather than volume were emphasized; for a rock show the whole thing was actually rather quiet and low key.

If in retrospect the possibilities would seem intriguing, Clapton's show with Traffic turned out to be a one-off. While Eric later made it clear that he would have actually joined the band if Steve had even hinted, no offer was made. He got the message – after Oxford, Eric quickly went on to form his own band, known as Derek and the Dominos. Interestingly, for the first few weeks (until an unforeseen personality clash erupted) the band's second guitarist was a guy named Dave Mason.

Back in the States some weeks later, in some ways Traffic's second U.S. tour wasn't all that different from the first. Playing many of the same venues, they drove most places instead of flying, which suited Chris just fine. Starting off this time on the east coast, they debuted in Philadelphia on June 9th, and then went on to New York, playing four shows in two days at Bill Graham's Fillmore East – whose stage backdrop was decorated with lighted traffic signals sequenced to go from red, yellow and then to green as Traffic walked on. While there, they also popped back into the clubs, still the best way to get a feel for the current music scene.

In New York, Chris and Steve hooked up with Jimi Hendrix again as he oversaw the final touches on his recording studio, "Electric Lady", on West 8th Street. Although the facilities were not finished, on June 15th Engineer Eddie Kramer called in a drummer (Dave Palmer) and set up a session. Even before Chris and Steve arrived, Hendrix was playing Traffic's "Pearly Queen". As usual, the musical rapport between Jimi, Steve and Chris proved excellent, but despite inspired jamming the only thing ever released was the least interesting – some backing vocals Chris and Steve added for a track called "Ezy Rider" (on the posthumous Hendrix album, *Cry of Love*).

Years later Winwood recalled an unusual jam with Chris and Jimi happening around this time. With the expected drummer failing to show, instead of cancelling, Steve took his place. The serendipitous arrangement changed everything. With Jimi's guitar and Chris's tenor sax each placed in a stereo channel as dueling lead instrumentalists, the three lit into an amazing, twenty-minute jam ranging from Spanish inflections to straight rock, to boogie, and then all out free jazz. The sympathy was obvious as the two chased each other, trading riffs and handing solos back and forth while Steve ably kept it all from spiraling into infinity. As excellent as it was, this recording like untold others would end up merely spooled onto a reel, stuck on a shelf and consigned to oblivion.

Before leaving New York, Chris again played saxophone with Jimi, jamming with Buddy Miles (drums), Jon Lord (organist from Deep Purple) and Steven Stills (bass) at The Scene. The session went so well they were asked to come back the next night, which they all did, playing only for free drinks.

Out of New York, Traffic drove into the Midwest. Rolling back into the old, even more decrepit Detroit they met Russ Gibb again, playing shows at his newer venue – the Grand Riviera. With Michigan's automotive industry in a death spiral, music presented the only light at the end of the tunnel for local teens such as Doug Fieger. Amazingly, the super-fan who had been so impressed with Traffic in '68 would now be opening the show with his own band, Sky. He was "thrilled" to be on the same bill, perhaps even more so to just hang; smoking hashish cigarettes 'English style' and making small talk.

Fieger recalled, "Chris was a sweet, sweet man, and really talented. I felt like he befriended me. Although he only said like, thirty five words, he liked me; and that to a young guy is kind of unreal." Backstage, Fieger was shocked to see how the quiet flute player readied himself to play, "I'll never forget, standing backstage with Chris, he had this kind of wry smile on his face, and he crushed up a tab of acid on a Leslie speaker cabinet, and snorted it, and walked on stage. That really impressed me, I went, 'Wow!' He walked out on stage, and played an *amazing show* – it was amazing!" Surprisingly, Chris would perform many shows on the tour exactly this way; for whatever reason, it seemed to work.

Easily pleasing the tough Detroit crowd once again, Fieger recalled, "They were the real deal and everybody knew it. Detroit's a hip town musically; especially back then, a very, very hip town. And if they didn't like a band, they didn't like 'em. Grand Funk were popular everywhere but Detroit – and they were from Flint (Michigan)! *Why?* They played that heavy metal, Detroitish, loud music. I saw them booed off the stage."

Other echoes from '68 were in the air as well. Oddly, it seemed that Dave Mason *just happened* to be in Detroit when Traffic came into town. At loose ends again after touring with Delaney and Bonnie he met up with them at the theater and watched the show from the wings. He also stuck around for the after show party, but that would be as far as things went. For this tour at least, the trio was a complete universe with no room for another star.

Sky accompanied Traffic to another event in Cincinnati Ohio on June 13th, billed as the 'Midsummer Night's Dream' Festival. In a year packed with festivals influenced by, or trying to emulate, Woodstock this was an especially strange, poorly-run event. Held at the Cincinnati Red's baseball stadium (Crosley Field), the fans were crammed into a dusty bowl beneath a merciless sun to see fifteen bands play in a festival lasting just one day. Packed in amid acts ranging from the unknown (Mighty Quick and John Drake's Shakedown) to the heavy (Mountain and Grand Funk Railroad), to over-the-top 'shock rock' bands of the day (Alice Copper and the Stooges), Traffic – sweating and cramped on a crowded stage in the evening heat, got in only a fraction of their usual set. Wisely, one was "John Barleycorn", which worked its usual charms on the cranky, exhausted crowd.

While Sky was bumped off the playlist altogether, the trip south was still worth it, since back at the hotel the night would be spent playing music with his heroes. Fieger recalled, "Everybody ended up in our room, and we jammed acoustically. I had a Hofner bass which I could play acoustically and someone else had a guitar, and someone had a tambourine – Chris was there with his flute, and we were just playing!" Although Doug would go on to have widespread success with his next band, The Knack, his formative time with Traffic instilled memories he would never forget, "I can't say enough about them… they were a true creative energy."

Zigzagging across America, from there the path would lead to Chicago, Minneapolis, Salt Lake City, and three cities in Texas. They even played Toronto Canada, where they hit the last gig of the famous 'Festival Express' train tour that had chugged in from the west. There was a lot of talent on board including The Band, the Grateful Dead and Janis Joplin, but Traffic capped the show with a fantastic, captivating set in near darkness.

The end of June found them back in California, where once again, Bill Graham awaited. At his Fillmore West in San Francisco, they played two sets per show as Graham had desired back in '68 – this time not forgetting to divide up the songs. Like a band with something to prove they watched each other, taking the timing to a fine, honed point. But even when Steve somehow lost his step, mangling a song they'd played a million times – "Dear Mr. Fantasy" – the audience proved forgiving. With the sympathy flowing both ways, they played a cross-section of everything, including a Blind Faith number – "Can't Find My Way Home". With Steve on organ, and Chris on flute and sax, it felt like a cover version from some long lost band, which in a way, it was. This was Traffic's night, at their home away from home – and all was well.

Anna Capaldi (her last name recently changed from 'Westmore' via English law's 'deed poll'), traveled with Jim on the tour and confirmed that the Fillmore shows were luminous, "I remember one at the Fillmore West – with "Glad", when they clicked on that, it was really tight – they could have gone on forever… absolutely incredible. They'd just go off in places, and then build up and drop down again – amazing, amazing." A recording reveals that the band was in fact 'on' as she remembered, with "Glad" by turns hypnotic and exhilarating. Paired as usual with "Freedom Rider", the fifteen-minute tour de force created a mood boosting the whole show. And if the music fulfilled the audience, Anna recalled the band's reward as well, "In places like the Fillmore West, to hear people applauding and absolutely loving it – it was a high in itself."

But the best was saved for last. Played since their first concert as a band, "Feeling Good" had somehow grown even more personal and compelling. The dynamics were now so powerful that the song was impossible to top; here as everywhere the audience hung on every note. The lyrics of the chorus gave a sense of summing up the still hopeful American experience of 1970, for the band, the audience and the youthful generation: "It's a new dawn, it's a new day, it's a new life for me, and I'm feeling… goooood." With Steve stretching the last word out into a cry entangled with Chris's highest notes on the flute and Jim's crashing drums, the musical state of grace left tears in the eyes of many. As a single song, this would prove to be perhaps the deepest experience Traffic would ever offer their audience.

Still closely following the band, *Rolling Stone* sent a reporter to talk. Chris was as usual friendly, but also talked about his uneasy situation vis-à-vis songwriting, "I'm not a song writer. I think most songwriters are singers too. They have to get into lyrics and use their voices. But my voice is my instrument. On reeds and woodwinds, you see, the mouth is still used. It's like singing to me, but it's hard to write songs that way." Like a typical Traffic fan, he also marveled at what the band could do when they all gave their best. Remembering "No Time To Live", he said: "I listened to that a while ago, and I couldn't believe it. When we did it, I had no idea it was that good. Fantastic."

Driving from gig to gig, the wide open spaces gave them the chance to experience the country more intimately. Listening to radio stations drifting in and out as they rolled past head-high cornfields, wide plains, mountain ranges and the small towns in between, the culture merged with the landscape. Anna recalled, "There would be great music stations as you went through different States. You'd hear different music like country and western and bluegrass. That was all part of the great experience to come to America and tour."

Having played from shore to shore without major strife or disruption, things had finally gone as intended. With audiences, critics, and fellow musicians expressing their appreciation, and waves of warm applause washing over them nightly, Traffic was able to bask ever so briefly in a time when rock 'n roll seemed to make good on its promise to move society toward a better place. Unfortunately, savoring the moment was not in the cards – across the ocean on the European continent, yet another tour beckoned.

*

Flying directly from America to Germany, the opening act was Free, with whom Chris had recorded before taking off for New York in the summer of '69. Chris hung out with Free's guitarist, Paul Kossoff, whose inventive, fiery lead playing belied a quiet, sensitive soul. Like Chris, 'Koss' was having difficulty adjusting to fame and the music business. Part of the problem may have been that, in a world of rock stars often physically much smaller than they seemed on stage, at barely five feet Kossoff was perhaps the shortest of them all. At least one friend thought that his diminutive height definitely affected him psychologically. But framed by music, friendship and their respective insecurities, Woody and Koss formed a tight bond that would last to the bitter end. Another member of Free, Paul Rodgers, appreciated Chris's mellow presence, but also recalled a hidden darkness, even many years later: "He was a sweet guy, and a great player, but underneath it all I sensed a tortured soul."

As for Steve – his restlessness was resurfacing. As good as everything had been going, on stage and off, lately he'd begun mentioning possible additions to the band. The ideas ranged from the farfetched – a French horn (perhaps an inside joke) – to something more practical – a bass player. Always a kind of weak spot for the band – Steve either covered bass on the pedals of the organ, or Chris did with his octave divider on the Gibson Maestro. Either way it was confining, and more than the others, Steve felt the strain. These days, the name of Ric Grech, Winwood's old Blind Faith compatriot, kept popping into the conversation as he mused about the future.

With the short European tour that took them into Germany and Holland completed, Traffic headed back home. The respite was again brief; another trip was scheduled. But this one was the stuff of dreams – they were heading into the desert sands of Morocco. Somewhere back they had agreed to do the score of a movie, by a Dutch Director named Antoine Coyas, and the recording was to be done on location.

Traffic's success with films had so far been abysmal. After initial success of a sort with *Here We Go Round the Mulberry Bush*, somehow they'd lost their whimsical scene in the *Beatles Magical Mystery Tour* film, and although asked to take part in the Rolling Stones *Rock 'n Roll Circus*, that too fell through because of the breakup of '68. So here was another chance.

Details regarding the plot of the proposed movie *Nevertheless* are today, as then, quite thin. The basic idea revolved around the travails of a wandering guitar player, to be played by an American actor, Michael J. Pollard, who had come to fame for his sidekick role in the movie, *Bonnie and Clyde* in 1967. Traveling the world in a VW bus shaped like a guitar (the neck of which stuck off the back like a tail), his quest would take him into the heart of the Northern African desert, where he would end up doing, well, something... Traffic's proposed role was to watch the scenes being filmed and make up music on the spot; recording it right there with mobile equipment. The idea was indeed intriguing, and having just spent the summer improvising music every night, it should have been a breeze.

As it turned out, the project was, at best, an ill-conceived mess – at worst, a delusional fantasy. Jim Capaldi shook his head at the memory, "It was just madness, total madness. I mean, nothing ever got done – nothing happened. Everybody just got too stoned. These Dutch guys were kind of amateur film makers, and they'd got a student kind of grant from the government – like an Art Council." It seems that Coyas, having sold Traffic on the idea of improvising the musical score, believed that he too could simply wing it. But, disturbingly, while the band finally made it on location following a flight to Casablanca and then a hair-raising car ride over the Atlas Mountains, the equipment needed to record them was nowhere to be seen. The problems would mount from there.

A friend to Coyas and Traffic, Dick Polak, was hired to assist the project only to find himself stuck uncomfortably in the middle. Having designed and constructed the aluminum framed guitar/bus himself in Amsterdam, once in Morocco he was distressed to learn that the film cameras had somehow ended up in the Canary Islands. What *was* on site included a van full of random props (a stuffed polar bear, fireworks and axes), as well as the crucial guitar/bus, which now lacked either a windshield or the keys to start it.

With Jim keeping an eye on the unraveling production, Steve and Chris quickly lost interest. Unfortunately, they couldn't even jam – their musical instruments hadn't arrived either. Instead, they wandered the streets of the local town, smoked loads of kif – the strong local hashish and listened to local musicians who serenaded them at their castle-like hotel. At some point Chris would also take a horseback trip into the desert with photographer Michael Cooper, the details of which remain tantalizingly unknown. As for the film they were supposedly making, even Jim would ultimately deem it hopeless: "They filmed shit and stuff. (Then) they lost the tripod in the desert – suddenly they had no fuckin' tripod!"

Somehow the situation only deteriorated from there. "It all ended in total chaos", was Polak's recollection, "One of the guys that worked for us, a Moroccan guy, was threatened to have his balls electrocuted by the local police; he was suspected of stealing money from us – which was not true. I felt responsible for Traffic, so I decided to take them out of there... things had become quite hairy."

CHAPTER TWENTY

So they left. Chris, who traveled light (he'd arrived in Morocco with only a toothbrush), exited the way he came, reprising the scary ride back over the winding mountain road with the others to Casablanca. Before leaving, Jim spent time with actor Michael Pollard, writing lines, and trying to find a worthwhile theme. At the hotel, the two would encounter a woman tourist who, having never heard of Traffic, asked Pollard what their music was like. He responded with a smirking non-sequitur: "They sound like the low spark of high heeled boys" – a phrase quickly scribbled into Jim's lyric book. Later he would cite the enigmatic quip as the only useful thing to come out of the trip.

('A popular man about groups', Chris Welch, Melody Maker, 3/14/1970)

('I was pissed off after Blind Faith', Rolling Stone, 5/28/1970)

('Report from the Hollywood Festival', Richard Green, NME, 5/30/1970)

('Traffic, Continued', Jon Carroll, Rolling Stone, 8/6/1970)

(John Barleycorn Lyrics, Traditional)

CHAPTER TWENTY-ONE

FAREWELL JIMI

As Chris finished the crazy expedition, Jeanette was finding her way home as well. On tour with Ginger Baker's Air Force, they had crisscrossed much the same ground as Traffic that summer. But Baker would prove a difficult taskmaster; multiple personnel changes later and the band was floundering. To top it off, Jeanette had what would turn out to be a serious injury. Coming off stage one night, she tripped over the drum kit, falling hard and hitting her head. Knocked unconscious, she came around and seemed alright. But thereafter she would be plagued by lingering headaches and then more serious complications. With the fall being perhaps the last straw, before the scheduled Air Force trip to Europe, Jeanette dropped out and went back to England where she and Chris were reunited.

But the joy was tempered with festering issues which soon re-emerged. While living with Chris, Jeanette had never resolved her feelings for Jimi Hendrix. Reveling in telling her friends that Hendrix had written the ethereal song "Little Wing" for her, she saw herself as one of the select few women that Jimi had ever *really* loved. Indeed, just before she was to join Chris and Steve in Air Force, Jeanette had jetted off to Toronto Canada at Jimi's request to meet up with him at his trial for heroin possession, at which he ended up being acquitted.

By the fall of 1970 Hendrix was back in Europe, playing at the Isle of Wight to a huge crowd, then touring Scandinavia and Germany before ending up again in London. Lodging at the Cumberland Hotel, he jammed around town while pondering his musical future, including the notion of forming a band with Steve Winwood, Remi Kabaka and Love's Arthur Lee. While that idea apparently never got past the fantasy stage, Jimi did seem genuinely torn as to where to go next.

As for Jeanette, she somehow wanted both men. Stuck firmly in an edgy love triangle, how did Chris feel about it? His emotional response might not have been as cut and dried as one might surmise. Eleanor Barooshian insisted that Chris was okay with sharing Jeanette, "I don't think that Chris minded that Jeanette went with Jimi – because she was with Jimi before she even knew him. There was no competition thing there between them, Chris wasn't like that." Still, she paused to consider how Chris could tolerate the split affections of the girl he dearly loved. "He was very calm about that, the way he took it. I think that's why he took more drugs."

By the second week of September, Jeanette was starting to feel wedged out herself. Hoping to see Jimi, she had gone to the Cumberland only to find him occupied. The depths of Jeanette's feelings were revealed in comments she made later, "Monika Danneman came and said she was madly in love with Jimi and had this ring and they were going to get married. I fell for it unfortunately and left the country. Jimi said: 'Please wait.' But having heard it from this girl right in front of me, I didn't have a leg to stand on."

How well Danneman actually knew Jimi was questionable. As for his alleged 'proposal', it was almost certainly like others made to any number of girls in the last couple of years – a form of self-illusion. In the stressful and sometimes flat out crazy world he inhabited, Hendrix's easily tendered (and almost as quickly forgotten) marriage offers provided a comforting projection of future stability, however temporary.

It was a tangled and confusing time for them all. Georgiana Steele-Waller, a friend of members of the Who, claimed to have dropped by Chris and Jeanette's place around this time to see Chris injecting heroin under his skin – 'chipping' – with Jeanette, while Hendrix visited with Danneman. Despite, or perhaps because of the heavy drug use, all apparently got along just fine. While there are multiple and conflicting reports about what Jimi did in his final days and hours, Steele-Waller says that this visit, which Jimi ended by saying he needed to go to sign a contract, was in fact the night of his death.

One way or the other, by the second week of September 1970, Jimi Hendrix's wild ride in the fast lane of rock 'n roll was about to end. Taking Danneman's strong sleeping pills and wine, a tired and wired Hendrix tried to rest while visiting her room at Hotel Samarkand in Lansdowne Crescent, Notting Hill. Lying on his back in the bed, too sedated to be roused, he vomited and suffocated. And so it was that despite the crush of people always seeking his company, Jimi Hendrix died on the morning of September 18th, in part because no one was paying enough attention. Near his body, on the night table lay his last writing, a poem whose final lines summed up all the weariness his frenetic lifestyle had led him to: "The story of life is quicker than the wink of an eye, the story of love is hello and goodbye, until we meet again."

According to Jeanette's later (and logistically implausible) account, the encounter with Danneman caused her to depart for Amsterdam just before Jimi's death. Upon hearing the news she rushed back to find London in an uproar. While Eric Burdon found Jimi's bedside poem and mistook it for a suicide note, Jeanette took it a step further, "The night before he died, somebody told him that I had gone away. In the morning he was found dead. I think it just had to happen." In her version, Hendrix had interpreted her leaving as abandonment, precipitating an impulsive act which resulted in his death. While apparently only Jeanette truly believed this, the circumstances were indeed a swirl of confusion, made more so by statements by Monika Danneman shown only much later to be false. In the end, perhaps only one fact truly mattered – Jimi was gone, and it was a crushing blow to both her and Chris, each of whom loved him in their own way.

All they could really do was console each other. Jeanette would later say that Jimi's death caused her to have a nervous breakdown that lasted a year. She and Chris would self-medicate with Mandrax – a sedative which, when combined with alcohol, induced a hypnotic-like state. Over time, some people noticed an odd metamorphosis. According to writer Chris Welch, by the time he interviewed Jeanette, she had taken on Jimi's body language – talking and even walking in a way that was noticeably similar to the late musician.

Apart from Jeanette, Chris had little to say about Jimi's death, especially in public. It was simply too painful. Even years later, when asked by a friend how it had affected him, Chris's expression darkened as he held his hand forward to stop the questions, saying only, "*Please* man!" Later still, he could only shake his head and mutter, "Awful, terrible... Oh god, that was *so* dreadful."

As time went by and the grief finally subsided, Chris's regard for Jimi was evident as he talked about the music they had made together – only a small fraction of which was ever released. Paying the highest compliment he had to offer, Chris would tell the jazz magazine *DownBeat* that above all Jimi was a collaborative artist who just happened to play guitar, "As far as combining elements in a kind of collage way, to me, the only guy that could do that without losing himself was Hendrix. Working with him on the few things that we did was probably the most eye-opening thing for me because he was so uncompromising in one way and yet so compromising in another. Like he'd be listening to you and you could still play your own licks; it was strange." Beyond that he could only remind people that Hendrix was a shy and gentle man, and not the flamboyant caricature often portrayed.

The losses they'd suffered drove both Chris and Jeanette to desperate lengths to find answers. Reading *Black Magic* magazine and studying the occult, séances would be held with friends in an attempt to part the curtain of death. One of these rituals, which included Jim Capaldi, gave an unexpected and intriguing result – supposedly making contact not with the spirit of Jimi but another recently lost friend, Brian Jones, the former Rolling Stones guitarist who had died the previous year. Having known each other perhaps as far back as the Elbow Room days, Brian and Chris's eclectic approach to music had put them on common ground. Certainly by 1967 they were friends, sometimes forming a social trio with Jimi Hendrix at London's 'Speakeasy' club. On the road with the Dr. John tour when the word of his death spread, Chris had been quite upset. And as with Jimi, the circumstances surrounding Jones' passing were shrouded in mystery and lingering questions.

At the time it was determined that he had accidentally drowned in his own swimming pool, but to many of his friends his death seemed improbable – Jones was known to be a strong swimmer. The official death report called it "Death by misadventure" and the ultimate cause of death an asthma attack while under water.

Strangely, it would only be in 1999 that a confession seriously countered the official verdict of an accidental death. Frank Thorogood, a builder who was renovating Jones home was reported, on his deathbed, to have admitted killing Jones as they tussled in the pool.

But as far as Chris was concerned, from 1970 forward he already knew. Hearing a friend (Vinden Wylde) casually comment on Jones's 'accidental' death, Chris quickly returned a terse disagreement: "*No*, Brian was murdered, he was murdered, definitely." When asked how he was so sure, he was equally emphatic, saying simply: "Because Brian came and told me himself."

As for Hendrix, the spiritualist efforts proved fruitless. After many months, Jeanette finally gave up hopes of reestablishing a link. Her last published thoughts on the matter were accepting. "...I finally realized he wasn't coming back. People say he's still here. But mentally and physically he isn't here. That's why he said: 'When I die, just play the records.'"

Around the time of these dreary goings on, Chris and Jeanette moved into another, larger apartment in Notting Hill Gate, a third floor walkup flat near Island's offices. There was an interesting irony in the new living arrangements. With Jim now living in a quiet village and Steve settled into his country estate, Chris – the one who loved and appreciated contact with nature most – was the only one of the three living in London. Forced into a tough decision (as previously with art vs. music), in the end, his love for Jeanette would leave no option – she was a city girl, through and through. And if he dreamed of the country and desperately needed it, Chris wouldn't be leaving town for a long, long time.

*

In late fall, Traffic regrouped, rehearsed and went out on the road again. Even before Jimi's death, Steve had decided on changes; the long surmised addition of a bass player came just before the ill-fated trip to Morocco. While it was Ric Grech, rather than Eric Clapton that came into the fold – in the end Traffic would have a taste of Blind Faith after all. With a sense of security in knowing what to expect, initially at least, Grech would smooth out the rough edges on stage.

Amazingly, speculation arose that the newly ex-Beatle George Harrison would also join. The *Palm Beach Post* exposed the notion to the world, throwing out the most thinly grounded report: "Now gossips say it'll be Harrison, a longtime friend and frequent guest in Traffic jams." But that particular fantasy proved short-lived; back on the ground in America that November for a short tour which included a Fillmore East gig recorded for a contractually obligated 'live' album, Grech was the only newcomer.

After Christmas, they hit the road yet again, playing some dates in their native country – mostly university auditoriums, and a couple of shows in Scotland. But if the band was hoping for an uneventful tour, a respite after the recent hardships, it was not to be. If Hendrix's death had been more Chris's personal tragedy to overcome, Jim Capaldi's time to suffer was now at hand.

It began with visitations, repeated phone calls and other unwanted communications from a figure from the past – an insistent voice that cajoled, cried, pleaded and then threatened. Jim was being hounded by Danielle, the French girlfriend that he had broken up with over a year ago. For whatever reason, she had refused to accept that Jim was out of her life and was desperate to change his mind. Calling over and over to remind him of the good times, she tried to rekindle a fire grown cold. At first Jim shrugged it off, either laughingly ignoring the calls, or exasperatedly hanging up. Nothing worked.

Christie Nichols, nearly ready to graduate from College, was spending her last months in England with Helen and Patrick Hamilton in Blewbury. With Chris now with Jeanette, her association with Traffic was nearly past as well, but she took a last road trip with the band and recalled the time as particularly rough for Jim, "We were going to a Spencer Davis performance, and Steve was going to play with them for fun – it was a festival, and a lot of people were going to play. Danielle kept calling him, over and over again. She got really possessive and crazy, and she scared him a lot. She must have called him, like, twenty times." Finally, she would present him with an ultimatum, the only threat she had left. As Jim held his hand over the mouthpiece of the phone, he told the others, "She's threatening to commit suicide unless I go back with her." But after all the months of haggling, and trying to disentangle himself civilly, Jim had had enough. Christie recalled, "He finally said, (something like) 'Go ahead!'" Slamming down the receiver, he could only sit and fume, hoping that she got the message. And it seemed so, from there on the phone sat silent.

While the festival proved a fun night out, for Jim it was also a welcome release from an old girlfriend's harassment. Afterward too, all remained quiet, and it was only later they found out why; Danielle had indeed carried out the threat and taken her own life in her London apartment.

Somehow, even worse news lay ahead. Jim's partner, Anna would give birth to a son that they called Damian Thor Capaldi. The child was Jim's first, and he was a proud father. But within two months Damian suddenly died of the mysterious, but not uncommon cause of 'crib (cot) death'.

The twin tragedies would plunge Jim into a state of utter devastation. In later years, he would never talk about directly about Danielle or Damian's deaths, only admitting that he was a complete mess in early '71, "I was going through a very spaced out patch, and I wasn't sure that I was going to be able to carry on." Friends like Paul Medcalf knew that he had been essentially crushed: "Jim went through a bad time – it really cracked him up completely. He couldn't play drums; he'd lost all confidence as far as I could see." Spending untold hours staring vacantly, Jim took to mumbling and obsessively pulling at strands of his hair as his situation played over and over in his mind.

As for Traffic, with all that had happened in recent months, the band's future was suddenly quite uncertain. Desperately they tried to carry on, but as his playing unraveled, a sad Capaldi offered to quit for the good of the group, "I said, 'I should just step down you know', I was *not* together as far as playing. We were struggling."

In an act of compassion, Steve declined the offer. But Jim's disability also presented an opportunity. The band survived by growing around the problem, adding one new member, and then another until the rhythm section was rebuilt from the ground up. Jim noted, "The funny thing – it wasn't planned or conscious – it was almost like controlled abandonment. Sometimes we didn't know what we were doing, not in a mindless way, but we had the ability to not know, to not be preconceived or second guessing. We just walked into the valley of progressiveness with a couple of compasses, but nothing specifically battened down." Although done out of desperation, it was daring as well. If in the end they *did* fall, at least they would be falling forward.

The first addition was perhaps the biggest gamble of all – they hired Anthony 'Reebop' Kwaku Baah – a percussionist from the Konongo Township of Ghana. Although given a traditional Ghanaian name – Kwaku meaning something like 'Born on a Wednesday', his family were also well off enough to send him to a western school, which he quit at age fifteen to play in various bands. Playing with furious precision yet seeming abandon, his tribal drum training and natural rhythmic inclination made him a stand out, even in a country filled with drummers. Emigrating from Ghana to England in '64 at age twenty, ostensibly to go to college, Baah quickly fell into the burgeoning music scene, jamming with Freddie Hubbard and Roland Kirk before joining Jimmy Cliff's band. Moving to Sweden in 1968, he became a session player, at the same time forming his own band – something called Dzabado! ('Wow!'). Although only five foot three, Baah was a musical powerhouse, and none other than jazz master Dizzy Gillespie bestowed the moniker 'Reebop' – recognizing his unique ability to synthesize jazz and African rhythms. Traffic met up with him in Stockholm and according to Jim he simply played his way into the band, "Reebop joined by just jamming every night in Sweden, and suddenly he was in the band, nobody needed to say yes or no. He found his own place."

Jim's account became part of the Traffic mythos, but Reebop was no stranger. Before moving to Sweden, he'd been all over the London rock scene, spending time at the Cottage, and had even joined Traffic recording sessions. Having the highly energetic, usually smiling African expatriate join Traffic was in no way a random move, but it was *smart*. Like Chris, Reebop naturally grasped the spirituality at the core of making music. Equally important, he also had heaps of the 'mad energy' that Jim had lost. A shot in the arm just when they needed it most, Reebop's beats added a new dimension to Traffic's music – grounding and opening it up at the same time. Unfortunately, it wasn't enough. What they really needed was another rock 'n roll drummer.

By April of 1971, the band that Eric Clapton had formed in the wake of trying to join Traffic – Derek and the Dominos – had just broken up. Although only together for about eight months, the group had managed to rocket higher into the creative stratosphere than any of their contemporaries. Their sole album, *Layla, and other assorted love songs* was an utter classic of the rock genre and the title track, "Layla", possibly the best single song of the 70's. The fuel that drove them on was a volatile combination of Clapton's broken heart (he pined for George Harrison's wife, Pattie), heavy drug use by all, and a perfectly aligned constellation of talent. Besides the musical core of the old Delaney and Bonnie band, for a brief but magical period, the Dominos snared the incendiary talents of Duane Allman – guitarist for the Allman Brothers Band. The unprecedented synergy allowed the creation of a nearly perfect rock/blues album. But following the pinnacle came the crash: Allman returned to his own band, egos clashed, arguments flared, and drug-induced paranoia soaked all to the core. After a failed attempt at a second album in London without Allman, a burned out and heroin-addicted Clapton locked himself in his mansion in Surrey, while keyboard player Bobbie Whitlock sat in the driveway and screamed in vain for him. Afterward, remnants of the band floated around the London scene, waiting to see what would happen next.

Jim Gordon had been Derek and the Dominos' drummer. The lanky, curly-haired American started out as one of L.A.'s top session men, having played with everybody from the Beach Boys to the Everly Brothers. In the Dominos, Gordon had been confident enough to accompany Clapton anywhere musically. And it was he who had come up with the all-important piano coda for "Layla" – a serendipitous touch making the song one of the most epic and enduring in rock history. In light of Traffic's desperate need for a solid timekeeper, Gordon looked like a natural. Quickly accepting when asked, the rhythm section was now revamped and seemingly ready to roll.

A question still lingered. With Jim Gordon on board, what did that leave for the other Jim to do? Rehearsing with the new lineup, his primary instrument was now a tambourine. He did still sing – and was currently working up songs featuring himself as a lead vocalist. He could also take on the stage announcements – something Steve didn't care to do. While the public would never know why Jim was no longer drumming, there was clearly something odd about the new arrangement. For the press it was papered over: it had all been Jim's idea.

Knowing he would have to make himself useful, Jim now redoubled his lyric writing efforts. And with recording sessions for *John Barleycorn Must Die*'s follow-up scheduled, he also hedged his bets by writing with Grech and Gordon, both of whom were hoping to contribute tunes. Bringing Gordon home to Marlow, Jim and Jim would work up a demo called "Hard To Find". The song had initially been meant for Derek and the Dominos, and for Gordon the tragic end to that band still lingered; Anna recalled hearing him play his haunting "Layla" piece on Jim's piano late at night as he sat alone in the dark.

If Traffic's overall situation seemed patched together and uncertain, having entered Island's studio that Spring, like a butterfly from a chrysalis they would emerge transformed, "Sometimes at your weakest, you are also at your strongest – the strength comes to get you through," Jim Capaldi recalled. "My contribution at the weakest point of Traffic's entire career; I came up with 'The Low Spark Of High Heeled Boys.'" Having rediscovered Michael J. Pollard's quip from that desert oasis in Morocco, Jim would be inspired to build an extraordinary song around it. Couching the lyrics in a metaphor of the music industry's threat to an artist's soul, the work was actually suffused with strains of Jim's very personal loss and sorrow.

Winwood would be inspired as well, coming up with music unlike anything he'd done before. Based around a long, almost desultory piano track, 'Low Spark' would be punctuated with sudden dynamic swings that turned things around with a rush of intensity. His singing had changed as well. Since 'Barleycorn' he'd evolved a wistful quality that couldn't have been further removed from the brash blues shouting of the Spencer Davis days. Ultimately, 'Low Spark' would prove a nearly unclassifiable statement. Or as Jim put it, "For a thirteen minute track, it's so unusual and so special. It kind of sums up Traffic in a way… the eclectic-ness, you can't put your finger on it at all, yet you know it's familiar. It's jazz, its blues, its rock… it does give one a Polaroid of Traffic's tapestry."

Like so many things, Chris Wood's role in the making of the song was not quite as it seemed. The long, freewheeling, intense solos in the middle and the end of 'Low Spark' was (and still is) cited by critics as being his finest saxophone work – the place where his playing broke through to a level worthy of a great jazz artist. But while the playing is indeed extraordinary – it wasn't him. Steve Winwood actually did the famous solos. Using a Moog synthesizer, an electronic instrument that he was experimenting with, he simply mimicked the sound of a sax and did a thoroughly amazing job of it.

There was a little more to the story however. Chris did indeed play all over the first take (the same one used for the album), including a long solo near the middle. In the wake of Winwood's overdub it would be mostly covered over, though wailing, atmospheric lines would remain, initiating the song's melancholy mood. An outtake tape reveals that, with Gordon's drums rolling and skittered behind him, Chris actually envisioned the solo akin to a smoky late night jazz club jam with ample space hanging between the notes. But if, in the end, most of his work would serve as the muse for Winwood's mesmerizing solo, then so be it.

After all was said and done, each had contributed their best, and regardless of the change and strife, the fragile magic of Traffic still wafted in the air. "The Low Spark of High-Heeled Boys" released late in the year, and became a huge hit on FM radio. In America, it would become nothing less than one of the defining rock songs of the decade.

The creativity kept flowing. In the wake of their son's death, Anna, always spiritually minded, was heavily influencing Jim, and by extension, Traffic. At her urging, Jim read and was jolted by the philosophical writings of Herman Hesse. After finishing *Siddartha*, Hesse's tale of a man's struggle to find the nature of his inner being, Jim wrote a lyric reflecting his own search called "Hidden Treasure". Strengthened by Chris's flute and Steve's acoustic guitar and softly keening voice, the resulting song would prove one of Jim's most beautiful and insightful works.

CHAPTER TWENTY-ONE

Struggling with her own grief, Anna wrote a poem she titled "Many A Mile to Freedom". Visiting the Capaldi's house in Marlow, Steve discovered Anna's poem on a table then went to the piano and wrote a tune to accompany it. The spiritual twin to "Hidden Treasure", it contained lyrics that joined Jim and Anna's separate journeys into one: "Together we flow like a river, and together we melt like the snow…" With pain and loss turned into beauty – both songs shimmered with the spirit that permeated Traffic's best music.

With no songs of his own to add, Chris still gave his all, absorbing the emotions and merging his feelings with theirs as he played. Looking back, Jim remembered how Chris rose to the occasion, "Very, very strong; that was where he'd arrived at a great place. He'd reached a peak. His flute on 'Hidden Treasure' is wonderful. His sax – just his little intonations and licks in 'Low Spark' are great. Chris knew how to play a sax, and play solos without playing solos. He just put statements in, he put colors in. He was an expressionist, and he used the sax like a vehicle for just giving you a sudden shock, a jolt, a sound or a color. Chris's whole mindset and spirit was in wanting to break ground and to find… wanting a different angle, and a different direction. He'd come up with something that made you look twice. His whole persona was that. He lived that way."

Staying with Jim and Anna during the sessions, Chris enjoyed spending time with Eve, Anna's child from her previous marriage. Sometimes acting as the babysitter, he often read her bedtime stories. Even decades later, Eve recalled the whimsical evenings with a longhaired Chris, and his special nickname. Anna laughed when she relayed the tale, recalling why Chris enjoyed being around children, "Yeah, 'cause he was a little boy too. He'd say, 'I'll go read her 'Jack and the Beanstalk', or whatever. She used to call him 'Auntie Chris!'"

Back in the studio, the music poured out in a creative torrent. Spooky Tooth's drummer, and friend of Traffic, Mike Kellie was around during the sessions, playing (uncredited) on some tracks. Kellie remembered Chris's special, nearly intangible role, "He was more influential than people realize – I don't know if I can be more specific… There's a track on *Low Spark* called "Rainmaker", which I played drums on. We did it virtually live; Ric on bass, Chris playing flute and me on drums. And the atmosphere is *so much* Chris's flute. His solo in the middle of it is *so* wonderful. Now if you go back and listen to it (the solo) – a wonderful piece of music, and so simple – if you take it away – in your mind, there's not a lot left. He was so expressive – that hunched back, sort of… yeah."

In the wake of Hendrix's death, Albert's tragic injury and all the rest, a protective surface had been stripped away, freeing a conduit from within. Having located an ephemeral balance point between lines that set the overall mood and solos which lifted things beyond, his phrasing (especially on the flute) now verged on the sublime. Tone-wise, the flute also managed to mirror Steve's winsome vocal approach, strengthening the sympathy between them.

With Traffic moving in the direction Chris had tried to steer since the late '69 reformation, and even before ("Feeling Good"), the best of the new work would not have been possible without "John Barleycorn"'s influence. "Rainmaker" especially, had vibes straight out of the lost Cottage, in effect Barleycorn's successor. Set alongside "Hidden Treasure" and "Many A Mile to Freedom", Traffic's nature-based mythos now flowered fully, redefining the character of the band. While the shift in emphasis may have been Chris's greatest overall contribution to Traffic, the influence was subtle enough to be invisible to anyone on the outside. Yet the power of the vibe would be clear to all – Traffic's musical apogee had been reached. While it was a place they would all would have liked to stay a little longer, the finely-tuned equilibrium was already about to be tipped to one side.

With the album almost, but not quite completed, management booked the band for gigs at Universities across England. A test of both the new songs and the rearranged group, it was a chance to see how all the changes would translate to the stage. As such, the tour would launch a whole new phase of Traffic. But before this could gel, something as inexplicable as it was inevitable occurred. Having quietly returned to England for the first time in a couple of years, Dave Mason had come around; he wanted another shot with Traffic.

On the surface, it made little sense. Having been unceremoniously kicked out, and rebuffed any number of times since, Mason had gone on to become a legitimate success on his own. His *Alone Together* album, released in 1970 was packed with excellent, hook-filled songs and made a showing on the charts. Getting good play on the hip FM stations, he subsequently put together a hot band to play his music the way he wanted it done. Clearly, Mason didn't need Traffic's hassles and interpersonal dramas to be successful. And yet there was something there he couldn't quite leave alone, a nagging drive to see if the puzzle pieces might somehow be rejigged into a better fit. So, despite the headaches and rejection he was back, believing it worth one more try.

By this time, Dave had settled down a bit, gotten married. His wife Lorraine was there when the initial reunion took place. She remembered that the circumstances which brought them together again as either fated or wildly coincidental, "Dave and I went back to England and got married. We popped in – Chris's place was always the meeting place, 'cause Steve's place was out in Cheltenham, and Jim had a really cool house in Evesham (sic). Chris was really the only person who lived in London. It was a third floor walkup, you'd ring the bell and yell, and he'd buzz you up. When we first saw them, it was totally spontaneous – we thought we'd stop by and surprise them. And the weird thing was, either Jim and Steve were already there, or they arrived soon after. It was just like – whoa! Everybody is showing up at the same time, after not seeing each other for so long. (We) sat there and drank wine, smoked a lot of hash joints and gossiped about everybody. They just played some music – acoustic music, and hung out."

Musically, there was no problem, the separate parts quickly slipped back into the four-arrow Traffic symbol – whole and spinning once more. But, as always, the psychology was a little murky. With Dave's pattern of being nearby whenever he thought they might have him back, it seemed unlikely that chance played any role. Having noticed the path they'd taken for "John Barleycorn" the acoustic guitar he'd brought to Chris's place also made perfect sense.

Underlying motivations aside, in the end Mason would be invited to the tour rehearsals. But with a now long chain of Mason-related hassles in their history, what exactly was Traffic thinking? It certainly wouldn't take long for the two Taurians to lock horns again. While Dave saw his return as, if not permanent, at least open to negotiation, Steve made it clear to the press that Mason would be around for the six or seven University gigs that they had lined up across England, and no more. And while he might have been upset to hear his return characterized as little more than a lark with an old friend, Dave also wouldn't chance spoiling things by overtly complaining about it either.

Getting the slightly unwieldy, seven-piece group ready ended up requiring a lot of rehearsal – so much so that the first dates had to be cancelled to give more time to prepare. The more or less expected issues aside, there was a more disheartening problem – despite efforts to firm things up, the rhythm section wasn't working. Somehow, despite their combined years of experience, Gordon and Grech weren't meshing. With the timing slippery and unsure, the band had now fallen into a raggedy, error-prone mode. As puzzling as it was frustrating, it would only be further down the road that the causes would surface.

Jim Gordon proved especially volatile. Traffic would record the song he and Jim had worked up – "Hard to Find" – but it didn't go smoothly. Although trying mightily to dress up the track up – adding violin, harpsichord, piano, acoustic guitar and other instruments – in the end there could be no disguising the fact that Gordon couldn't really sing; at least not in any way that fitted into Traffic. But no one had the nerve to tell him. After repeated attempts to get his vocals right, Gordon himself seemed to finally recognize it. Expressing an unbridled fit of frustration, at the end of the last take he would punch out the red recording light. The efforts were all in vain. By the time the album was released, Gordon would already be out of the band and "Hard To Find" quietly moved to the out-take list where it remains today, buried in Island's vaults.

There was more bad news. Once finally on the road, the reviews were harsh. The British press, while not always positive regarding Capaldi's drumming, were unrelentingly negative toward Gordon's. Adjectives like "sloppy", "disastrous", and even "abominable" were sprinkled throughout various reports. The *New Musical Express* was perhaps kindest: "One thing is certain. The rhythm section was in dire need of rejuvenation."

While Steve was said to have been distressed by the reviews and the unexpected instability, the band played on. Surprisingly, a mobile recording unit was taking it all down for posterity, allowing the best tracks to be saved as they emerged. And with that, the *real* reason they'd agreed to have Dave back – the man they swore they'd never play with again – was revealed. Having been contracted by United Artists, their American distributor, Traffic needed to deliver a 'live' album. With recordings from the previous quartet tour having been squelched (for various, conflicting reasons), now they simply needed to get the damn thing done – a mere (as Jim and Chris would both later refer to it) 'contractual obligation'. Subsequently, an accountant must have worked up an equation to show how many more units would sell if the name 'Dave Mason' appeared on the cover. Could it have been that simple – and mercenary? Not long after, Jim would basically admit to it in the press. If a more altruistic reason existed, no one ever articulated it.

What must have been the highlight of the short tour, especially for Chris, was the date scheduled for the summer solstice – June 21, in the middle of the beautiful countryside at Glastonbury in Somerset. The

'Glastonbury Fair' essentially took everything people like Chris believed about the mythical/magical nature of the British countryside and tried to harness it for a music festival.

Sent by *Rolling Stone* to cover the event, for Chris Hodenfield the Glastonbury Fair lived up to its billing; he reported it straight as a quasi-mystical event, "About ten miles south of a town called Downhead, Andrew Kerr decided to put on a festival. He found the sight in the hazy farmlands of Somerset, and as he looked in one direction he saw an energy lay line (sic) that ran from Stonehenge to Glastonbury Abbey. And as he looked above him, he saw the alignment at the center of the Zodiac from Butleigh Church… it was an exact interception of the summer sunrise and the central sun of the galaxy…"

Set to run for a week, with Traffic's appearance coming at the climax of the solstice, the event turned out to be a mini-Woodstock, but even better since it was free from the start. To literally top it off, Kerr built a wooden framed pyramid around the stage. Overlaid with white cloth, it was exactly proportioned one tenth the size of the real thing in Cheops Egypt. Shimmering in the sun amidst the trees and farm fields, the stage emanated good vibes to match. For a major rock festival, the organizers also managed to keep things on a very human scale. With only about ten thousand people in attendance and good (mostly free) food, spirituality was also high on the list of priorities; Chris's hero, the great Ley hunter and *View Over Atlantis* author, John Michell was there, as well as an Indian Swami named Santji Maharaj. Most importantly, the music offered was very much in sync with the times – newly emerging 'prog rock' bands like Gong and Soft Machine improvised with creative abandon into the summer sky as a peaceful audience sat and listened. Writer Holden, who had by now seen his share of 'rock festivals' was nearly ecstatic, "The Glastonbury Fair leaves all other festivals in heavy disgrace."

It couldn't have been a more ideal scene for *the* band identified with the Berkshire Downs, and the announcer indicated as much: "What better band to have in the English countryside but – Traffic!" And yet, having reached the pinnacle of the image that they'd organically grown, the band had somehow slid past it into the insulated, twilight world inhabited by rock aristocracy. Rather than showing up early to soak in the atmosphere, they would arrive only at dusk, just before going on. Rolling up in Winwood's four-door Aston Martin, the core of the band sat inside until show time, the car so filled with hashish smoke that none of the passengers could be seen. As the back door finally opened, Chris waved the cloud away as he emerged. Smiling but disoriented, he asked a couple of young roadies standing by the car: "Hey guys, have you seen my boots? I'm about to go on stage." Snickering and pointing, one replied: "*Is these them?*" Chris had been holding the boots in his left hand the whole time.

However high they were, once centered within the pyramid, the magic everyone hoped for flowed freely. With a stoned and happy audience lounging in front of them, Traffic put on a superb show – with even Jim Gordon finally fulfilling his promise of unalloyed excellence. Playing nearly everything they knew, from "Medicated Goo", and "Forty Thousand Headman" to "John Barleycorn", they even did songs off the not yet released album. Then there was "Dear Mr. Fantasy". Always a powerhouse, the song now had Dave and Steve dueling each other on lead guitar – their combative egos finally put to good use. But as the long set reached its climax, the pagan gods that everyone at Glastonbury had tried so hard to invoke suddenly seemed to stir. And when they finally spoke, the voice would seem to be directed at Traffic, or at least one of them.

Steve Hyams, the young guitarist who'd witnessed the comeback show at the Roundhouse the year before observed the finale from the side of the stage, "It was a great gig; you couldn't fault it musically – although I preferred the feel of the three-piece. Dave Mason had got out his (acoustic) guitars. He had a pair of twin Martin D-45's, a twelve string and a six string – really expensive, beautiful guitars. Steve had gotten out a couple of really nice guitars too – a Les Paul and a Gibson upside down Firebird, and just kind of stood them up against the amplifiers. It was in the days when you had your amplifiers on the stage and the sound system for the voices on the far side – the P.A. system. They did 'Gimme Some Lovin' at the end."

Beneath the stacks needed to send the music across the fields, the band played on. Excited to hear the marching rhythm of the reinterpreted Spencer Davis Group classic, audience members climbed on the stage to revel in the music. A joyful, if chaotic scene ensued, with the skirts of the hippie girls swirling like leaves on a blustery day.

Then it happened. Near the end of the last song, the wall of amps began to perilously sway before crashing forward in a heap. Amazingly, no one was killed, or even hurt, but there was damage. Steve Hyams witnessed, "With all the people dancing around, this whole lot crashed down – Dave Mason's guitars were smashed to pieces. He had just dusted them and put them back in the cases! And of course Winwood's were untouched.

He had just sort of put them there, while Mason had made a point of being meticulous. They kept playing… I was amazed that he could carry on. But I can remember afterward, when they were all finished and people were clapping, he (Dave) was just standing there. He picked one up – it was like the head, and everything else was just hanging there – strings and bits of guitar. His face was like… it was a free concert, I hope they had it insured."

Insured or not, the mangled guitars would prove an apt metaphor for Dave's experience in this band. His dream of returning to Traffic, like the beautiful acoustic instrument he'd hopefully dragged up three floors to Chris's flat now lay crushed and utterly destroyed. While he would make a handful of encore appearances in future years, by the end of this short tour, Dave Mason's days as a *real* member of Traffic were really over.

Serving as a reminder of the last fling, within a month and a half that hastily recorded 'live' record was out in the stores – with Dave's name in big print on the cover. *Welcome to the Canteen* could be viewed either as a decent souvenir of the time, or a vinyl headstone. At least it all ended with a bang.

Actually, it was a close call for the lot of them. Despite Glastonbury's glory, in Dave's absence things only deteriorated. The last English concert, at the Royal Albert Hall was considered an outright disaster. Even "Barleycorn", always a concert highlight, didn't work, with writer Joe Mitchell describing it as "…mistimed, off key and with words misplaced." Turning in an article for the *Record Mirror*, Mitchell (previously an ardent supporter) couldn't disguise his dismay, "I wonder how much longer the name (Traffic) will retain the old magic, when it is accompanied by this sort of performance?"

With the tour stuttering to a conclusion, the hints, vibes and psychic rumblings that presaged the last break up of Traffic were also reemerging. It seemed that the grand musical experiment begun when Jim quit drumming had careened onto a ditch. Even before anything was said, the signs were ominous.

But with another tour already booked, a legal vice would prevent any rash conclusions. Jim Capaldi would tell a reporter, "Steve wanted to cancel the forthcoming American tour, but we couldn't." The importance of 'contractual obligations' was something Chris Blackwell had tried to impress on them, and this one was crucial. They were now on the cusp of a self-reinforcing cycle that would likely rake in the cash – an American tour sparking interest in the album, whose release would create excitement for further touring, stoking further album sales, etc. It was 'breakthrough time' if the game was played right. So the situation was quite clear – the road waited.

While Jim brooded and twisted his hair, Chris Wood's response to the uncertainty was predictable. The country sanctuary long gone, and bound by love to Jeanette, his life in London would prove the opposite of the rejuvenating Downs. Having scaled a creative peak with the Low Spark sessions, a gradual yet seemingly inexorable decline now took hold as alcohol and drugs became his coping mechanisms for a life slipping more and more off kilter. Curiously, it was Dave Mason who claimed to have earlier suggested Chris might need something like an "intervention", only to have the idea rebuffed by Jim and Steve. Perhaps they were once again, a little too close to the trees to see the forest.

One person, a little further removed, did get a clear glimpse. In a chance encounter, Rosie Roper, the village girl from Aston Tirrold that had formed a special bond with Chris back in the Cottage days, ran into him again in the fall of 1971. As Chris had long ago encouraged her to do, instead of 'ruining her life' as an uneducated barmaid, she had returned to school and become a nurse. Stopping into a pub called the 'Waterloo' between Cholsey and Moulsford at the Berkshire border with some friends, Chris and Traffic happened to be there too. She was shocked by what she saw. "I'd gone in for a drink, and I looked over and thought, 'Under all that hair, that beard and moustache – I know that guy.' He looked like a tramp – and it was Chris. (He) couldn't even stand up. He'd gone from sitting up to lying down on this bench. I walked over and I thought he was dead." Glaring at the scene, Rose was indignant that no one else seemed to pay any mind. "I looked at them all and said, 'Don't you think you should get this lad home?'" Watching him dragged out the door, Rose recalled the clear-eyed, smiling Chris she used to know, and pondered the price he'd paid for *his* career choice, "I thought, 'My god, what has he done to himself. Oh, what is money if that's all it does to you?' I could not believe it – *that* isn't the lad I'd seen four years ago." It would be the last time she ever saw him.

If Chris sometimes seemed uncomfortably close to death's door, others within his extended circle also approached that threshold. 'Twitch' (Michael Jones), the Elbow Room DJ once known for his Jamaican patois and ill-fitting suits had since undergone a transformation. Entranced by the powers of LSD, he had become a kaftan-wearing hippie before morphing into a robed, Christ-like figure. His unsteady eyes filled with an inner wisdom, he now dispensed advice along with drugs that he sold or simply gave away. On a trip to India with his wife, flying high on LSD, Twitch thought he'd found a disciple on a sunny beach in Goa. Giving emphatic assurances that he could not be killed, Jones supposedly solicited a traveling companion to stab him with a long knife. But with the offer taken up, his blood would indeed soak into the Indian sand. Twitch's death hit the Traffic crew hard, with Jim writing and recording a song about his fateful path called, "How Much Can A Man Really Take". And while Chris would add a heartfelt flute track to this, the song could easily have been about him as well. While still able to impart his feelings into music, the steady drip of personal loss was taking its toll.

The dark shadow seemed to have even drifted across the ocean. Back in America yet again, the happy, almost idyllic days of the 1970 trio tour now felt a million miles away. Only a little over a year later, in New York City, usual comforting haunts like The Scene and the Fillmore East had closed. Across the country too, the tone was quite off. While '69 and '70 had been chock full of rock festivals all trying to extend or recapture the innocent charm and glory of Woodstock, by 1971 many that took place were plagued by problems – a combination of poor management, tired acts and an overall lack of enthusiasm. Looming over it all was the administration of Richard Nixon – now into its third oppressive year. Having campaigned heavily on the promise to end the Vietnam War "with honor", the conflict inexplicably raged on. With mangled veterans on the streets and body bags coming home weekly, there seemed no light at the end of this tunnel – and the effect was chilling. The free and open feeling that had previously been so much part of the American experience now seemed fragile and waning.

Stardom was exacting its own cost. Drugs aside, the insulation from reality and the simultaneous re-enforcing of the mythic nature of the artist was becoming smothering, and for some, intolerable. With Jimi Hendrix, Brian Jones, Janis Joplin, and just recently Jim Morrison gone, the destination they'd all sought – fame – had revealed a new and horrific face.

David Bowie, who had performed nakedly alone with an acoustic guitar on the recent bill with Traffic at Glastonbury, sought to survive the madness by paradoxically embracing it full-on – creating an otherworldly persona called 'Ziggy Stardust' to protect him. Although fairly new on the scene, Bowie had insight into the soul-killing intellectual void that the culture had evolved into. He later mused, "There is such a lack of substance that your ego becomes the whole world. You come to think that the only defense is to believe in yourself." But where did that leave those whose ego wasn't as strong, or perhaps couldn't quite believe their own mythology?

For Traffic, myth and reality were very much in conflict. While a much larger band, somehow they had become reduced as well. On this tour, consistency became the primary, if sometimes elusive goal. Considering their size and the various drug problems any number of things could and did go wrong. Still, if not quite as nimble as in the past, the initial shows proved much better than the previous British disasters. With the new studio album still unreleased, they played most of the songs from it anyway, finding acceptance and often enthusiasm. Having seen so much more of Traffic then their English counterparts, American fans still very much loved and appreciated this band. That much at least could be counted on.

They hit the usual places, from New York, Boston, Chicago, and back to the west coast. At Bill Graham's Winterland on October 28th, it was almost like the old days. The announcer began the show by shouting, "From England, the incomparable Traffic!" Kicking off with "Medicated Goo", they dug in with verve and passion, winding up with a long exploratory "Low Spark" that Jim had enigmatically introduced, "This is dedicated to everybody who gets put down for doing something right." Somehow, no matter what they'd been through San Francisco always made everything worth it, and the show left everyone up once more. But behind the scenes, the road was much rockier.

Richard Feld was co-owner of Activated Air, the sound company that the band was using this time out. While loving Traffic's music, he remembered a hard and sometimes quite unpleasant edge to this particular trip, especially after the shows. "Back at the hotel, sometimes members of the band are partying – in this particular case it was always Gordon and Grech. And there was *always* a lot of smack, and really scuzzy groupies around. I remember grabbing my partner by the collar and saying, 'Let's get the hell out of here, this is poison'. You know, everybody is shooting up – it was ugly."

Entangled in the situation, Chris was in full retreat mode. The once seemingly boundless landscape explored so freely back in '68 had now shrunk to a universe of airplanes, flood-lit stages and the four walls of whatever hotel they were in. Tailed by a roadie everywhere he went, he couldn't wander far. If getting high, talking and listening to cassettes provided a mere pseudo-oasis, in the netherworld of the road, it would have to do.

Fairport Convention was the opening act. Their bass player, Dave Pegg, the guy who'd unknowingly almost gotten Dave Mason's Traffic slot back in the Elbow Room days, recalled that consumption-wise Chris was a match for anybody. "Chris was a bit of a 'party animal', I think it's fair to say that he kind of out-partied everybody else. You could always have a party in Chris's room. They'd have all the spirits; they'd have their own bar." Playing the larger arenas, there was no lack of cash to crimp the lifestyle. Pegg recalled, "They'd have their own accountant following them around. Chris would buy a different hi-fi every day. He'd send the accountant out to buy a new hi-fi, 'cause he'd left it, or he'd thrown it out the window. It was literally every day," Pegg noted.

Soundman Feld observed what came out the other end, "Chris Wood – he was a sweetheart, an absolute sweetheart, I never heard a bad word out of him. He was though, drunk – all the time. We would get up for breakfast, and he had been up all night. He would always sit down with us, and more than likely he would fall asleep in his eggs. To make conversation with, he didn't always make a lot of sense, but he could play. He was *very* Traffic – jazzy," said Feld.

Chris himself would say almost nothing about the period, recalling only that the tour "ended with a lot of friction" and indicating that much of it emanated from Jim Gordon. And it was true. By that point, the drummer's violent tendencies had emerged full-blown; eventually he would commit the unpardonable act of losing it in front of the audience – ending more than one concert by stalking off the stage in a seething rage. "Gordon threw a shit fit on stage a number of times near the end of a gig – kicked his drum kit over, did all kinds of ugly stuff," Feld recalled.

But Jim Capaldi also laid blame on the increasingly hollow-eyed Grech, telling a reporter, "Getting Ric in wasn't the greatest move we ever made. I think Steve asked him because he was in Blind Faith with him. He wasn't right at all. The whole thing eventually got worse and worse." He noted that even the plane rides were becoming tense and problematic.

Careening down the road, it wasn't long after San Francisco that the wheels fell off. With the 'contractual obligation' now complete, no time was wasted – both Grech and Gordon had screwed up too many times. As Richard Feld witnessed, "Those guys came to no good… We finished up that tour I think in Minneapolis/St. Paul – they were fired that night."

Sadly, the future prospects for both were dim: Ric Grech's career would drift ever downward, and by the time he died in 1990 of liver and kidney disease his most recent job had been selling carpet. As for Jim Gordon, his mental status was eventually diagnosed as schizophrenia, the seriousness of which was only fully appreciated after he stabbed his mother to death in 1983 – believing her responsible for the chatter of evil, controlling voices in his head. Institutionalized in a men's facility in California, Gordon remains there to this day.

Back in '71, the plane ride home from America was somber. With two members already gone and Winwood wanting to step away from it all even before the tour, the others now waited for the other shoe to drop. Once back in England, Jim was succinct about where he thought things stood, "I could see it coming… By the end of the tour Steve had decided to break the group up." But instead of a dreaded phone call and press release, weeks would drag by with only silence – painful, but far better than the alternative.

Trying not to dwell on an uncertain future, Jim decided to push forward and make a solo album. While a couple of songs were already in the can – leftovers from the Low Spark sessions, most of the work still lay ahead. Seeking to help him along (and perhaps with the outline of a grander scheme already in mind), Manager Blackwell would offer a suggestion.

('Beatle star in Traffic?', Tom Campbell, October 4 1970)

('Chris Wood in talk in', Steve Peacock, Sounds, 5/12/1973)

('Traffic Jam', Ray Townley, DownBeat, 1/30/1975)

('Endless party at Glastonbury', Chris Holden, Rolling Stone, 7/22/1971)

('Hendrix, A Biography', Chris Welch, Flash Books, New York, 1973)

CHAPTER TWENTY-ONE

('Live! Traffic and Seatrain', Record Mirror, 10/2/1971)

('Traffic Back On the Road', Mary Campbell, Waycross Journal Herald, 10/17/1974)

('Men Of words, Men of Music. The ascent of Bowie, from myth to reality', Alec Ross, Trouser Press, 10/1979)

('My Life, So Far…', Georgiana Steele-Waller, self-published, 2007)

('The Story of Life', Jimi Hendrix)

('The Trouble In The Rhythm Section', Tony Stewart, NME, 3/25/1972)

CHAPTER TWENTY-TWO

'ALABAMA MEETS GHANA'

If a former casket warehouse in Sheffield, Alabama, was an exceedingly unlikely place for Jim Capaldi to find himself, there was a connection. Only months before, Chris Blackwell had used the place at 6314 Jackson Highway (now known as 'Muscle Shoals Sound Studio') and its resident session musicians to record music with soul/reggae singer, Jimmy Cliff, for his next album (*Another Cycle*). The resulting single "Sitting in Limbo" was a jewel, holding a lilting melancholic sound tinged with reggae and other harder to define influences. Jim liked it, a lot.

So having made up his mind to do a solo album (his first) and finding London filled with only dreary uncertainty, the guy who stood in awe of Chris Wood's brave attempt to 'go it alone' in America in '69 was now motivated to take a risk. With Blackwell along for support, and a sheath full of tunes written during the *Low Spark* period, he would shack up at the local Holiday Inn, drink (illegal) whiskey with the guys, and start knocking out songs.

The musicians he worked with – the Muscle Shoals Rhythm Section, while nearly unknown to the public were still legends of sorts, having cut their teeth supporting many of the great Soul and R&B acts at nearby Fame Studios. The experiences of Chief Engineer, Jimmy Johnson, still in his 20's, illustrated why Jim sought them out. "I'm the guy that mixed 'When a Man Loves a Woman', and also 'Sweet Soul Music' by Arthur Connelly," Johnson recalled. "And those were in mono. 'Sweet Soul...' was no overdubs, I had one overdub on 'When A Man...', and that was it. Once we got it, and the balance was right – that was the finished record. When I cut that out it went straight to the presser to be mastered! See, that's how we learned it – and 'Sweet Soul...' was one take. We did everything live, it was an Otis Redding production..."

His collaborators were equally skilled; David Hood's bass playing was both solid and nimble, while the drumming of implacable and bespectacled Roger Hawkins was precise yet funky. And Barry Beckett's fluid mastery of the keyboards allowed him to slip comfortably into any contemporary genre of music. Besides engineering, Johnson also played the electric guitar with a clipped rhythm fitting neatly into the talents of the others.

In a nutshell, the Muscle Shoals cache was based on excellent musicianship paired with a clear mission: to make great and, if possible, 'hit' records in an efficient, timely manner. As Jimmy Johnson recalled, "We thought it was our duty – for everyone – to cut a single that would sell well. Stuff that we were known for was mostly hit records – hit singles."

As for Jim, his gamble very quickly paid off; *Oh How We Danced*, his first solo album, was essentially finished in less than a week. And he almost got his hit too. The single "Eve", written for and about Anna's daughter, broke into the top 100 on the U.S. record charts during early '72. Not a bad start to a solo career that he never really expected to have.

Meanwhile, Traffic's own album, *The Low Spark Of High-Heeled Boys*, with its unique sound and hexagonal-shaped cover (designed by artist Tony Wright) was getting great reviews. More importantly, the title song in particular was working a mysterious jazzy magic across the airwaves; the buzzing Moog notes floating out of underground radio stations and into the headphones of stoned teenagers from coast to coast. For a band who'd never courted the commercial path to success, the enigmatic looking/sounding record was now well on its way toward selling a million copies. By early February, *Billboard* would declare the album 'Gold'. Amazingly, the beginning of 1972 would find Traffic, for the first time in their career, the hottest band of the day. With even more money and fame sitting on the table just waiting to be picked up, there would never be a better time to push the whole thing again, hard.

Yet a formidable obstacle remained. Did the band even exist? While the others didn't know if the last tour's 'break up' was final or simply Steve's emphatic reaction to the previous lineup, at the very least they lacked a rhythm section. But having returned to the motherland, Capaldi and Blackwell hadn't come back empty handed. Besides a briefcase full of Jim's master tapes the two also carried a possible solution to the 'Traffic problem'.

CHAPTER TWENTY-TWO

The sales approach likely had a couple of angles. With a tour already booked (possibly a planned continuation of the last jaunt), the obligation itself was difficult to dodge. But Jim's experience with the Rhythm Section also held the promise that things would be different this time, and better. Recreational beer and whiskey aside, none of the Alabaman musicians were drug users, much less abusers. Great music minus the hassles would prove a hard deal to refuse. And, as the album peaked in the charts, the combined logic would take things to a conclusion that would later seem quite natural, if not inevitable.

The plan, such as it was, was straightforward. Chris, Jim, Reebop and Steve would fly to northern Alabama, rehearse for a few days with a new drummer and bass player and then play gigs. And while Steve was on board with the plan, Chris suddenly and unexpectedly balked. While later he would fault Muscle Shoals for being too predictable, his fear was likely the opposite at first – the distinct possibility of another crash landing, which might very well kill the band for good. He was definitely concerned about the rehearsal time – a mere three days slotted with people he'd never met seemed quite deranged. Putting his foot down, for once Chris actively resisted, vehemently arguing with Steve and Jim to reconsider.

Eventually he would acquiesce, and in the end the Muscle Shoals Rhythm Section proved as solid as a sunbaked brick. But Chris's fears weren't entirely unfounded either. Although Winwood, Wood, Baah and Capaldi never knew it, the whole enterprise came perilously close to disaster right at the outset. Fortunately Hawkins and Hood were too polite (and likely too embarrassed) to let on how they'd nearly bailed on the whole 'Traffic thing' in the middle of the very first show.

David Hood spoke for the others in insisting that they still had almost no idea who Traffic was. In fact, he wasn't even sure that he really liked the band. "We didn't know who the hell they were. I had heard, through a friend of mine, like "Forty Thousand Headmen", a few things. I thought, 'Yeah, well, they're *pretty* good.'" But with Blackwell paying up front for a solid month of studio bookings, traveling around the country and playing a few songs with an eccentric British band seemed like a pretty sweet deal. Used to coming into new music cold and quickly sorting things out, it wasn't all that different from what they were used to – at first. David Hood recalled the first meeting, "They showed up, like two or three days before we were supposed to go out on the road with them and said 'We want to do these songs', this and that. We made our little chord charts – and the songs were *long*, some of them, like ten or fifteen minutes long – and they'd have like two chords in them or something. I thought, 'This will be a breeze.'"

Traffic needed only two players for the tour, bassist Hood, and drummer Hawkins. Jimmy Johnson was hired to engineer the sound and would be manning the mixing desk, while Beckett stayed behind. Hawkins and Hood had played together so long that they could practically read each other's minds, so even with minimal rehearsal, they would leave Sheffield with a calm confidence the job would get done. Instead, they would step into a rock 'n roll maelstrom which juxtaposed their skill against chaos, naïveté, and naked fear.

The first scheduled show was at Yale University, in the first week of February. It also happened to be the week that *The Low Spark Of High-Heeled Boys* went Gold in the Billboard charts. The auditorium held twelve thousand, and it was packed – in their time away from the States, Traffic's popularity had peaked. Waiting to go on stage, Hawkins and Hood finally took a moment to reflect on their situation, although it probably would have been better if they hadn't. Despite all the sessions and years immersed in music, they had somehow *never* played a concert before – this would be their first.

"I've got my little notes, charts and stuff," David Hood recalled. "We went to New Haven Connecticut, at Yale. First night, this is funny, we were down beneath the stage in the dressing room, and we hear this 'raaargh!' – this roar. So, I go upstairs and peek out, and they're throwing a Frisbee. The place is mobbed – full, and they were just cheering because they were throwing a Frisbee back and forth. I thought, 'Good lord!'"

From there, the magnitude of their situation became suddenly, chillingly clear. "And so we go out there – and it is *so loud*, the music's loud, the crowd is loud, the lights were dim, I couldn't see my little notes – I'm scared to death. I don't know what the shit is going on. Man, I thought, 'What have I got myself into?' And I looked at Roger, and he's the same way." Retreating to their musical instincts the two gritted their teeth and simply hung on, until the midpoint of the concert when they had a break. Here Steve, Chris and Jim took their trio moment for the now iconic "John Barleycorn". Minds reeling as they stepped off stage, a nearly frantic Hood locked eyes with Hawkins, "So, we got a break, we went off stage and I thought Roger was going to *leave*. His face was white; he didn't know what to do. And I thought, really, that he was going to go get in the car and just leave." But the pause allowed both a moment to gather up their wits and ultimately, finish the job. If

Steve, Jim or Chris noticed the distress, nothing was ever said. Compared to the previous road trip, everything was going just fine.

After that, they learned to go with the flow, adjusting to life as rock 'n rollers. David Hood recalled, "Yeah, we were part of Traffic! It seemed kind of funny, because here were these guys from Alabama, our accents were so different. You can imagine a group with Reebop, Woody, Steve, and me and Roger…" Or as Jim labeled it: "Alabama meets Ghana."

In reality, the changes were seismic, with the self-professed "steady home guys" more than a little shocked at how their lives had been transformed. Jimmy Johnson, hired to produce the sound for the concerts, was shown a mixing board he'd never seen just before the first show and expected to simply make it work, "It was incredible… I had never mixed live before. They just threw me in, like a little kid thrown out in the water and told –'swim'. I had never seen a board like that… it was straight up, like a strange looking early 'Mackey' board."

As for David Hood, he admitted to being "appalled" by the lack of structure and laissez-faire attitudes of the others. "We'd say, well, we've got to be down in the lobby of the hotel at 10, because we have to catch a flight at 11 to be in time for the show. So us guys, being businessmen in our own right and studio guys – if we were booked for a session at 10, we were there before 10 to get stuff set up. So, we'd all be down in the lobby, waiting, waiting, waiting. Pretty soon, someone would stagger out, someone else would stagger out. Pretty soon, someone would be *carrying* Woody out – dragging his stuff. We couldn't believe it! I'd probably get ulcers worrying about the missed plane. They didn't care you know, because somebody was taking care of them every moment. They had roadies – Wood had a roadie assigned."

Burned into the minds of the ultra-responsible Muscle Shoals men were memories of just how *different* the lifestyles of their band-mates were from their own. Having climbed the ladder to the upper reaches of rock's elite, these musicians were now pampered geese required only to lay more golden eggs. "They were just children," Hood concluded, "who could just not have any responsibilities at all. Woody was a pretty big partier – alcohol, drugs, everything. He lived like there was no tomorrow, so when tomorrow came, they'd have to go get him – drag him."

Having a straight, tight band behind him, by show time Chris was typically sober enough to play his arsenal of flute, saxophone and keyboards. But having slid into a full-on dependency, these days a special kind of equilibrium had to be maintained, or else. Tony Curtis, a long-time roadie for the band, recalled that Chris now required a carefully measured dose of alcohol to keep things in balance, "I think he used to get frustrated. I know you had to give him a controlled quantity of scotch and coke on stage. You'd try to limit it, but he'd want more – you just try to limit it. That bit had to be just right."

Once, deprived of his usual quota on management's orders, Chris went into what was for him a unique fit of pique – hurling his prized flute javelin-style at Curtis, who casually reached out and caught the projectile in mid-air. Thereafter, experienced roadies stood by with the correct formula, since above all – the show had to go on.

But, unlike the last tours' consistently edgy state, this time around the show was satisfying and getting better all the time. They even had a new 'star'. Center stage, amid his spread of drums and colorful garb, Reebop was now the visual focal point. Smiling broadly as he threw his head back and forward in time to the music, in early '72 he was beloved and at the top of his game. Jim Capaldi recalled his reception, "He went on to become a great piece of Traffic in that period – where we'd walk on stage and ten thousand people would be going, 'Reebop! Reebop! Reebop!' He walked on with the African clothes… he was a monster. But then, he went through all that to being an absolute fucking nightmare!"

Reebop's antics were legendary. Although short and thin, he was both incredibly strong and able to go for days without sleep. David Hood remembered some long, confusing evenings, "He was a fun guy, but he was further out than the rest of them. I spent many a night, all night, talking with Reebop and would walk away thinking, '*What did he say?*'" His energy wasn't all natural though; a consumer of cocaine, he was capable of ingesting vast amounts. Not surprisingly, his mood could veer pretty far off kilter, and he too could pitch a fit, being known to hurl sharp-edged metal timbales like Frisbees at hapless roadies. But having witnessed Gordon's unceremonious ouster, he never created a scene in front of an audience.

Through it all, Steve Winwood was friendly and welcoming to the new band members, but as usual kept a distance from any mayhem. Like many rock stars seen up close for the first time, David Hood noticed that the physical form didn't match the legend. "Winwood is a really nice, easy-going, soft spoken, quiet kind of guy. When we knew him, I bet he didn't weigh 100, maybe 120 lbs – white, skinny, he looked frail, like a good wind would blow him away."

In fact, Steve wasn't feeling well these days, which became increasingly clear as the tour continued. The symptoms were vague, and shifting – at time his abdomen was tender, his appetite poor. At other times, his throat would be sore, his singing strained. A number of doctors were consulted, but it remained unclear what, if anything was physically wrong. One concern was that he might have a serious problem with his vocal cords. Penny Massot recalled, "I think a lot of it was to do with (that) he smoked too much dope. So that didn't help, and he wasn't feeling well. He went to a lot of doctors in New York – throat doctors, and there was nothing wrong with him." Even so, the sense of physical unease continued.

The tour ended up in California, and as usual for the west coast, they turned in great performances. Hood confirmed that things had turned completely around since that first frightening gig, "It took me a while that first tour to get used to it, Roger too. As we did it, it got good, and by the end of that tour it was really good." Having seen the rising tide of potential, a film crew was there to meet them at the Santa Monica Civic Auditorium. With the musical gods smiling, a confident performance was indeed captured. Naturally, much of the footage was centered on Steve, but everyone got a moment to shine.

Chris's profile came during "Rainmaker", and the choice of shots was providential. The song's lyrics – a plea from a farmer to a shaman to help end a crop killing drought, was one that he connected with; like 'Barleycorn' before it, Chris understood where 'Rainmaker' was coming from. And, as the camera came in tight, he went there – intensity contorting his face as he leaned into the microphone to begin a keening flute solo. Head cocked to one side, the notes spilled forth as his eyes shifted far to the right, as if trying to catch a glimpse of his own emotional vortex. Dramatically sucking air between streams of sound, his energy would crescendo before fading back into the melody. And just that quickly he was backing away; it was done – just a few torrents of air through a metal tube. But a moment of strange beauty had also been captured – an all-too-rare visual documentation of Chris's creative passion.

Watching the performance on DVD more than thirty years later, the intervening time allowed David Hood a deeper appreciation for his ex-band mate, "He played great, very intense; it was thrilling to watch. I think he went off his own feelings quite a bit. He colored the music – he didn't really play melodies in the music, he colored it. He created moods. The eerie sounds he would get on that flute on some things… it was perfect; it had a different, spiritual quality."

CHAPTER TWENTY-THREE

NOTES FROM THE EDGE

As good as the '72 tour had been, its wake would leave waves of uncertainty curling off in all directions. Feeling poorly, Steve headed straight back to Gloucestershire and more doctors. Jim and Chris too simply went home, returning to their own peculiar states of limbo. As for the Muscle Shoals players – dropped abruptly back into their now strangely sedate lives in small town Alabama – they were left with no indication when or if they would be invited back. "We did the tour, and then it was 'See 'ya'", was all that David Hood could recall being told.

Back at the London flat in the depths of a rainy English winter and needing to restore a sense of normality to his life, Chris brought a dog home one day – a whip-thin Saluki whom Jeanette would name 'Jasmine'(subsequently nicknamed 'Jazzer' by Chris). Having always had dogs as a boy, the contact with a being asking only for food and affection helped ground lives grown removed from day-to-day concerns. But the dog could only do so much. With a lifestyle still including drugs and a near-constant stream of visitors – the mix was, at best, inhibiting to Chris's creativity.

Meanwhile, suffering and still unable to get a satisfactory explanation for his ailments, Steve had gone to ground. The condition progressed to an acute stage as he woke in agony one day, doubling over and grimacing. Penny Massot recalled, "I had to call the doctor. This doctor that I called for him didn't diagnose it at all, and in the end I said, 'Let's go in the car.' He was in terrible pain and I drove him to Cheltenham General. When we walked in there, the doctor said to me, 'You know, he's got a 50/50 chance.' At the end of the day what was wrong with him was that he had a burst appendix – and he nearly died. He had peritonitis."

Sent home to convalesce, the illness and surgery would prove quite debilitating; very weak for months, he only slowly regained strength. The brush with death apparently shook him up. For Penny, the extended duration together became quite claustrophobic. "I was with Steve, holed up in Gloucestershire, where we never moved. He didn't really want me to leave him. He didn't feel safe unless I was around."

With months dragging by and nothing happening, Jim grew concerned, again wondering if his band still existed. Unable to rouse Steve from his lair, he turned to Chris. At Notting Hill Gate, he found Jeanette, Chris and Jazzer living a decidedly unhealthy lifestyle – the hangers on and drugs looking more and more like a noose tightening around his neck. Long overdue perhaps, Jim finally comprehended the transformation that had taken over his friend, and it scared him, "When I met him, I would never, in a million years – I would have bet any money in the universe – that a sensitive guy like that could ever get into really, really dark, dangerous stuff. But he started going out and hanging out, doing shit I could have never… stuff that would have frightened the life out of me… heavy, needles, heroin, you know." Appalled, Jim hauled the couple (and dog) back to his protected home in Marlow for some respite from the toxic London scene.

While a step in the right direction, the taste of life outside the big city didn't work any miracles. Long talks and pleading to lay off the drugs finally turned to harangues – "What are you *doing* man!" But, by deflecting any notion that he had a problem, Chris was incapable of changing anything. His method of getting off heroin merely involved a substitution – a bag of pills that accompanied him to Jim's house. And it didn't help that in his relationship with Jeanette, there was no 'strong one' to help pull the other out of danger. Jim literally tried to do it for both of them, but finally had to face the futility of the task. "They were living with me, hanging out and whatever. I'd pop out, up to town or something and come back and they'd both be in the kitchen. It was in the days of Mandrax, the sleeping pills – downers. I'd be in the kitchen to make tea and Jeanette would be on one side, saying something, and Chris would be over by the sink. Then Jeanette would eventually get down on the floor, and I'd try to lift her up – 'hang on' you know – and prop her up. And as I'd prop her up, Chris would slip down on the other side of the floor. Then I'd get him up, then *she'd* slip down again – and I said 'Fuck it!' and went on and made a cup of tea! Exactly what happened one night – I just stood there laughing."

His mirth soon faded. The longer Chris and Jeanette stayed, the clearer it became that their path had become a well-worn rut, "He lived with me for about three months, him and Jeanette. And you know, you get to that stage where you really have taken that extra step – over to the other side. You can shout, but you're never gonna get them back over. He was already…"

Bleak as it seemed, Jim would seek another route to reconnect. With summer approaching, Jim, Chris and his dog (but interestingly not Jeanette) took a road trip to the coast. Driving in Jim's big American Pontiac Firebird, they headed toward the Welsh coast to reach Padstow, on the coast of Cornwall. The traditional site of the Wood family's in-country vacation, the two were to meet up with Steph, Muriel and Stephen Wood. Although the Cornwall holiday was something the Wood family did nearly every summer whilst Chris was growing up, it had now been years. As a partial return to the innocent days of his youth, the trip was welcome and very much needed. But as was the norm, a major complication would emerge.

Winding through narrow country roads in Jim's Firebird, the skeletal hand of mortality that nearly grasped Steve, now scythed toward Chris and Jim. Never a great driver, Jim's reputation behind the wheel was such that many of his friends wouldn't even get into a car with him. While not overly concerned, Chris did follow Jim's lead by strapping on his seatbelt. As they neared the coast, Jim noticed a group of bicyclists eyeing his bright red 'muscle car' and decided to show off. Hitting the gas and smiling broadly as they roared by, a dip in the road followed by an unexpected bend loomed as they reached peak velocity. Losing control, the front tires would leave the road coming out of the depression before the Firebird struck a stone wall bordering an adjacent field. Sloped with centuries of accumulated dirt, the wall acted as a ramp, launching the car in a twisting trajectory which ended as they slammed back into the road, inverted, the roof partly crushed, sparks flying everywhere.

Jim recalled the aftermath, "The next thing is, we're upside down, the wheels are spinning round. The dog's in a bit of a bewildered state, with its tail wagging in our faces, 'cause we're upside down, strapped into the car. In the next ten seconds, I envision the petrol tank exploding, and I'm trying to open the door, which of course is all buckled, it won't move. I'm banging and kicking with one leg and arm, and I'm freaking out. And Chris calmly winds the window handle – and the window goes *up*, 'cause we're upside down, you see. I'm panicking, kicking my door and fucking screaming, and Chris, of all people, he just calmly wound the window… But the dog and me and him just crawl out that side of the car. I'm sitting on the side of the road with my neck fucking killing me – I'm going 'Oh man', holding my head. The next thing I know, while I sat there, some old lady had appeared. And I look 'round, there's the old lady, Chris with the lead in his hand and Jasmine following behind him, and they're wandering down the road to have a cup of tea! Chris just wandered off, in a kind of dream, with the dog following him…"

Dazed or not, Chris did call Stephanie to pick them up as well as arranging for Jim's prized car to be towed to the local scrap yard. As a penance for his egotistical act, Jim spent most of the holiday in bed trying not to move his sprained neck. At a cottage overlooking the beautiful coastline, the drummer known for his manic energy could do little more than listen to surf and seagulls. Still, it could have been much worse.

If the vacation went rather poorly for Jim, Chris would get a vital boost from his time away from London. Grounded once again by family and calming sea, he would return home determined to find another path to writing music – either something he could submit to Traffic, or if necessary, for a project of his own. Almost immediately, a helping hand appeared.

At Island sessions for Reebop's solo album, Chris met a young guitar player called 'Junior' Hanson (full name, Donald Hanson Marvin Kerr Richards, Jr.). Hanson was playing with Toot and the Maytals, who had recently recorded a song called "Reggae Got Soul" for Island. Heavily influenced by Jimi Hendrix, Junior was also a big Traffic fan. Invited back to Chris's apartment for a jam, they hit it off right away – extraordinarily so – for months thereafter the two were rarely apart. "Chris was a great friend of mine, I used to go out with him *every* day for a long while – every night," was Hanson's recollection of those times. "We'd be up every night, when everyone else was in bed." Finally, liberated from the role of almost side-man that he'd slipped into with Traffic, Chris plowed headfirst into making his own music with Hanson. "He played flute and keyboard, saxophone and whatever," Junior recalled. "He bought a bunch of equipment and we started writing stuff every day – also for his wife, he was writing stuff. We were very close, all three of us, very good friends." Still a teenager, and living at home with his mother, Hanson made the most of his time with Chris and Jeanette. "I'd stay all night with him, and go to mother's house in the morning before the rush hour started – get some sleep and come back and start again."

The three quickly dialed into an eclectic but productive methodology. "We did everything. We'd start the song with just the lyrics, sometimes we'd start it with a bass line, sometimes it would be a sequence of chords.

Sometimes it would be a melody he'd play on the flute – so it wasn't one way of writing a song. By the end of the week you could have a full song, and start putting the words in, and before you know it, you have the full deal – the melody, the bridge, the chorus, the solo; Jeanette would come up with some words, she'd sing along and write them down. I guess she had a little book to keep whatever words she came up with."

Having helped spark Chris's creativity back to life, Hanson soon realized he was dealing with a rare sort of musician. "Chris was at a level where he could play with somebody like Jimi Hendrix, or maybe Miles Davis… He had a kind of 'bird thing' where he could fly – he could help the music fly. Chris had the ability to catch you in a couple of notes, and you pretty much knew it was him. Whereas a lot of people who played the same instrument were very technical, but once they start playing you lose interest very quickly, because they didn't dig into your soul like Chris would. He would go into a trance when he played. People like Hendrix, and sometimes Clapton – they actually go into a trance when they play, and Chris was that kind of player. He preferred to be musically hypnotized, I think, rather than technically blown away. He was more economical in what he gave you, so that you could actually feel it, and remember it. He was always like, very sensitive with music. He knew when to play… and you'd feel really good, he'd really kind of suck you in – the Pied Piper. He created atmospheres – like birds, clouds, sunshine. He'd make sounds like *nature*. If you listen, you'll hear it…"

Change was in the air. As the fall progressed to winter, Steve finally began to stir, prompted by Penny, Blackwell and especially Jim – who kept showing up at the house, sheaths of lyrics in hand. The time, it seemed, had come; Traffic would have another go.

Reconvening at Island's offices, Chris came prepared. Between all the jamming and the musical nights with Junior, his creative resurgence had borne fruit. Out of all of the reels of tape, one piece stood out. Based around piano chords in a minor key, the track had no lyrics although Chris's voice, as always, came through his instrument. The sax figure that crept in carried a melancholic tone, followed by a gradual ascension to a plateau and then briefly on to something higher, seeming to peek above the clouds at the radiance beyond. As the seven-minute tune progressed to a conclusion, sax cries gave way to an almost jaunty horn-driven refrain that signaled, if not resolution then at least acceptance.

As to the "Tragic Magic's" subject matter, Jeanette thought she knew, later telling a journalist that Chris's first ever tune for Traffic, was actually about heroin. Whether a warning or a hymn to it, he himself would never say; it was likely a little of both.

As the strands of his musical life came back together, Chris's relationship with Jeanette also took a big step – they got married. Although many people assumed that they'd done that long ago – and it was an illusion they both fostered, it didn't happen until November 22, 1972. The ceremony was brief and non-denominational, done before a registrar at the Kensington Registry Office in London; Steve witnessed, while Jim acted as 'Best Man'. Although there is a 'wedding photograph' showing Jeanette in a beautiful white dress, it was apparently done after the fact for the families. On the day, it was a much simpler, seemingly impulsive event. Jeanette's friend and former Cake collaborator Eleanor was there, and helped Jeanette get herself together, "She was late, and I was trying to get her dressed. I had a pair of jeans on with my boots on top of the jeans – and she did the exact same thing: my friend Jeanette, my sister."

But why now? Suzette Newman, an assistant to Chris Blackwell at Island, and someone who knew the couple well, thought she knew. She recalled that at the time Jeanette, still a non-resident, was coming to the end of her work visa, and would have to leave the country unless she married an Englishman. With the loss of her father, the New York apartment, and her band, the combination was unsettling. Suzette believed that if Chris hadn't agreed, Jeanette would have looked elsewhere, "Jeanette got married because she *needed* to get married! It was between Chris and another guy. She was seeing Chris, but she was already seeing someone else too." Regardless, Chris loved Jeanette far too much to let her go. In a practical sense, the marriage changed nothing. Married or not, Jeanette remained an iridescent butterfly, flying where she willed.

By early December, Chris's *other* open marriage was also starting up again. At Steve's house and then in London they went over the new songs as a plan solidified – knock a new album out with the Muscle Shoals Rhythm Section and hit the road again. Although the core members of Traffic had been separated for many months, Junior Hanson confirmed that the connection between them all, but especially Chris and Steve, remained strong, "They were really close, you know. They had the kind of connection where they really didn't need to talk to each other. They just looked at each other and they knew what the next move would be; very close."

Seeing his friend off on his trip to America, Hanson suspected that he and Chris might never be quite as tight again, and it was true. While they would certainly play in the future, the planned album would slowly fade from view, with even the reels already recorded somehow disappearing. But there was an upside. Between the non-stop wood-shedding and contacts made via Chris, Junior ended up making his own album for Island. Later still, he would change his last (stage) name to Marvin and hook up with yet another artist famous for weaving hypnotic spells. Coming out of the other end of the 1970's, Junior Marvin would be best-known as the lead guitarist for Bob Marley and the Wailers.

*

Sheffield, Alabama, December 1972: With a strong sense of déjà vu hanging in the air – the multicultural gang quietly reconvened. Yes, Traffic was back in town, ready to make their next record – *Shoot Out At The Fantasy Factory*. Oddly though, publicity in the rock press regarding the trip was nil because officially, it never happened. When finally released, the back cover of the album would say only: "Recorded at Strawberry Hill Studios, Jamaica." Reminded of that, David Hood could only laugh and say, "Well, I've never *been* to Jamaica." There was a reason for the deception. Like the Rolling Stones back in December of '69 – who recorded a chunk of *Sticky Fingers* incognito at the same location, Traffic lacked work visas – rendering them unable to legally record in the U.S.A. If that made them rock outlaws and pirates, at least they were in good company.

Split by an ocean for nearly a year, once reunited they all simply got to work. "We were happy to see them, they were happy to see us – we recorded", was David Hood's recollection. The album came together incredibly fast. For a band used to dribbling out sessions over months, the Muscle Shoals methodology proved a lesson in economy. Listening to demos, the session team huddled and drew up chord charts, after which track after track tumbled forth. And, as had happened previously for Jim's album, within a week or so (minus a few overdubs), they were done. Hood recalled, "Due to our method, we changed their way of recording – added structure to it, and we got it all done pretty quick."

There was one puzzling, non-negotiable concession the Muscle Shoals Studio had to make. Ever since the watershed "Dear Mr. Fantasy" session, a vital lesson had been learned – whenever possible Traffic recorded together, unobstructed, as a band; the crucial nonverbal communication between them simply required it. With all the changes that they'd been through, more than anything else this might explain how they maintained that consistent, identifiable, 'Traffic sound'. So counter to modern norms, there would be no drum or vocal booth, no baffling to separate the players. David Hood recalled, "With them we just set up in the middle of the floor – like a band – it meant that there was leakage. That was something that we would never let happen in our recording place." While complying, the Americans were quite dubious. And when all was said and done, their well-practiced ears could hear the lack of separation that went counter to the crisp, well defined sound they were known for. Only later would Hood appreciate why things had to be that way. "But that was part of the sound that they had – that's how they got some of their sounds." And Traffic's sounds had both moved forward and looked back – the question being if and how they would all fit together.

The title track, a fuzz-guitar powerhouse, would open the record with an ominous sounding roar. Paired incongruously with comic book lyrics, the song would prove loud but shallow. If lacking true menace, "Shoot Out..." would still be saved by a groove fueled by Reebop's drums.

Up next was the stately "Rollright Stones", bearing lyrics born of a spooky night at a stone circle of the same name from back in the Cottage era. Jim portrayed the Stones (in existence as far back as 4,000 B.C.) as repositories of the human spirit, binding generations across time. Based around Winwood's ebbing and flowing piano, the long (thirteen minute) track, wisely left Woody plenty of room. And having a large canvas before him he painted in contrasts, with brash, percolating sax figures beefing up the chorus, and contemplative flute lines reaching out to nestle the verses. Deep into the track, the sax would surge again, gurgling in an unknown but affecting tongue. With "Rollright Stones", the 'Traffic vibe' would emerge once again, clear and strong.

In some ways, "Evening Blue" was the purest song of the lot. Jim's tale of a sleepless night spent in front of a crackling fireplace, sung by Steve in a high, clear voice was set against a sparkling acoustic guitar. Chris's straight tenor solo was economical yet full of feeling – playfully illustrating the sound of the wind rustling around a darkened house. A mellow jewel, Evening Blue affirmed that the 'Barleycorn' vibe was still part of their vocabulary.

Sitting at the piano in his leather jacket, an unshaven Chris would finally play a sketch of his song as the others gathered around. Always laser-focused on making "hit records", to the Alabaman musicians "Tragic Magic" seemed pretty far out. David Hood recalled, "The chord changes don't go where you think they would go. They don't follow 'standard procedure' – weird. And there's no real melody to that song, it's all feel and adlibbed things. It's all chord changes and feel – no melody." Cognizant of the cliché of the jazz sax solo, Chris's horn work would remain restrained, working to serve the overall dynamics. If Chris's musical path had, at first, seemed an unlikely one, in the end it all came together. Cleanly captured by Muscle Shoals' well-placed microphones, "Tragic Magic" would shimmer with a low-key yet undeniable authority.

And with that, Chris Wood was finally a songwriter for Traffic. Just as gratifying, with no concessions at all made to commerciality, fans would be quite accepting of "Tragic Magic", a song played many times over the next two years.

Having loved *Low Spark*, *Rolling Stone* magazine could only manage an ambivalent review of the new album. The songs were dissected one by one, as if in pointing out the flaws, they might somehow go back and correct them. The comments regarding "Evening Blue" were typical: "There's a wonderful, soothing touch to this song. Chris Wood has a keen, well-phrased solo against Winwood's organ. Steve's vocal is good... but unnecessarily inhibited and sometimes a bit amateurishly inflected." "Tragic Magic" received similar comments. Having been darlings of the magazine since its inception back in '67, the review must have stung a little. But by the time this issue was out, the band was well into another, even more massive U.S. tour where the fans were voting with their money and feet every night; the auditoriums were packed.

*

On the road in January of 1973, Traffic had morphed yet again – keyboardist Barry Beckett had been invited to play Hammond organ. Although done to allow Steve to concentrate on piano, guitar and vocals, Chris too would no longer have to cover that spot on things like "Empty Pages", or "Dear Mr. Fantasy", a role he'd held since 1967. With Jimmy Johnson still mixing sound, the original core of Traffic was now literally surrounded by competence and reliability. On-stage the songs now rolled with a well-oiled proficiency; sound-wise they were fantastic.

Still, Chris found reason to fret. The downside was subtle, and seemingly contrary to common sense. Besides finding himself squeezed into a more limited role, in a way Traffic was never supposed to be *that* good. Back in the trio days, the danger of it all falling apart on stage tended to keep everyone on their toes. Now, with the rhythmic component rock solid, the predictability took them near to a fully prearranged product, a dangerous place in Chris's view. But if a return to the genesis point was his deepest desire, currently no one else seemed to care. Certainly, for all the typical fan could see or hear, the band was playing great – in fact, better than ever.

In America, L.A., Frisco and then Chicago and New York City were always the highlights, with the cities between sometimes referred to merely as "the hinterlands." This time they started on the west coast, and the reception was glorious. As the 1970's unwound, audience appreciation for Traffic only grew – they were one of the few great bands who hadn't broken up, burned out or had a crucial member die. And with every tour seemingly a topper to the last, the expectations remained high.

At Bill Graham's Winterland in San Francisco for shows on January 25th and 26th (also the home of *Rolling Stone*) they seemed to defy the lukewarm album review by opening with a charged version of "Shoot Out At The Fantasy Factory". From there, they would play every song from the record, released only a week or so before – all the tracks would be received with unbridled enthusiasm. Of course, the expected "old ones" as Steve liked to call them, such as "Glad/Freedom Rider" and "John Barleycorn" were there too.

Then came the capper – on the first encore on the 26th, Carlos Santana, and members of his band showed up to jam on "Dear Mr. Fantasy". For the second, Dave Mason also joined in for a rousing "Gimme Some Lovin". While this was the very song that made the tower fall at Glastonbury a couple of years before, this time around the karma veered toward rock nirvana. Graham, having hosted their very first performance in America back in '68, was certainly in seventh heaven. Knowing that the band was making its way toward New York, he would send a Western Union telegram ahead to the promoter there to let him know what was in store:

CHAPTER TWENTY-THREE

To Frank Barslona at Premier Talent Associates, New York,

To let you know that, based on their performance at Winterland this past weekend, my opinion is that the present Traffic group is by far the most outstanding band playing contemporary music today. The addition of a keyboard man has freed Steve Winwood to focus on guitar and vocals and the man is absolutely brilliant. But it is the unit as a whole that mesmerized San Francisco for two evenings.

You should be as proud to be their representative as I am to produce their shows.

Cheers, Bill Graham, Fillmore Productions, 01/29/73.

Strategically planned by Chris Blackwell, the tour started with big auditoriums in places like Providence and Boston before swooping into a more intimate venue in New York. This time around, Traffic would play multiple dates at the Academy of Music in Brooklyn, an old orchestral hall and opera house holding only fifteen hundred people. Here they would play two shows a night, the last of which could be extended as long as they felt like it.

Longtime roadie Tony Curtis remembered one of these shows ending in a similar fashion to those in San Francisco, only better, "Half of Santana jammed with us. That was quite a night, it was absolutely amazing." Curtis also noted that the jam affected all on an almost spiritual level, especially Reebop, "I remember that the stage was full, 'cause it was quite a big lineup with Traffic at the time, and then seven or eight of Santana – and Reebop, he was crying because he was so happy! Crying on stage. That was such a good sound, absolutely wonderful…"

Hearing of the revitalization, the British rock press sent emissaries to cover the Academy shows. They too were blown away, and effusive, "Now with Barry Beckett on organ, David Hood on bass and drummer Roger Hawkins, Traffic are the world's greatest band." Having been absent in Britain since those notoriously bad gigs with Gordon and Grech, the reporter from *NME* wanted to forewarn fans in the homeland what was heading their way, "Just wait till you see them in April. Hells bells, you'll never believe it."

With the acclaim and focus aimed mostly at Steve, only a minor note concerning Chris was made, saying: "Chris Wood was blowing magnificently until he disappeared from the stage." Happening near the end of the Saturday night gig, most ominous was the fact that with the rest of the band playing so well, his presence was hardly missed. Perhaps it helped that Dave Mason stepped in, seemingly out of nowhere, as they played the encore – "Heaven is in Your Mind".

For Chris, the incident would demark a period of lingering instability and stage fright. While the cause was clearly complex, success itself was part of it. Now playing mostly massive places, he was firmly stuck in a system in which fans interacted either through an unintelligible roar or else fawned and pawed at him when up close. Lamenting the situation, Chris mentioned his longing to return things to a more human scale to reporters, but also knew it was unlikely. Such as it was, from here life on the road would find him either transforming his angst and fear into great performances or dealing with the dark prospect of falling apart in front of thousands of people.

Christie Nichols would glimpse the trap he'd fallen into. By now, the American girl from Helen Hamilton's Blewbury refuge had finished college and returned to her hometown of Chicago. Hearing that Traffic would be playing at the Arie Crown Theater she felt compelled to go, needing to know if those highly charged days in Berkshire had been real or some kind of dream. While relieved to be warmly welcomed backstage, she quickly understood that the once strong current was also gone, an artifact of another time and place.

Following a short conversation and a hug goodbye, Christie would look over her shoulder to see something that even decades later held a melancholy feeling – Chris was literally being swept away. "I wasn't overwhelmed with emotion, it was like closing a door to the past – letting go. As I walked away from Chris, the groupies closed in on him, and I actually felt sorry for him… he was resigned to them. He was so passive."

After America, England and then continental Europe were lined up for tours. It all began on home ground – Birmingham (at the old Town Hall), then York and Manchester before dates in Holland, France and Italy. And that was just March. April took them to Austria, and a slew of dates in Germany, before circling back to London's Rainbow Theater. Old friends and Island label-mates Spooky Tooth were the support group for much of the tour, with Don Carless, the proprietor of the old Elbow Room along as well – all traveling in luxury buses. In some ways the tour harked back to the chummy days of the 'package tours' across the British Isles, although the hotels were now all four-star. Accommodation aside, the road was still quite punishing; for the nearly month long tour, they had exactly four days off – two of which were spent in travel.

Back home in England, the 'bad show' curse that had haunted Traffic for the last two years was finally broken. The first couple of concerts, nearly three hours long and spellbinding, left fans ecstatic and the rock press heaping praise. *Melody Maker* was at the York University show on March 21st. The correspondent made special note of Chris's contributions – especially "Tragic Magic", exclaiming: "Traffic Mark IV (I think), is possibly the best band to appear live under the Traffic banner since Winwood first quit Spencer Davis."

Bumps were, of course, inevitable. The next day, in Manchester, Chris came on drunk or high, and seemingly disturbed with the stage equipment – which one fan recalled him kicking repeatedly. Another noted him embroiled in a verbal altercation with someone in the audience that continued throughout most of the show. In either case, both agree that Winwood ignored the fracas, steering the band around the problem member, barely missing a beat. If Chris was perhaps subconsciously testing to see how far Traffic could go without his involvement, the answer came back unambiguous – all the way.

By the time they got to the continent Chris had righted himself, and the shows only got better and better. Seeing the potential brewing, Chris Blackwell arranged for multi-track recorders to be available for the last few shows. It was time for another 'live' album, and one that would hopefully capture the definitive, though still evolving 'Traffic sound' so far eluding tape. Indicative of the changing times, reggae tapes and Miles Davis's newest album, *On the Corner*, repeatedly played as the bus rolled on. The jazz trumpeter's move into rock and funk produced an intense, beat-driven music that ultimately pervaded the mindset of everybody – echoes of which were soon reflected on stage. Gliding seemingly effortlessly across Europe, the music was rich, full, and honed to a cutting edge.

An anthem everywhere they went, these days "The Low Spark Of High-Heeled Boys" was the capstone. It also exhibited the yin/yang of Steve and Chris's approach to music, a prime example being the version played at the Rheinehalle in Düsseldorf, Germany, on April 9th. While "Low Spark" had always been a vehicle for Winwood's range of skills, this time out his voice – strong, calm and clear, soared over pounding chords and fanciful, extended piano runs. Balanced and centered, he unhurriedly sprinkled notes, slowly unfolding a panoramic sense of space and time. Chris would gradually but inexorably disassemble this mood. His tenor solo, begun with straight, pure tones, would mutate to feral, warbling cries and finally staccato, trumpet-like bursts as the switches on his effects box were flipped again and again. Amid the musical bombs exploding on stage, a sense of desperation permeated; Chris was playing as if his life depended on it.

If his band-mates were too preoccupied doing their jobs to appreciate the heights being reached, soundman Jimmy Johnson calmly took it in from mid-hall. In an already long career in which he'd witnessed – and helped create – some of the best Soul and R&B, Johnson recognized a musical/psychological thread that ran deep. "On that sax, man, he was… you know what it was? It was like reckless abandon. He just came up with all kinds of ways to change the sound. He used different textures at different tempos, it was wild; it really was. It was like a real soul inside him, almost like he was screaming and living through it. And I think, he was such a nice guy, that sometimes he would get *mean* on that horn – 'wah, wah, wah' (like a dog bark) – he would talk back and shit. He would never do that to anybody, or be rude. (But) he would be rude with the horn – it was like a burst. I felt like, inside, I was seeing how he really wanted to show his feelings, but he couldn't – except through his horn."

Photographer Dick Polak also recalled his old friend's idiosyncratic, underappreciated approach, "I don't think that Chris was particularly valued by the public for what he really was and for what he really brought to that band. I think his input was underestimated. He did his solos and they were very good – but they were also a bit off the wall! It was like 'what was that Chris – where did that come from?' But there was an incredible, technical aspect to his performance. He was always fumbling with his amplifiers and his effects boxes, and not getting it right, not being in time – yet the whole thing was *perfect!* But it didn't look like that, didn't appear like that. I think his mind just worked in a different way than most of us."

If he was speaking in a musical language few truly comprehended, it also seemed the only portal Chris now had to express his innermost self. And as the tour rolled on, show after show, he held nothing back.

For better or worse, others were going through their own changes. Reebop, as always a free spirit, was by now quite far out on a limb. In Paris he made enough of a scene in a restaurant that the French gendarmes later pulled over Traffic's bus to arrest him. While Blackwell defused that situation, the problems didn't end there. His drinking and drug use, always considerable, were escalating, and like Chris he was now less than reliable where it counted – at the shows. On more than one night, he simply passed out on stage, falling forward over his drums, to be carried off by waiting roadies. In Cologne, although his drums were set up and waiting, Reebop was missing until the last couple of songs, when he finally dashed on stage to laughter and applause. Not impressed, Winwood laconically remarked, "Well, now that everybody's *here*, were gonna do a number called 'Light Up Or Leave Me Alone'".

"Light up…" was Jim's song, and with his 'spaced out patch' finally fading, he was doing better all the time. Although Winwood was, as always, the brightest ember, Jim had free run of the stage, introducing songs and band members – still the 'master of ceremonies'. Back behind the drums most of the time playing a small kit in tandem with Roger Hawkins, Traffic's rhythm section now sounded like something out of the Allman Brothers Band, or even the Grateful Dead. With long, jazzy arrangements – "Low Spark" now stretched to twenty minutes; they were a band at the height of their renaissance.

Just getting around was part of the experience. After all these years, hashish remained a staple of the band's medicine bag, but getting aromatic 'Nepalese Temple Balls' past borders and airports also required a certain kind of theater. With up to thirty-five people in tow these days, Traffic's hippie, gypsy tribe would seem a natural target for airport security scrutiny, but somehow it didn't work that way. Hood recalled, "I was really amazed at how they were able to get their drugs everywhere. This was right prior to when the big hijacking scares came down, so security was much more lax. We had all of these people that would go with us… just friends of the band that would go with us for a while. We would go places, and it would always seem that we would arrive at the airport in the last minutes, just seconds… They would cause so much confusion at the gate that we were flying people with us who didn't *have* tickets. In my naive way, and also in my structured life, I was appalled. I'd say, 'Oh shit, we're gonna miss the plane!' But they weren't worried about it, they were *trying* to create the situation where they could take advantage of the whole thing. It was funny, looking back on it."

Not all of the airplane rides were as humorous. Reebop specifically, was well on his way to becoming the "absolute fucking nightmare" that Jim recalled – a trend begun back in America. "Reebop knew no rules, no boundaries, anything… he was a totally free person, and he'd take anything." Hood recalled. "One time I thought we were all gonna get arrested. We were flying somewhere, and he was real fucked up, and he started hollering on the airplane, stuff that you'd *never* get by with these days. He said, 'I want you to stop this plane, *right now*, or I will bring it down – I will destroy it!'" With a torso and arms bulked by a lifetime of vigorous drumming, there was reason not to treat his behavior as a joke; Reebop was a force to be reckoned with. "He was little bitty black guy, but he was as strong as two elephants; he was the strongest guy I've ever seen that size. If he hit you, he'd kill you – he was a powerful man. I don't know how in the world we got off that plane and got to the hotel without any problems that night."

While genuinely liked by his band-mates, Reebop's presence could also create a sense of unease bordering on dread. Hood concluded, "He really had us… there were times when I saw him coming, I went the other way, 'cause I knew that something was gonna happen." Roger Hawkins, in particular, seemed most affected, averting his eyes when Reebop walked by. Seeming more and more frazzled by his band-mate as the tour went on – to some observers Roger looked on the edge of a nervous breakdown.

A final straw of sorts came as Reebop commandeered the bus P.A. one day and using the driver's mic, rapped over the music, mile after torturous mile. With no one brave enough to tell him to shut up, at the next stop nearly all simply voted with their feet – quietly filing out, heading to the other tour bus.

Closing the circle in London, Traffic put on the concerts that they'd been anticipating since the start of the tour – a two show blitz at the Rainbow on April 12th. With many friends and relatives in the audience, they pulled out all the stops. Tony Stewart, who covered the gig for the *NME* opened his review with superlatives, and went up from there, "Traffic have, at last, stitched up England, they really have. I was there at the finest gig by, in my opinion, the greatest band in the world. And I've been wanting to say that for a long time." Stewart praised the stage act as "almost perfect", and took time to profile each member's contributions. As for Chris, special note was made of "Evening Blue", and especially "Tragic Magic". "With "Blue", Wood was superb, proving for all to hear that he's truly one of the finest sax players in the country. Incidentally, "Tragic Magic" was played with even more excellence… it received top honours."

It wasn't hyperbole; opening with loud wallops of Reebop's drums and bracketed by sprightly piano trills and the rhythmic unity of three drummers, Chris was as free and expressive as he'd ever be. Cutting loose with verve and precision, he rode the tune's rolling pattern until Steve picked up his guitar for the final vamp. From there the tune soared higher and higher as the two alternated leads. Finally secure in the pantheon of Traffic – "Tragic Magic" was jazz, rock, and something beyond either.

With the last crooning note, Chris simply took the sax from his mouth and stepped back from the spotlight. With no bow or acknowledgement, as always he simply prepared for the next song. In concert, "Tragic Magic" was less about attention than restoring his dignity. Long removed from the songwriting co-op Traffic had been founded on, he was once more demonstrating his worth as a contributing member, even if it meant starting again.

By the time the band started "Low Spark", the audience was clapping along from the very first notes. Twenty glorious minutes later, the union of the group and the audience at the Rainbow was complete – the triumphant return they'd dreamed of had become reality. But as the last notes faded into the night, another phase of the band was at an end, although perhaps only one person knew it. As it had happened many times before, with the tour concluded, the group too just dissolved. With no references to future plans or promises, to work again, for now it was simply over.

As the Muscle Shoals musicians packed their bags, their minds now turned to the empty and quiet studio awaiting their return. Of all the side men and ex-members that Traffic produced, these would walk away the most unscathed from the experience. But having partaken of the rock 'n roll lifestyle this time around – with the groupies, hash smoke and the mind-blurring travel schedule, David Hood would later concur about the risks, "Being on the road for a long time is dangerous to your health… I was lucky to have survived it." In the end they all did considerably better than that – with chops built up from the road, the Muscle Shoals Rhythm Section actually came out of the experience better than they went in. There was one major letdown however; back in Sheffield after the non-stop intensity of a rock 'n roll tour, their hometown felt slower than dripping molasses for a long, long time.

Less fortunate were others like Traffic's old Producer, Jimmy Miller, who by 1973 had fallen deeply into the mire. The once energetic and imaginative guy who'd done so much to shape the group's early sound was now on the cusp of being fired by the Rolling Stones for being too 'out of it' on heroin to finish work on their current album (*Goats Head Soup*). According to Keith Richards, what was left of Miller's once boundless energy was spent carving a swastika into the top of the recording console at Island's Basing Street studio where the Stones were recording. While Jim Capaldi held great affection for the Producer who had done so much to help shape Traffic's early sound – he too was dismayed. Linking Miller's downfall to his association with the Stones themselves, Capaldi would say, "Jimmy Miller was stout, healthy, (all) handsomeness and strength. After us, it was great. The Stones! After three or four albums with the Stones – gone, Jimmy – junkie, gone. I never thought he'd go like that." But of course Jim's own band-mate really wasn't far behind.

('40,000 Headmen And Some Sweet Rock 'n Roll', Tony Stewart, NME, 5/21/1973)

('Dear, Mr. Fantasy', NME, 3/3/1973)

('Shoot Out at the Fantasy Factory Review', John Romasco, Rolling Stone, 3/15/1973)

('Traffic In The States', NME, 2/24/1973)

('Traffic Problem solved', Melody Maker, 3/31/1973)

CHAPTER TWENTY-FOUR

THE SHADOW OF MARBLE ARCH

If the pace had slowed dramatically for the Muscle Shoals musicians, Chris and Jeanette's post-tour period found them very much on the move – and not entirely voluntarily. It seemed the non-stop music and constant comings and goings in their Notting Hill Gate flat had caused issues with the neighbors and more ominously, drawn unwanted attention from the authorities; it was time to vacate.

Living in a hotel for a while, they finally got a place near a famous London landmark – the huge, ornate Marble Arch (located at the intersection of Edgware Road and Oxford Street). Ironically, the Arch too was only here due to a forced relocation. Originally serving as the entrance to Buckingham Palace when completed in 1833, a Palace expansion would later render it out of scale. So it would be moved – stone by stone – to the new location. Close enough to be in its shadow, the Wood's flat, a two-storey place on a semi-circle street at 14 Great Cumberland Mews, was also just steps away from Jimi Hendrix's last residence at the Cumberland Hotel.

Previously occupied by Island Producer Guy Stevens, for better or worse this would be Chris's home for as long as he lived in London. Being only a block away from Hyde Park, the grass and trees of the expansive commons provided some peace in the heart of the busy city, not to mention being a good place to walk Jazzer, who'd gone quite stir-crazy in the confines of the previous flat.

As impressive as Marble Arch was, and is, the historically astute Chris certainly knew it was only the last in a series of fascinating structures that once defined the neighborhood. The first was an enigmatic basalt monolith known as Oswulf's Stone (or Ossulstone). Once planted in the ground near a crossroads in the pre-Roman era, its purpose is lost to the mists of time. But someone clearly didn't like it; eventually the stone would be knocked over, and unceremoniously buried nearby.

The structure replacing it would have a much darker story. In the 1100's the corner was known simply as 'Tyburn'. Unparalleled in British history, a unique triangular gallows would be erected, serving to execute prisoners condemned by generations of Judges, Magistrates and Kings. With stands for audiences to watch, bound prisoners from Newgate Prison were brought by horse drawn wagon for hanging, sometimes cut down alive to be drawn and quartered for good measure. Incredibly, at least 50,000 people would eventually die at Tyburn, many unceremoniously dumped into nearby unmarked graves. The carnage continued until the hanging of one John Austin, a highwayman, in the fall of 1783; after which the horrific tripod would finally be dismantled. But centuries of bad memories lingered, and in 1851 the great Marble Arch was moved to the spot, ostensibly to serve as an entrance to Hyde Park – which it never was, but more likely a clever means to re-brand old Tyburn.

In a final twist to the saga, in the early 1800's the long-buried Oswulf's Stone, was somehow located and disinterred. Roughly leaned against Marble Arch by unknown excavators, the two were thrown into a crude embrace – and left that way until one day in 1869, when the elder standing stone again vanished. Weighing many tons, its removal would be witnessed by no one; Oswulf's Stone has never been seen again.

Naturally, by the early 1970's the semi-circular street, set slightly away from London's usual bustle, was quite peaceful. With brick walls less likely to disturb the neighbors, Chris and Jeanette quietly settled in, installing recording equipment in an upstairs bedroom 'studio', and modestly furnishing the rest of the place. Naively hoping to leave the stream of drug-crazed people plaguing Notting Hill Gate behind, Chris halfheartedly covered his tracks by hinting in the press that he'd moved out of London altogether. But shrouded as they were in a millennium old shadow of mystery and death, trouble would locate him and Jeanette in no time at all.

With another English summer stretching in front of Steve, Jim and Chris, a plan of sorts arose from the amorphous haze: all would work on solo albums. With Traffic in its usual post-tour limbo, for Jim and Chris at least, it was always prudent to have alternate plans. Of the three, only Jim had managed one so far, and if Traffic was on hiatus, as it apparently was, what else was there to do?

Not long after the triumphant Rainbow show, a reporter snagged a rare interview with Chris, gleaning some insight as to where he was at these days. Whereas Steve rarely exposed any depth to the press and Jim tended to spin things positively so as to not rock the boat, Chris freely aired some of the ambiguity that went part and parcel with his band, "Traffic to me isn't a group, it's a name – a name that can stand for any combination of people. I know there'll always be four, Reebop, Jim, me and Steve, but it's not a group as such. The word 'group' is revolting to me – the way it's taken." Would Traffic record again? More vagueness, "I could never use the word definite – as I say, you never know what's going to happen. I know there's another tour planned…"

With questions about his proposed solo album arising, he mentioned "sympathetic" people he wanted to work with – Junior Hanson, perhaps Mike Kellie, and of course Jim and Steve. But his notions about writing credit (no doubt based on his experiences) also made it clear that he would do things differently than Traffic, "See, I would give everybody a royalty – because what they're going to be playing is really their own solo, improvising."

Being Chris, before it was over, a bit of musical metaphysics would enter into the conversation: "It's the *contact* between your body and the instrument which gives the expression of you. The easiest part is learning the fingering on sax or flute, the hardest part is this point where it makes contact with your body."

But when it was all said and done, how much truth had been revealed? When it came to making the solo album – something that Jim had done before and Steve seemed poised to do, Chris was surely a lot less self-assured than he seemed. With only one self-written song thus far having made it to a record, the thought of pulling off a whole album by himself must have been daunting, if not paralyzing.

As it would turn out, the good of all intentions came to naught. But if none of the three would get their own album together that summer, recordings were made. In June, Steve got involved with an old Air Force mate, Remi Kabaka, ostensibly to act as a Producer for an all-African musical project called Third World. Roped into playing on all of the tracks, they would be quickly released by Island under the title *Aiye-Keta*. Critical reaction was mixed, with a review calling the album "a minor release, but an interesting one."

Trying to recapture the spark of his previous visits, Jim would fit in some time back in Muscle Shoals. As before, he got a lot done in a short amount of time but the album, punningly titled *Whale Meat Again* would not be released until the following year, perhaps so not to compete with Traffic's own product slated for the fall. *On The Road*, a 'live' recording from Traffic's recent European tour, exhibited a combination of epic jams and dead-on precision. Interestingly, with only six long songs, spread out over four album sides, one of the tracks was Chris's "Tragic Magic"; deemed worthy to stand beside other Traffic classics.

Trying to get his own project off the ground, Chris went looking for Junior Hanson. But in the interval since those fervent nights of jamming and writing music in the old flat, he'd gotten a band together. Known simply as 'Hanson', the rock/soul outfit was already working on their debut album for Island. Turning the tables, Chris would be asked to add a flute part to a song they were working on ("Mr. Music Maker"), which he did. Soon after that Junior was gone – off to the States to try to make a name where it would do the most good.

With that door closed and the other 'sympathetic' people perhaps too busy to help, Chris was left with too much free time and no shortage of companions to help him kill it. The people he saw these days were the likes of Keith Moon, Mitch Mitchell, Ric Grech, Paul Kossoff, and Trevor Burton. If together they had the makings of a superstar band, mostly they preferred to hang, relax and of course get high. Knocking at Chris's front door after a night at the clubs, the company would be bearing bags of pills and powders, or be looking for the same; it was the same old scene all over again.

Vibes player, John 'Poli' Palmer, ran into Chris during this period. Having known each other since the Elbow Room, Palmer too was at loose ends. Having passed through a succession of bands since Deep Feeling, he was now solo and somewhat desperate to keep his career alive. Meeting up at the ever-popular Speakeasy, he and Chris commiserated. Hearing of Poli's struggle, Chris was sympathetic, providing contacts and small recording jobs to work on, to which Palmer was grateful.

But Chris had problems of his own, something made clear one day when Poli's phone rang, "I think he was rehearsing for his album. He called me and said, 'Can you help me with it?'" Having seen Chris's erratic lifestyle up close, Palmer wasn't sure that he wanted to get entangled in it, and tried to beg off. "He was heavily into his bits and pieces, and I thought, 'Do I need this?' you know. It was him and Paul Kossoff, he arranged this thing. And I said, 'I'm a bit busy at the moment Chris', and he went: 'Please, *please* man.' When somebody says *that*, you've got to do it, so I said 'Yeah, okay man, alright, I got me vibes…'"

Meeting up with the others at a studio, Palmer perked up – with Kossoff onboard he realized that the elements were in place for something interesting to happen. But the promise proved fleeting as the desire for drugs trumped the creative impulse, "It was me and a bass player, and Chris and Paul turned up. We had a strum for about ten minutes, which was very nice, and then he (Chris) said, 'I'm just nipping off to see the man', and like four hours later me and the bass player are looking at each other, like, 'What do we do?' And I said, 'I think I'm going home now.' It was such a sad thing…"

Noticing his mate stuck in the mire, Jim Capaldi continued to invite Chris out to the house now and then for a few days respite, a place he enjoyed being; perhaps aware that going to Marlow was an act of self-preservation.

But if the converted Parsonage could usually be counted on as a safe-house, this time things were different. To start, his usual protector wasn't there. Having since separated from Anna, Jim was again living a bachelor's life – which took him elsewhere at times. Noggie Nolan, a mild mannered Irish Traffic roadie who worked mostly for Jim, was minding the place. Nolan recalled, "We had a few weekends… Jim would do a lot of traveling. Jim wanted to find the magic, the beauty, the women. He just couldn't leave women alone… So, I'm the butler, or whatever, and Chris would turn up, he's got his own room – I called it 'Flat 14.'"

He wasn't alone long. Next to arrive was Viv Stanshall. Musician, poet/songwriter, actor and vocalist, Stanshall had been a member of the avant-garde, parody rock group, the Bonzo Dog Band, and recently had also begun thinking about doing his first solo album. Long suffering from severe stage-fright, like Chris, Viv also self-medicated. Appreciating Stanshall's sophisticated humor and deadpan upper-crust diction, the two enjoyed the drink, banter and perhaps a little music. Then Graham Bond showed up.

Of all of Chris's associates, his relationship with Bond was always the most edgy. While the two clearly shared a musical affinity, spells, candles and incantations filled the other side of the equation. While sometimes unnerved, Chris could never quite turn his eyes away. In the intervening years since they'd met, Bond had not mellowed, quite the opposite; as his mental stability eroded and his career floundered, his reliance on Magick only deepened. In earlier years, his belief system usually came off as an earnest, if strange, attempt to improve the musical vibes, but now he seemed intent only on making a last stab at regaining some control in his life.

Noggie (Chris) Nolan shuddered recalling Bond's presence, "Weird, weird, weird…Vivian Stanshall, he was another great character, he was similar to Chris in a way, but Graham Bond was, I don't know – very, very heavy. Not at all anybody I'd been used to knowing that'd be Chris's friend… a total nutcase."

Lately Bond had delved into something known as "The Enochian System of Magick". The so-called system involved the manipulation of an "Enochian Alphabet" involving letters placed in a 'magical arrangement' specifically to attract and harness the energies of non-human entities ranging from 'Angels' to 'Elementals'. Keith Bailey, a drummer who had been in a band with Bond in the late 60's called 'The Graham Bond Initiation', knew better than most what Bond was up to, having studied Magickal practices with him for a while back in the day.

Around this time, Graham had approached Keith again, telling him of his exploration of the Enochian System. The meeting left Bailey fearful for Bond or anyone else who went in that direction, "Everyone who touches it comes to disaster, and there is nothing good whatsoever about it. But for some reason it is very enticing to those who get involved in it and it quickly absorbs them into it beyond their capacity to resist it." The disaster that Bailey referred to was the supposed opening of conduits to other realms, allowing these entities to attach themselves to whoever made the mistake of inviting them. Sure that Graham had already done this; Bailey theorized that Chris may have been touched as well.

A dark cloud of foreboding did seem to accompany Bond to Marlow, one nearly overwhelming to roadie Nolan. While not aware of the nature of Bond's practices, what he saw was enough, "Although he was a great musician, it was quite shocking how he was, in a heavy way, indoctrinating – 'My spirit, my thought…', and that was it, (he was) gone, defunct. I just felt it very, very excruciatingly strong – which I didn't go for."

With his own nerves badly shaken, Noggie noticed that Chris seemed to keep his cool, able somehow to "sort of over-ride that, he could just plod along, Chris. But it really used to freak me out. Chris was quite aware of it, so I can't bridge the gap there – I never had any reason to cross Chris on it, 'cause he was such a nice guy."

CHAPTER TWENTY-FOUR

What exactly transpired, and exactly how much this affected Chris is unclear, but the mad weekend apparently took a toll. After all of the goings on were said and done, did Noggie believe that Chris left Jim's house frightened by the experience? "Yeah, yeah … (pause), yeah."

Whether any of this magical minefield was 'real' in the objective sense or just an elaborate mind game, Chris believed – which made it real enough. But if his curiosity could lead him to situations that rattled his wits, he was also capable of counterbalancing dark influences with his intellect. Island's Suzette Newman, who saw all sides of Chris over the years recalled, "He was an intelligent guy! For a start, he read books, while the others didn't. And he was into mysticism and magic. He was way ahead of any of them on that. Way ahead."

Esoteric Astrology written by a woman named Alice Bailey was very possibly one of those books. A contemporary of Aleister Crowley's, Bailey (no relation to Keith Bailey), was born into a well-off family, becoming spoiled and self-centered before seeking spiritual illumination. Where Crowley veered into the manipulative world of the occult, Bailey's studies (beginning with Theosophy) ultimately led to teachings she felt would spiritually benefit the whole of mankind. For Chris, the attraction would have been understandable – having been into astrology from way back, he'd never given up on the practice, since it seemed to capture the essence of people's characters in uncanny ways. Over the years, he'd progressed from having his chart read by astrologers, to being able to create them himself, a task that he would often do for friends.

But Esoteric Astrology opened up whole new vistas. The practice, as constructed by (or in some cases supposedly merely *through*) Bailey combined the structure and language of astrology with symbolic aspects of Christianity and Buddhism. As in traditional astrology, Bailey believed that the zodiac allowed practitioners to discover the purpose of their inner being. Her advancement was in aligning the individual with the cosmic, compelling for Chris since the concept of Ley Lines was already so deeply engrained in his world-view. Importantly, Bailey's message was positive – emphasizing the "Seven Rays", which streamed to the Earth from the deeper regions of the Universe. Literally interconnecting everything, hers was a metaphysics based on light; an affirming, if complex, path to personal and ultimately global enlightenment.

Inspired, one night back at the apartment, Chris picked up his tenor sax and switched on the tape machine. With *Esoteric Astrology* roiling the waters of his mind, he drew a breath and slowly blew a long heraldic phrase, evoking an imaginary matador, cape on arm, approaching a shifting bull. The muse having descended, once again the music began to flow.

*

Waiting for Traffic to stir again, at home the routines went on as before – work slipped in, somewhere between visits with friends, drugs, and socializing at clubs like the Speakeasy. While Chris might have craved a more normal family life, the conditions in and around 14 Cumberland Mews made that unlikely. Neither he nor Jeanette appeared to care much for cooking or cleaning, and with no regular help, the flat was often a mess. Their relationship had similar qualities. While, by all accounts, the love between Chris and Jeanette was real and in its own way, quite deep, theirs was always a free-form jam of a marriage. But if on the surface there seemed little beside love keeping them together, the impulse to grow a family regularly bubbled up. As such, it didn't seem at all odd that one day a lost 'daughter' would be found, rescued and brought home to stay.

Attempting to get her own career going again, Jeanette was working with a female duo (percussion and keyboard) who lived together just down in the Kensington High Street region. Amidst this arrangement was an eighteen-year-old American girl named Holly Beth Vincent. A budding drummer and songwriter, she had recently relocated to England to see if London still had a viable music scene. Living for a while with the female couple, Holly then met Jeanette and they quickly hit it off, collaborating on bits of songs and spending free time together. But as Holly prepared to attend a birthday party for Jeanette, things suddenly turned sideways – she found her bedroom door bolted from the outside, "They had me locked up in their apartment on Ken High Street, I was not allowed to go to (Jeanette's) party, god knows why." Later she theorized that the women were jealous of her growing closeness to Jeanette.

Upon hearing of the situation, the typically passive Chris rushed over with a plan already in mind. Rather than deal with doors and locks, he took a dramatic, more chivalrous route to save the girl in distress. Holly Beth recalled, "Chris rescued me from imprisonment. He climbed up the fire escape, several flights, and freed me… Jeanette threw everyone else out, mostly, and wanted me there, and Chris came and got me."

And just that quickly – she had a new home. Chris and Jeanette enjoyed having the musically minded girl around, and invited Holly to stay as long as she wanted. Right off, it became a family-style arrangement. "These people raised me, or tried to. I was 'adopted', and given my own room, an allowance, and chores – restocking the candy supply, vacuuming the blow off the carpet, helping to chase the dog when it escaped onto Oxford Street…"

Her presence brought a sense of normalcy previously unknown at the flat. Holly recalled the period as peaceful, with Jeanette acting the glamorous mother and Chris, the eccentric musical father, "I liked them both a real lot, they were both really good people in their own ways. She taught me about wearing velvet and kohl eyeliner. He was my 'Dad'… If Jeanette and I were hanging out, writing songs together, he would join in. One time he was taking a bath, and he got out, wrapped a towel around himself, picked up his sax, and laid down a sax solo on something we were working on! He was a very creative, and really soulful – more like a jazz musician, old school… he was a very deep person."

Of course the normalcy was all relative; perennial issues still influenced everything – cocaine, mandrax, heroin and alcohol were very much part of the equation. While aware of it all, Holly was sheltered too – the losers and dealers somehow kept mostly at bay while she was around. On top of that, both Chris and Jeanette maintained a watchful eye, not wanting Holly to enter the land of the damned as they had, "The way that they treated me… I would be curious, like 'Oh, I want to try that!', and they'd just be like '*No*, you can't.' When I say that they treated me like their adopted child, I mean that literally – they were protective of me, to a very large extent. I have a good memory of Chris and a fondness for him. For a couple of drug addicts, they were really conscientious! That was just in their better nature I suppose. Ultimately they were both really, really great, special people."

But underlying it all, Holly also observed Chris to be "kind of lost", living in a state of sadness for all that he perceived wasn't right in his life. Vincent noted, "He was not in a good place, he was not happy. He was really in love with Jeanette and her behavior affected him badly." But that aside, change for the better was in the air too. As had become the pattern, the late fall brought hints that his band was stirring, if tentatively. Holly remembered that, "Jim and Steve, the Traffic people – they were coming over to see how he was doing, to check up on him."

Holly's 'adoption' was just the latest in a string of attempts by Chris to fashion a 'family' amidst the topsy-turvy world he inhabited. All the way back to Rosie Roper, and Helen Hamilton, Chris's survival instinct had led him to people that provided a sense of kinship, even if each was short lived. This would be no different, nor the last.

In fact, about the time that Holly moved on, another young American would enter their lives. Mick Lee, about twenty, and also a musician/songwriter, met Chris via a near-random incident involving a bag of cocaine. But the two quickly hit it off, building a relationship based on listening to, playing, and writing music. As someone just beginning a career in music, meeting Chris would provide Mick with a conduit to people he had only read about in magazines. Lee recalled, "Woody's house was kind of like 'Musician's Central', it was an amazing scene. On any given night you might have Mitch Mitchell, Winwood, Remi, Rosko Gee, Ric Grech, Mick Taylor, and John Martyn – it was just a 'who's who' of musicians in London at the time. We'd sit around, late at night and just fucking play music! That's where I got my musical education."

Interestingly, the one famous musician Mick already knew was Graham Bond. Considering him a "tortured genius", Mick's experience provide insight into Chris's own fascination. "We were at a friend's house, and he wanted to learn the song's that I'd written. He'd get me to play to him, then he'd have me put the guitar down, and for ten of fifteen minutes, he'd talk to me about the song in a way that nobody before or since had talked to me. It was 'Alright Mick, the song is in the key of 'C', the color of the key of 'C' is green, and it relates to water…' And he'd go off on this long thing that I didn't understand … I just tried to absorb it on an unconscious level, without trying to make a logical understanding of it. After ten or fifteen minutes of this, we'd start playing the song together. Ever since, I've had the impression where, to give an analogy: if it was a book, instead of a song – what I'd done was, I'd written the name of the book and the titles of the chapters, and Graham wrote everything in between! There was stuff in the chord progressions and in the music that I thought I'd written, that I had no idea was there! Graham would just sit down at the keyboard and wring all this *stuff* out of this idea I had taken him. It was just – he was just, phenomenal…"

As the relationship with Mick strengthened, Chris would actually suggest that they form a band with Graham Bond, Ric Grech, Paul Kossoff, and a drummer named Paul ('Funky Paul') Olsen – who played double kick drums in a style reminiscent of Ginger Baker. Player-wise, the plan looked fascinating – it would be a jazz/blues fusion of the most unusual sort. But while Chris put some effort into organizing things, before it could go anywhere a tragic incident would seal the unborn band's fate.

*

As it happened, with all of the youthful energy flowing through Great Cumberland Mews, Chris got some good work done. Beside the demos with Jeanette and Holly and later, Mick, he finished off that astrologically-inspired track that had started so promisingly way back. Like "Tragic Magic", the new music was jazzy, deeply personal, and indicative of where his life was at. So the visits from Steve and Jim came at the right time – they dug what they heard. If Chris wasn't exactly straight drug-wise, musically he'd gotten it together, and that would have to do – it was time to give Traffic another go.

Reconvening at Steve's rural Gloucestershire house that fall, it was clear that the band stood at the nexus of conflicting forces and mutually exclusive paths. For one, the Muscle Shoals Rhythm Section was out of the picture, for good. While they hadn't been promised more work at the end of the '73 tour, at the time it hadn't been ruled out either. So, when they had called up Island's office to enquire about the upcoming year it seemed reasonable that they might see their English mates again. In response, a handwritten letter from Steve was returned, apologizing for the lack of contact and then respectfully letting them know that their part in Traffic was over.

If the Rhythm Section were somewhat shocked, they weren't the only ones. Jim Capaldi wracked his brain to understand how Steve could dismantle what critics had called 'the best band in the world'. Later he would become suspicious that Steve was trying, consciously or not, to sift the group down to a point where there would finally be no one left, except himself. "It was such a *powerful* band then, with everything covered – the extra piano, the proper bass player, and Steve went and knocked it on the fuckin' head again. And I could never understand that... I just know in my heart that whenever it got really comfortable, really good and solid, he was thinking, 'Well, a lot of it comes from my talents' – which it was – and I had a feeling that he thought, 'I just don't want to be a part of this, even though it's really good, because I'm just like a member of something... I want something to be more of me somehow.' Blackwell and me – I turned to him one day and he looked at me, and it was like 'fuckin' hell', this is *so* good, you know what I mean? Then he (Steve) said, 'We can have a four piece', and it wasn't 'cause he wanted a four piece. I think he was just slowly wriggling down, to get rid of... not wanting... kind of knocking it on the head, and I don't know why..."

But Chris was with Steve all the way – if not having subtly instigated it himself. Having earlier questioned the wisdom of having that much musical predictability in the first place, he often cited the three-piece as the freest and best expression of Traffic. As such, the new arrangement was a much closer fit to the past ideal. Steve sensed it too, and said as much in his letter to Muscle Shoals. So, if Jim saw the changes as something akin to Traffic's death rattle, from another view it was a rebirth. As for Chris, the new arrangement gave him another chance – perhaps the last – to reclaim the promise of the original band, and just maybe, his place as an acknowledged musical force in the band he helped create.

The next phase would be a departure on many levels. For the first time, Steve brought in another composer – Viv Stanshall. The drunken poet who shared the crazy weekend with Chris and Graham Bond now hung out with Steve too – bringing him a surrealist lyric called "Dream Gerrard" around which Steve created a piano track. The marriage created a magnificent musical dreamscape, and the song's jazzy vibe seemed to inspire other songs Traffic would work on. Of course, Jim had a number of lyrical pieces to contribute, the best of which was a kind of bookend to Stanshall's piece, called "Graveyard People". The long, exploratory tracks would form the spine of the album and concerts to come.

Jim's songs also included a couple about his band-mates. The weaker was something called "Memories of a Rock 'N 'Rolla"; a fantasy tale about the life arc of a rock star. Although likely about Steve, it applied to Jim as well. As a biographical sketch, the song was a good idea, but the execution dragged somewhat. Although retrofitted with an upbeat 4/4 ending, "Rock 'n Rolla" remained kind of flat and, uncharacteristically for a Traffic song, almost trite.

"Walking In The Wind" was the other. The title came from a facetious response that Jim had given back in 1968 when asked by a rock reporter about his hobby. However, most of the song actually concerned the lifestyles of Chris and Jeanette, and it was an unsparing assessment. The opening referenced a drug addled rock star surrounded by sycophants, while subsequent lines described his consort as a 'Plastic Princess'. If Jim was now publicly (if cryptically) voicing his disapproval of the couple's mutual dissolution, at least he was artful about it. With the pre-recorded sound of wind prefacing the track, a distinctive bass track and Steve's keening vocal phrasing, the song imparted a sense of beautiful desolation. One of the best songs on the forthcoming album, "Walking In The Wind" would also be released as a single.

At the time, Jim would only discuss the song's meaning with vague generalities, never admitting to the real source of inspiration. Even so, Chris and Jeanette had little trouble figuring it out – though neither let on at the time. Later Jeanette would confront Jim, but still he would deny its true meaning.

Interestingly, an early take of "Walking In The Wind" had an extended soprano sax part by Chris, a more or less continuous blow which flowed into a beautiful jam with Steve's guitar and an overdubbed tenor. But ironically for a song written about Chris and his wife, very little of his distinctive contribution would survive the editing knife.

The two songs (both instrumentals) Chris brought to the sessions could easily be seen as a yin/yang of his life in the past year. The darker side was represented by "Barbed Wire", a long, slow dirge sounding like an extended coda to "Tragic Magic". Chris would later say that the track was about being "tangled up in life", a mood the music clearly expresses. Starting at an almost funeral-march pace, the tenor line sounded like a weary sob until a sudden tempo shift when the tune jumps to life amidst a frantic scramble of conga beats, splayed piano notes and horn honks – as much a coke rush as a true escape from the pain. But even this upbeat, if nervous, interlude seemed to burn itself out as the mood shifted back to aching despair. In a life in which bleakness often pulled at him with a ferocious tenacity, "Barbed Wire" was Chris's heart's cry, a mournful horn/voice that said all there was to say on the subject.

In contrast, "Moonchild Vulcan" was brightly lit, sprightly, and brimming with optimism. Also known as "Wood's Bolero" (as written on some of the tape boxes), the tune began with that tenor sax 'bullfighter' motif, joined together with a drum-march beat. Ascending in a swirling pattern before fading back to quiet, the silence punctuated a mood shift as a funky strut emerged – a musical landscape explored by Chris's straight tenor sax solo. Soulful, soaring and even sassy, his playing was confident, full, and affirming. To conclude, he let the marching drums and horn theme rise once again after the track had faded to silence. With the tenor finally cut loose from gravity, the notes would float higher and higher before fading into the ether.

While "Moonchild Vulcan" was indeed the document of a man with something to live for, like "Wind", it also held its share of secrets. In Alice Bailey's complex astrological scheme, the Moon conceals or 'veils' another celestial object – the planet Vulcan.

The very existence of Vulcan – a small (and presumably very hot) orb closer to the sun than Mercury, was controversial. 'Discovered' in the late 1800's by French astronomer Urbain Jean Joseph Le Verrier, Vulcan, while never seen (although others claimed to), was predicted based on deviations in Mercury's expected orbital path. Oddly, other astronomers were at first supportive, before later dismissing Verrier's claims. While he continued to assert its existence, over time serious debate regarding the reality of Vulcan would fade away. In Alice Bailey's view though, the planet was out there (although possibly *most real* as a metaphoric object).

It all lined up for Chris in that his astrological sign, Cancer, was ruled by the Moon, which in turn veiled Vulcan. As much as Chris identified with the Moon, even calling his song publishing company Lunar Music, Bailey described it as a dead, decaying planet that when removed as a spiritual obstacle (i.e. 'lifting the veil'), would let energies (the "First Ray") of the 'sacred planet' (Vulcan) shine through – illuminating the way for the person truly on "the Path."

So "Moonchild Vulcan" was Chris's self-portrait, or perhaps a portrayal of the life he desired – a fearless push into the unknown, followed by a joyful, fully realized experience that concluded with a final leap past the veil of death. It's possible that he also saw the song as a kind of totem to block the darker forces that sometimes threatened him and Jeanette.

Well-hidden metaphysical implications aside, Chris had a good piece in hand, something that could be honed on tour. It all worked to plan; in many ways a reaction to the Muscle Shoals era just ended. With an album's worth of tunes in hand, rather than rushing to record them and then touring, this time they would reverse the order – touring with the new songs, letting them grow and mature, and *then* making the record. The recording methodology was new too. By taping the shows, they could pick the best take/performance, overdub where necessary, and build the album from that. It certainly wasn't intended as a traditional 'live album' either, since the tracks contained no trace of audience reaction. Put into a seamless mix with songs already recorded at

CHAPTER TWENTY-FOUR

Steve's studio –"Walking In The Wind", "Love" (grown from a studio jam initiated by Reebop), and maybe even "Rock 'n Rolla", and/or "Barbed Wire", the finished product would be united (hopefully) with a common vibe.

The overall feel was of a departure as well. Rather than re-treading the well-worn rock/folk path, they veered deeply into jazz/rock fusion. Consciously or not, Steve and Chris were reviving some of the elements present even before Traffic existed – the jazzy jams done with Dave Mason and drummer Frank Devine back in '66 were done in a similar spirit. In a crucial way, they had finally returned to the primal source that launched everything.

Most importantly, an overall sense of enthusiasm had returned. Some of it had to do with the addition of Rosko Gee, but Chris's improved condition was the crucial catalyst. Long weeks of sessions and rehearsals at Steve's home/studio had put enough distance between Chris and the London distractions to allow him to straighten up to a degree. With his blurred mind sharper again, the sense of potential returned.

Jim's roadie, Noggie Nolan witnessed Chris re-emerging as a creative force, concerned that the music came out, as he always required it, *right*: "Chris's involvement was magic, especially the sound – the double track saxes… he played tenor, soprano and alto. When Chris was asked to go into the studio to overdub something, he might look like 'the pits', but he knew his part. He could be critical of himself, saying 'Look, let me do that bit again.' And Chris was the sort of person, where it was very hard to drop him into something. He'd rather take it all again. He could be very stubborn in that way. He'd rather go from the top, and play it all over again. The basic track was always done as – 'that's the one'. He was very, very much into music, believe me." Nolan summed up his paradoxical friend this way, "Chris crossed a lot of musical spectrums. I think he was very, very futuristic and very, very old-fashioned as well. The past probably meant something that could help get him to the future – especially musically."

The sudden renaissance was helped by the fact that, as in the old days at the Berkshire Cottage, being surrounded by friends in a womb-like space allowed him to focus on music. Here in the countryside, the outside world – with its clocks, schedules and money-grubbing ways – could be held at bay, forgotten, at least for the moment. For a man for whom the proper location had always meant everything, Steve's studio was more than a room with microphones and an eight-track recorder – it was the place where Traffic could uncover its muse. So it was only fitting that Chris would come up with the name for the place; with much thought to place, and a little punning humor he would christen it *Netherturkdonic* – a moniker that has stuck ever since.

The planned tour would begin and end in Great Britain between which they would travel all over Europe – from Germany to Switzerland, Holland, Belgium, Denmark, France and Italy. At more than forty dates spanning February to the latter half of May, this would be the longest road trip Traffic would ever do. Just to plan such a thing meant that the band's confidence had to have been pretty high, but with Chris's history of inconsistency, threads of doubt couldn't have been too far below the surface.

It might have helped if he didn't have to worry about what would be happening at home in his absence. Before leaving, he sought out Jeanette's old band-mate, Eleanor Barooshian, pleading with her to watch out for his wife, "When he went on tour he used to *beg* me to stay with her – so that she wouldn't run off and get into trouble." Pondering the deep-seated restlessness of someone she'd known since they were both sixteen, Eleanor found no easy answers, "It's just the way she was. She was always that way. I don't know what she was looking for, but she was always a wanderer."

This time in particular, there would be good reason to worry. That autumn, not long after Chris had left for rehearsals with Traffic, Jeanette would experience something as frightening as it was inexplicable – and it would happen right at home.

In the second week of September, the Rolling Stones were in town to play their first London dates in two years. Someone from the Stones camp contacted Jeanette, offering not only tickets, but backstage passes and a limo ride to the event – an offer she couldn't refuse. Young Mick Lee, now a close family friend, was the lucky guy chosen to accompany her; well dressed and excited, he was at the apartment in the blink of an eye. Jeanette of course was in no hurry. In fact, the limo driver sat in front of the flat so long that Mick finally invited him in to bide his time as Jeanette got herself together upstairs.

Then it happened.

Mick recalled, "Eventually, Jeanette is ready and she's coming down the stairs, and the phone rings. She was halfway down the stairs, so she turned round and went back upstairs to get it in the bedroom, and I thought 'here we go, it's going to be another half hour at this rate', and I was getting a bit antsy at this point. Literally thirty seconds later, I hear this blood curdling scream – it was scary. So I run up the stairs to see what's going on, and Jeanette is passed out on the bed, with the phone in her hand, and the phone is dead, it's just a dial tone, and she's out cold – clammy and in a cold sweat.

I was young and inexperienced, I didn't really know what to do, I got some brandy and a cold, wet cloth, and I tried to bring her around – it took about ten minutes. And the minute she wakes up, she bursts into uncontrollable tears, hysterics. It probably took me fifteen minutes to where I could get her to where she could talk – she was still in total distress. And I said 'Jeanette, *what is going on?* And somehow or other, I got it out of her: she was convinced that it was (Jimi) Hendrix on the line. Hendrix of course was dead. She said that he called her a name that only he had called her; and she just freaked. Needless to say, I had to send the limo driver away. I spent the evening consoling Jeanette, because she was just inconsolable."

Having had many years to think about that night, Lee concluded, "I am not convinced in any particular direction about the hereafter – I'm neither a believer nor a non-believer, but I will say this – I believed Jeanette. It would have been impossible to fake what happened to her, and I believe that she experienced what she experienced. It was very, very freaky."

While Chris would return as soon as he could, there really wasn't much that could be done. Was Jimi really still around in some fashion – and if so, what did it mean? Having previously tried so hard to establish contact after his death – and coming as it did only about a week from the third anniversary that day – the phone call from 'the other side' was obviously deeply disturbing. But in accepting the paranormal at face value, perhaps these things simply came with the territory. Still, while it was neither the first nor last unexplainable occurrence at the flat, this particular incident simply cut too deep – it would never be mentioned again. And from there, with the financial security of both of them at stake, Chris had little choice but to return to work.

*

Fortunately the work was quite satisfying. Pared down to Steve, Chris and Jim plus Reebop and Rosko (who neither drank nor took any drugs), the nimbleness and flexibility lacking since the old trio days had almost returned. Increasingly enthused about the possibilities, Chris told a reporter, "When we do numbers they're never the same – the arrangements are always the same but we might do something a little differently each night. And we can do this certain way of going about it (without) people tending to get lost, panic or something…" The extensive rehearsal time had given them a large repertoire to choose from – supposedly including their glorious psych/pop single, "Paper Sun", for the first time since '67. With this hard earned musical capital in hand, the time had come to go out and spend it.

The first gig was booked for Glasgow, Scotland on February 21st. On that afternoon Burt Muirhead, a Scottish writer who had arranged to interview Jim Capaldi for his rock fanzine *Hot Wacks*, ran into Chris sitting alone in the lobby of their hotel. Just a short walk from there to the venue where Traffic would be playing – the 3,500 seat Glasgow Apollo – he was waiting to go over to the sound check. "He wasn't wearing socks, he was just sitting, one leg over the other, reading the newspaper in the hotel foyer, like someone waiting for a taxi," Muirhead recalled.

Chris and Burt chatted amiably as hotel patrons walked by, including members of the Monty Python troupe, who had spent the day filming scenes for their movie *Monty Python and the Holy Grail* at nearby Loch Lomond. Chris had socialized with several members the night before in the hotel bar, but now, pretending that he didn't recognize them, did a double take as they walked through the lobby, still dressed in their chain-mail (really plastic) armor. Waiting until they passed he leaned in to ask Muirhead, "Who the fuck is *that?*" with a bemused smirk before turning back to sip his tea. Clear eyed and relaxed, Chris seemed quite sober, even sanguine, and ready to play.

Muirhead recalled that the first show, heavy with new material and just enough older stuff to mollify the fans went over very well indeed. As for Chris, "He was absolutely spot on, he was fine…" So far, so good, but with the long road stretched before them, all of the real tests lay ahead.

For a major rock group of the day, the set-list was audacious. Rather than roaring out with a recognizable hit, the show opened with an un-named instrumental simply referred to as "Intro". The tune had several distinct sections – the first with Steve on electric piano and Chris on sax, followed by a deft switch where Steve would pick up the guitar as Chris sat down at the keyboard. In the third part, they switched again, with Chris soloing on tenor – first straight, and then wah wah'ed to Steve's piano accompaniment before wrapping it up by returning to the start. All of the back and forth was classic Traffic – their very personal form of low-key musical theater. If nothing else, the tune served as an upfront reminder that the dynamics that made this particular band tick were very much alive in 1974.

The rest of the set would be just as adventurous. Sometimes it was a straight roll into another instrumental – Chris's "Moonchild Vulcan", or a slowed down version of "Dear Mr. Fantasy" – a song previously held in reserve for the 'big finish'. On some nights, they wouldn't play 'Fantasy' at all. Instead, "Heaven Is In Your Mind", from the first album or even the spooky lost classic, "Withering Tree" would be pulled out. On top of it, every song off the album that they hadn't yet released was performed – letting previously unheard music form the bulk of the concert. Often the show ended with an epic (up to forty minutes) "Graveyard People", followed by an encore of an un-named guitar-based, riffy instrumental. If they left many fans pleasantly scratching their heads over the unconventional show, Traffic, after all these years had finally become the band they'd always intended – a jazz-rock combo playing purely for the art of music – commercial expectations be damned.

The tour map outlined a route that took them from one end of England to the other, not once, but twice – punctuated by the trip across the continent. A determined effort was made to win back the hearts of their home country, a place long forsaken in favor of wooing America. And it was working. While all of the new and overtly jazzy material put off some, the sheer musicality of the performances nearly always saved the day. Reports from the road confirmed it. Spending a couple of days with the band, *New Musical Express's* Tony Stewart would go away converted: "I was left with the distinct impression they're now rid of those terrible gremlins, and have a more clearly defined purpose. For the first time since the trio of Winwood, Wood and Capaldi was enlarged there's a *band* instead of an itinerant bunch of footloose session musicians."

Stewart noted an overall air of health around the group this time out. In recent months, Steve had started walking and bicycling, while Capaldi took handfuls of vitamins every day. Happily, he was back to playing the drums with furious precision. The most transformed though was Chris. Recalling the broken down musician from the previous year's tour in America, Stewart said, "I found it sad to witness Wood's slow but sure physical deterioration… it was touch and go whether he'd see his next birthday. Now the change in him is as remarkable as the change in Winwood… on stage, his performance is consistently excellent." Stewart also noted that Chris's visage as well as his personality had evolved, "He's plumper in the face and gut, and at the same time more introverted. Hiding behind a pair of shades, he tends to sit alone in the dressing room, reading the paper."

With the dark glasses serving as the thinnest of shields to protect against the dealers and groupies, Chris exerted his limited willpower for the sake of the band, and his own future. Checking his gadabout tendencies must have been difficult, but the payoff was a reinvigorated Traffic.

The real wildcard at the outset was Reebop – unlike the others he wasn't particularly interested in a lifestyle refit. Still drinking and snorting whatever, he remained an unrepentant link to the out-of-control days of past tours. And it was telling – as they moved from city to city, he was still losing it, trashing hotel rooms, initiating physical confrontations with the roadies, and worst of all, screwing up on stage. Unbidden, he had taken to vocalizing along with the songs, or continuing to play on after the rest of the band had left the stage. Not surprisingly, Steve wasn't pleased.

If Reebop's behavior was the first real crack in the wall, it wouldn't be the last. Chris had never stopped drinking – an undiagnosed alcoholic, it just wasn't in the cards. As before, keeping himself together required a precarious dance with the liquid spirits. Sometimes he slipped. In Paris, a reporter noted Chris regularly visiting a line of beer bottles on his amp during the concert. By Italy, he would need considerably more.

Roadie Noggie Nolan recalled that while the Chris of old tried to find time to explore the ancient Italian cities, other forces pushed back: "We went to Venice, had a look around. Chris was very much into architecture, he was into a lot of things. But I remember in Naples, it was such a chaotic scene… there had been some demonstrations with students or something, and the Italian police were a bit over the top. We were playing in this big amphitheater – and the police were just throwing tear gas through the windows. Considering that no one was hurt, you just took things like that with a pinch of salt."

And yet, Traffic's day in the ancient city had started out on a far gentler note. At the sound check, Chris met a shy fourteen-year-old Italian fan named Elena Iglio. She recalled an encounter with a Chris who "looked ethereal – his eyes were focused on you but also went beyond you – something that I could not fathom." Mesmerized by his "Christ-like" quality and insecure of her ability to express herself in English, Elena would nearly whisper her request for the show – "John Barleycorn". Tousling the girl's hair, Chris smiled and promised to play it for her before walking away. And they did.

But at the concert, Traffic's usually calming musical spell didn't hold. A few songs past Barleycorn, as protesting anarchists pounded on the doors and tear gas wafted amid drunken U.S. Servicemen jostling with local cops, Steve suddenly had enough. In a rare public show of anger, he lifted a middle finger to the auditorium, turned and walked off stage. Chris followed, as did Reebop, leaving Jim and Rosko to finish "Dream Gerrard" alone; the show had lasted a mere forty-five minutes.

The mixture of the violence and Steve's intolerance to it was followed by Chris's sudden loss of self-control. While having more than once talked Noggie Nolan out of quitting during various bumps on the road, he now found difficulty saving himself. Noggie recalled, "It all came to a head in Italy. Chris was really, really out of it. Rosko was a very stabilizing person, because he didn't drink or take drugs, whereas Reebop was totally – I think Reebop and Chris were in competition to see who could get the biggest thing up their nose." Somehow, amid the external and internal chaos, the band would complete the remaining shows and move on.

With the Italian craziness finally behind them, the rolling ship righted once again. Back home in England the remaining shows were all good, with the band lauded (if belatedly) by their countrymen for the return of the "Traffic Spirit".

Underneath it all though, unseen forces were shifting; more turbulence lay ahead.

As the tour neared its conclusion, the word suddenly spread around the touring party: Reebop had been fired. The drugs, his antics on and off stage, and perhaps his unhealthy influence on Chris had finally taken him past the point of no return. With just a few shows left to play on the tour, Steve told him to leave.

Unable to process the situation, Reebop would be at the next gig, ready to play. Confronted once more, this time Steve said, "What are you doing here? Reebop, you can't play with us anymore." Desperately trying to put a positive spin on what he was hearing, the drummer replied, "Oh, you don't have to *pay* me, I'll just play!" But the money saving offer was in vain, henceforth his space on stage would remain vacant.

With the African congas silenced, unseen reverberations knifed through the band. Having been in Traffic so long, prior to this it was assumed that Reebop was as permanent as any of them – perhaps the "wriggling down" process that Jim had feared had begun. Asked by the press soon after, Chris couldn't even admit Reebop's leaving had been Steve's call, laying the departure on the drummer himself and minimizing the impact, "I really think it was really down to the fact that he wanted to go. I thought at first we'd feel the loss but I can't honestly say we do… it wasn't like losing a limb or a kidney, it was just like another dimension. I thought we were going to miss him – we don't."

Having had to rationalize one bad vibration, another quickly emerged that was even more unsettling – Graham Bond died. Having tumbled into dissolution in recent years, on May 8th, 1974 Bond's life would end suddenly and violently on the tracks of a London tube (subway) station, where he was torn apart by an oncoming train. It happened the night Traffic was playing their hometown of Birmingham. In fact, the tube station where he died (located at Finsbury Park, London) was just steps away from the Rainbow Theatre, where Traffic would play their final gigs in less than a week. While most viewed it as the suicide of a broken man, rumors of all sorts ran wild. Ascribed as being everything from a simple accident, to a hit job from a drug dealer, to some kind of vengeful Black Magic attack; the real reason Graham Bond met his fate where he did will likely never be known.

In the press, Chris would make only one vague, wistful comment about Graham, implying more distance between them than there really was: "Bond was a bit beyond me, I mean, having known him, God rest his soul, he was a little beyond." In truth, having had years of encounters, some musical, but others magical and/or frightening, Chris was rattled by the way Graham left this world. While the extent of the unfinished business between them remains unclear, many years later, an incident reported by longtime friend Brenda Bryan [see Chapter 28] would suggest Chris believed Bond's spirit still retained the power to locate him

And on that melancholy note, the tour begun as Traffic's jazzy renaissance sputtered to a funereal end.

*

When The Eagle Flies, produced by "Chris Blackwell and Traffic", was finished off in the post tour break. The idea was to have it out for the next set of tours, which would dwarf the recently completed trek. Revisiting the United States (for the eighth time), South America, Japan and Australia were to follow – places Traffic had never been. The trip would extend to the year's end, and perhaps into 1975. The assumption was that the combination of strong album sales and relentless touring would finally take Traffic into the elite realm of bands such as the Rolling Stones and Led Zeppelin. For Jim Capaldi at least, that had always been the goal, something they'd never quite achieved.

In the final stages of the album's preparation, a few changes were quietly made. It began with the cover. A pen and ink drawing had been made showing a blighted cityscape, above which hovered an avenging eagle, wings spread wide. In the forefront stood the band – a leafy vine representing nature connecting one to the other. In the original, a smiling Reebop stood at the far left, his arm linked around Jim's. But by the time the final proofs rolled off the press, he'd vanished. Like Dave Mason back in '67, he'd been literally removed from the picture – airbrushed out and sketched over. While having done all of the sessions, the tour and ultimately at least a couple of the album's songs, it was as though he was never there. While it made a sort of technical sense, the erasure was also a chilling reminder of how quickly and profoundly things could change in the world of 'Traffic'.

For Chris, losses of a more personal nature were yet to come. First, on "Dream Gerrard", the long, spacey song with solos from Steve, Chris and even Rosko – Chris's sax part was cut about three quarters of the way through. With each side of the record able to hold a maximum of twenty minutes, the format required a sacrifice. There were other slices. "Walking In the Wind", of course, had only ghostly traces of Chris in the final product, while "Love", which opened with Chris's audible question: "Are you playing in 'E' Steve?", would be faded down just as a flute-led jam was getting started. But harder news lay ahead.

At the last minute, "Moonchild Vulcan" – Chris's pride, his life affirming celestial prayer – was removed from the album. He later told a close friend (Vinden Wylde) that it had come down to either having room for his song or the weakest (but more conventional) Winwood/Capaldi composition, "Memories Of A Rock 'N' Rolla". Although jazz/rock had been a conscious approach, was a calculation made that the instrumental "Vulcan" would tip the album into being a little *too* jazzy for a record-buying public? If so, the sense of déjà vu should have been overwhelming – it was all eerily and sadly similar to the 'commerce over art' decision regarding the dreadful "Hole In My Shoe", way back when. And while it was true that Traffic wasn't the same artistic co-op begun in '67, the deletion of "Moonchild Vulcan" showed little respect for Chris's crucial contributions to the band. Viewed from that perspective, the move was quite cold indeed.

Amid the retraction and cutting, small hints of what had been remained. The drawing of Chris on the album cover was interesting. It showed him looking past Rosko to lock eyes with Steve, his left hand firmly grasping the still mystical Traffic symbol. But perhaps more important, in the center of Chris's tweed hat, pulled down against the winter chill, was another small artifact overlooked in the retouching process. Just above the brim the faint image of a crescent moon can be seen – a most obscure reminder of Chris's lost song.

Traffic only played one more gig in England, the Reading Festival in August. Then after a short break (during which the new album was released), they were off to begin that long slog around the globe. If Chris loathed flying early on, years of drinking and self-medication built up a tolerance. But now Steve decided that surface travel was the way to go too. To get to America, he would take a boat (the Queen Elizabeth II), after which he planned to use a Rolls Royce Silver Cloud sedan (also shipped on the boat) to drive from gig to gig – no matter how far apart. Always up for the leisurely approach, Chris went along – bringing his usual bag of odds and ends and a shortwave radio. More practically minded (and utterly unafraid of flying), Jim saw no reason to waste days on a boat; he and Rosko would take the plane.

But for Chris and Steve, the five-day boat trip did a world of good. Reconnecting as friends, they hung out and talked, perhaps delving into topics such as the role of Middle Eastern influences and ancient Pythagorean scales in the new songs (subjects both had referred to in the press around this time). Pythagoras' (Greek philosopher and mathematician born 570 BC) scale produced music not only mathematically harmonious (pitch intervals in 'perfect fifth' ratios) but was also veiled with metaphysical connotations. By changing the tuning of 'A' from the modern 440 Hz standard reference pitch to 432 Hz, the esoteric benefits supposedly ranged from the mundane (making listeners feel more tranquil) to the cosmic (harmonizing music to the speed of light). Was this new ground for Traffic to explore?

*

The United States of late 1974 was shuddering through a downward spiral in self-confidence. The previous year's Arab Oil Embargo set the stage by plunging automobile owners' collective faces in a bucket of cold water – the culture of cheap driving would never be the same. The long-hated Nixon regime's recent collapse would have been welcome except for the psychological burden of a paranoiac, self-induced funk known as 'Watergate' that accompanied it. Meanwhile in a far off continent, the pointless, bloody and seemingly endless Vietnam war finally sputtered to a close – an utterly lost cause, at the cost of fifty-five thousand American dead.

The mainstream rock scene reflected the country as a whole. Perhaps most disturbingly, it had also come to embody the ethos that the idealistic hippies had rebelled against so long ago – big business. Huge stadium shows, merchandizing and an increasingly homogenized radio format all helped concentrate the revenue stream into fewer (and increasingly greedier) hands. Yet the exploitive model came with a high cost. Having been scaled up, over-hyped, and milked to the hilt by big promoters, the enterprise was rapidly running out of steam.

Many artists were following a similar trajectory. While some, like Led Zeppelin were still enjoying their heyday, many of the biggest acts of the 60's era, having spent their youthful creativity, were shamelessly cashing in, such as Crosby, Stills, Nash and Young's album-less stadium mega-tour. Having lost their fluid lead guitarist Mick Taylor, the Rolling Stones had recently jettisoned worn out satanic pretensions for a safer 'party' approach (*It's Only Rock 'n Roll*), while the happy go lucky hippy band – the Grateful Dead, would play only a few shows in the upcoming year before going on an indefinite hiatus. Emerging from his heroin haze, Eric Clapton had finally returned, but was still battling demons. These days he often walked on stage blind-drunk, and on at least one occasion in the next year would be reduced to playing from flat on his back. Joe Cocker could perhaps stand as a human metaphor for the lot. In a career always precariously balanced between inspiration and excess, he'd literally staggered over the line to fall off more than one stage recently. More than anything, dissolution seemed the emerging paradigm for the aging rockers.

What about the group that had started the whole 60's rock revolution – the Beatles? While long gone as a band, mid-decade found the individual members all struggling in one way or another. Yes, Ringo and Paul each released solid albums in '73 (*Ringo* and *Band On The Run*), but the rest of the decade would be downhill for both. John, just now coming off his infamous drunken 'Lost Weekend' period in Los Angeles, was also creatively spent and soon to be quitting the business for a home-life refuge. Only the most road reticent of them all – George – toured in '74. While playing to full arenas with Indian sitar master Ravi Shankar, he would be dogged by a chronically hoarse voice and a lackluster response to his eccentrically rearranged songs. Profoundly disillusioned with the 'rock life', Harrison's first major tour would also be his last.

Despite the diminished states of the once-fab four, an intense, almost pathological nostalgia had set in for the Beatles of old. Recently, offers of all sorts had begun pouring in to entice a reunion. Amongst these was one for fifty million dollars for a single concert – with profits to be reaped from a closed circuit broadcast encircling the globe (coinciding with a merchandising blitz on an unprecedented scale). Apparently, some moguls viewed the emerging musical era as so barren that only the resurrection of this one particular band – at nearly any cost – could possibly save it. The Beatles response to this madness was (thankfully) – silence. All in all, the last quarter of 1974 was a weird, unsettling time.

In this context of diminishment, many rock fans looked to Traffic as one of the last of the great sixties British groups left standing; despite the near constant shape-shifting, the band's talent, appeal and mystique remained intact. As such, back once again on American soil, some of the old rock excitement lingered and expectations ran high. But almost from the beginning, cracks were showing too.

Rolling Stone, still holding on to its place as the definitive arbitrator of the scene, had been up and down on Traffic over the last couple of years. Reviewing the new album, they were again ambivalent. While recommending *When the Eagle Flies* for its "somber intensity", the reviewer had no time for the jazzy tangents, saying, "the extended jam on the Dadaistic 'Dream Gerard' is laughable. Winwood attempts an awkward jazz solo and Wood's saxophone is skimpy." While recognized as the main creative force, Steve was also singled out for the most criticism – his famous vocals now referred to as sometimes "weak or flat." Ultimately, Traffic was described as having the same systemic problem that rock had in general – unclear direction. The magazine concluded with a recommendation that they ditch the jazz for shorter, conventionally structured songs. The bottom line: *When the Eagle Flies* was a little out of step with what passed for the American zeitgeist.

Jim Capaldi disagreed, thinking that they were actually in front of the curve. Recalling the sense of disconnect that threaded through the reviews, he said, "It was ahead of its time, the synth, the mood. The critics didn't really get behind the record… I think it was over their heads, you know." But perhaps the relative gloom of *Eagle* was a little *too* in tune with the times, something the critics either didn't understand or were loath to admit. Arriving in a damaged America in the fall of the year with an album featuring songs like "Graveyard People", Traffic simply mirrored the approaching cultural winter. And if the critics couldn't appreciate the societal subtext, it didn't bode particularly well for the audiences to come.

Be that as it may, a reporter was sent along to cover the first few dates. David Rensin met them for the first show at the Boston Gardens on September 13th, and was impressed. Backstage he saw evidence of the old camaraderie as Jim jokingly read a letter from a supposed American relative, while Chris sipped Courvoisier and covertly checked out the quality of the Promoter's chinaware. Chris Blackwell was in a good mood too, smirking as he revealed that he'd turned down having Dave Mason as the opening act in favor of Little Feat, saying only: "I've seen him before."

On stage, Rensin found the magic intact, "As Steve Winwood and Rosko Gee struck the first tentative chords, blood relations and Dave Mason made no difference to the 15,000 sweaty fans who crammed the Garden. Traffic had been sorely missed since their last swing across America nearly 19 months ago, and neither year-round hockey ice just inches beneath the plastic floorboards nor the groups return to a four-man format would cool the hungry Boston crowd."

Amid all the cultural uncertainty, the reception must have been a huge relief. Just to be sure, the set list had been modified for the American audience. While still opening with the same instrumental played in Europe, most of the lengthy, jazzy explorations were gone (including the now homeless "Vulcan"). The set list now strategically mixed enough familiar songs amongst the new to keep the restless Americans from squirming too much. And yet their best known song – "Dear Mr. Fantasy", would, for the first time since '67, not make the list at all.

Early on, they'd seemed to have gotten it right. And Rensin was correct in viewing the first shows as mere prelude to the big nights ahead in New York City. Indeed all eyes were focused straight ahead for a special venue – the Academy of Music – where they would soon be playing four shows over two nights. The Academy had been one of the hotspots of the past several tours – and this time was no different. New York City, Chicago and San Francisco were still places where Traffic felt they had to prove their mettle – and where they often played their best.

But as well as the Boston show had gone, with its conclusion a strange fragility hung in the air. Perhaps it was that odd intensity the audience displayed, the palpable restlessness of the uncertain scene that Traffic had stepped into. Or it might have had something to do with the dynamics of the band itself. Whatever the cause, something was now slightly, if indefinably, off. Hunched down in the backseat of the Rolls, Rensin caught up with Steve as the door was closing, asking for any final thoughts on what it was like to be the leader of Traffic, to which he responded, "I've taken it upon myself. Sometimes, if a band fucks around too much, people will ask, 'What's going on?' I think if I didn't keep things together – which is the leader's role – they wouldn't be together." And with only a few inconsequential words to add, he was on his way back to the hotel.

In the dressing room, Rensin found Chris alone, in a reflective, philosophical mood. While seemingly at peace with the current state of the band, he also hinted at the possibility of a cataclysm that the others couldn't yet see, "Every move we've made might have seemed self-destructive at the time, but it's because of those very moves that we are where and what we are today. That's why we're around – even though it often seemed like we were breaking up. Sometimes now, I've gotten the feeling that things won't last much longer, but more often I think that we'll go on for quite some time – as long as we've got the courage to keep together through strong decisions and remain honest about how we feel."

It was all eerily parallel to the conversations the same magazine had taped back in the dwindling days of the Cottage, back in '68; Steve sending out vibes concerning a change in his state of mind, and Chris countering on an almost subliminal level – justifying why Traffic should live on. While both used almost the same words as before about 'keeping the band together', this time around Chris added that crucial plea for all concerned to be honest about their feelings. Ironically, despite all the years gone by, it was very unlikely that the two ever talked about it face to face. And that was unfortunate, because the crisis point was a lot closer than anyone realized.

September 18th, 1974, Academy of Music, 42nd Street, New York City, early show: In a hall packed with a rambunctious audience, Traffic stepped into their usual relaxed and happy concert scene – or so it seemed. As Jim adjusted his drums and Steve settled in behind his keyboard, a tone of confusion ran through the crowd as some caught sight of Chris unsteadily approaching a microphone. His slurred words at first sounding like a joke aimed at Howard Stein (Promoter of the concert), he soon trailed off to an incomprehensible mumble. Stein, waiting on stage to introduce the band, paused for an awkward moment before talking past Chris, "I want to speak for everybody Stevie, in saying, and we never thought we'd say it again – 'Thank god we're back in Traffic!'" The resulting applause was equally enthusiastic, but as the band started the usual warm-up tune, it was already clear that all was not well.

The intro jam's usual nimble 'switch around' was the first obvious problem; When Steve picked up his guitar, Chris was slow at getting in place at the keyboard, and once he was, played a reckless spray of notes. For his sax solo, he was again late, coming in with the wrong key amid a blast of feedback. Quickly recognizing the problem, Steve began a pattern that would continue throughout the show – at the first opportune moment, he simply played over Chris, cutting him off as a way to guide the tune to completion.

The rest of the show wasn't any better. From his demeanor and playing, it was clear that Chris was 'out of it'; with no way to hide or put a positive spin on it. Larry Geller, a longtime Traffic fan in the audience that night was shocked and dismayed by Chris's behavior. "He was just wandering around on the stage, walking back and forth like he didn't know where the hell to go. So you could just tell right away that something was wrong. And then he would just blow a note here and there, and just stand there. He was barely playing, especially with the sax. He was incoherent basically, and because of that Winwood and Capaldi weren't so great either. They kind of just rushed through the show – it was heavy on "Eagle Flies", which was not their best material anyway, so that was part of the problem too. The whole thing was falling apart; it was as loose a show as you would ever see."

Filled with a dense haze of cigarette and marijuana smoke that nearly obscured the stage from the rear of the hall, the Academy had become a nightmarish scene leaving nowhere to go but forward. In the face of Chris's condition, and the crowd's increasing hostility, Steve pushed the band on. Some songs were passable; "Graveyard People", "Pearly Queen", "Who Knows What Tomorrow May Bring", had enough solidity to placate the audience. But others were near train wrecks; "Something New", in particular, found Chris blowing jokey notes from Stephen Foster's "Camptown Races" in the middle of an already disjointed solo.

For his own "Tragic Magic", Chris was wobbly, but managed to find the theme, even showing a few moments of grace by ending his solo with extended crooning low notes. Even so, Steve took no chances, moving from section to section to a hasty conclusion. Although they got decent applause, the audience quickly reverted to catcalls and shouts. Unnerved by the unremitting negativity, Chris began to lose his cool, scolding and then pleading into the microphone, "Shut up, shut up, please, please…" Soon after, he disappeared from the stage.

With whistles, shouts and frustrated shouts coming at the stage from all directions, a besieged Winwood halfheartedly laid blame for the situation with the rude audience itself, complaining in a weak, defeated voice: "Well, ah, I must admit, New York's not really with us tonight. Not totally, but um… (More yelling)… What? We'll try…" As he began his intro into what should have been the saving grace, "John Barleycorn", it was clear that nearly every aspect of the concert was jinxed – his acoustic guitar was far out of tune, requiring that he stop to fix it, amid more jeers and drunken laughter. Still, with only Jim at his side he carried on, playing two verses until, somewhat miraculously, Chris reappeared (to some applause) with his flute for the final stanza. While he was there for "Forty Thousand Headmen", managing to play enough of the ghostly flute notes to keep that song alive, within seconds of its conclusion the shouts returned and continued unabated.

There would be no respite. Winwood's attempt to introduce "Dream Gerard" was met with a cascade of verbal abuse, and when it came time for his solo, Chris's saxophone sounded like a raw, wounded voice crying out in pain. Ending with a passable "Low Spark", the band was able to leave to real applause, but as much as they might like to put it all behind them, the awful night wasn't over – they still had the late show to do. Almost certainly they would have been better off had they cancelled.

CHAPTER TWENTY-FOUR

In the interval, Chris's condition only worsened. And by show time he was absent from the stage or if he did make it on, he wasn't there long. In any event, Steve decided to simply carry on without him. Trying to cover all of the crucial musical parts as best he could, Winwood strove mightily to maintain a semblance of normalcy – but it didn't last. By the end of the fourth song, members of the crowd began to talk and gesture toward the stage as it became clear Chris was missing.

Jim tried to defuse the issue, but instead opened a Pandora's Box. Addressing the audience, he got as far as: "Chris is sorry that he couldn't be here…" before the angry retorts flooded in: "He better be!"; "What happened to Wood?" Fearing the return of the previous show's hostile atmosphere he then tried to distract with a compliment, "How are you? It's good to be back in New York…" (Loud heckler): "Where's Wood?" Jim: "Chris is laying, as they say in Jamaica, cool and easy." (audience): "Bring him out!" Jim: "So, it's the trio for a bit…" (audience): "Bullshit!"

For a band used to receiving love and acceptance from their American audiences the intense negativity must have stung badly. Playing on, the heckling gradually subsided but the restlessness remained. In Chris's absence, it seemed that Traffic's sound was, for the first time, too thin to maintain interest. While they could get by without him temporarily, during the Muscle Shoals era, this time out there was just not enough flesh left on the bones to pull it off. While ostensibly Steve's group, without Chris's contributions, it was clear that Traffic as such could not exist.

So a crucial paradox finally revealed itself – for tonight at least, they couldn't play with Chris, and yet they couldn't really play without him either. Jim seemed to sum it up as he tried to introduce one of Traffic's classic songs that night, "The situation in which we recorded it is similar to tonight… it gets more fitting every year… it's called 'Who Knows What Tomorrow May Bring.'" That was indeed the pertinent question – the band had two more shows to play the following night.

While Chris was back for both concerts on the 19th, the instability lingered. If not 'out of it' as on the previous night, his nerves were shot to pieces, the playing shaky. Technically, there were problems too; electronic squalls of sound emanated from both Steve's synthesizer and Chris's effects box. With forward momentum impossible, the band struggled as though mired in quicksand, with Steve often ending songs early just to avoid further trouble.

Just before the last song of the early show, after Steve had introduced Jim and Rosko, Chris came up to the microphone and attempted to apologize for his absence on the previous evening. Interrupted by a loud shout of "Mr. Fantasy!" by an audience member, he seemed to have to overcome a lump in his throat to begin, almost stammering: "Um, yeah, I wanted to have a chance to say, I was just, ahh… I couldn't get on the stage – alright? (pause of several seconds) I really feel bad, you know? I really feel bad…" His last few words were obscured by further shouts from the audience, many of whom had no idea what he was talking about: "Low Spark!", "Rock 'n Roll Stew!", "Gimme Some Lovin…" With any real communication impossible amidst the chaos, there wasn't much point in continuing. As far as Chris's apology went, that was the end of it.

Or it should have been. The last show of the run, held later that evening, was in some ways the roughest of all. From the second song, crazy feedback plagued them. Nearly from the outset too, elements of the audience were back to shouts and taunts. The combination of the two distractions caused something to snap within the band, inspiring a rare return reaction. Interestingly, Jim, the usual on-stage wordsmith, fell into silence – for once unsure of what to say. Instead, with catcalls falling over them at the end of "Graveyard People", it was the mild-mannered Chris – no longer chastened by his own transgressions – who went back at his tormentors. He began with a dose of pure sarcasm: "Thank you. You're very, very kind – for *this* type of audience." Seeming to pause to consider the remark, some finally applauded before the hecklers redoubled their taunts. Jim, struggling to introduce the next song, "Pearly Queen", was cut off, and then drowned out.

From there, it was war. By "Who Knows what Tomorrow May Bring" Winwood was ignoring the crowd except to sing and play with a fierce intensity. Meanwhile Chris kept up the cutting remarks: "Thank you, New York, although it would be better if you kept quiet…" Fed up, he seemed willing to go as far as necessary, but Steve played over him, moving on to the next song.

He finally got another chance when introducing his own composition: "This one is off the "Shoot Out"… album, and it is especially dedicated to New York, it's called 'Tragic Magic.'" For those that knew of the song's drug addict message – and some clearly did – the comment was a slap in the face. The response, an interesting combination of applause, knowing laughter and fierce retorts, including an audible: "Fuck off!"

which Chris also didn't let slide. Feigning innocence, he replied: "Why'd you say 'fuck off' when I said 'Tragic Magic'?" Before they could start the song, he got his answer from one audience member: "You're the one that's fuckin' stoned baby!"

After that, there didn't seem much more to say. The show looked to be a write-off, an utter catastrophe needing only to be finished so they could move on. But suddenly, as if from nowhere, things began to turn around. Perhaps, not surprisingly, "John Barleycorn" started it, casting its usual calming magic spell, even though a nerve-jangled Chris really struggled at first. "Forty Thousand Headmen" took them the rest of the way, with Steve soaring vocally and strumming furiously, followed by the classic fluttering flute notes floating and darting high above the heads of the audience. Somehow, the resulting vibe mended everything, settling the audience into a pleasant reverie. More importantly, the heckling dried up and the resulting applause was the most sustained of the night. "Dream Gerard" worked too; with Chris's confidence returning, he played his longest and best sax solo of the whole run of shows.

Not taking any chances, Steve didn't wait for an encore, moving them right into "Low Spark". But having turned some kind of corner, he needn't have worried. The version that followed was fantastic – by turns edgy and hypnotic, with Chris jumping in for an early solo, then playing sax notes off Steve's spiraling synth figures. As the song moved toward its conclusion, Traffic was back in full flower. Having veered away from utter disaster, the spirit had inexplicably returned. Finishing the set to a deafening roar of approval, the relief was palpable on all sides.

Although "Low Spark" was the last planned song, the need to savor the victory won out. Conferring backstage, the four emerged to play one more – that frantic, riffy instrumental used to close the European shows a few months back. The guitar and sax powerhouse – full of punchy chords – perfectly closed out the bitter chapter by rocking the house. It was also the last time the tune would ever be played.

If the run of shows at the Academy ended on a note of grace, nothing could erase the memory of the tortuous trail of broken glass preceding it. The next morning an attempt was made to patch things up before they left town; Jim went on a local radio station, apologizing and promising that they would play a free concert the next time around. And with the last bit of unsavory business tidied up, it was finally time to get the hell out of the 'Big Apple'.

But the reverberations would linger. An incredibly harsh review would soon be filed back in the homeland in *Melody Maker*. Entitled "Terrible Traffic", the piece chronicled the bad shows and clearly singled out Chris as the culprit. For the first time, a major music paper had slammed Traffic hard; Chris Blackwell, now home in England, felt the blow and wouldn't forget it. But strangely enough, back in the USA, something about the whole mess also drew them closer – at least for the time being. Besides, there was too much work left to do; next up was Maryland, Pennsylvania, and then a safe haven – the west coast.

On this tour, there was a new American face amidst the mostly British crew. Chris Blackwell had recently hired Candice Brightman as the tour's Lighting Director. What did she think of the rough start to the tour? Having previously worked a long stretch with the Grateful Dead, to her, Traffic's odd off-night didn't seem worth mentioning. In fact, in later years, she couldn't recall those Academy shows at all: "No, no, I don't remember it. Remember, I worked for the Grateful Dead, and I've heard some *really bad* shows."

Brightman actually thought that Traffic's playing was not the real issue of concern. She did however notice more consistently troubling patterns as the band moved west: "I thought that they were playing really well, (but) the audience was not paying attention. Nobby (Clarke, sound mixer and Road Manager) and I would have this thing, where he would turn the sound down and I would dim the lights, in an attempt to get the audience to stop talking – to notice that they can't even hear the music – and maybe they would shut up." The other big issue was probably related. Many of the shows were not selling out, or even close. The combination of circumstances cast a pall as the tour continued. "It was a rough tour; people didn't come to the shows. They had just released an album that was kind of dirge-like. I liked the album, but it was kind of down. They were doing that thing where you'd go into an arena, and curtain it half off. People were kind of depressed about that," Brightman recalled.

So, maybe the critics had been right all along, the new music just wasn't right for the time. For all the effort to stay true to their jazzy muse, they just weren't attracting enough of a new audience to balance the lack of enthusiasm from the old fans. With so many dates still to be played, and generally weak advanced sales, the psychological effect of their first real sense of decline exerted some weight. Brightman was sympathetic, "Kind of a heartbreaking experience – it must have been, for them."

To balance the downside, the band and crew enjoyed each other's company. Brightman saw both sides, "I think it was sad and difficult because of the crowds – they weren't coming and when they did they didn't pay attention. So that was tough, but there was certainly a lot of camaraderie amongst the crew and band. What I remember was that these people were profoundly funny; my face hurting, my stomach hurting from laughter. I just remember Chris being funny to be around… They could do all the 'Monty Python' – word for word, they could do whole shows. So, a lot my time was spent just crying from laughter."

On stage, it wasn't all gloomy either; some very satisfying, even great shows were turned in. Not unexpectedly, the west coast concerts ranked highly. In San Francisco, a fan recalled a show that included Chris sitting on the drum riser to play an intense, exploratory sax solo for "Graveyard People". At the Long Beach Arena, the local paper noted: "Each selection was greeted with genuine, appreciative applause from the sell-out crowd. 'Forty Thousand Headmen', a Traffic classic, featured the finely tuned harmony of Wood's flute along with Winwood, both giving the piece a mythical quality." In Tucson, Chris visited a western clothing store and was outfitted as a cowboy – duds that he happily wore on stage for several dates. He also inspired smiles from his band-mates by rolling under Steve's grand piano to play a solo one night.

Brightman had only fond memories of the Chris she knew from the tour, "Woody was kind of a mystery. He was so mild mannered and laid back, but he played beautifully – that was always my favorite part of the show. He wasn't afraid to be really pretty… lovely." By the time they got to Texas, everyone was relaxed, taking in the landscape as the open plains rolled on mile after mile. Perhaps as a result, one of the best shows took place in Fort Worth on October 12th.

But even here, wistfulness hung in the air. After Chris's economical yet nearly transcendental flute on "John Barleycorn", Jim spoke up, proudly saying "Chris Wood – the magic piper… thank you." But as the band prepared to launch into "Forty Thousand Headmen" he added more, "That's an old English story, of the passion of the 'corn – where they're reaping the corn, and they're getting drunk. This one is about passion – not quite, or paranoia." As Steve began the guitar intro, Jim went even further, his own passion evident as he concluded with a note aimed straight at his own band, "But you've just gotta stand up and keep going – no matter what the odds."

Three days later, in Tuscaloosa Alabama, Traffic met up with the Muscle Shoals Rhythm Section for the first time since April 1973. There were no obvious hard feelings; the Americans drove many miles to see their ex-band mates play. David Hood gracefully recalled the four-piece Traffic as quite good, but afterwards – back at the hotel – noted something amiss relationship-wise. "That was the last time I saw Chris. He was okay, but kind of melancholy – I think Winwood was trying… they were not really together. He (Chris) came up to me and said, 'Gosh, I wish I was still playing with you guys.'" Whether remorse or from interpersonal dynamics within the band, Chris needed Hood's friendship that night. But the reunion was brief – by morning the band was on their way to Georgia.

Looking back on it, Hood mused that perhaps Muscle Shoals had gotten off the rollercoaster at the right time, "The times had changed, and music was changing. What everybody had thought was so cool at one time, the next time around… people were getting tired of twenty minute jams, that kind of stuff, it had been done so much, it was time to move on."

Little Feat opened for Traffic at the Omni in Atlanta on October 16. It was a hot town for them – they'd always done well there, and had even written a song ("Oh Atlanta") about the city. So the crowd was up and primed when Traffic hit the stage, but unfortunately it was more like déjà vu of New York; Chris came out, according to one witness, barely able to stand, much less play. Seeing where things were likely heading, Steve didn't wait for the meltdown to play itself out. About twenty-five minutes in, claiming firecrackers had been thrown at the stage, he abruptly got up from the piano and walked off. The others followed, and that was that – the show was over.

The tour went on – although it was clear that the tolerance level for instability had lowered. But once again, things firmed up. Crisscrossing the Midwest – first came Bloomington, then Detroit – where Chris finally returned a beautiful extended flute coda to "Love" – Cleveland, Cincinnati, and on to St. Louis. Then another big night loomed. October 27th was scheduled for Chicago, the lynchpin of the heartland, with some major rock press waiting. The well-respected jazz magazine *DownBeat* asked for an interview, to which both Steve and Chris quickly agreed; honored that Traffic was considered worthy by the premiere scribes of the jazz world. On the rock side, the new hip rock magazine on the scene *Creem* also sent a reporter, Cynthia Dagnal, to review the Chicago show.

If there were any nerves, they didn't seem to be showing. Chris gave a long, lucid interview to *DownBeat*, covering all stages of his career. The magazine also briefly but glowingly reviewed the concert, calling Traffic's concert presentation "a well-paced, almost perfect set."

Creem's Dagnal seemed to have witnessed a different show altogether. As a longtime Traffic fan, she was, to say the least, disappointed. Her first issue was with the audience, which she described as wildly bipolar right from the start, "Chicago can be the most demonstratively grateful audience in the universe when welcoming a returning legend, just as it can be the most devastatingly rude bunch of fuckers this side of Armageddon... this night they were faced with all of the above." In her report, the band too came in for a share of criticism, with Rosko's bass solo referred to as "embarrassing", while Chris's note-sustaining sax playing said to have, "left everything to the imagination." She faulted the structure of the newer songs too saying, "What was once rich, sure footed and complex... is now sparse, tentative and tellingly simple." But some high praise would be reserved for "Barleycorn" whose appropriate use of simplicity "set an exquisite, otherworldly mood – a gem among the bottom heavy rhinestones." Overall, the fundamental problem was just more of the same – restless audiences and a lack of enthusiasm for new material. In a place previously a stronghold, the sign of things to come was hard to miss.

The body of the concert concluded, the band stood in the wings, listening to the applause wash over the auditorium. Then Steve called out "Heaven Is In Your Mind" as the encore. While rarely performed in recent years, ironically, this song was one of first ever played by Traffic in America back in '68 – a circle now complete. They followed with the usual closer "Low Spark", and it was over.

Immediately afterward, a dark omen – Steve's stomach was hurting. According to what he told *DownBeat*, it was bad enough to consult a local doctor. In the past, some type of physical aliment typically presaged intentions to make a big change. And so it was again. With many dates scheduled yet to play, Steve had decided to go home.

Meeting up outside the hotel, as far as the others in the band knew, it was time to move on to the next show – Knoxville, four hundred and fifty miles away. Jim recalled seeing Steve climb into the Rolls, ostensibly for the long drive to Tennessee, "He walked out in the middle of America. It (Chicago) was the last gig. I waved him off, thinking I'd see him at the next gig, and I never saw him again."

As on previous occasions, the bad news would be broken by others. It was only when Jim, Chris and Rosko arrived in Knoxville that afternoon that they heard that Steve was on his way home. In a state of shock, they instinctively moved on to Chattanooga to watch Muhammad Ali fight George Foreman on closed circuit T.V. – a match Jim had been looking forward to for weeks.

Four days later, *When The Eagle Flies* would go 'Gold', the RIAA designation for having sold a million copies. Too late to save Traffic, the album had finally been deemed a certifiable success by the record-buying public.

('90 Minute Traffic Jam', Denise Kusel, Long Beach Observer, 1974)

('Chris Wood in the talk in', Steve Peacock, Sounds, 5/5/1973)

('Esoteric Astrology, Vol. III, A Treatise On The Seven Rays', Alice Bailey, Lucis Publishing, New York, 1951)

('Freedom Riding Again', Bill Henderson, Sounds, 9/14/1974)

('Traffic, A New Cycle', Tony Stewart, NME, 5/11/1974)

('Traffic: Coming or Going', Cynthia Dagnal, Creem, 2/1975)

('Traffic is a Spirit', Mojo, 1994)

('Traffic Jam', Hohman and Townley, DownBeat, 1/30/1975)

('Traffic Lightens Up for American Tour', David Rensin, Rolling Stone, 10/24/1974)

('When the Phoenix Flies', Bill Henderson, Sounds, 9/21/1974)

CHAPTER TWENTY-FIVE

THE BEGINNING OF THE END

There is no light without shadow and no psychic wholeness without imperfection. To round itself out, life calls not for perfection but completeness; and for this, the 'thorn in the flesh' is needed, the suffering of defects without which there is no progress and no ascent. C. G. Jung

Exactly why Traffic shuddered to a grinding halt when and as it did remains, to this day, open to speculation. Interestingly, in later interviews the one who should know has had little to say. While rarely mentioning the stomach ailment, Steve often referred to a sense of being trapped in a "cul-de-sac" of albums and endless road trips – and that was certainly true. Beyond that, a constellation of forces were aligned – Chris's erratic condition, the lack of ticket sales, long car rides, and the sometimes deranged and/or apathetic audience response – all could have contributed to the tour ending as it did.

But back home among friends, it was clear that more than a road trip had been severed. While no Traffic break-up was ever announced, to those in the know, the signs were there. Paul Medcalf, one of the band's primal associates, would talk to an exasperated Steve who, while never flat out saying the band was over, made it clear he'd had it with Chris's excesses, "Well see Paul, he can't do the job anymore – he's too out of it – he's falling asleep on stage…" Medcalf elaborated, 'the trouble is, Steve was a perfectionist, musically, and Chris was bumbling around… unless he was sharp as a knife, like he used to be, it didn't work. I think that was it basically. I think Steve wanted the band to be respected."

Gordon Jackson had similar recollections, "I was working for Steve at the time and I remember him coming home from that tour – and it wasn't very nice. The flavor that I got from it was that Steve had just had enough. He couldn't risk going onstage and have that happen anymore – because it was going to ruin his career as well."

So it was Chris's unreliability – in particular those train-wreck shows in New York which helped swing things past a tipping point. And if Steve couldn't work with Chris anymore, Traffic also had to fall – Chris's personality was far too embedded in its fabric to exist without him; that much at least was clear.

But how did it all come to this? Certainly underlying issues had been festering for years – if not from the beginning. While Chris's substance problems caused obvious issues, a vicious cycle was also at work. Island Records employee, Suzette Newman noticed the dynamic, "When he was 'out of it', he was nervous around Steve because he knew that Steve didn't approve. I think he got crushed along the way. The more insecure he felt about Steve the worse – the more of a state – he would get into. But none of these things would've been talked about – people didn't talk."

Indeed. As much as Traffic relied on that psychic link to work their musical magic, verbal communication was another matter. Chris, of course, rarely confronted a touchy area even if it affected him directly, while Jim was the master of spinning nearly any situation in a positive direction. And Steve's vague restlessness had for years kept the others in a state of near constant uncertainty. The fear that he would pull the plug – for whatever reason – created a very particular type of stress that Jim and Chris each dealt with in their own way.

Musically, the issues weren't cut and dried either. The tension between Steve's desire for a more controlled presentation versus Chris's need to be freely expressive (for better *and* worse) – an apparent weak spot of the band – was also not exactly what it seemed. In the end, the fuel that Traffic drove on very much required that volatile mix of imperfection and talent; two seemingly irreconcilable states that were actually inseparable. But in severing the ties for good, was Steve aware of the creative loss to follow?

Penny Massot pondered that very question. Having acrimoniously broken up with Steve herself earlier in the year after being a couple since 1966, she would later question his understanding of Traffic's value, "I don't think Steve realized that actually, how important it was, those times. They were so close, they were like brothers – and he left them adrift. It's a shame, a real shame. I began to wonder if he had any idea about what was good and bad in those days. Maybe it was Jim, Chris and I that understood – 'this is great'. Maybe he didn't know the difference."

CHAPTER TWENTY-FIVE

Jim held similar feelings. While acknowledging Chris's weaknesses, he also vehemently felt the bad nights were an acceptable price to keep this unique band alive, "It don't matter! Miles Davis ended up just spitting on stage and playing the odd note – deeeep! And everybody was going fucking mental." Recalling the night that both Joe Cocker (opening for Traffic) and then Chris fell over on stage, Jim believed the alternative – a polished, artificially perfect stage act – to be much worse, "We toured with Joe Cocker, alright? And Joe was in his terrible phase. And the review was, 'Joe Cocker came on and fell over, then Traffic came on and Chris Wood fell over.' He fell backwards off the organ – the organ seat, he just went backwards, and 'boom!' and Joe Cocker had been on and just fuckin' collapsed you know. But who wants to see dancing, and all of this – dry ice? I'd like to see *that* – because it's fucking real. And I don't even mind embarrassing myself in front of you…"

Above all, Jim felt that, when it came to Chris's overall wellbeing, losing Traffic was the worst thing that could have happened to him. "It was bad man, it was bad. But the two break ups like that were wrong – to be at least very upfront and say 'this is it', you know. Chris *was* falling apart, I know, but – you know what I mean, it would have been better to keep going. It would have given him something to grasp on to. He did (have stage-fright), and his condition was deteriorating – but he could play, he could perform, and it would have given him something… it would have given us more ammunition to keep Chris on the straight and narrow a bit more. I mean, I was prepared to do it. I don't know if Steve could face it, I don't know, but my attitude is like, 'come on, let's be fuckin' positive… why walk away from it?' Chris was a bit flaky sometimes but it would have been better to give him something positive to do. It was better that he could like, work. And when it was all over, Chris just went downhill completely… he just absolutely sank then, there was nothing to keep him going."

But an invisible door had already swung shut. As much as Jim may have pleaded, and Chris simply hoped, this time there would be no going back; the brotherhood was broken. Hurt and uncertain, with only a gray, British winter looming in front of them, where exactly could Chris and Jim go from here? As far away as possible: Brazil.

In a move reminiscent of the later days of '68, the shattered remnants of Traffic would regroup to see what could be salvaged, or to at least help console each other. In mid-November Chris, Jim, Chris Blackwell, Chris 'Noggie' Nolan and Island executive Tom Hayes flew to Nassau, then Miami, the Bahamas, and finally to sunny Rio de Janeiro. More than a vacation, the trip was a kind of ghostly continuation of the truncated tour – Rio was scheduled to follow the U.S. dates. And Traffic or no, the record business and press people were still interested in talking.

But Jim and Chris would arrive in an awkward, limbo-like state – unsure of exactly who or what they were actually representing. Unable to even consider forming another group this time around, they settled for being feted by the record executives and making the rounds of numerous parties. Jim tried to make the most of it, talking up the Brazilian girls, meeting local musicians, and jamming here and there. He and Chris also hung out with other ex-pats escaping the English chill – Cat Stevens and Dudley Moore were in town as well.

Besides the parties and sitting by the pool, Chris would wander the ethnically diverse city streets and beaches, attend football (soccer) matches at the huge city stadium, and seek out local sights and sounds. Noggie Nolan recalled Chris becoming absorbed in a lifestyle far removed from anything back home. "Chris loved it to death – (it was) so humane, so real, so detached from England; the be all and the butchery. We went to a lot of the samba schools; Chris was fascinated by the rhythms – really fascinated by the rhythms."

At times, the mosaic-like aspects of the city overwhelmed his senses. Since its Portuguese beginnings, this city had always been a confluence between humanity's greatest reach and its deepest flaws. Surrounded entirely by nature's embrace – Rio de Janeiro unselfconsciously juxtaposes rich and poor, deprivation and joy in an urban notch nestled between a boundless blue ocean and the deep green Amazon rainforest. Even more daunting is the inescapable image of an omniscient being standing high above it all. Perched atop Corcovado Mountain, the 130 foot tall statue known as O Christo Redentor ("Christ the Redeemer"), embraces Rio and all its contradictions with the outstretched arms of a savior of souls.

Noggie recalled Chris still scheming for some kind of adventure, "We did sit up one night in Copacabana. We sat up at the window, with the old-fashioned shutters, rolling down – and it's just belting down with rain. We were sitting in this room, and Chris had out this big map of Brazil – the Amazon jungle. He was very, very much into nature." But tracing out possible routes on a map is not the same as going there, and despite the allure of Brazil's complex beauty, he could never quite clear his head enough to act. Certainly this wasn't the comfortable and secure woodlands of England he knew like the back of his hand. More importantly, the same record executives escorting them to meet the local celebrities and elites also kept the alcoholic spirits flowing and the cocaine bowls full. Sad, high and distracted, he wasn't really up for a deep forest adventure – the map on the wall was as close as he would get to exploring the Amazon.

In all, Jim, Noggie and Chris stayed for nearly three months – doing a little bit of everything, including writing some music. While Jim insisted that they were "having a ball" – and *he* clearly was, Chris remained mostly adrift, frequently staring off into the distance in a dream-like state. One day, perched before his hotel window as another dawn broke over the Atlantic Ocean, he witnessed something so incredible he rushed to rouse the others. Jim recalled, "He woke up one morning and claimed that a wave had come over an island which was out there in the bay – a massive wave. We were all going, 'Chris!' He swears he saw this wave swamp the island!" Looking out the window himself, all Jim and the others could see was calm, unbroken sea on a clear Brazilian morning. Later, Jim would chuckle as he pondered how Chris could be so emphatic about something so clearly impossible.

Whether Chris ever came to understand his vision for what it actually was is unknown. Certainly, the tableau makes most sense as a rather chilling visual metaphor of his own alienated condition.

Soon after, their plans for the future no further along, it was time to go home. While Chris returned to England with his jangled nerves somewhat soothed, other than that not much had changed. Like that giant wave, any insight he might have gleaned in Brazil would be wiped away by the cold reality greeting him in early 1975: his band was defunct, Jeanette typically restless, and the Marble Arch apartment again filled with parasites. Surveying the all too familiar scene as he walked in the door, any thoughts Chris might have had about repairing his damaged life quickly evaporated into the cool London night.

*

A young guitarist named Pete Bonas from Bedfordshire clearly remembered the circumstances leading to meeting Chris Wood, "I was with a group called Brand X – a jazz/rock band at Island Records. I'd met Chris, Jim, Reebop – all of those people at Island at the time. They'd all be hanging out at the café, the studio rehearsal rooms and all of that." But the heady atmosphere didn't last. Having decided that Brand X wasn't their cup of tea after all, Island unceremoniously dropped the band in early 1975. As bad as the news was for Pete, it only got worse. Given a disproportionate share of the blame for "not playing fast enough", he soon found himself kicked out of the band as well.

Not long afterwards, Pete ran into Chris again, venting his frustration, "I said, 'I've just been sacked by the band, dropped from the label, and I can't pay my rent.'" With Pete's situation paralleling his own, Chris was sympathetic, saying: "You know, you can come stay at my place – no problem." Bonas moved in the same day. But as humbled as he was to be invited, Pete soon discovered the reality of life at the apartment was far from glamorous: "It was a nice place… but pretty much a 'halfway house'… you know, anybody and everybody came 'round in the middle of the night. It was a bit crazy really, a lot of drugs."

Still, he was grateful to be taken in. With his roadie companion 'Two Sheds' Jackson, Pete surveyed what was needed to be done around the place, and without being asked, simply got to work: "He was surrounded by a lot of dodgy people you know, and we tried to kind of clean the place up and get rid of some of these hangers-on, and for a while we did that, my friend Sheds and I."

As mundane as it was, keeping the apartment livable was always the first order of business. Normal day-to-day chores – vacuuming the carpet, washing dishes and clothes, and taking the dog to Hyde Park for walks otherwise had lapsed for extended periods. The latter might have been the most important. Often confined to the kitchen, and lacking a yard to use as a toilet, Jazzer simply relieved herself there. Jeanette's old friend Eleanor Barooshian, still a frequent visitor, would eventually come to refer to the place as 'Dogshit Mews'.

The chronically disordered state of the apartment was in fact, simply a mirror of Chris's own condition: having lost his sense of purpose, his once vibrant personality was now rapidly fading as well. Invisibly but unfathomably wounded by the path he'd taken, Chris was for all intents and purposes, a man dying by degrees.

During this period, he sought the company of others in a similar state – getting not so much high as obliterated in the hope of forgetting both the past and a similarly harsh present. The core included two old friends. One was Trevor Burton, the bass player so entranced by the magical life at the Berkshire Cottage that he left his band, The Move, for a solo career that had now stalled. The other was another long-time mate, the ex-guitarist of Free, Paul Kossoff. 'Koss' was especially down and out these days, his drug problems causing him to lose out on one opportunity after another. Although ostensibly the leader of 'Backstreet Crawler', (whose members played as best they could around Paul's deficits), his best chance to shine brightly again had slipped away about a year before.

Steve Hyams, a friend to both Chris and Kossoff, (and an associate of Mott The Hoople) recalled the essential paradox of the talented but troubled guitar player, "I mean they all wanted Kossoff. Bad Company – they had a rehearsal – Mick Ralphs told me they'd had a rehearsal, and he came, but it just didn't work because they just couldn't rely on him." And it seemed that Koss was quite aware of his diminished situation. "The guy that ran the rehearsal studio took him home and said to me a few days afterward, on the way home he noticed Kossoff was crying, and he said 'Paul, what's the matter?' and he said, 'When you've played with the best – what do you do? Where do you go?" Of course, Chris could have said exactly the same thing.

While often inundated with depressive characters, some positive influences served to balance Chris's situation to a degree. Pete Bonas and Junior Marvin (who was recently back on the scene) – both only moderate imbibers, actively tried to get him back into playing. Jamming with friends at the Speakeasy seemed a comfortable way to ease him into the game, but Chris desperately tried to beg off. Finally cajoled into a car, he muttered excuses all the way to the club. "We had to drag him," recalled Pete, "'Come on Chris!' He was *very* reluctant, but we did get him down there, and we managed to get him up on stage. But it was like he had some sort of agoraphobia or a major anxiety about even getting up on stage and playing. That's how bad it was." While neither Marvin nor Bonas understood at the time, in the wake of Traffic's last shows, Chris's long-standing stage fright had evolved into an invisible iron maiden leaving little room to move without inflicting intolerable pain.

More comfortable at home, he and Pete often jammed late into the night in an upstairs room in the flat. Bonas recalled Chris's love of unfettered free expression. "His own compositions would be minimal themes, and all atmospheric – complete groove, and that's it. He had a good understanding of music from that point of view – really that (freedom) is the essence of performing and playing." And when he was feeling secure and relaxed, the old Chris could finally reemerge. Playing tenor over Pete's jazzy guitar figures, deep lines oozing feeling and soul would flow, his trademark squeaks popping up around the edges as punctuation. It was obvious that he was having fun too – several jams ended with mutual chuckles audible on tape. A few times, they managed to make it into the studio to do more. One especially productive session happened when a suddenly inspired Chris requested that the old Traffic session tape for "Barbed Wire" be pulled out of the vault. Rushing over to the studio with Bonas, he would add additional tenor sax parts to fill out the sound while Pete played a new bridge in the middle. Along with the old "Moonchild Vulcan" track, at least two worthy pieces to start the solo album were now in hand.

So while the intent remained, progress only came at a glacial pace. In fact, a terrible catch-22 was at work: with Traffic gone, raising Chris's self-esteem hinged on making a record of his own, yet with his confidence at an all-time low, headway was difficult. While it was clear to Pete that Island was willing to support the effort, they also seemed strangely unaware how much help he really needed. "Chris Blackwell and Island were like, 'Okay, get your act together mate and the opportunity's there.' But there was nobody pushing him, getting a producer... I would spend a lot of time with him, with the cassette players – just sitting around and playing. We spent a lot of time doing that, 'cause I was trying to get some material together to try and get an album – that was the plan – but it was hard work, nailing him down. He didn't have the will or the organizational capability to get it together."

The unexpected arrival of Dr. John shook things up in a good way. Having recently rolled into London town, Mac was bubbling with ideas, wanting not just to hang out and get high, but to play. With his dynamic and quirky personality filling the space of the apartment, everyone rose to the occasion – the possibilities crystallizing into action. Pete recalled, "Dr. John came and stayed for a week. He was really cool actually – it was nice having someone sane in the house. He was a genuinely nice bloke, down to earth, no bullshit." The fact that he was also quite superstitious became clear as he set about protecting the entrance to the house in his own unique way. Pete noted, "He had a little stick, a little Juju stick with a little skull and stuff on it. I went to move it, and he said, '*No*, leave it by the door... leave it by the door...' He was into that stuff."

Mac quickly and forcefully rallied the others. Rehearsing a tune called "Diggin' On You", he kicked it off by barking to Chris, "Get your horn man, where's your fuckin' horn – one, two three..." the old bandleader taking charge once again. Although only a rough run through, in one way at least, the song was also quite remarkable – with Mac on keyboards, Chris on soprano sax, Pete on guitar and Jeanette on vocals – Chris was actually given a verse to *sing*, something he hadn't done since 1967. Laughing through part of the line, they all loosened up, and the next one, "Out Of Tune with the Universe" was much better. Taking the lead vocal, Jeanette's voice had found a silky, slinky quality that fitted with the moonlit vibe that Chris brought to his flute part. In no time at all Dr. John's New Orleans hoodoo vibe was working wonders.

For his part, Mac – quite used to living in rough conditions – was somewhat taken aback by the situation at Marble Arch, saying, "It got *real* bad. Everybody was crash padding at their place, and it became a hang… they were asking me for help, but I was in trouble my own self. But I did some recording dates and stuff, trying to help." Still, before any solid results were achieved in the studio, he would drift out as he'd come in; picking up his magic stick and tipping his hat as he moved on to other adventures. Unfortunately, Dr. John's brief morale boost wasn't enough to get the album rolling.

What about his old band-mates, Winwood and Capaldi? While their assistance had once been a vital assumption in Chris's album plan, that now seemed impossibly remote. From Pete Bonas's perspective, "I didn't see him getting a lot of help from positive people, I can tell you that. Even Jim and Steve, they avoided him because of the company he would keep, the drugs and all of that. And I thought at the time, 'Come on, somebody's got to help this guy.'"

But things had gotten complicated. With career issues of his own, Steve was quite occupied sorting out his own always promising but still uncertain post-Traffic path. To keep his chops up he found time to work with various artists who asked for a little of his deft touch, but re-entangling himself with the down-and-out Woody was likely very close to the bottom of the list.

Even Jim backed away. Although he said he'd been willing to carry on indefinitely with a wounded Traffic, by steering around Chris these days, he too had come close to giving up. After years of trying to reconcile the contradictions that defined his old friend, Jim's feelings had progressed to the point of utter frustration, "In the end, you get angry – you get angry because it becomes so unmanageable. And you are going, 'Why are you doing this? Why can't you be fucking together, be *normal*'…"

As a kind of last attempt to reach out, Jim wrote a song about (and to) him called "Boy With a Problem", that would appear on the album, *Short Cut Draw Blood* released in 1975. By turns, sad, scolding, hopeful and resigned – Jim would bluntly lay his feelings on the line. Chris's response to the song is unknown. Perhaps feeling that he'd done all he could, Jim would then move on. Ultimately, he would go so far as to turn Chris away from entering a social gathering at his home one night. Pete Bonas was there. "I saw Jim do that. I was at a party at Jim's house, Chris turned up, I think he was told in no uncertain terms to go and get his act together. They didn't want to embarrass the other guests…"

While Chris's ability to work again depended on cleaning up his personal life, the complexity of that situation offered no easy path. While Jim actively courted the societal elites these days, Chris still allowed anyone in – from people he met on the street, to drunken tramps, and rowdy Hell's Angels. As the self-appointed guardian of 14 Cumberland Mews, Pete Bonas had a hard time keeping order, but tried, refusing to admit or removing people that he deemed trouble makers. Lemmy Kilmister, bassist for Motorhead, who Pete considered a "hustler", was asked to depart the premises more than once, while others needed more encouragement. "I punched a guy one night, literally punched him and kicked him out," Pete recalled. Observing, but in no way helping, was Chris, who, rather than thank Pete, later remarked, "I didn't know you were violent!" Bonas wasn't the only one resorting to force on occasion. Anna Capaldi, who dropped by to visit one evening with Don Carless from the old Elbow Room club had her own run at removing a drug dealer – knocking him down a flight of stairs after he refused to leave.

What was almost certainly worse was facing what remained when the uninvited guests did finally depart – primarily the state of his marriage, which was utterly dysfunctional. A string of men rationalized that 'rescuing' Jeanette was a chivalrous or romantic thing to do, not acknowledging her equal responsibility for the situation. Worried about losing her for good, Chris would fret during her absences, but rarely voice displeasure. If unable to keep her as near as he would like, he counted on their spiritual connection and underlying love to somehow keep the marriage alive.

There was one more strand that held them together, and it was the strongest of all – fear. Jeanette was progressively turning into an epileptic. The condition, having begun with the fall she'd taken during the long past Air Force days, had progressed from headaches to incapacitating seizures. Watching them occur on an unpredictable but increasing basis, Chris could only cradle her head as she writhed and worry as he waited for the episode to pass. His need to protect Jeanette now took on a new, if confounding, urgency.

Similarly irresolvable, Chris's deep-seated anger about the perceived injustices from his Traffic days would bubble back to the surface as well – leaving him brooding for untold hours. In a band where others got the lion's share of the credit and artistic acclaim, a red-faced Chris would fume to Pete Bonas about how he'd been slighted. Although many years had passed, he was still incensed about "John Barleycorn" – the song that had done so much to re-launch Traffic's career. Bonas noted, "I remember him, going on at me – how he'd brought that whole idea, and that album, and didn't get any credit for it. He was *very* upset about it. In fact, he went on quite a lot about that – calling 'em names, 'Fucking bastards.'"

But the occasional bursts of anger weren't enough to rouse the will to move forward from the current mess – quite the opposite. His sense of powerlessness instead led to a fundamental disregard for his own well-being. The precarious thread on which Chris's life hung became more and more obvious to those who still stood by him. 'The girls' from Island's office saw many scary episodes. Chris Blackwell's assistant, Denise Mills, reported finding Chris face down and turning blue more than once – calling the ambulance in a panic. Suzette Newman noted that Chris's condition would slide further and further downhill until he could no longer take even rudimentary care of himself, requiring a call to his family to take him back to Birmingham to recover. Besides the loss of Traffic and his troubles with Jeanette, Suzette also perceived a complicated nature deep inside, "There was a part of him that was drawn to this terrible squalor – junkie-type people, and there was the other side who really knew good things, art, beautiful things, travel – good quality stuff. So there was this conflict in him all of the time."

The list of life-threatening incidents during this period is mind bogglingly long. Folksinger and heavy drug user Tim Hardin supplied him with what was later determined to be a horse tranquilizer (almost certainly PCP), which first made him comatose and then stopped his heart for some period. Brought back from 'the dead' at a nearby hospital, the drug would leave a distinctive tattoo on his nervous system – a permanently dilated pupil in one eye. Another time, Junior Marvin found him slumped over the steering wheel of his car outside the apartment, his lips again blue. This time he was lucky – pulled up and shaken he was eventually roused without professional help. Around Chris more than most, Pete Bonas witnessed a string of incidents serious enough to require ambulance rides to the hospital, tersely recalling, "It happened at sort of regular intervals." Once he accompanied an unconscious Chris, watching as a doctor casually glanced at the inert form on the gurney before quickly diagnosing the problem, "Oh, Tuinol, right, put him over there…"

The most frightening episode occurred when Chris unexpectedly went into a seizure in front of Pete. "Scared the hell out of me – we were sitting there, just me and him in the Mews. We were playing, he had the sax, I had the guitar. And suddenly he just flipped over backwards and went into convulsions. His spine was twisting, he was convulsing, and it was the most horrific experience. It was like 'Wow!' you know? Because Jeanette had epileptic fits as well – *she* had fits! What a crazy scene. He scared me. I thought he was dying. It was all over quite quickly; he got up, sort of didn't know where he was, and was freaking out… I thought, 'How can he have a fit like that? What's wrong with him?' I didn't know."

Neither apparently did Chris who, after groggily coming around, declined to take stock of where it all seemed to be leading. According to Pete, "He didn't want to get into it. He'd say, 'Oh, that's okay, I'll be alright', and then change the subject. He would *never* address the problem." After witnessing numerous episodes, Bonas finally came to understand how dark it had all become for Chris. "It was sort of fated. He was like… doomed, which is a pretty grim sort of thought. He had that doomed, spaced out look sometimes. I remember sitting with him when he was sort of 'out there', you know. And I think he really didn't care, to be honest."

Once Pete tried to impress on Chris how ridiculous his drug behavior had become. Cannily, he used a language Woody should have appreciated – humor. Aware that he was about to catch a cab across town to buy more dope, Pete was inspired; "I left him a fake line of coke. I remember it like it was yesterday, standing in the kitchen, and just saw this mirror and razor blade, and I mischievously thought, 'Yes! 'Andrew's Liver Salts'! (an 'Alka Seltzer'-like medicine that furiously bubbles in water). He [Chris] was putting on his coat upstairs, and I hurriedly chopped up a line, *two* big lines, and left the rolled up note next to it, and the razor blade, then hid, knowing he was coming down the stairs. And when he came I was peeping at him! When he saw it, it was classic – he looked both ways, you know? The he went straight over to it, and hoovered it up –

then quickly out the door, into the cab. Ten, fifteen minutes later we got a call from the people he'd gone over to – they called, 'what's up with Chris!? He's foaming at the mouth and nose!' They were totally freaked out – the 'Andrew's' had all bubbled up and foamed out of his nose." But did Chris get the point? The outcome was inconclusive, "He came back, like a day later, and yeah, he didn't really say much... we had a good laugh about it."

But the unremitting bleakness could sometimes lift when he spontaneously snapped out of it, transformed somehow back into the old Woody that had so amazed and amused his friends in the 60's. Hiding his tape recorder, he would entice people to say outrageous things, and then play it back to them, laughing and mimicking the victim's unintentionally silly comments. On days like these, he might take Pete and Jeanette out to visit family and friends, his charm and polite manner winning over recipients of his attention as he delved into a range of subjects.

Then there were the car rides. Pete had one that was quite unforgettable: "It was a nice BMW, (fuel) injection thing that he'd got – it went like a *rocket* – it was a brilliant car. And I thought, 'He's got a car? He's not gonna drive it!' And he did, he'd suddenly kicked in, and he was okay. He was doing 140 miles an hour with Jeanette standing with her head out the sunroof! I remember thinking, 'This guy can't be *that* out of it if he can drive a car 140 miles an hour.'" But the beautifully lucid intervals were all too brief; a relapse of one sort or another was never far away.

Somewhere about this time, the upper levels of Island finally tried to see about relocating Chris and Jeanette into a rural estate they could call their own. Moving out of the big city had certainly worked for Steve and Jim, and a quieter, more sedate environment looked to be an ideal change for the nature-loving Chris too. This would also kill two birds with one stone by parking Chris's Traffic income somewhere where it couldn't be frittered away by drug and clothes purchases.

The designated place was a spacious upscale house in Woburn, located close to the ancient Woburn Abbey in Bedfordshire. With a prominent ley line running through, it seemed a perfect fit. But timing is everything, and by now it was quite late – the rural life proved far too slow for over-medicated nervous systems. Spending exactly one night at the house, the next day found the couple back in London. Later, Chris would sarcastically refer to his beautiful but always vacant country home merely as "the tax dodge."

While stuck in a seemingly static netherworld, on the horizon a storm of change brewed. Subjected to a series of progressively stronger blows, in the end, like it or not, Chris and Jeanette's lives would be forcefully rearranged for them. The first loss was in some ways the hardest to bear. Chris's dog Jasmine departed – not through death, but more akin to an escape. Tasked with taking the perpetually pent up dog to Hyde Park for much needed exercise, one day Pete watched as she took off, running purposefully across the open field into the trees. Calls after her were all in vain; the long-suffering Jazzer would never be seen again.

Then it was Pete's turn. After nearly a year of living in the mad 'half-way house', keeping the peace and repeatedly saving Chris's life, Bonas needed to attend to his own career and future. Working for a while with Jim Capaldi on sessions and some appearances, he then received an offer requiring extensive road work. He took it – filling the guitarist slot for the touring band of a singer named Jimmy Helms. With the apartment cleaned up and seemingly stabilized for the moment, it was time for a change, "The place was pretty quiet, and I thought, 'right, I'm gonna head back out for a while... so I joined Helm's group for about a year." While Chris must have been quite upset to lose someone who'd become his close friend and guardian angel, in the end he only wished him well. "He was really supportive, 'cause I'd got a gig – he was happy about it," Pete recalled.

Soon after, Chris's other musical partner, Junior Marvin was given his own job offer, being asked to join Bob Marley's group, The Wailers. With Jeanette joking that, "Bob Marley stole our guitar player!" Junior then jetted off to Jamaica – another protégé whose rising star had eclipsed their own.

Left to fend for themselves, Chris and Jeanette could do little more than carry on, and hope for the best. But the entropy crept back in the wink of an eye. Bereft of meaningful plans and adrift once more, Chris's only comfort was to seek out mates to whom he could relate – especially old friends like Trevor Burton and Paul Kossoff.

Burton recalled a dreary period with Chris and Koss that no drug could fully erase, "I think a lot of it had to do with loneliness – and nobody to look after him, like today – no teams of people – you had to look out for yourself. I think Chris was lonely, and I think Paul was lonely. And they just sank deeper into the pit – with the drugs and booze – and couldn't get out."

But having shared countless indistinguishably blurry days and nights with them, Burton finally came to realize that the lost trio was actually caught in a trap of their own making. In that moment of clarity, he did what the others could not. "I left London. My Manager came 'round, and said, 'Here's some money – go back to Birmingham, or else you're gonna die!' – 'cause we were all in the same state – Paul Kossoff as well. We were all doing mandrax, heroin and shit. And I did. I went home and got myself together and started again. I managed to slither up the wall and get away from it. If I'd stayed in London, I'd have probably died."

Kossoff wasn't as fortunate. On a trip to the U.S. to tour and finish up an album with Backstreet Crawler, on March 19th, 1976, he would pass away on an airplane in mid-flight. Drummer and band-mate Tony Braunagel was with him, and recalled his final moments, "I look back on my memories, as one does, and I say, 'I lived through that?' I was with a guy who overdosed on a plane – Paul. He was sitting in the middle seat, next to me – we took a red eye out of L.A. to New York. We were gonna be there a couple of days and go back to London, and Glyn Johns was gonna mix the record. And Paul never made it to New York. He was sitting next to me when we took off, and we'd had a couple of drinks. Then he got up and went to the bathroom – and that was it. When I heard we were landing in New York, I looked around and he wasn't there. We got off the plane and they were prizing the bathroom door open… I tried to keep an eye on him; I thought sitting next to me was close enough!" Paul Kossoff was twenty-five years old.

Attending the memorial service in a daze, Chris later spent time hanging out with Paul's old band, re-christened 'Crawler'. While never openly discussing the issue, Tony Braunagel observed that Chris was "devastated" by Kossoff's passing, and thought the time spent with them provided him with some solace. In tribute to Paul, Chris would play on some sessions, with one of his solos ultimately ending up on the first Crawler album. They would prove nearly the last recorded notes played by Chris Wood in his lifetime.

CHAPTER TWENTY-SIX

THE RISE AND ECLIPSE OF VULCAN

For a musician whose early career was built around non-stop jamming, the once joyful practice was now something Chris went to great lengths to avoid. Although nearly all of his time was spent hanging at Island's offices and studios, having lost one friend too many to premature death, playing was close to the last thing on his mind.

Occasionally, a musician passing through would recognize Chris, praise his work with Traffic and ask him to add a sax or flute part to a track. Inevitably, he would beg off, rolling out one excuse or another as to why he couldn't at the moment. When cornered he might actually go ahead and agree to a session, but then claim to lack the proper instrument or equipment. Promising to go get said instrument/part Chris would take his leave and of course not return.

His utter lack of productivity became more and more noticed. An Island brain-storming session was called to come up with a way to make *something* happen for him. A session musician often used by the studio recalled engineers culling through old Traffic tapes looking for sections of Chris's playing that a tune could be built around. Supposedly very little deemed worthwhile was located. At one point, Chris was called in to record a part over a salvaged track, but arrived so 'out of it', that he played in the wrong key – and worse, never seemed to notice. The project was ultimately abandoned.

But even at this dismal low, his ears were open for underappreciated talent. With players like Hanson (Marvin) and Bonas, he'd found up-and-coming guys who were happy to play with a recognized 'star'. By treating them as equals, Chris was able to get their best efforts working on his behalf. In turn, he would both educate as well as provide them with opportunities to ply their trade. Both Pete and Junior significantly benefited from knowing Chris. So, it was not surprising that as 1976 rolled on, yet another discovery was made – a seventeen year old keyboard prodigy named Phil Ramacon. Overhearing him play with a reggae band at Island's basement studio in Hammersmith, Chris instantly recognized strains of a musical influence that he loved – that of classical composer, Claude Debussy.

As Ramacon recalled, things progressed quickly from there, "Chris got to know me through the band that I was in, and we used to hang out and play pool. And whenever I played piano solo, he liked it. It was only a short step, since we were hanging out together there anyway – he invited me out to play." The bond deepened as they discussed their mutual admiration for Debussy's unorthodox compositional techniques. "I was probably the only reggae guy that he knew that was into Debussy, not just to call the name, but to play in that style. I come from a classical background, and my study of Debussy comes from that... he uses unresolved suspensions; he uses modulations that don't actually modulate where they're supposed to – it gives you that feeling of suspended time. The melodies that come out of that are unusual as well."

In turn, Ramacon recognized in Chris a person with a rarified level of musical appreciation, "People like that, they don't come along very often. I haven't met many people who – they don't just say that they like it – they actually like it, they have it in their record collection and talk about it. And I think, 'Yeah, there's a kindred spirit.'"

The classical approach was a mode Chris had always wanted to incorporate into his music – and something Traffic managed only to a limited degree. As such, some very interesting potential now brewed. But while the two set about discussing plans, the barriers were quite high. Having been downtrodden for so long, Chris was in no shape to organize his own sessions. He needed not just a catalyst, but a translator – someone to synthesize ideas into a platform he could play to.

According to Phil, the music would be typically conceived not by jamming but over a meal (usually at an Indian restaurant), where the two discussed musical structure. "I think he enjoyed bouncing ideas off me, and most of our ideas would be formulated by talking – going for curry – before every session, religiously."

From there studio time was booked. Island Engineer (and trumpet player) Dick Cuthell would gather session musicians, while Ramacon oversaw the development of the backing track. Only then would Chris come in –

alone – to add his parts and finish the song. It was an unorthodox style, and as far from the traditional 'Traffic method' as could be, but it was the only way Chris felt comfortable these days.

As iffy as it might have sounded, the intellectually-driven, open ended process actually worked; over the course of weeks, several songs got done. The best was a track Chris called "Don't It" (later, "Indian Monsoon"). Beginning with an inverted heartbeat rhythm wrapped in filmy sheets of synthesizer notes, Ramacon added airy vocalized 'aah's to give the track a contemplative quality, leaving a lot of space to fill in. Chris completed the aural imagery by weaving keening soprano saxophone notes throughout – hinting at a melancholy bird singing itself to sleep in the canopy of the rainforest. As finished, the song was entrancing and utterly unclassifiable; not quite jazz, nowhere close to rock. Of course it was also un-commercial in the extreme, a fact that would soon figure into where things would go (or not).

Ramacon remembered how it came together, "He did trust us, trusted me, trusted everybody really. A lot of those tracks had unusual chord progressions; they are chord progressions that you can't do with the average guy. 'Indian Monsoon' is an unrelated minor, and I used it in his stuff. So that was exciting to have someone like him trust me, and I was able to use parts of my knowledge that I couldn't use with anybody else. And then he came in and did his free extemporizing on top of it, and it was like – 'Wow!' It was good, it was very exciting."

Well below the radar, the sessions continued. Engineer Cuthell aside, it seemed that no one was paying much attention to the fact that Chris was working, much less creating interesting music. Some of the sessions were not even done at Island, but at Pathway, a smaller, nearby studio. Even the relatively inexperienced Ramacon recognized that the situation was unusually informal. "I didn't get an official call, like I would now, from a manager or the record company; I think they left it up to him (Chris). He could call and say, 'Do you fancy coming down to the studio tonight?'… So it was an organic thing."

Next up was a track built around several distinct sections known as "Birth In A Day". Powered by tight, driving horn riffs alternating with languid passages, "Birth" easily fitted into the approach Chris had worked with since "Tragic Magic" – contrasting deep melancholy against glimpses of the sublime. This particular song meant a lot to Chris; over time he would labor again and again to overlay solos that would adequately express his emotions. Eschewing his Gibson Maestro box or any other electronic effects, he relied only on his breath and fingers, uncurling deep tones out of the tenor sax that crooned against a trumpet riff seeming to chant the words, "Birth in a day." At over eight minutes, it was yet another affirmation that music survived at his core regardless of the turbulence swirling at the surface.

Furthest out was something called "Jam in Butter" (later "Grasshopper"). Arising out of a jam between Chris, Phil and Dick Cuthell, "Butter" was a classic study in contrasts. With an electronic rhythm machine setting the pace, Phil played a ping-ponging synthesizer phrase throughout (which Chris described as "jumping all over the place"), on top of which a soothing flute line flowed. Without vocals nor an obvious beginning or end, once again no concessions at all were made to the 'music of the day'. And therein lay a big problem.

The period from 1976-77 found the paradigm of modern popular music, especially in England, shifting violently in a new direction – punk rock had emerged, or better – erupted. With a musical style predicted on outright destruction of all that had come before, groups like the Clash and Sex Pistols, while crude in approach, also effectively rewrote the rules. By 1977, the impact had been felt throughout the music industry, leaving many rock veterans shocked to find themselves supplanted so quickly by rank amateurs.

Crawler's Tony Braunagel recalled that unsettling time, "I lived on King's Road, when the Sex Pistols were in the sex shop ('SEX' boutique). I lived two doors from that shop, where they started out. You'd see somebody in the pub and go, 'What the fuck is *that*?' And we did see the change. We were all career musicians, and here were these people who went to art school and could not play an instrument – and everybody's diggin' it, because of the energy." If Braunagel felt slightly paranoid about where all this was leading, he had every reason to – Epic would soon nix sessions for Crawler's third album, and release them from their contract. As he recalled, "The big wigs intervened and decided that we didn't have the material that they wanted. We weren't quite as commercial as they wanted us to be."

Even closer to home, in July of 1977, Steve Winwood finally released his first solo album – a record anticipated since Traffic's 1974's swansong. Yet despite a decent amount of P.R. hype by Island – a typical rock press ad declaring with iconic authority, "The Voice, The Feel, The Sound" – sales were much softer than expected. Reaching only as high as the 22 position in the charts, *Steve Winwood* was nowhere near the huge 'hit' the label hoped for. The underlying problem wasn't that Winwood had advanced too far 'ahead of the curve' as *When The Eagle Flies* might have been, but more the opposite. Although Jim Capaldi and Viv Stanshall were called in to help as lyric writers, the new album would hold precious little of Traffic's grit. In the end, Winwood's first solo statement would prove far too safe and 'old school' to compete in a market awash in brash chords and youthful vigor.

So, with even Steve unable to readily reignite a career with well-constructed tunes and a familiar voice, where exactly would that leave a confidence-shot, flute and sax player piecing together an all-instrumental, jazz/classical fusion album?

Phil Ramacon maintained a positive view; thinking that running counter-current to the trend-of-the-day might have been the way to go, "It would have been hot, because that was where punk was – right in the middle of punk – and it would have been great to do that. And not only that, Chris's collaborator was reggae!"

But in a studio bustling with more viable prospects, little heed was paid. Suzette Newman, who tracked Chris more closely than most, could barely remember anything at all about plans for a 'Chris Wood' album: "I *think so*, yes – he wanted to, but it didn't quite happen. He did sessions, 'cause he was around the studio a lot… he didn't formally work in any given period to say, 'this is gonna be my record.'"

Phil Ramacon's recollection of the aftermath of that productive period was only slightly clearer, although more conclusive: "What happened was, it all of a sudden fell dead. I don't know if the 'powers that be' recognized what we were really doing, and who was involved. It just suddenly ground to a halt really, and it was such a shame. At the time, we never got any feedback…"

Thus the wall of invisibility Chris had built around himself revealed its downside. Lacking the personal drive to claim his place at the table, the work would languish. The vote of no confidence merely pushed him back home. And that was unfortunate, since more and more home was a desperate place to be.

By the summer of 1977, Chris's other partner Pete Bonas was back in town, just in from a long North American tour. Jazzed up to see his old friends, Pete bounded up the steps and knocked on Chris and Jeanette's apartment door. But once inside, his hopeful smile quickly faded. "I remember going back and being quite shocked. I was glowing with good health, vibrancy and energy, and I remember walking in and seeing Chris and Jeanette looking absolutely like death, you know? I remember Jeanette was crying. It was a bad scene, a drug spiral of decline. It was not good." While the pair obviously needed rescuing, having almost singlehandedly kept them afloat for so long, Pete concluded he no longer had the wherewithal. "I was fresh and feeling good, and walking back into that, I was like '*No*, I don't want this, I've been here.' It's not like I didn't like these people – I loved Chris. I just thought, 'I can't do anything here.'"

The drift and decay might have moved at an imperceptible pace, but the toll was mounting. Lacking productive paths to follow, Chris and Jeanette were in fact shattered to pieces, though neither seemed to possess the will to make needed changes. The passage of time, rushing forward for everyone else, remained only an abstraction inside 14 Cumberland Mews. Within those walls a tenuous stasis persisted, one which would have to give some day, for better or worse.

*

Perhaps sensing the danger looming, Chris finally made his first conscious attempt to break from the heavy drugs. Undergoing a round of therapy involving an artificial coma – something he called 'The Big Sleep', he finally sought to detoxify himself from heroin. And it worked, *sort of*. While he would manage to edge his way off that drug, the pull of addiction was stronger than he had anticipated – soon he would merely substitute heroin for a morphine-based cough syrup, which he drank by the bottle. Still, for someone who had previously brushed off any suggestion of a problem, it was a step forward.

With the often empty apartment unbearable, he bounced back to the Island offices and studios – roaming the halls like a flesh and blood ghost unable to move on to a better place. Playing pool, reading books, talking on the phone for hours on end to persons unknown, all the while sipping brandy and cough syrup – Chris hid his condition as best he could. On good days, he popped his head into sessions to see what others were up to. Finally, a friendly face invited him in.

Tyrone Downie, the keyboard player for the Wailers was back in London, having recently fled Jamaica in the wake of a near tragedy. On December 3rd 1976, bandleader Bob Marley had been attacked – shot and badly wounded in a politically motivated murder attempt. No longer feeling safe in Kingstown, he departed for England and took the members of the band with him. But as Marley laid low for the time being, London held only uncertainty for Downie. With months dragging by, Island finally gave the go ahead to make some recordings. Tyrone recalled, "I wasn't sure what my future was – I was stuck between. Did I have a solo career? Was I still with the band? So I started doing this stuff, so as to not go crazy."

Noticing two struggling souls, Denise Mills had the foresight to bring Chris and Tyrone together. Tyrone recalled, "Denise was kind of the 'babysitter'; she was for me too, at the time. So she thought, since we both had time, and were both kind of 'lost in space' – that if we got together and started playing it would be good for both of us therapeutically."

Mills' instincts were right on. As Chris and Tyrone jammed, a camaraderie based on musical eclecticism quickly formed – each discovering in the other a willingness to bend or mix any genre in the pursuit of a good sound. On a human level, Tyrone could see that Chris was in bad shape, but chose to simply accept him as he was, "He didn't look really healthy, I was kind of worried about him. I don't know if he had relationship problems – I heard that he did. But love can make us want to hurt ourselves, you know? So I think he was in a lot of pain, because you could see it in his face, and in his actions and stuff. But it didn't stop him from playing brilliantly." Tyrone recalled the early collaboration as inspiring both, "Woody would jam, and said, 'Let's start recording some of this stuff.'"

With Tyrone's help, Chris was able to transform some of his pain into music again. "Sullen Moon" came first, a tune Chris had written with Jeanette. Her lyrics began with a poignant line: "Sullen Moon, take this love and make it easy…" encapsulating the ache residing at the heart of their relationship. Chris and Tyrone concentrated on the arrangement. Before long, a meandering jam resolved into form – a stark, manic keyboard jangling furiously in a stutter-start rhythm, contrasted with a mellowing (and sublime) flute line. Yet another crazy, classical/jazz fusion – "Sullen Moon" was again perched at the fringe, but the creativity was infectious. And as the energy level rose, quite unexpectedly, an entirely new musical avenue opened up.

Kicking around London, a young Venezuelan bassist named Jorge (George) Spiteri was looking for a break. Having grown up poor in South America, Jorge and his brother Carlos (Charles) loved the English rock sound, and although that scene was across the world, both dreamed of somehow being part it. Surreptitiously making their way to England in the early 1970's, the dream was suddenly a reality. Recruiting a core of English players – Steve Alpert (keyboards), Dave Early (drums), Dave Ulm (congas) and a floating horn section, Spiteri founded a band that lived and breathed a fusion of British rock and samba/salsa rhythm. Wood-shedding in the local clubs of London, they began attracting attention from local musicians and an increasingly avid fan base. Coming as they did in the middle of the punk revolution, Spiteri sounded – depending on the listener – as a band either utterly out of place or a welcome change of direction.

Tyrone Downie was in the audience one night at Ronnie Scott's nightclub when Spiteri played, and sought Jorge out after the set. As Jorge remembered, meeting Tyrone led him straight to Chris Wood, "Tyrone came to see us and liked our playing, and said he was doing an album – and would I come play bass for him? I said, 'Well, you have 'Family Man' (Aston Barrett), and he's great', and he said, 'No, I want that Latin thing that you do.' I went to the session, and to my surprise, at the same session was Chris Wood."

This was a big deal. Having grown up listening to Traffic, Jorge not only loved Chris's playing, but fundamentally knew where he was coming from, "He was a very magical guy – something else. You can hear that in the song he did with Hendrix on *Electric Ladyland* – he was drawing figures. Or on "No Time To Live" by Traffic, he was like an elephant screaming… he was artistic, drawing music – an art form." Chris also picked up on the connection. When they first met, Jorge played him a Spanish language version of "Forty Thousand Headmen" – a song that the brothers did as teenagers on the streets of Caracas. As Spiteri noted, "We showed it to Chris and he flipped."

Tyrone and Chris wasted no time combining the available talent with their own wide-ranging interests. As Downie recalled, "Being that I had met this band, 'Spiteri', because I was always a fan of Latin music – I really got excited. I was originally into classical and jazz and blues, as well as Latin or Brazilian – I really explored a lot. I wanted to create new music around the music that I liked. Spiteri were really good musicians, with percussion, rhythms and stuff."

With all of the pieces in place, the multicultural amalgamation took off into the stratosphere. The first song typified the 'World Music' philosophy by melding salsa and sangria into a third, unique entity – something

Downie called "Sangua." Kicking things off with a sparkling polyrhythmic pulse followed by Downie's slippery synthesizer, the Spiteris came through with everything that they had. Carlos in particular cut free on various percussive instruments, producing exotic, animated sounds ranging from nimble timbale runs, to bird-like chirps (using a water filled Victorian era bird-whistle instrument) to tinkling bells. The there was also a 'special guest' – Reebop Kwaku Baah who turned up at the last minute with his drums. As he had done many times with Traffic, Reebop nearly stole the show, playing his congas with verve while singing an exuberant impromptu chanting vocal over the top. Chris's part was more subtle, a little sax and later flute which floated over the synthesizer lines. As a musical experiment, and nearly twenty minutes long, "Sangua" proved as successful as it was ambitious – it bowled them all over.

The floodgates now open, more sessions followed, and before long "Steph's Tune" would emerge – an upbeat, reggae-fied ode to Chris's sister. Carlos remembered the new music as universally satisfying: "We were happy, Tyrone was happy, Chris was happy. He liked us; we were playing music that he could relate to." Indeed, after all the depressing years since Traffic's demise, Chris's excitement for playing with a band had finally sparked back into life. Spiteri's organic, nimble approach quickly drew him in, opening him to fresh ideas.

The Spiteri band was ideal in another way as well – they were all straight arrows. Having already seen too many musicians ruin themselves with various substances, bandleader Jorge enforced a strict no-drug policy – banning even cigarette smoking. In his own way, Chris respected this. While his impaired condition was sometimes obvious, he also didn't do anything in front of them. Carlos Spiteri noted, "I never saw him with a bottle in his hand – drinking. People told me that he drank or took some pills or something, but I never saw him. He was such a nice guy to us – really pleasant, decent, polite. He would never raise his voice for anything."

But musically it was a different story. These days, the mild mannered Chris was speaking up, suddenly quite sure of himself. This became clear as the Spiteri band kicked off a song they were calling "Cinnamon Girl". Hearing potential in the song sketch, Chris fetched his alto flute, returning with ideas for the arrangement. Rehearsing with pianist Alpert, Chris played a lilting, soulful melody over the chords that immediately set off a buzz among them all. From there the evolution of the tune was rapid, and quite natural. Beginning with a contemplative, easygoing rhythm, the song ascended quite naturally to a plateau where a full, funky sound kicked in. Following a final huddle, the band knocked out an elegant, ten-minute masterpiece as the tape rolled. While fundamentally Latin, "Cinnamon Girl" now had a jazzy tinge, and a final section that throbbed with Santana-esque energy. Pulsing with a soundscape of artful flourishes, this was the best music Chris had been involved with since Traffic, and he was quite aware of it.

A title change was then proposed. Jorge recalled, "It was supposed to be called 'Cinnamon Girl', and Chris said, 'No, let's try *See No Man Girl* – it's more exotic. It's got to be 'See No Man…'' He was a very sweet guy, but at that point he became very adamant that it should be 'See No Man Girl.'" The only real vocals (aside from Chris calling out "Samba, samba!" to indicate a tempo change) was a repeated chant: "See no man, see no man girl – no romance for the cinnamon girl." Although intended to have a full set of lyrics, Chris again insisted that the single line was just fine as it was – and joined them singing it as well. Later learning of Chris's problems with Jeanette, Jorge then understood Chris's vehemence: "And I got his point, 'cause he was suffering, right? He was probably saying 'see no man girl' to his wife. In retrospect I thought, 'fuck – it's true.'"

Like "Sangua" before it, "See No Man Girl" was utterly unique for music being made in England in 1977; on an artistic level, the Spiteri/Alpert/Wood collaboration was very much a success. The organic magic Traffic had always been known for materialized, seemingly out of thin air, with Chris once again the catalyst. Jorge recalled, "He was a very dreamy guy, Chris. He recorded it originally on a bass flute that he had – a very long, bass sounding flute. He recorded 'Forty Thousand Headmen' with that flute. He was very keen on that sound – of that flute. It was a very dreamy sound. With Chris, the natural thing was to get the magic out without having to ask him for it. With others, you have to ask them to get on that kind of thing, while Chris had it. He sounded so *natural*, it was amazing."

Certainly the fit between Chris and the Spiteri band was quite natural as well. Aside from their unqualified acceptance – crucial in allowing Chris to open up again – the Spiteri's were willing to drop everything else, to devote themselves to an album, even to tour as his band. Carlos had recently been asked to go on the road with another group, Santa Esmeralda, who had scored a hit record ("Don't Let Me Be Misunderstood"), and wanted to capitalize on it. Hearing about the offer, Chris asked him if he would be leaving, to which Carlos smiled and replied: "I'm *not* going, I'm gonna stay here with you!" For once, the signs all seemed to be pointing in the right direction. With some real support finally behind him, more and more ideas were bubbling to the surface. In particular, there was one long-cooled ember that he became quite anxious to reignite.

While Chris had long considered his rejected Traffic track "Moonchild Vulcan" a finished piece, he now had second thoughts. As much as a Traffic version could have been 'definitive' (especially from a marketing point of view), it was apparent to him that the Spiteri band had the chops to make it better. Rather than just adding some overdubs to the existing track, he would call them in for a new recording. Huddling around the speakers to listen to the original, Jorge and the others already knew where to go with it; the new version came together in a single session.

While retaining its basic form, the reggae lilt Spiteri supplied to "Moonchild Vulcan" was more authentic than anything Traffic had managed, while the Latin rhythmic and percussive influences lifted everything to a new level. As in "See No Man Girl", subtle touches abounded, with chimes sparkling and bird-like percussive effects darting in and out before nestling next to Chris's flute lines and then the tenor sax solo, whose marriage of tone and soul was near perfect. And with that, the title for the album Chris very much hoped would follow now came into focus: *Vulcan*.

The ease and confidence displayed was inspiring to all involved – collectively they had somehow achieved the sound of a veteran band. Pianist Steve Alpert noted the boost given to the previously down and out flute and sax player, "All I saw was Chris's reaction – he thought he'd tapped into something that could revive his career basically – a positive sort of vibe." Pausing to consider where it all could be leading, thoughts began to emerge of someone Chris thought should join them.

Jorge recalled that Chris seemed to suddenly wake to the possibilities, "With us he wouldn't drink, and he'd be more musical. He started really doing some good things, and at one point he got so excited, he said, 'Look, I want to go to Steve Winwood's house… I want to talk to Steve about getting involved.'" Unable to drive himself due to a recent car crash (his 'rocket-like' BMW having been first driven into a lamp-post, and then a less forgiving brick wall), Chris asked Jorge if he would drive him out to Winwood's country home. The cassette he tucked in his pocket before they left was crucial – it represented something long absent in Chris's professional life – a sense of hope. Could the new music be the key to resurrecting a working relationship with his old partner?

Pointing out historical places and discussing the mysteries of the British landscape, Chris was clearly up for the trip. Once at Steve's, he quickly got to the point. Popping in the tape of "Moonchild Vulcan" and "See No Man Girl" his first comment cut to the chase – "Listen to this, the magic is back…" before making the case for Steve's involvement. But while Steve seemed to appreciate the validity of the work, in the end no commitment would be made.

This wasn't the only option that lay before Steve these days. Amazingly, something resembling a Blind Faith reunion also looked like a possibility. Coming out of a rehearsal room at Island, the Spiteri brothers and Chris spied Steve conferring with Eric Clapton and Ginger Baker at a table in a corner of the cafeteria. Leading them over, Chris would tell them, "I think these guys are reforming…" Carlos then overheard what sounded like Baker and Clapton pressing Steve for material, "They were hanging out together, and jamming in the studio – but they were all expecting Steve… 'Okay Steve, where are the songs?'" While the ¾ 'super-group' would retreat to a rehearsal room that afternoon, in the end, nothing would come of this either.

If disappointed with the outcome of his overture, Chris would refocus on the productive collaboration with Spiteri and Downie. And another small but important step was also made. Knowing that Spiteri had a local gig (at a pub called 'The Red Lion', on Fulham Road), Chris actually went along – jamming with the band on the pub's tiny stage. His old friend Mitch Mitchell happened to be there and sat in as well. Against all odds, perhaps getting Woody to play 'live' again with a band was more than just a fantasy.

Another fantasy, perhaps the most improbable of all, happened that year too: Traffic – of a sort – came back, if only to play their own farewell. Having recently fallen in love with, and marrying, a beautiful Brazilian girl named Aninha, Jim was now entranced by her country as well – they would move there. At his going away party, a jam session was arranged with an ad hoc house band featuring members of Bad Company, (and Jorge

Spiteri on bass) supporting Steve Winwood, Jim Capaldi and Chris Wood. And although none knew it, this would be the last time the three would be in the same room together.

If the long awaited renaissance now seemed possible, if not actually at hand, a cold reality pushed back. The unfortunate fact was that Downie and Spiteri's positive influence had not liberated Chris from his problems. As inspired as the music making was, his life remained stubbornly complicated and conflicted.

Spiteri's pianist, Steve Alpert, noted that while the potential to move forward existed, Chris remained fragile, a point made clear one night when they all went to dinner. In the midst of talking and eating, Chris suddenly passed out, his face landing in his plate of food. Alpert recalled, "For Chris, obviously we would have done a whole album if he'd been able, physically or emotionally. But that was not a good time for him. It really wasn't – we saw the effects of drugs. You find yourself… having to prop somebody up whose head had just fallen into a plate of curry. I thought, 'I don't understand it, this is the guy from *Traffic* – what's going on?' It was very sad, because he was like a lost sheep."

In fact, the worst possible setback was about to be let loose upon him, a concise constellation of negative forces poised – seemingly knowingly – to strike Chris just when it could do him the most damage.

Financially, the fortified walls built from his long association with Traffic had started to collapse. With no money coming in from gigs or new recordings, the long delayed implications from the paltry writing credit he'd received during his tenure in Traffic suddenly hit home. Amid the societal and generational changes in musical tastes, these days precious few royalty checks were coming in. On top of that, people like Phil Ramacon noted that Chris was being pressured for taxes he somehow missed paying from way back when. "He owed a lot of money to the I.R.S. … a *lot* of money. To me, at the time, it was really an astronomical figure. And that was one of his biggest reasons for being depressed – he just didn't see how he could repay it." While still able to record at Island, cash for other things, like food, was now chronically short. He was constantly being taken out for his meals by better off friends and associates.

But the worst was still ahead. Perhaps directly related to his financial woes, the everlasting crisis of his marriage suddenly snapped. Quite unexpectedly (at least to Chris) Jeanette moved out. First taking a plane to Greece for a holiday, she called from there, making clear that when she returned she would be living with someone else. The news broke when Chris was rehearsing with Spiteri. Although knowing nothing at all about Chris's personal life, Steve Alpert observed what happened when the call came through. "There was an announcement, something to do with the wife. I remember there was a bunch of people… probably the people looking after him at Island, there was a bit of a scene, a telephone call. There was a thing to do with the marriage, because I remember him crying, breaking down. And then they had to get a car for him…"

The band could only watch as Chris was led away, for once unable to hide his grief. Now much of his 'out of it' behavior made perfect sense. Alpert could only shake his head in sympathy, "I remember talking to Jorge – 'cause you've got a guy who is not able to function properly – so what is going on is that you have one thing after another crashing in. How much can a person take? It was quite a dramatic moment, I can say."

What brought Jeanette to the point of finally leaving Chris? The sudden money shortage was likely the final straw, but a mix of factors obviously contributed. Jeanette would live the rest of her life with a recording studio engineer named Larry Bartlett, although she and Chris would never divorce. Amazingly – since friends had long ago assumed she was infertile, within a year she would be pregnant. In mid-1979 she gave birth to a boy she called Damien James, the names chosen to honor two souls lost at the other end of the decade: Damian Thor, Anna and Jim Capaldi's son who died as a newborn in early 1971, and her first real love, Jimi (James Marshall) Hendrix.

At Island's offices, the eclipse that had fallen over Chris reached totality. Even before the tumult of the marriage collapse, there were signs that the innovative music made might have all been in vain. While there had been some ripples of excitement as the new tunes emerged, now that the dust had settled, the possibility of taking things further seemed remote. In light of the perceived poor prospects for Chris, the un-classifiable fusion of reggae/jazz/latin and rock so far produced would be all that there was.

By December of 1977, Jorge Spiteri recalled that after an initial period of encouragement, the lights suddenly dimmed, "People were excited, coming into the studio, hearing the thing and thinking, 'Oh shit, he's really done something good.' Then at some point he (Chris), said, 'Look they're not going to bring out our stuff, or Tyrone's – because of the punk thing.'" While Island didn't handle punk artists, per se, the genre's influence –

compact, simply structured, high energy songs – was clearly the trend record companies were most interested in.

With the news that his recordings were unlikely to see the light of day, the broke, wife-less Chris saw only one route left – escape. With only weak promises made to the Spiteris to carry on in the New Year, he went back to the deathly quiet apartment and packed. Coming back to the studio alone on December 22nd, he would ask for the tape of "Barbed Wire" – his unreleased Traffic track about feeling ensnared by life. Overdubbing a final, heartbreaking tenor track he would listen back to it, and walk out. Knowingly or not, this would be the coda to all of his years recording at Island – he was finished.

Christmas day found Chris not in Stourbridge recovering with his family, but on a plane. Flying to Jamaica, Island's Suzette Newman confirmed that the trip was less a vacation than much needed therapy, "He hung out, he had his flute and things, and really – he was just trying to get healthy and have a good time in Jamaica. He spent some time with this guy named Countryman (Lothan), who lived by the sea, and this friend of ours named Dicky Jobson (who later made a film called *Countryman*). They all just… Chris needed to be with people he could feel okay around, just to *be* – you know; no pressure, no stress."

Meanwhile, back in London, the musicians who'd supported him now had to contend with their own loss. After a Christmas break the Spiteri band reassembled at Island Studios in January 1978. Despite all of the discouraging news, they still hoped to somehow finish the record they'd begun and maybe even take it on the road. But after a while, they realized Chris wouldn't be rejoining them; the dream-like musical adventure was over. With no satisfying answers forthcoming, Carlos Spiteri could only recall an aftermath of bleak disappointment, "We were supposed to come back in January, but then, nothing happened – the whole thing broke up. After that, we never saw him again. I don't know what happened really."

Around this time, Tyrone Downie would also abandon his solo project, due to a lack of interest by Island and because the Wailers had finally committed to reuniting. Though securely employed once again, Downie would remain troubled that the inspired music which had materialized out of the blue was just as quickly consigned to oblivion. "The stuff I worked on with Spiteri and Chris was based around a really nice feeling – which is probably why it never came out. At the time, it was unheard of, 'what are you doing – this other kind of stuff!' I was in the middle of nowhere. It was not like anything that was happening at the time. But I am glad that we shared that, even though people were not ready for that. We all wanted to taste the soup together, and it tasted good! The sad thing was that we couldn't share the soup with anyone."

Thinking back on Chris Wood and the air of misfortune that seemed to envelop his friend, Tyrone's feelings were close to the surface, even many years later. "My last vision of him in my mind was him being happy – that we were playing together – that I wanted him to play with me, and that I believed that he could play. Beyond all that, there was this guy, a wonderful guy and a sweet person and a great musician. Even though he was suffering, he could still put the flute or sax in his mouth and blow the shit out of it. I can't remember any bad experience with Chris. He was like a baby; I mean I want to cry talking about him. He was one of the sweetest people I've ever met, and ever will meet." Pausing, Downie concluded by saying, "When you are sweet, vulnerability is part of it – horrible people are involved."

CHAPTER TWENTY-SEVEN

RETURN TO THE MIDLANDS

According to his passport, Chris stayed in Jamaica for about three weeks and then, on January 18th, was admitted into the Bahamas (presumably Nassau) for a period not to exceed three weeks. Allowed into the country as a tourist, the immigration office stamp proclaimed: "HOLDER MUST NOT ENGAGE IN GAINFUL OCCUPATION." While exactly what he did is unknown, 'gainful occupation' was clearly not a concern. In fact, this trip would be the final mark in the book. For a man once intent on exploring the world, particularly the family mysteries that lingered in China, the rest of his passport would remain blank forevermore. From here his life would be fundamentally different; for all intents and purposes, Chris was now unemployed – an ex-rock star.

Once back in England, a period of vagueness settled in as he drifted around London, mostly avoiding the Island studios and offices he'd previously haunted. Although he'd later return to pick up the masters of his recordings, no further sessions were planned or scheduled. With Jeanette gone, his long tenure at the infamous Marble Arch apartment was coming to an end as well – things there were literally falling apart.

There are several, conflicting versions as to why Chris would have to leave the place he'd occupied for so long. One later-era friend (Graham Broadbent) remembered Chris mentioning a plumbing leak that might have wrecked the place. *Trouser Press* (January 1978) reported that 14 Cumberland Mews was raided by the police looking for drugs (supposedly finding none), that resulted in a broken door, which Chris managed to lock himself out of while trying to fix. Brenda Bryan (and Graham) also recalled an incident stemming from the London Hell's Angels, who made enough of a disturbance that the police were called. Supposedly the Angel's stash – including heroin and cocaine, were dumped on the premises as they fled – leaving Chris to face the law alone. Yet another friend (Nick Cannon) said the incident actually occurred at Chris's house in Woburn.

As tangled as the tale became over time, one thing is clear – at some point Chris was arrested on a drug offense (the records have since been removed), and arraigned in court. The resulting charges were serious enough to warrant potentially extended prison time. Instead, a sympathetic judge ordered a long probation. But the terms would prove restrictive, involving mandatory regular meetings with a parole officer and a drug counselor, with whom Chris was to try to work through the labyrinth of his underlying problems.

In a way, the whole episode might have been something of a break. In light of the sentence and the restrictions imposed, Chris was ejected from his worn-out routines. For the time being at least, it may have saved his life. One close friend disagreed with the efficacy of probation though, thinking that Chris might actually have been better off with a stretch in jail, where he could make a clean break from his addictions. Such as it was, the court imposed conditions stipulating close monitoring. Ultimately, a judge would also place all of his income in the hands of his parents. Without much choice, he soon found himself living once again very near the place of his birth.

But even home wasn't what it had been. The romantic and gothic Corngreaves Hall, which had always loomed large in his imagination, was no longer the Wood family's residence. The carefully sculpted lawn and dense grove of shady trees had only been a perk of Mr. Wood's job, and once retired as County Surveyor, the family relinquished the Hall as well.

Although Chris spent little time with the family in the 70's, the sense of obligation remained. Upon finding that they would be forced to move, Chris used whatever savings he had and bought Stephen, Muriel and Stephanie a house of their own – a much smaller, but quite comfortable place in Romsley, far outside the Birmingham city limits, known as 'Spindle Cottage'. Although next to the M5 Motorway, it was also abutted by farm fields that ran for miles. All in all, it was a rather peaceful place, with lots of room to walk the dogs (Labradors, Toby and Rupert).

Now, in Chris's own time of need, he came to live with them. With four bedrooms and a small but privately walled backyard with trees and a birdfeeder (as well as an indoor pair of parakeets), he at least had a place to regroup and reconnect to a simpler, family-based life. The first order of business was fixing up his room: a big bookshelf on the wall, a radio and cassette recorder on the nightstand, and an American flag draped as a bedspread. By necessity, his record collection and most of his instruments went in the basement. With a life now resembling that of a 16-year-old boy, it was almost as if the years as a rock star had been merely a long, strange dream.

But a magnetic tape thread to the past lingered. Away from London, his head clearer, Chris compiled a series of reference tapes – writing out track titles and recording dates in his neatest script, labeling each with colored sticky dots to tell them apart. One surviving tape labeled "Yellow Compilation, Rough Mixes 16/8/78" included nine songs, some familiar and some less so, including titles such as "Slow Hot summer Day On The Old Island", "Flutered", and "Tyrone and Me, Jamming". While there seemed to be plenty of material, the quality was all over the place. With more work to do and time on his hands, he got to it.

By autumn, a better notion of what was usable fell into place. Back in Island's offices once again, on October 1st, Chris watched as Terry Barham, an assistant engineer, compiled two master reels – one for each side of a potential record. A: "Song For Pete", "See No Man Girl", "Letter One", "Barbed Wire". B: "Jam In Butter", "Moon Child Vulcan", "Tone Blind, Rhythm Deaf" and "Birth In A Day".

Was this the finished album, or still "rough mixes" needing further overdubbing and producing? The answer is unclear. While "Song For Pete" and "Letter One" seemed more like sketches, perhaps the minimalist contrast was exactly what Chris intended. What is more certain is that Island – having taken the time to transfer tapes and put the material into the form of a potential record – quietly declined to go further.

Terry Barham could only speculate that the work might have lacked sufficient "focus" for release, and added, "It is, in retrospect, quite understandable that people would have listened to it and said, 'What the heck do we do with this?' All music has 'mood' and... the 'mood' was wrong at that time for the music Chris was making. But, here's the rub, listening to it now, it *is* more focused than it would have seemed at the time. And, strangely enough, there is a simplicity to it which is just resting on the playing."

But hindsight didn't have time to work to Chris's advantage; with the exception of a November session, overdubbing tapes recorded with Phil Ramacon, and an inexplicable one-off sax overdub for a Johnny Thunders track ("The Wizard" – a Marc Bolan cover), this would be the last work he would do in London. With yet another year waning, and his record dormant, if not dead, where exactly did that leave him?

At some point, it became clear that the best route forward actually led back. More than anything he wanted to revisit an old partnership – creatively speaking the only one that *really* mattered. The synergy between him and Steve had led to the genesis of Traffic, and Chris had never given up hope that something could still be conjured between them.

Signs that it might finally be possible were emerging. On August 19th 1978 – three days after Chris had put together his tape compilation, Winwood played his first ever solo show, a loose, almost impromptu performance at the 'Rough Hill Festival' – a very small local Gloucestershire musical gathering. His group featured a guitarist (John Porter), a drummer (Terry Stannard), backing vocals from his wife Nicole, and her friend Demelza on bongo drums. Despite the ad hoc band, Winwood played most of the songs from his solo album as well a couple of classic Spencer Davis and Traffic songs and even an Elvis cover ("Hound Dog"). The fact that Winwood was willing to play such an open-to-anything performance seemed to have encouraged Chris.

Steve was in fact going through – as his old partner Jim Capaldi might have called it – a bit of a 'spaced out patch' himself. Having been stung by the reaction to his long-anticipated debut album, these days he was almost as unsure as Chris. Although still doing sessions for others, in having delayed his solo career for so long, Winwood's own musical identity seemed to have been misplaced along the way. Set back by punk's energetic rise, he'd perhaps spent too much time in solitude – writing and tinkering with new technologies. In later years, he would admit to being genuinely tortured by his lack of confidence during this period, going so far as to assert that if his next album failed as well, he might give up on a musical career altogether. If the Rough Hill performance indicated anything, it showed Steve finally willing to look over his shoulder a bit. This time, Chris's call had the intended effect; the visit would be arranged for November.

How long Chris stayed with Steve, and most of what they did or discussed is (except to Steve Winwood) unknown. There would be no record that the meeting ever happened at all, except for one thing – a battered cassette tape with a shaky, scrawled legend: "Me and Steve at his studio, 11/78", found with Chris's possessions after his death. Infamous for his ability to lose almost anything – especially his tapes – Chris clearly treasured this… the worn label indicated that he had handled and played it many times. Listening to it reveals why – the tape contains one of the great lost jams of the 1970's.

While this music will almost certainly never be released, the surviving tape documented an important fact – years after it was assumed that he was 'washed up', Chris could still be a creative talent of the first order. It also illustrates exactly why he went to such lengths to rekindle the relationship with Steve: the indefinable musical current between them was somehow very much alive.

"Me and Steve…" began with a testing of the musical waters. Sitting behind the Moog synthesizer, Winwood switched on a programmed rhythm of bass notes, which played in a repeating loop. Over this, he playfully threw jaunty notes from the keyboard as if prompting a mood to emerge. Chris listened until he knew the next move. Forsaking his usual instruments, he walked over to sit at the drum kit. Throwing in little rolls and fills he skittered like a jazz mosquito – lighting on a pattern for a moment, and then darting away. Steve was still searching too, altering keys, improvising around the rhythm. Though only a two-man band, the sound would grow increasingly full, ebbing and swelling as if seeking its level.

About twenty minutes in, Steve's playing suddenly morphed into something deeper. Again, Chris responded. Getting up from the drums, in the moments of silence between ghostly notes, he picked up his tenor. Wrapping a strand of wind around the keyboard phrases, almost imperceptibly the separate instruments would blend into one, flowing like wind skirting a desert.

With the rhythm track suddenly turned off, the music simply glided free. Switching to flute, Chris added sad, furtive touches before returning to the saxophone. Setting another rhythm on the synthesizer Steve then walked over to take a turn at the drums. At first riffing on the dual rhythms, Chris coaxed deep organ-like sounds out of the sax before turning to languid, breathy notes. Contrasting the introspective mood, Steve held a swinging beat which finally trailed off as the jam slowly edged back to silence.

While the creative burst seemed to have suspended time altogether, it had actually been going on for the better part of an hour. Both avant-garde and deeply human, the sound was a product of the same mysterious matrix that had existed between them since the earliest days.

One of the few people still in touch with both Chris and Steve – Paul Medcalf – wasn't surprised that the two could still relate musically, "I think, Chris and Steve, it was part of the same old jam – they just jammed. I think that's really what it's about. The thing is, Chris liked his jazz and Steve liked jazz – so that was a connection."

Amazingly, there was more to come. Before the year was out, the two would go so far as to rehearse together with a band organized to play a live show. The reason behind the unlikely event was a mixture of the practical and, of a sort, spiritual.

Seeking a non-chemical means to ease his jangled soul, Chris had begun to involve himself in a local church. Asked to contribute to needed renovations, he came up with the idea of doing a small charity concert. Knowing that Winwood was himself contributing music to his own church (playing organ at the Sunday services), Chris pitched the idea. By early December, they were testing the waters.

The show was to be held inside the small recreation room (the Pastoral Centre) near Christmas. With the commitment made, the band consisted of a drummer and a bass player (both unknown), Steve and Chris. They rehearsed at Steve's and the resulting set-list, while lacking anything at all from Traffic, proved an interesting, low-key amalgamation of their collective backgrounds. With a cluster of songs based around blues, R&B, and jazz they mostly kept to the overlapping ground – with Steve at center stage, but leaving room for Chris's influences and one of his own compositions as well. More so than at any time since maybe '67, this song selection represented something like an equal partnership between Winwood and Wood.

The rehearsal day found Steve in prime form, playing deft runs on the synth and organ and singing as good as ever. Chris was less confident. While seemingly in a good mood, his tenor runs on "I'm A Man" were tentative. By the time they got into Eddie Harris's 60's jazz classic, "Listen Here", things were better. Reprising his multi-instrumental role from Traffic, Chris would play electric piano, then soprano sax, before plugging in his electric tenor. Always the common language, jazz once again proved the ideal medium – the tune glided on air.

Amazingly, Chris also seems to have taken lead vocal on the next song – "Knockin' On Heaven's Door", with backing vocals and shimmering Hammond organ chords from Steve. Being that it was a benefit for the church, and considering Chris's numerous brushes with death, the song was both appropriate and touching.

There were still bumps. On his own "Barbed Wire", a song that Steve barely recalled and nobody else knew at all, it is unclear if they would ever get it down well enough for a public performance. Likewise, "Sister Sadie" a great old Horace Silver tune, which Chris was clearly enthused to play, seemed to have never gotten past the intro. Even so, with the material in hand, an entertaining show looked to be in the offing. Chris particularly seemed to enjoy the intended encore – "Hound Dog", throwing in Maestro effects which added a unique feel to the creaky song.

With the ad hoc band closing in on a fascinating set, things certainly looked promising. And yet *something* happened to throw a roadblock, since the show they'd rehearsed for never took place.

Chris later told a friend that the proposed show "was cancelled due to snow" – an unusually heavy December storm that kept Steve from making it into town. And it may have been just that simple. Regardless, the random event would change everything; the concert would never be rescheduled. Despite the recent burst of goodwill between them, Chris's window of opportunity suddenly slammed shut.

Instead, refocused on redeeming his own nearly moribund career, Winwood would seal himself into his newly-upgraded studio and shift gears. Going for broke with a single-minded determination, he would play all of the instruments for his next album himself; something called *Arc of a Diver*.

The move would prove decisive. When finally released in 1980, the record produced a genuine hit single – "While You See A Chance" (#7 on Billboard's 'Hot 100' chart). With its well-balanced mix of confidently played synthesizer, soulful vocals and newly evolved pop sensibilities, "While You See A Chance", (whose lyrics exhorted leaving the past behind, and moving forward), proved an excellent fit to Steve's current ambitions. And the timing was perfect; the song slid easily into place in the newly-evolved 'adult contemporary' music market.

In the wake of punk's unsurprising burnout and the subsequent lack of stamina in 'New Wave', rock's old guard – if they were willing to play the game of accommodating trends – suddenly had a shot at re-emerging as viable entities. Only the vacuous influence of disco was of any concern these days, but compared to punk's anarchistic dagger thrust, the threat was manageable. Many pre-existing groups (such as the Rolling Stones) simply embraced the beat-driven style, unashamedly throwing it into their bag of tricks. While Steve never went that far, having whiffed something that smelled very much like the death of his career, fitting his music into a more polished, pop format was a step he was willing to take – and one that would pay off in spades.

*

With Steve absorbed in his comeback, Chris's own dreams of musical rebirth quietly receded. Restless and unsure, he now mostly floated around Birmingham, seeking peace of mind where he could find it.

He rekindled relationships with boyhood mate Mike ('Lewie') Lewis and Brenda Bryan – the woman whose tiny vial of liquid acid had helped inspire the creation of "Dear Mr. Fantasy" back in the magical summer of '67. Now living a more conventional life selling cosmetics, Brenda recalled that Chris also seemed to desire only simple pleasures, "He would just come around here and sit and play his flute. I was an 'Avon Lady' at the time and he used to enjoy running around with me to collect. He used to love women, talking to women – especially housewives. I used to invite some ordinary women around, and he used to chat them up, and have a laugh. That was the only time he was happy really. We used to go 'round to a local pub. He loved the madness – ordinary people, in an ordinary pub."

Seeking those who would not judge his past or question his present lifestyle, one of his best friends was a local Birmingham guy named Graham Broadbent. Acquainted from the Marble Arch days through his brother Lenny, Graham was currently a man of no fixed employment (thus, like Chris, with a lot of 'free time'). With almost no knowledge or interest in Traffic or rock 'n roll for that matter, the two hung out at Broadbent's flat or in the local village, watching the working-class people bustle about. Graham recalled, "We were like 'Observers', that's how we used to say it, we were observing. We were students of life. We'd go to the shopping center in Northfield, and we'd be in there for bloody hours watching people. You'd see all these things that you never see, unless you sit down on a bench and watch it – 'cause you'd be too busy about yourself. We'd have these conversations with people we'd never seen before in our lives, and see how much we could intrigue them, and make them smile."

Removed from the shallow and often damaging relationships of rock society, Chris's rediscovery of the working class world provided both relaxation and a source of wistful self-reflection. More than once he told Graham he wished that he'd been born into that stratum of society himself. "He came from a middle-class background, but he loved the working-class people. He used to sit in a room with older people and especially the 'Black Country' people, and hear these quaint little sayings. He loved the working class because there was no fakeness about it. He saw them as the real people. We used to laugh at pretentious people – middle class – and he'd probably got more money than them! He used to look at them and start smirking."

In some ways, he'd simply slipped back into some of the same interests from his teenage years at Harborne Collegiate. While he would occasionally run off to places like Birmingham's Town Hall (where Traffic had frequently played) to see old friends like Richie Havens perform, for the most part he now eschewed any mention of his rock 'n roll past. Graham noted, "He wouldn't actually tell people a lot of things. He wouldn't go on about what he'd done... If he went anywhere and he met people, they'd say, 'What do you do?' He'd say, 'I'm a musician.' He'd never elaborate, he wouldn't say, 'I was in Traffic'. He used to despise that – being laminated by that. He hated being viewed as some *thing*, not a person – like some kind of silly icon."

The retreat from his rock-star history was rapid, and nearly total. Immersing himself in a mundane society, drinking strong beer and brandy, for now mere stability would suffice as a goal. But there was one nagging desire that he couldn't easily give up, something the 'ordinary women' he associated with could never touch: the place in his heart still filled with love for Jeanette Jacobs Wood.

Although ensconced in a seemingly permanent relationship, as well as the mother of someone else's child, Chris maintained contact – writing letters, calling on the phone and popping down to see her when he could. Apparently, Jeanette's longtime boyfriend Larry Bartlett didn't object to the visits, during which Chris brought gifts and toys for the child, Damien James. On some level, Larry and Chris must have had a measure of sympathy for each other; mother or not, Jeanette was pretty much the same restless girl she'd always been. As for Chris, in truth, he'd never quite given her up, and never would.

Getting her back might not have been outside the realm of possibility. Even after all that had happened, Jeanette's oldest friend, Eleanor, thought that Chris and Jeanette would eventually end up together again, "They really loved each other, I'll tell you that. Jeanette never would have left him (for good). They never got divorced – she went to live with Larry, but she probably saw more of Chris than Larry. She left the kid with Larry all of the time. That's just how she was. I knew them too well, it was just sad, really, really sad."

Part of Chris's attempts at renewal came from places where he felt spiritually centered. While in the old days he might have sought a circle of ancient stones at midnight, now he needed more human contact. The St. Laurence church in Northfield, on the far southern edge of Birmingham, is known as one of the oldest in the region, with a structure dating back to the Norman era. Historical interest aside, Chris liked listening to the sermons and feeling the earthy tones of the organ-based music. He especially enjoyed the part of the liturgical ceremony where people were asked to turn and greet those beside them by shaking hands. Equally important was the pub on the church grounds – 'The Great Stone Inn', where he could meet friends and hang out.

While no doubt spending more hours in the pub than in the pews, over the years Chris became devoted to the wellbeing of the church. In fact, he developed a close relationship with two Reverends from the Church of England who attended to the local parishioners: Curate John Barnett and, a couple of years later, Vicar Peter Nokes. While Chris tried to help the church, the Ministers also provided Chris with opportunities to better understand the meaning of the searing experiences he'd endured. The commitment was long-term, on both sides.

If Chris's London life had proved a fast-paced blur toward oblivion, his time in Romsley was more akin to a hazy, alcoholic, second childhood. Between 1979 and 1981, the circuit he traveled was quite limited, as was his ambition. Having lost his driver's license, he now walked, took the bus or relied on friends for transport. Thus limited, he soon slipped back into the role of a son living at home; reading the newspaper over breakfast, checking the birds coming to the feeder, and going on unintentionally humorous shopping trips with his parents.

The ritual of the family vacation to Padstow, Cornwall, continued as well. Facing the ocean, his head tilted toward the circling gulls, he once again glimpsed tranquility. Back home he tried to maintain contact with nature as well – walking the dogs in the woods and fields, regularly borrowing *National Geographic* from a friend, and reading books on wildlife. He also became a member of the National Trust, an organization that bought and preserved important buildings and estates throughout Britain.

Distraction and mild adventure often comingled. Coming home from Birmingham with a metal detector one day, he called Graham over to examine a map before heading to nearby parkland (Frankley Beaches) seeking 'buried treasure'. While Graham was openly dubious, Chris tried to inspire confidence. Pointing to the knobs on the device, with a sly wink he said, "You can tell if it's gold with this thing…" Hours later, the sun beginning to set, loud beeps finally marked the spot; the two rushed back to the car for shovels. An hour or so later, illuminated by flashlight, their prize would finally emerge. Graham recalled, "We were up the bloody hills – Frankley Hill, and it gets bleeding dark… There we are, digging a hole in the ground – what do we find? A fence post – a steel metal fence post, and we're digging a hole around it! I can see him now, laughing his head off…"

In keeping himself amused, and perhaps to simply cope, Chris often slipped into a 'role playing' mode. Graham noticed that Chris often seemed to act from a script that he improvised as he went along. Visiting Spindle Cottage one day he observed, "It was a bit like one of these black comedies – if you ever went to his house, with his mom and dad, it was like some kind of satire. He would sit there, be reading the paper in front of him, and he'd look at me and be smirking – smirking behind it, like a little kid. The whole thing was like a game."

One night, Graham was unwittingly drawn into the game himself. At a house-party, gradually filled with a rowdy group of rugby players, Graham and a girl named Kate, eventually found themselves squeezed into a bathroom. Suddenly Chris burst through the door, seemingly in a rage, "He came whooshing in, and said, 'You bastards!', and I said, 'What are you going on about?' (Then) he whacked me in the face, and I fell in the bath. And I said, 'What's *wrong* with you?' He said, 'Are you alright?' I said, 'Yeah, why'd you just smack me in the face?' He said: (casually) 'It was a 'stage slap'.' I said, '*Was it?*' Then this girl got hysterical…"

His habit of stealth-taping re-emerged too. Spending the night at Graham's place, the next morning at breakfast, Chris popped in a cassette, and with a deadpan expression played it for his host. "He said, 'Listen to this', and I could hear this *noise*. I said, 'What's that?' He said, 'It's *you*, snoring." With his classic smirk/smile, Chris took in Graham's reaction, quietly chuckling. The next day, thinking he'd turned the tables, Graham instead ran into Chris's sharp wit, "So I taped him snoring, and I said, 'listen to *this*'. You know what he said? 'Yeah, but at least I snore in tune!'"

Chris would also record a visit from a Probation Officer, who'd come to the house to check on him and discuss his case. Knowing that he was about to arrive, the deck and microphone were hidden under a sofa cushion, capturing the conversation as quite serious legal issues were discussed with Chris and his parents. Later, playing it back to Graham, he could only laugh at the absurdity of his situation, saying, "Fuck it all – listen to this! You won't *believe* this!"

In retrospect, the contents of this particular tape are more poignant than funny, with Chris struggling to be understood while often being cut off mid-sentence. Much of the discussion involved hints and outright suggestions that Chris was 'playing the system' to his advantage. At first, trying to reassure, he reminded the officer several times that blood tests taken every three months would show if he was using illegal drugs or not. In the end, the frustration evident in his voice, Chris would be forced to spell out the stark simplicity of his current state of existence (before being cut off once more), "It's important for *me*, to live my life – to get it together – to do my job – and that's *it*, right? I'm not trying to duck out of anything. I'm not trying to…" How the meeting concluded is unknown; the tape ran out shortly after these comments.

While a normal life of sorts was re-emerging, the gravity of his past exerted a force which could no longer be ignored. While the threat of imprisonment helped him steer clear of illegal hard drugs, alcohol and cough syrup were another matter. And having kept himself sedated for so long, the toll was now showing. Instead of dramatic, life-threatening overdoses, these days his liver and kidneys, rebelling from years of abuse, simply threatened to fail. Seeing doctors in Birmingham and London, tests from both locations confirmed that he was heading for serious trouble. While they no doubt tried to convince Chris to go straight with dire predictions, they apparently failed to account for the sheer depth of his need to alleviate his mental stress.

Chris's underlying attitude toward addiction was likely revealed the time he noticed Graham Broadbent trying to quit his own long standing habit – smoking. Broadbent recalled, "I hadn't had a cigarette for about a week and he came to the house, and said, 'What's the matter with you?' I said, 'I've tried to stop smoking.'" Watching Graham's uncomfortable demeanor for a while as he fidgeted with his own pack of Marlboros, Chris finally shook his head and approached with the only solution that made any sense to him – insisting that Graham take a cigarette. In response to his friend's incredulous expression, Chris matter-of-factly said only, "It's not worth it."

But, as was typical for Chris, a more hopeful side was also at work. While seeming to have an utter disregard for his health, his complacency had in fact been shaken by the bad medical reports. Confronted with evidence of his mortality, a desire to live seems to have finally stirred. Having gotten off heroin, Mandrax and coke, for perhaps the first time in his adult life, he now took a hard look at his major, stubbornly enduring problem – alcohol. Initially unsure of where to begin, he first came home from a local bookstore with a couple of promising titles – an encyclopedia of herbal remedies and a medical textbook describing disorders and diseases. Seeking to understand his addictions and consequent health implications, Chris optimistically if naively sought a loophole – something both legal and non-harmful that might still give him a buzz.

Visiting Mike Lewis early one morning to use the telephone, he arrived carrying a bag full of natural remedies. Mike's then girlfriend (now wife), Becky, recalled that day, "I can see all these things from Holland and Barrett – alternative medicine. He was into whatever was new. I think that was a cry – some sort of trying to fix it. I remember shopping with him at Waitrose in Stourbridge. I didn't know him very well; he was just this nice, gentle guy. And we went 'round, and sat on the floor. I can see him sitting cross-legged with the basket on the floor, and he was giving me a whole lecture on the different types of alternative teas." Mike confirmed that Chris took this interest seriously, "His knowledge of chemicals or health foods was fascinating – he should have been a chemist. He knew exactly what was in absolutely every health pill."

But, practically speaking, few 'teas' could really cut it when the chips were down. One was something called 'Skullcap', a scary sounding elixir consisting of an herbal base laced with some kind of opiate. Discovering this, Chris used his knowledge of chemistry to manipulate the mixture to produce something quite potent. Graham Broadbent witnessed the procedure, "He would put so much of that in a teapot with boiling water – stick it on top of a flour sieve, put all the boiling water into it, and get some honey to take the taste away. He'd leave it to stew for a while, and he'd drink it. One night he was falling all over the place, and I said 'What's *wrong* with you?' I got him to give me a cupful, and I slept for eighteen hours!" Ironically, in its intended form, the benefits of the herb Skullcap (Scutellaria lateriflora) supposedly include alcohol withdrawal, and improving liver function.

Through it all, he somehow managed to find his way back to music. But like other aspects of his life, it had to be rebuilt slowly, bit by bit. With his trusty Sony recorder, Chris began to tape little piano and flute pieces at home, often just fragments, which he planned to develop later. Then one day while relaxing at the St. Laurence Church's Pastoral Centre (essentially a recreation room), he was introduced by Jenny Carless (former wife of Elbow Room Proprietor, Don Carless) to a young local musician named Stuart Carr. A modest guy who played acoustic guitar, wrote songs and sang, he dreamed of a career in music, but as of yet had gotten no further than entertaining at the local coffee bars and pubs. He and Chris hit it off right away. Before long, they played together on a regular basis, although at first, it was all quite private. Stuart recognized Chris's need to keep things low-key if they were to work at all, "When I was playing with him, it was like a different world – he was away from the bigger stuff and whatever that involved. We did a few covers for fun, and that was fine."

On days when his mental clarity was good, thoughts returned to his long lost album. Knowing that the bulk of the music was already on tape, the desire to finish it tugged at him. Stuart recalled Chris starting to make trips back to London to talk with people at Island about further sessions, and getting his music released. But after these efforts, he was once again frustrated. Carr noted, "It was something he got a bit pissed off with. He used to feel that sometimes he didn't think that he was getting the help and the push and so forth from the record company."

So if the relaxed life of the Midlands soothed his nerves, the irritation of London still rankled and confounded. Even so, in Stuart, Chris found an easygoing partner. After initial sessions when they did covers of Paul Simon's "Homeward Bound", and "The Boxer" – even reviving Dylan's "Knocking On Heaven's Door", soon more creative stuff was welling up. Edging back to the freedom of expression that came from jamming, Carr recalled, "He played flute with me more than sax. We used to have some jams. There was a mate, a friend of mine named Colin. He was playing fretless bass, like Jaco Pastorius – a great bass player.

CHAPTER TWENTY-SEVEN

We'd go to his flat and just play. There was quite a mix – I'd be playing twelve-string acoustic, there was Colin playing fretless bass, with some really good, 'hold you down' bass moves, and there was Chris just dropping in and out, making shapes with his flute. It was fun – they were wonderful times, and I know that Chris enjoyed them."

The pair also worked up songs to be played at the Sunday church services. Reverend Nokes recalled Chris taking his liturgical obligations seriously, "I remember him writing and leading the congregation in learning one or two rounds. He'd get different sides of the church singing different things that all worked together in a round."

As a measure of how far his confidence had eroded, even in this low key, non-judgmental atmosphere, Chris still fretted that he wasn't up to the task. As Reverend Nokes remembered, "I lived in a flat quite close to the church, and quite close to where he used to stay sometimes. And he would come around at all hours of the day and night if he was going to play something on Sunday, because he used to get into quite a panic. For someone who played flute to audiences of tens of thousands in his time, I always used to joke that he was getting into a state before performing for one hundred and fifty people."

But Nokes also came to understand the extenuating circumstances. As they talked late into the night about Chris's experiences, the price he'd paid was obvious to the cleric, "He really was under a lot of pressure in his life – for a lot of reasons. He was more or less 'shot to pieces' at that stage. Yeah, he was suffering from anxiety quite a lot. But he was always incredibly gentle and patient and affectionate. Even for the smallest of things he was doing for our church, he... it had to be right. He practiced and practiced and practiced to make sure that everything was absolutely right."

In a move quite surprising to his friends, Chris declared he was finally ready to give up drinking – or, at least, seriously try. Picking up a book called, *Am I an Alcoholic?* from a local bookstore he was attracted by a convenient checklist of symptoms, most of which he was forced to tick off. Of course, the execution would prove trickier than the plan. The final push may have been that his friend Graham had already made the decision to quit as well. Facing the task with a buddy must have looked like his best chance to pull this thing off. Certainly, without some kind of help, there was little hope.

Sometime in 1981, apparently at his parent's request, Chris moved in to Graham's apartment, where he stayed for some months. Given a room, he immediately repainted it to a color of his liking ('Milkweed'), and then settled in with Graham as his vigilant companion, "We used to go everywhere together. His parents left him off at my house, 'cause they couldn't put up with him, really. I wasn't drinking – I was 'on the wagon'. So, to keep him off the drink – I was keeping him off it myself. I had to watch him like a hawk, otherwise he would cheat."

After some time together in close quarters, Graham thought he understood why Chris needed his mind-mellowing substances so badly, "He was sad – he just wanted to hide it. He didn't want to be in reality. He was better off when he was half out of it, than when he was straight. He was very humorous, *but,* he was very shy. And basically he put himself into a cloud; then he was above it all. "

Unaccustomed as he was to any stretch of sobriety, Chris not only physically suffered, but the social/psychological component was dicey as well. Going around to the usual pubs where they socialized, Chris and Graham stood out by ordering lemonade or orange juice. While many of his mates respected Chris's attempt to clean up, with a pub-based social circle literally centered on alcohol, one test of resolve after the other would arise, some of which he would fail.

The public commitment to change had good and bad aspects. On one hand, people generally wished him success; some going so far as to spread the word that Chris was not to be bought any drinks. On the other, when he really felt the need, he simply became devious. Typically, he would make some sort of excuse, before sneaking out to another pub, or perhaps visit a nearby Chemist (Pharmacy), where he'd buy cough syrup – typically Codeine Linctus, which he would drink from the bagged bottle. Like Mandrax back in the old days, Codeine Linctus could put him in that hazy place where problems and sadness dissipated, however temporarily.

While some progress was made, the clock was ticking; his physical problems were causing noticeable symptoms: fluid retention in the abdomen made him look fat while increased perspiration soaked his hair as sweat glands vainly tried to compensate for his weakening liver and kidneys. These days the handkerchief in his pocket was constantly wiped across his face.

In an attempt to keep his balance on the more positive path – or perhaps suspecting that his time was short, Chris decided to be confirmed as a member of the Church of England. Prefaced with classes addressing the spiritual, philosophical and practical aspects of the denomination, at some point he finally felt ready. But even here he needed support, Graham and a female friend Cyndi would do the ceremony with him. On the day, Reverend Nokes recalled that Chris came dressed in his own special way: a dark pin-striped suit, neck scarf, and his bright red 'Kicker' shoes. Having picked new Biblical names to demark their spiritual transition (Cyndi took 'Mary', with Graham and Chris both opting for 'Joseph') the three were re-baptized at a nearby reservoir. Surrounded by family and a few friends, the ceremony would be officiated by the Bishop of Birmingham.

As someone who had explored every kind of spiritual venture; from pagan ceremonies, deep astrology, and on to Crowley's Magick, was Chris *really* committing to Christianity after all this time? Graham Broadbent for one, thought not. He saw it all as part of Chris's search for humor and his role-playing take on life in general, "He didn't believe it! It was an exercise in being somewhere; I don't think it had anything to do with religion. That was quite a bit of a joke… he thought it was funny." Sister Stephanie, too, believed Chris to be miles away from being "born again" as a Christian. Reverend Peter Nokes naturally disagreed, but also acknowledged Chris's unusually broad worldview. "Sure, I would say that he was a Christian, yeah… although I'm not saying that he swallowed wholesale all aspects of the Christian faith. But he brought to church a deep sense of searching really. He enjoyed the fact that he could express his spirituality in a non-cerebral way, there was a lot of color, music and movement, and I think he found that helpful. Chris was unique really – he had an unusual way of doing things. If he were alive today, I think he would be very drawn to the new-age movement, the kind of Glastonbury thing."

As if rewarded from above, his ability to move around freely suddenly returned. Having been revoked for years, his driver's license was finally restored, and Chris savored the mobility. For a man who really loved fast cars, it must have been difficult to restrain his right foot – especially considering that his car, a Renault Gordini – could easily do 130 MPH. But he tried to be good. Stuart Carr recalled one humorous ride with a cautious Chris at the wheel, "The speed limit was 30 MPH in one area, and he purposefully and specifically drove precisely according to the speedometer at 29! Can you imagine the people behind him, queuing up?" But of course, there would be other times when he was much less conservative with the accelerator.

As far away from the London music scene as he was, reminders of his Traffic past continued to find, if not haunt him.

In the early 1980's, music videos were beginning to emerge. Although groups like The Beatles (and Traffic for that matter) had been doing creative promo films way back in '66, these days, cable television stations (such as M.T.V., which launched in '81) were beginning to realize that videos – the place where sounds and graphics merged – were the next wave in entertainment. Right off it was a win/win situation for the industries involved: advertising revenue for the networks shot up while the record companies moved more product. Soon, all the big labels were cranking them out.

With Steve Winwood's comeback finally in motion, Island got on the bandwagon. Logically enough, his first ever video was "While You See a Chance", the wistful, synth-driven hit. Having already had a successful run on the radio, the video presented an opportunity to take things further. Back in Birmingham in late '81, even some of the local pubs were joining in, their TV's blaring out the latest offerings to entertain the patrons. It just so happened that Chris and Graham – still sipping only orange juice – were there as the clip came on.

Considering the history involved, it was indeed an odd tableau – beginning with a stylishly suited Steve, his hair short and well-groomed, standing stiffly at a small keyboard, lip-syncing to the music. Behind him on a two-toned stage, a lit pyramid was slowly scaled by two androgynous figures – flashing lights at each other before tumbling to the bottom. More than anything the video seemed to pose a question – could the still youthful-looking Winwood be recast as a pop idol to a new generation?

Watching in disbelief, Chris's eyebrows raised as his finger tapped on the bar table. Many years later, Graham would clearly recall the heated exclamation that followed, "Chris and I were sitting in the pub – they had these videos and we sat there and he (Steve) came on. And Chris was going off: 'How could he prostitute himself like that?' That in itself shows what he thought – (Winwood) had given up their sort of sound – what he (Chris) liked – to go into 'jingles' – commercialization really."

CHAPTER TWENTY-SEVEN

In a way, the incident might have actually been beneficial. Chris seemed to finally comprehend that any musical future he had would have to be of his own making. Realistically, with Steve so heavily invested in the mainstream – and Chris both physically weak and hopelessly outside of it, there wasn't much to go back to anyway. But if that dream had died, some anger still lingered below the surface. It wouldn't stay there long.

Out of the blue, another reminder of his Traffic past suddenly appeared. Jim Capaldi – having also disentangled himself from Chris before moving to Brazil – was now back in the motherland. Reclaiming his home in Marlow, he quickly set about re-building his career, persuading Steve as well as another old Traffic mate, Reebop Kwaku Baah, to contribute to his next album. Wanting to see what else might be possible, Jim made his way north, stopping at the Wood home in Romsley. Hoping to inspire a musical contribution, Jim would hand over a cassette of acoustic demos when they met. But Chris merely tucked it into a pocket before suggesting that they go to a nearby restaurant/pub.

If Jim was expecting a pleasant visit, catching up with each other's lives and laughing about the 'old times', it was not to be. Having been down for so long and forgetting none of the ways he believed he'd been marginalized – Chris was actually primed and ready to explode. And once settled in at their table, he let it out – unleashing a torrent of grievances that caught Jim off guard, "He just vented all these kinds of feelings, from like where we stopped being that tight trio in the Cottage, and where we started living separately, and I just started handing lyrics to Winwood…" Especially rankled by how he believed he'd been edged out of the shared approach to writing music, Chris had long felt that he'd been left with no viable way to contribute. But now, with Jim sitting across from him, trying to articulate his words amidst the rage proved futile; he lost his composure completely. Jim recalled, "He said, 'Oh, you and Steve were writing, and I never got… *arrgh!*', and he came over the table at me." Grabbing Jim by the collar and pulling him close, he "let it all out, how he felt we'd fucking left him." Suddenly catching himself, Chris would finally loosen his grip and slump back in his chair, red-faced and distraught.

Jim tried to explain how the split in their brotherhood came to be. "I could see he was quite hurt, but at least we shared that, and had it out. And I just said to him, 'Chris, we were living separately and I was just writing something, and I'd give it to him (Winwood), and there was nothing else I could do. If you wanted to put yourself more in there, we should have gotten together more… tried to arrange get togethers and writing.'" Although Jim believed that blame rested with Chris too, for his prolonged, uncontrolled drug-related behavior, that would remain discreetly unspoken. Instead, he was contrite. "I said, 'Listen man, it was nothing intentional, you know – that was just the way it was – and I'm sorry, that's not the way it was meant to be." Placated somewhat, Chris tried to relax as the two finished their drinks. But a sense of finality hung over the meeting as well. For better or worse, it would be the last time they saw each other.

"It was good that I visited him," said Jim. "I wanted to see him, and see how he was doing. He had a go at me, you know, but at least I was there for him to have a go at me."

CHAPTER TWENTY-EIGHT

SEASON OF THE SULLEN MOON

With the year drawing to a close, Chris took some tentative steps back toward a life in music – one at last free from lingering attachments to the past. Rehearsals with Stuart Carr, although sometimes "blurred" by setbacks with alcohol, had gotten more productive – they were starting to write songs. Thinking that Chris was closer to visualizing a solo path, Carr said, "The direction was certainly to play and to be adventurous with different types of music – to move on from the great Traffic material, to move on to other people. I know that he missed playing as he used to with Traffic, but it only spurred him on in some respects to try something else." And part of that was working up plans for another benefit concert for the church.

Just lately, something else quite amazing had happened. After years of owing money and being utterly broke, a gush of funds suddenly poured in – something in excess of eighty thousand Pounds Sterling. That "tax dodge" in Woburn – the house he'd only slept in once, was finally sold. To avoid more problems, Chris would need to invest most of it; it just so happened that a local recording studio just starting up needed a partner with cash.

Having a place to record when he was ready instead of having to deal with the distant, often estranged situation in London was indeed appealing. Perhaps his long defunct album could finally be resurrected and finished on his own terms? Chris was clearly excited at the prospect. Already fiddling with the title, he told friends that he was considering both "Barbed Wire", and "Mood Music". Making one last trip south, he came back with a large box of tape reels and a sense of hope – things finally seemed to be moving in the right direction.

Then Jeanette died.

The details of Jeanette Jacob Wood's passing are today quite thin. From what is known, on December 31st, 1981, she left her home alone to attend a New Year's Eve party, presumably somewhere near Kent, where she lived with Larry and Damien. At the party, she was supposedly accosted by a (presumably drunk) man, who, having been rebuffed, hit her in the face with a glass. As a result of the physical and emotional trauma, she collapsed into a series of seizures. On somehow returning home in the middle of the night – her face bandaged in gauze, she was calmed by Larry, who left her sleeping on the living room couch. On the morning of January 1, 1982, he found her in the same place, dead – of causes apparently directly related to her seizures.

On hearing the news, Chris was quite understandably distraught, even frantic. One of the first things he did was to rush back to Graham Broadbent. "He was off his head about it. He came in and was in this dramatic thing – screeching and screaming. I said, 'What's the matter – what the fuck's the matter with you?' He was going on, and throwing his arms, but he was pretty cut up about it – obviously he was. We talked about it. I said, 'Well, there's nothing you can do about it – what can you do? He wanted always to get back with her, you see. And now, 'it was never gonna happen', he said. And I remember looking at him, and the whole thing was sort of like… you know. He hardly came down to see me after that."

Prior to the terrible day, Chris had been working with Graham on a poem for Jeanette, appropriately titled "Born To Be Free". He had also asked his sister Stephanie to make Jeanette a specially-designed leather purse, which she did. Intending to present both to her in the New Year, now they would remain tucked away in a drawer in his room.

However destroyed, Chris would fulfill his duties: buying a cemetery plot and large black granite headstone (leaving room for his own name), and playing flute at the small service. Only after completing the necessary tasks would he implode – burying his sorrow as might be expected, with alcohol. And now he went straight for the hardest stuff he could find, typically vodka, which he consumed by the bottle.

Wandering the streets of Stourbridge in a near-blind haze a few days later, Chris would unknowingly pass an old friend. John (Jack) Priest, knew Chris well from the art school period, but almost didn't recognize him now, "I walked past him, and went 'whoa, whoa, that's! I turned around, and here's this guy, who's getting overweight, he stuttered, and was unsure of himself. He'd lost the plot somewhere, and I thought, 'What a shame, he's in a really bad state.' He told me on the streets what happened to him, and I said, 'Okay, let's get together sometime.'" When they did met again in a local pub, Priest and others tried to help Chris regain his footing from the horrible blow. But from here, 'recovery' became a more relative term, since as Priest succinctly put it, "his main preoccupation was trying to stay off the booze, or using booze."

*

Chris lived another eighteen months. Witnessing the pit of despair that he plunged into in the aftermath of Jeanette's death, the memories of even his close friends played tricks; with some recalling that he died broken-hearted only six months later. The effect of the loss was, of course, beyond measure. Having said that she was the only woman for him – "I don't want anyone else", in the wake of his love's permanent absence, his future looked dim indeed. While it might seem that the event sent him into an irreparable downward spiral – and many obviously believed it did, reality was more complicated. As before, his life would be filled with ups and downs. But, even as the end approached, his will to live, and more astoundingly, his desire to create music, was sometimes stronger than it had been in years.

The recording facility financed with his money would help him shift focus. The place to be known as 'Sinewave Studios' (for the undulating line that sound produces on an oscilloscope) actually began in the basement of a guy named Pete King. Having managed and produced the first three records for the reggae band Steel Pulse as well as recording tracks for UB 40 – who subsequently ditched him for a big label, King had taken his knocks in the music industry, something he had come to see as "a terrible business." Now he wanted to start again. Although he'd located a more appropriate studio space a couple of blocks from the Birmingham Town Hall at 51 Gas Street, King lacked the funding to renovate. As such, his dream studio remained just that.

That is where Chris came in. King's credentials with Island and being a brother-in-law to Paul Medcalf made the partnership seem natural. With more money in hand, equipment was purchased, rooms outfitted with sound baffling, and a studio was born. Having set up the financing, Tony Hughes, an accountant who handled the cash from the sale of Chris's house, stayed on to help run the place. According to King, despite the large amount of money Chris put into the venture, he was *not* the sole owner of Sinewave, "We got 80 (thousand pounds sterling) financed, so he was in the development, but it wasn't his studio. He put some money in; he was a partner, but not an active partner on a daily basis." Still, without Chris's cash, it was highly unlikely that Sinewave would have got going at all. And yet, almost from the beginning – and most unfortunately – confusion about his role, and what exactly he was entitled to, led to problems.

Besides a place to make his own music, Chris came to the enterprise with a singular managerial principle – one which immediately put him at odds with the others. According to what he told close friends, Chris envisioned Sinewave as a resource and hangout for young, local musicians; a place where they could jam, learn and get their foot in the door of the music business without going broke or being exploited. While generous and artist-centered, this model obviously wouldn't be the most profitable. In contrast, Pete King wanted Sinewave studios to be a prestigious, high-end recording facility, on par to the best of those in London.

Chris, of course, lacked the personality to push his agenda very hard; before long he would settle for simply having a place where he could feel like a working musician – whether he was one or not. But even this proved problematic.

While the studio was built with comfort in mind, particularly a recreational waiting area (with pool table) modeled after that of Island's, it seemed that Chris Wood's mere presence quickly became bad for business. Pete King recalled, "He'd come into the studio with a two liter bottle of Bitter Lemon, and it'd be about a quarter bitter lemon, and the rest vodka. And he used to sit there in the lounge, one or two bottles of vodka disguised as Bitter Lemon. It was quite sad really, he reeked of alcohol. It got to the point where we'd have clients there – quite well known bands, and they'd say, 'Who the hell is that guy?' They'd never heard of him. There came a point where we'd say, 'If there's a paying session in, you need to be scarce.'"

King insists that the requests for Chris to be elsewhere were actually few, and blown out of proportion by Chris (and later his family). Contrary to the perception that they only wanted his money, King was adamant that he and the others actually desired to help Chris, "We were the only people that still believed in him – he was part of us, you know. We used to say, 'Hey, c'mon, let's do some work', and it was 'No, no, no – I don't think I can do it.' So, we didn't say, 'Fuck you', we said, 'wait till tomorrow' – and we'd have him there for an hour or two in the afternoon."

Six months or so after Jeanette's death, equilibrium remained elusive. But an important morale lifter would surface. Around this time, Chris was asked to do a Radio Birmingham interview for a show called *Coming Home*. With Stuart Carr along for support, Chris was treated with a respect he'd seen little of in recent years. Following a Traffic medley, he would be welcomed as an elder statesman of rock, and responded with a lucid, if often melancholy sounding, dialog with the DJ.

Asked first about the origins of Traffic, he was not overly expansive – only briefly emphasizing the importance of the Elbow Room jams in bringing the members together. He did however betray a tone of wistfulness, revealing how important those days had really been, "And there was born the idea – 'wouldn't it be nice to play together?' It was an idyllic sort of thing – a dream which came true."

As the interview wound down, Chris seemed eager to make one point clear – his disdain for the state of over-commercialized music. Having witnessed the unsavory evolution of the industry, not to mention having been heavily stomped on by it himself, he suggested a more humble, workman-like approach, "I think people want to – what's the word – to sort of deescalate from this intense selling drive, money making spree, money-making racket, and get back to kind of sanity, by where you're making a comfortable living – where you're working for it, *crafting* for it. And this I believe can be done."

With the passion rising in his voice, Chris – talking mostly to musicians just starting in an era based more and more on production, sheen, and track 'perfection' – called on them not to lose the essence of their art, and perhaps their souls amid the technological advances, "It's the atmosphere of the *sound* that makes it, and if you can get that… When we were in Traffic, we used to put things, sort of demo-down on a small stereo tape in the room at the Cottage, and we came into the big studio and we could never recreate that actual feeling that we had there – there was no low ceiling, or door open to a field with birds chirping… I'm not one to stop progress, but one has to be very careful that progress isn't taking over you, you know."

*

Having met Chris so soon after Jeanette's passing, John Priest knew that his old friend needed a boost, and in late May of '82 he thought he had a way. He was planning a charity concert to feature locals who had made the big time. Having already gotten commitments from Robert Plant, Steve Gibbons, and Sounds Of Blue (and later, Chicken Shack) alumnus Andy Silvester, Priest wanted Chris to be part of it as well.

When asked, he was, as usual, disinclined. Still, as the date approached, Priest persisted. "I asked him to play, a few days before, I said 'Come on, come on – bring your sax, man' cause I thought this may… sort of chivvy him along, give him something – to be part of the thing, instead of being a spectator." Reassured that he would only have to play as part of a show-closing jam, Chris finally agreed. There at least he could just blend in with the others, an arrangement he deemed tolerable.

On the evening of June 1st 1982, the Kinver Community Centre was already abuzz with several hundred revelers and musicians when Chris arrived. Meeting him outside, Priest was relieved to see him open the boot of his car and retrieve his tenor. What he couldn't fully appreciate was that a small miracle was in progress – this would be his first performance before a paying crowd in nearly six years.

Inside, Chris mingled with friends as he walked his instrument backstage. Meeting Andy Silvester by the bar, he seemed to be in a good mood as they talked before the show. He was also trying to *be* good. Facing an internal struggle no one else understood, Chris had apparently decided to see if he could play without an alcoholic crutch. Approaching the bar, he made a show of ordering an elaborate drink that according to Andy Silvester, "had every ingredient you could imagine, *except* alcohol. He was doing it as a bit of a joke – having fun with the barman by getting him to concoct those drinks." It was also his subtle way of announcing that he was trying to stay sober.

Having not seen his old friend for some time, Andy couldn't help but notice the transformation, "He was always a good looking dude really, he'd got lovely blue eyes – but he had put on a good deal of weight by then." He also saw a measure of fear behind the jokes. "He was nervous. I'm sure that he liked a good drink before going on stage – and being deprived of that would make him feel even worse."

For Robert Plant, this low key gig would prove a triumphant first step of his comeback after the death of his Led Zeppelin band-mate John Bonham. With a tight band and comfortably familiar songs, he re-invented himself as a solo performer and regained his confidence. Soon after, an album with the Honeydrippers would be out with their single, a version of "Sea of Love", destined to be a hit.

Chris found no such turning point. Instead, as the evening went on, his nerve to play slowly but surely evaporated. As the finale approached, he did force himself on to the stage, clutching his tenor with grim determination. But, as the other musicians filled in around him, he drifted further and further back. John Priest watched, "His heart wasn't there at all. He wasn't playing. He came on, got onstage – but where everyone (else) was up front, kind of jumping about on stage – he kind of lingered behind the curtain, kind of offstage, to the right of the stage."

Out of view, he tried to compose himself; but when he put the mouthpiece to his lips to play – nothing musical emerged. Flustered he would try again, only to falter. As Priest recalled, "It was a very sad kind of performance. He kind of honked his sax – it was kind of… he seemed to be lost and blue. That was about it."

A physically imposing instrument, the tenor saxophone requires both muscular strength and an attitude of confidence to play – neither of which Chris had to offer. Beyond the usual performance anxiety though, he now had an even greater problem. The pressure of the fluid accumulating in his abdomen was now pressing against his lungs as well. As a result, Chris barely had the necessary wind. Perhaps unaware of these limitations, in the end he would give up and simply stand behind the curtains, embarrassed and silent.

With finale concluded, he finally emerged as a DJ came on to spin records and people drifted back to the bar. Priest met him there, noting the confusion on his face as they stood in uneasy silence. Feeling partly responsible for Chris's distress, Priest said, "He (only) did it as a favor for myself… He wasn't strong, he was a sad guy." Moments later, in his time of supreme weakness, a man known to both walked over and addressed Chris as John watched, "This dude, said to him, and I will not forgive him for it – he said, 'Do you want a drink man?' And Chris said, 'yeah, yeah, I'll have a brandy, I'll have a brandy'. And I said, 'No, no, man, what are you *doing*?' He said, 'Just this one time, I'll have a brandy'. And this other guy said, 'Come on! Have a brandy, have a brandy!', and went off and bought him a brandy and came back."

The dam burst. As Priest observed with a mixture of sorrow and revulsion, Chris's resolve collapsed completely. Looking at the drink, Chris upped the ante, "Could you make that a double?" As he was heading back to the bar to recharge the drink, "Chris came on, put his hand on him, with some money slapped on the table, and said, 'Can you make that a treble?' And of course, treble followed treble…"

The pain and humiliation that Chris tried to drown that night was not to be denied. Later he would travel with a carload of others to someone's house to continue the party. Arriving at their destination, he fell out of the car, only first able to crawl up the drive. Finally righting himself, a woman approached, asking, "Aren't you Chris Wood, the famous musician?" With one last reminder of a past which had fully overshadowed his present, Chris's composure crumbled. As Priest later heard from a friend – "He just exploded. He wasn't violent, but he was so emotional, he (lost) his cool."

With his breaking point seemingly at hand, later Chris would climb unsteadily out a second story window. There he would precariously teeter on the ledge, his eyes staring into the blackness as he recited lines from *Romeo and Juliet* into the night sky.

But oblivion wasn't quite ready to swallow him. As such, the aftermath of the bad night was sadly familiar. Having crashed over and over, the routine was now well established: whatever the horror, pick yourself up and carry on. But re-engaging with life very much required an ally to help stabilize things so he could move forward again. As it happened, one was a lot closer than he imagined.

*

Walking into a still-under-construction bathroom at Sinewave, Chris stopped to talk to the plumber, a local guy named Vinden Wylde. The day job aside, Wylde was also a sax player, as well as a longtime Traffic fan. He vividly remembered the day he met his hero, "I talked to him for four hours! We stood there, and were waving arms and jumping up and down. It was an amazing chance to meet him."

The two got on so well that, before long, Chris took Vinden into an unspoken but serious master/apprentice relationship. For Wylde, this opportunity to learn from "the master" was one he was thrilled to have; with years of weekly semi-pro gigs under his belt, he was more than eager to get to the next level. Soon he would be making weekly stops at the Wood home, where Chris seemed in a rush to pass on everything his pupil needed to know.

Over the next few months, Chris revealed that he was interested in putting a band together. Wylde recalled that it was to be, "Latin jazz, really – two saxes, two flutes, playing harmony. He was teaching me harmonies on the flute – like on "Dealer" (from Traffic's first album). He was showing me things all the time, all these mechanical tricks on instruments, flutes, or saxophone; raising my game up to what he wanted." By investing his time and energy, Chris lived in hope that he'd found a loyal partner that would see him through when the time came.

His confidence stoked, he now wanted a fresh listen to some of the old Island tapes to see what might be improved; on August 2nd (1982) Sinewave accommodated. With his instruments in hand and Vinden at his side, the master tape of "Birth In A Day" would be loaded. Playing to the original eight-minute track made with Phil Ramacon back in '76, Chris first lightened the mood with a keening, ascending soprano sax track. Then a lyrical (and quite beautiful) flute solo would be laid down between the horn vamps, imparting a wistful interlude. Crucially, the song was also radically shortened, faded down at almost a third of the original length. Adding a last subtle touch – a slight echo applied to the flute – he was done; "Birth In A Day" had been reborn.

More compact, concise, and most importantly, memorable, "Birth" was still miles from anything acceptable to popular radio. But that, of course, never figured into the equation – Chris was quite happy with his jazzy jewel; perhaps it would help bring his long-delayed album back to life.

While dismissive of the drunk that too often merely wasted time at the studio, even Pete King couldn't help finding himself impressed. "I remember one of the tunes that I was working with him on, even now, in my head. I can remember the vibe of it. It was like, beautiful jazz, but really – not avant-garde or anything like that – it was crossover jazz. It wouldn't have sounded out of place in America or anywhere… It would have been on an album that could have stood next to Ronnie Laws (Texas jazz/funk saxophonist), or any of those people. It was on the same level as that kind of stuff."

King also insisted that if Chris had been a little more together, a genuinely good album would have emerged, "The gaps when we could get something out of him were fairly limited. He wanted to play music, and we had a plan: get this album out – put him in a bracket where he belonged, which wasn't in a 60's pop band, but as an ace jazzer – a great jazz musician. If the album would have come out and had done as well as I think it would have done, the hope was that it would be enough to help him pull himself out of the mire." Good intentions aside, some of Chris's subsequent experiences at Sinewave weren't as encouraging.

At the dawn of 1983, Chris Wood appeared, depending on the observer, to be either very close to his doom, or on the cusp of a musical breakthrough. The truth, as in so many aspects of Chris's life, was fully embedded in the paradox. On the one hand, he was becoming more and more serious about all aspects of music. On the other, one year after Jeanette's death, having lapsed over and over again, he now seemed to have given up any pretense of abstaining from alcohol. As he'd told Graham Broadbent regarding cigarettes, Chris seemed to have decided that, in the end, sobriety was just 'not worth it'. Subsequently, the long precarious balance of his health would soon nose-dive; heading full-on toward the precipice, now only the exact distance remained unknown.

There would be one last, unfortunate push in that direction. On January 12th, his old friend, Anthony 'Reebop' Kwaku Baah died suddenly of a cerebral hemorrhage while on stage in Sweden. In the not-too-distant past, the African drummer had in fact made the trip north to see Chris, with one friend recalling the two actually playing a set at a local pub. As such, his death, coming as it did, very near the one year anniversary of Jeanette's passing, hit hard. Vinden Wylde recalled being told of it by a dejected Chris, who could only hang his head and mutter, "Poor Reebop", over and over.

Around this time, Chris began what looked like a slow review of the key people and places he'd known; physically circling back to resolve or perhaps just close chapters from the past. One stop was to see his old Cumberland Mews house-mate and musical partner, Pete Bonas. Unannounced, Chris showed up on the doorstep one rainy day. Pete was saddened at the sight, "It was tragic – that was the last time I saw him alive. He came up to Highgate, at the flat – he had a little mac on – sweet, but he was wasted – not sort of on downers, but it looked like his mind had gone a little bit. We had a little put-up bed in the living-room and he slept on that. In the night, he got up, looking for the toilet, and he wandered out into the street – he was wandering around in the road. I had to go and get him. He was desperate, he wanted for somebody to help him. I mean, what could I do? There was nothing I could do."

CHAPTER TWENTY-EIGHT

Chris would also visit a much older friend living in London –Trevor Jones, the steady mate who'd stuck with him through thick and thin all the way to the Royal Academy. While they found things to laugh about, he also noticed Chris worriedly clinging to his dictionary of medical terms, and that beneath it all, his friend "was in a terrible emotional state." Trevor remained unconditional in his friendship, handing Chris a key to his house and telling him that he could come back any time.

Together, Chris and Trevor dropped in on the art teacher and mentor who had done so much to help both – John Walker. On seeing Chris again after so many years, Walker too was alarmed, but tried to cover it with humor – reminding him of the time his hair fell out back in '65 as he fretted about leaving Art School. Walker, "I said, 'what happened to the spot' or something. We kind of joked, made light, but it was sad, it wasn't a nice time. I was concerned." Reading Chris's expressions, Walker thought he saw something that looked like regret for the road not taken, "I'm sure that there was something there – that he was reaching out. He probably was reaching back to see… we certainly didn't talk about painting, (but) it was in my studio, and he was there… (pause)… You know, I think he'd felt he'd made a mistake. He didn't *say it*, but he kind of implied."

Continuing to sort out the tattered threads of his life, he would also return to the place where his spirit had been freest – Witley Court. Essentially in the same state as in '66, the enormous decomposing mansion seemed to await, if not beckon his return. Vinden Wylde recalled, "He was still interested in it. He showed me the drawing that he did (of Witley), and said that he'd been there at night, and that I should go there." A photo from this period would capture him standing in front of the ruins (in the day) in a pressed shirt, tie and long grey trench coat, the hint of a smile on his face.

Finding peace there was important, since elsewhere it often proved elusive. Despite his recent confirmation in the Church of England, his interest in the realm of the occult certainly hadn't ended. He still did horoscope readings and charts for friends, as well as the occasional séance. More significantly, he was never able to rid himself of concern from a long-dead figure that literally haunted him still – Graham Bond. Whatever had happened between them years ago left entanglements he'd been unable to fully shed. Brenda Bryan recalled Chris's visits bringing an energy which manifested in strange ways, such as in seeming to cause household lights to flicker on and off by themselves. At first, Chris appeared mystified by the phenomena, saying: "What's that – what's that? Look!" But before long, he was more sure of the cause, and frightened. Brenda recalled, "He (Bond) hung around with Chris. Whenever the lights used to flash – which doesn't happen anymore, which is strange – but it used to happen a lot when Chris was here, he'd dive on the floor, and do these *signs* and stuff. And I'd say, 'What are you *doing!?*' He'd say, 'Oh, it's Graham, it's Graham…' And I'd say, 'Oh don't be ridiculous.' It was totally Black Magic."

Even at home, a spiritual conflict seemed to be playing out. A cassette tape discovered after his death held two short pieces of audio, each pointing in an opposing direction. The first was a crazily sped up and oscillating voice (seemingly Chris's) reciting a warning amid a heavy background hum: "It's not safe to be in the house, for the next four hours or more. For the sake of anyone who might be there – leave. Leave immediately. This is no joke. Remember, any time in the next four hours – so leave, immediately. It's not safe, especially for you…"

Directly following was an open mic recording Chris made of an Easter Sunday church service radio broadcast. Over an angelic sounding choir, an announcer began by intoning sacred words: "The Easter Hallelujah, the Hallelujah of the resurrection. This is the will of my Father, that all who believe in his Son shall have eternal life. I will raise him up on the last day says the Lord, Hallelujah." As the choir returned – welling up in full voice, Chris's flute would join them, playing modest, mellow phrases to the heavens.

Whether he was trying to reconcile the conflicting currents that ran through his life or simply acknowledge them is unknown. But as it had been since the 60's, his cassette recorder helped him capture, replay, and examine his life. As his days grew short, he seemed to need it all the more.

Perhaps the most poignant piece of audio he would leave behind was a fascinating self-documentary style recording. It captured a road trip Chris made by himself to a destination that held memories and perhaps mysteries he still hoped to unravel. It began with the sound of a microphone rustling when the machine was turned on. Getting into his Renault Gordino at Spindle Cottage on Romsley, Chris is heard giving his father a goodbye honk before heading off, the engine humming as the windshield wipers cleared away rain. Driving on, he talked to himself about the weather and driving conditions before stopping to sit quietly at a park bench. For a full ten minutes, the local birds would fill the tape with their comforting and familiar voices.

Later he would make another stop, soliciting comments from an unknowing woman and a little girl before driving to a gas station to fill up. Continuing his sojourn, he eavesdropped on the local police with a scanner as they talked back and forth about a local theft suspect on the run, before switching over to a BBC jazz program. Hearing Horace Silver's classic "Song For My Father", the sax player in him couldn't resist, he turned it up, singing the horn parts as he drove.

Finally, arriving at his destination, the mystery location turned out to be nothing less than the birthplace of his creative life. Narrating the conclusion to the drive, he began, "Now I'm going to turn into Corngreaves Hall, reminisce a little tiny bit… (sound of a turn signal and rough road surface)… this is rather pitiful (road noise), I can see one or two of the trees I painted (road noise)… they've certainly got potholes in this place… I've really just come to look, not fart around…" And with one more comment, almost under his breath; "My god it's heavenly…" he turned off the key.

In a very crucial way, he'd finally returned home – to his *real* home. But it certainly wasn't the same place that he'd left so many years before; the bumpy road only the first indication of the disrepair the dwelling had fallen into. While the County always had plans to subdivide the once elegant structure into new, high-end apartments, for whatever reason, in 1983 nothing had been done. Instead, like Witley Court, Corngreaves Hall was slowly being ceded back to nature.

Having come to "reminisce", would he take the opportunity to muse on the unforeseen twists of his fate as he walked around the husk of his old home? Of all the tape rolled over the years, this one, more than any other seemed likely to expose something of the hidden nature of Chris Wood. But it was not to be. Seconds after cutting the car's engine, the recording too abruptly stopped as the side of the sixty-minute tape ran out – and the other side was blank. With the Sony C-60 FeCr cassette holding no easy answers, in the end, whatever thoughts and feelings this final visit to Corngreaves Hall conjured would be kept very much to himself.

*

If all of the recent soul searching had uncovered anything, it must have reminded Chris that he was, above all else, still a musician. Although his confidence had been battered bloody, and he could only manage with an alcoholic boost, the desire to play was still in there, and with the right encouragement could be drawn back to the surface.

One pub that Chris frequented was 'The Vine', just outside Stourbridge. Here he would meet old friends like Robert Edwards, and Mike Lewis whom he'd known from his earliest art college days. Better known by its colloquial name, 'The Bull and Bladder', the pub had a tiny stage and a seating area the size of a modest living room. Frequently hosting local blues and jazz acts, Mike Lewis recalled one band, the Paul Woodhall Trio, inviting Chris to sit during their upcoming appearance. Against all odds, instead of dismissing the offer out of hand, he agreed.

Naturally, on the night he was much less sure. Aware of Chris's predictable reticence, Mike decided to drive them both, "Christopher had a habit of being late for everything, seriously late. The night that we were supposed to go – it was a Monday night, 'Monday Night Jazz Night', he was late, and I phoned up his Mum and said, 'Is Chris there?' She said, 'He's on his way.' I said, has be brought his sax – or flute?' She chuckled sadly and said, 'Michael, he'll never play that (tenor sax) again.'"

While Chris did only bring his flute, it was one he'd done his best work with – the long alto he'd used on "Forty Thousand Headmen". While Lewis was excited, Chris hadn't yet committed to playing, saying only: "I'll tell you when we get there." Once they did, he was still very hesitant, anxious and perspiring in a heavy coat that he wouldn't take off. No doubt remembering the previous disaster, he seemed close to bolting. Lewis was equally tense, "I thought, 'Oh my god' – he was nervous – pacing up and down, smoking and drinking. And I thought, 'If he drinks any more he definitely won't play it.' But he played it. This guy introduced him, and he played three, twelve-bar blues. And once he started, you couldn't… the guys were getting off the stage, 'cause he was really into it, the sweat was pouring off…" Robert Edwards, who ran the event, remembered it too, "He had to be encouraged, he didn't want to do it, he had to be persuaded, you know. When he got up and started, he was fine. In fact it was nice to see him play, because I hadn't seen him play in years."

Having given his all, the toll of the exertion was clear, but Chris was heartened by the reception. Mike Lewis recalled, "Of course, when he had finished, he sat there – absolutely drained, and didn't look well, he looked ashen. It had obviously taken it out of him. But he was *so* pleased with himself. I said, 'That was fantastic, great – you've done it!', and he said, 'Yeah, yeah.' And I think, if they had asked him to do more – and the audience wanted more – he would have carried on all night. He was *that* into it at the time.'"

Instead he would simply savor the rare sense of satisfaction. Perhaps the night held a sense of closure as well – the short set of jazzy blues numbers, played in a small pub had taken him very close to a full circle from where he'd started back in 1962. From here, pleasant memories would have to suffice – this would be his final public performance.

Back home he worked to complete a tune sketched out the previous winter, something he now called, "Spring Can Really Free You". Starting as mere fragments on the piano, the piece evolved into a fully-fledged song akin to "Tragic Magic" or "Barbed Wire". Like these, "Spring" would express the path of his moods. Using just piano and an overdubbed flute, the song alternated sad, nocturne-like passages with jaunty up-tempo sections that almost danced – each dovetailing into other as naturally as the seasons of the year. The cyclical structure imparted a sense of optimism *and* acceptance. Although instrumentally uncomplicated and a little tentative, the tune was also heartfelt and beautiful. Sadly, while he lived, it seems that no one (perhaps his parents aside) ever heard it.

As for his mother and father, while essentially forced to live with them, it was obvious that Chris deeply cared about both, though his relationship with Muriel remained complex. While she kept at him for his bad habits, and wasn't afraid of saying things in front of his friends like: "Well, look at how much damage he's done. You can tell he's got brain damage – look at his eyes," Chris often called when he was out to reassure her that he was okay. And heartened by his participation in the Northfield church, Muriel began attending as well, enjoying the opportunity to worship with her son again. Chris's friends like Graham Broadbent also noted that Chris and Muriel were, in fact very similar, "Chris was very much like his mother – in looks, and the humor of his mother's was exactly the same as his."

As for Stephen, although he'd initially advised Chris against going into music, once the decision was made, he would become his son's biggest fan. Besides Chris, only he knew the titles for all of Chris's solo, instrumental recordings, and was equally concerned that they someday be released. Over time, many of the father and son's interests seemed to merge. Chris's love of architecture had of course come from Stephen, and while the elder Wood had always maintained the birdfeeder, in later years he joined a bird watching society and would discuss avian interests with Chris. He also became a huge jazz fan, buying records, and taping live broadcasts off the radio – each neatly labeled and meticulously stored. It was his father's accepting, if emotionally reserved, nature that made it tolerable for Chris to be at home again.

His enthusiasm to play elevated again, plans were made for a proper recording session at Sinewave. Vinden recalled, "I was desperate for recording time, because I'd played some afternoons in his house and he was still in good condition – playing-wise – doing unbelievable things, and he had all these ideas, all this stuff he wanted to do." But the execution obviously required some studio time, and here they ran into a wall. "I knew one of the engineers, I said to him, 'Look, can Chris Wood and I just come in and have a blow – with just a drum machine or anything?' And he said, 'No, the book's full.' The place was always empty, there was never anybody in there – okay, maybe there was a band in there late at night, until the early hours of the morning – I don't know, I never saw that. Every time I went in there – 'the book's full, the book's full.'"

Distressed, Chris worked himself up enough to actually go back and have it out. Arranging a meeting, he then asked Vinden to drive him up to the studio. Not surprisingly, his nerve wavered the closer they got to Gas Street. Vinden recalled, "He said, 'Right, I'm going down to sort them out…' And then we go down there in the car… to the studio in Birmingham, at the studio, and he had terrible hiccups before he went in there. He couldn't really deal with… the hiccups persisted. And then he had to go home, I had to take him back to his mother's house. He said, 'Oh, I'm sorry, I had a shepherd's pie yesterday, and it's given me terrible hiccups' – but it was nerves…"

With plans made and exciting music in the offing, Vinden decided to return to the studio alone; he had a bargaining chip held in reserve. Having previously plumbed water lines for a washing machine for one of the studio engineers – a job for which he hadn't yet been paid, Vinden went back for another chat about the studio log books, "I went down there one night, and I was really peeved, and I said, 'Alright, I'll let you off what you owe me for the plumbing that I've done, if you'll let me have an hour – just one hour with Chris Wood in the studio.' He said, 'Sunday, you can come down next Sunday.' It's funny how everything changes when you have enough money. It really angered me, but that was it."

So it came to be that on April 17th, Chris had his only formal, full band recording session at Sinewave. Having been graced with a short window of time to get something done, an ad hoc group including a drummer, a guitarist, and a bass player was rounded up. In addition, Chris's friend Nicky Cannon was also there to play congas. Chris brought his alto flute, while Vinden would play the shorter 'C' flute, and tenor sax.

The session was to be built around a single song: "Sullen Moon". While previously recorded with Tyrone Downie, the result had been more of a jam. Now Chris was intent on redoing it, and for a very special reason. Having recently found Jeanette's original lyrics, the completed song would serve as a tribute to his beloved, departed wife. Having roughed out the tune at the Wood home, Chris and Vinden were very much ready to go. Wylde noted, "I'd go down to his house in the afternoons, and he would play the arrangements through on the piano, and I'd write them down so when we'd go into the studio I knew exactly what to do."

Once there, however, Chris was of course hesitant. But having experienced that fear so many times, he now worked through it in a practical manner – sending Vinden in to get the band warmed up while he listened in the lobby. After ten minutes or so, he would finally enter, flute in hand. Vinden recalled, "Once the ice was broken by me going in there, he came in. He walked in saying, 'Oh right, okay, we'll do this...' it was very good, he was telling people what he wanted, getting the chords sorted out and getting the bass lines sorted out. He was producing it, telling me what he wanted on the flute, and he really got it. He was away and doing it and it was fantastic."

With a band backing him for the first time in years, there was indeed a tantalizing sense of potential brewing, but a problem nagged. While the mix of instruments was basically what he'd had in mind, the session players, while eager, were not quite up to the task. To get the tune together, Chris went around the room, patiently speaking to each as they sorted out the parts, hoping loose-limbed enthusiasm would compensate for lack of acuity. But having directed the chord sequence and tempo over and over again (at one point clapping it out), at some point the cacophony resolved into a semblance of what he had in mind.

As a full run-through got underway, "Sullen Moon" finally gelled; rolling along with a Latin rhythm, somehow the elegiac quality it was always intended to have emerged. The vibe, at least, was right. Pushing on, he tried to get Jeanette's lyrics into the mix as well, but the allotted time ran out; in the end he would settle for a more or less complete instrumental jam. Imperfections aside, with Chris's passionate alto flute singing out the melody, the song was already a gem in the rough.

Completed as intended or not, the session was a major accomplishment. Having found it in himself to direct the musicians with authority, Chris had at long last taken on the role of 'band leader'. Flushed with pride, and patting each other on the back, he and Vinden would take some satisfaction that they were indeed on the right path. But the glow didn't last; the undeserved kick in the teeth that always seemed to be waiting for Chris came even before they were out the door.

Out of concern for his feelings, Vinden had never told Chris about the plumbing quid pro quo. But that didn't stop some of the recording staff from doing so. As Wylde recalled, "At the end of the session they went in and told him that the only reason he was in there was because I'd let him off some money from the plumbing. They rubbed his face in it and said that it was only because of the bloody washing machine! (They) said that he would have to pay for any session work that he wanted to do."

Little more than a week later, Sinewave would get an assignment to complete a 'song' BBC 4 wanted to use to promote the upcoming basketball season. The tune consisted of a backing track of drums, bass, and a synthesized keyboard accompanying a cheesy female vocal chant singing, 'Lay it up, you gotta lay it up' as a chorus. Art, it wasn't, but the BBC was willing to invest some money in the belief that a little added saxophone would catch the ear of radio listeners.

Wylde would receive a call from the studio asking if he'd take care of it. He agreed, but once again thought of his mentor, "I said, 'Can I bring Chris Wood, can I bring my mate?', and they said, 'Alright, bring him'. So I phoned him up and said, 'They want us down at the studio Chris', and he said 'okay'. But when I got there on the night to do it, to actually pick him up and take him there, he didn't want to go. He was scared stiff about going there again." Muriel stepped in to help flush him out the door, saying, "'C'mon Christopher, I want to clean up, to tidy up, I don't want you around my house, I want you to go out." With the studio now looking like an easier situation to deal with, he got his horn and went. "He didn't want the hassle," Vinden recalled. But that didn't mean walking back into Sinewave would be easy – the bitter lemon bottle, filled mostly with vodka, went along for the trip.

CHAPTER TWENTY-EIGHT

Once there, the job was explained as requiring two saxophone parts – a repeated refrain and some kind of more expressive lead line. Chris, of course, had no intention of playing on the corny tune, and motioned for Vinden to go into the booth while he sat outside. Handling the rhythm part on alto sax was no problem, but when it came to the lead, Vinden faltered, unable to fit an appropriate phrase into the allotted spot, "It's a real fast number, and you've got a really short section where you can get a solo, get some riffs in, and it was something I couldn't do."

Walking out of the booth unhappy with his performance, he asked Chris to step in, "I was crap, what I did was terrible, and I said, 'Oh Chris, come on!', and he said, 'No I don't think I can do any better.'" But like an echo of his mother, Wylde persisted, nagging, "I said, 'C'mon – *you* do it instead.' And he said, 'Oh, alright.'"

But, by this time, Chris had drunk enough that he was threatening to topple. "There's a mike standing there – like a straight mike, and he had the soprano sax like that (hunched forward), and to balance and play, he couldn't do it. He said, 'Can you stand behind me, and hold me up?' So I held his shoulders." With Vinden literally supporting him, the tape rolled while Chris finally put the horn to his lips. Far from what might be assumed possible, he tore into the task with a peculiar ferocity. Picking out the openings in the tune, he played energetic runs, including a couple of honking phrases sounding like something from an after-hours jazz club jam session. Watching at such close quarters, Vinden was amazed: "It was just one take – all hell let loose – it was kind of like a swansong…"

Although it had only been for a radio commercial (and one he'd never live to hear) Chris still gave it everything. Slumped once again back in his chair, he was exhausted but satisfied. "He was happy with that, yeah, he was happy…" Vinden recalled. This time, even the recording engineers were gracious. "We left there that day very different to the previous week, where he'd had the wind knocked out of his sails. The people in the studio were very positive with what he'd done, and everything had been put to right, I thought."

As brief as it was, the April 26th recording session proved another small but important buoy for Chris's self-esteem. But a cost would be exacted for the moment of grace, and it came high – Vinden saw that that all was not well with his friend, "He was very, very ill, and I didn't know – I didn't know what was happening to him. He was hemorrhaging slightly, out of his mouth. I didn't understand what was wrong – it was like he had lipstick on, but it wasn't, it was blood." There is actual evidence of this; long after his passing, his family would take the sax out of its case and discover the mouthpiece still crusted in his blood.

Returning to Spindle Cottage once again, his body failing fast, Chris began easing himself away from the concerns of the world at large. These days he was prone to keeping mostly to his room, where he read, listened to music and played a little flute. As for the drinking, in the last year or so he'd been jotting anguished little notes about the state of his relationship with alcohol, referring to it as "the demon drink", acknowledging that he "couldn't get out of it", and that he was "slipping down and out of control of it." But, practically speaking, stopping now would change nothing, a fact that Chris understood. As such, the grocery list nearly always included vodka.

And now he would slowly disengage from many of his friends, a process already ongoing for one reason or another. Having reunited with his girlfriend, Graham Broadbent recalled that, out of respect, Chris had quit coming around in recent months. Similarly, he tapered off his visits to Mike Lewis and Becky after Mike got a new job that kept him occupied.

In May, he did pop in to see Brenda Bryan, bringing a case of beer and a few records he wanted to listen to. These days he sought simplicity and spiritual messages; the two listened to the Staple Singers ("What The World Needs Now Is Love") and Woody Guthrie. Brenda recalled that the romantic and earthy Guthrie had captured Chris's imagination these days, "He thought that the music in England was terrible… Chris loved Woody Guthrie – 'The Oregon Trail', he used to play that over and over again." With the song's promise of deliverance from poisoned plains to a western paradise, Guthrie's affecting dust bowl tale held an obvious appeal for the world-weary Chris. The last verse was especially powerful: "Well my wife gets sort of ailin', when that mean old dust is sailin', and she wishes for the days beyond recall, if the work's there in the future in that north pacific land, we'll hit that Oregon Trail this coming fall." The relaxed and wistful visit was his last, though her then boyfriend, Nick Cannon would visit Chris the next month.

Concerned about his wellbeing, sometime in late June, Nick took him out to a local pub where they made small talk. Here, Nick noticed what looked like a serious physical problem, "As we were sitting down – looking out over this balcony which overlooked some woodlands and things – quite a nice view – I saw him cough into his hanky, and he just turned 'round, trying to hide it – it was great big goblets of blood. I said, 'Chris, what's that?' He said, 'Nothing, nothing', then he went to the toilet, and he came back out, and he did it again. And I said, 'You're not well Chris, you're 'gonna have to go home', and he said, 'No, no, I'll be alright.'" But in the face of Nick's increasingly jittery distress, Chris finally relented.

Once back at Spindle Cottage, Chris would make a mundane request, the outcome to which would remain etched in Nick's memory ever since, "I remember driving him home that day, and his mother wasn't in. He had two Labrador dogs – Toby and Rupert, brothers, white Labrador dogs; he used to adore them. He poured himself a drink and said, 'C'mon, let's take the dogs for a walk.' In the back of his house, where Day House Bank is, there's a big cornfield, and we walked across the cornfields there. As we were coming back he picked some wildflowers – a bunch of wildflowers. He had them in his hand, and threw them up in the air, and said, 'That's my life.' I thought it was quite odd, and he looked at me, quite sad. And I looked at him, well, confused – you know, what's going on? He'd just tossed these flowers into the wind that blew by, and said, 'I'm gonna die Nick.' I said, 'Don't be ridiculous Chris.' And he said, 'I know, I'm gonna die. And I want you to help my mom and dad with the house,' – because I used to do building – 'make sure the house is looked after, and in good shape, if you can.' I said, 'Of course I will, of course I will, but you're not gonna die anyway.' Then we sat down, and I think he had another drink. I didn't know he was that ill. I guess really, I should have, but I didn't."

In May, Vinden's wife had given birth to their daughter. Quite naturally occupied with his family, he hadn't seen Chris for a while. But on his birthday, June 25th (only a day after Chris's), he would be rung up by his mentor, wishing him well. Less than a week later, another, more worried call came from Muriel Wood, asking him to come over – which he did. On his arrival, it was clear that his parents were concerned; Chris had holed up in his room. Vinden recalled both almost pleading, "'He won't come out of his bedroom,' they said, 'You'll get him out, you'll get him out of the bedroom.' I think the deterioration had happened slowly, I don't think his parents realized how really bad he was."

Chris clearly wasn't prepared for the visit, "He jumped out of bed. I don't think he was very happy about me being there in the room." In turn, Vinden was so taken aback by what he saw as to be almost panicked, "He looked *so* ill – his stomach was swollen, the whites of his eyes were yellow. He'd got a t-shirt on, his upper arms were black. He had shorts on – his thighs were black, he'd got blood clots on his tongue – it was terrible. I thought 'My god, I've got to get out of here, I've got to go.'"

Aware of Vinden's distress, Chris tried to soothe it. Saying that he'd meet him downstairs, he got on a robe and followed. Of course, having long ago studied the symptoms and prognosis of his disease, Chris knew full well what was happening. With liver transplant surgeries (and the crucial development of anti-rejection drugs) only on the cusp of standard practice – and certainly not available for unrepentant alcoholics, he was in a blind-ended corridor with no time to turn around. Even so, protecting the feelings of people he cared about was still important to him. His elaborate plans to put a band together had mostly been made to keep his young protégé hopeful. Lately he'd gone even further, calling up several local jazz clubs and booking dates for upcoming live gigs in the coming months.

Meeting his mate in the living room, Chris continued the charade. Wylde recalled, "He deliberately came downstairs and tried to be as normal as possible. The last thing he said to me was, 'Look, I'm going into hospital tomorrow, and when I come out, we're gonna do a lot more sessions, and we've got a gig at 'The Junction' in Harbourne to do in August – we're gonna play there. We'll come out and we'll conquer the world' – that sort of thing." Smiling and touching his shoulder, Chris reassured his friend one last time that he was indeed "coming back", before saying goodbye. Then, on what would be his last day at home, he settled on the couch to watch the Wimbledon tennis tournament on television with his father.

The next morning he was admitted to the nearby Kidderminster General Hospital, where he would spend the next few days. Getting around-the-clock medical treatment, his family was initially encouraged; with his worst symptoms temporarily alleviated, Chris rallied. Keeping his hospital window open in the hot summer weather, he sat in his bed, reading and visiting with family and Curate John Barnett from St. Laurence's Church. Seemingly stabilized, Muriel spread the word, calling his friends and people at Island with updates on his condition.

Meanwhile, back in London, Steve Winwood's life was undergoing a transformation of a different sort. Having just finished rehearsals with his new band, he was now embarking on his first ever solo tour in England. Island's Suzette Newman was closely involved as the tour got underway. But amid the good vibes at the first shows, she also became aware of a dark cloud in the north – the news filtering in from Birmingham was dire. Newman recalled, "Chris was very ill, and Steve was on tour with his new thing, and I kept saying, 'Chris is in the hospital, we have to go see him'. I think we knew Chris was dying." Perhaps believing that there would still be time to visit later, the tour would continue.

Within a few days of his admittance, Chris's condition deteriorated, requiring a move to Queen Elizabeth Hospital in Birmingham. Here, possibly at Chris's request, visitors were limited to family and clergy. Confined to bed, he spent time reviewing his life's path and sought to direct his mind to a place of peace. During her last couple of visits to see her brother, Stephanie Wood recalled, "I remember him saying, 'I wish I could go to Cornwall'…"

Phone calls from Mrs. Wood to his friends continued; at first hopeful and encouraging, they suddenly turned bleak. Graham Broadbent, who had already tried unsuccessfully to get in to see Chris, was with Nick Cannon when Muriel rang up, clearly unable to come to grips with her son's precipitous decline. Graham recalled, "I said, 'How is he?' She said, 'Oh god, they had to give him a sedative, he was screeching and screaming about. He's made a big fuss that he's dying.' And I thought, 'Fucking hell…' He *knew* that he was dying. She said, 'Oh he's being silly.' She wouldn't show too much emotion." Indeed, this was very much Muriel's way. While internally destroyed by witnessing Chris's last struggle, she still did her best to keep her emotions under wraps. Regardless, the news was bone-chilling to hear – no longer able to protect the feelings of others; Chris was staring his death in the face, even if his mother couldn't.

As dire as it seemed, somehow he rallied. On the night of July 11th, Steph, Muriel and Stephen visited again to find Chris subdued but alert and seemingly stable. With no state of emergency to hold them, the family finally returned home for the evening. But around 2 AM the phone rang. Christopher Gordon Blandford Wood died before what would be a warm summer day, July 12th 1983. He had turned thirty-nine just three weeks before.

In the hours after his death, Muriel again had the dreadful job of conveying the news. Although friends were obviously aware that he was ill, it was a testament to how well Chris disguised his condition that nearly all reported being stunned to hear of his death. Nick Cannon recalled, "His mother phoned me up and said, 'Christopher died last night in hospital.' And I said, '*Oh no…*'" As crushed as he was to learn of Chris's passing, Nick also had to listen as Muriel finally came unraveled, "She said, 'I told him, I *told* him, if he didn't stop he was gonna die! What a silly man he is…' And she just kept going on and going on about it – and I just put the phone down."

Vinden Wylde heard from her that morning as well. Having never understood the seriousness of Chris's condition, he had a difficult time processing the news, "It was a complete shock, I didn't expect it. He told me that as soon as he was well enough, we'd start playing again, and so I was waiting like a good soldier for him to come out of the hospital and we'd start again… I think he knew all along, and he was just doing that to save me pain."

The day before Chris's death, the word of his condition finally reached the last of his old friends. Pete Bonas got a call from Jim Capaldi who had apparently just learned of Chris's hospitalization, "Jim phoned me up, and he said, 'Look man, he's in hospital, he's real bad – we've gotta go'. I went, 'Yeah, yeah. Let's go.' Then Jim phoned me back: 'It's too late – he's gone'. And I thought, 'Fucking hell'… I was absolutely floored, maybe we could have done more, you know? Very, very sad."

The funeral ceremony was held on July 20th at St. Laurence's Church in Northfield. With a casket surrounded by flowers ranging from a saxophone shaped display (Island), to a handpicked bouquet of wildflowers (Brenda Bryan), the diverse palate of textures proved a fitting representation of Chris's life experiences. Similarly, the church was packed with a cross-section of people he'd known, from childhood pals and college mates to musicians and local friends who had served as his support network in the last years. It would be the first and only time all the strands of his world would be in the same place at the same time – although in a fundamental way they weren't really together at all. While sharing a deep grief at Chris's death, the cultural divide remained – the pre and post-fame friends forming one group, and the rock aristocracy the other. Ginger Baker came, as did Pete Bonas and Phil Ramacon. Of course, Jim Capaldi attended, as well as Steve Winwood who agreed to play the organ during the church service as well.

The ceremony included two traditional hymns separated by a prayer, and some words by Reverend Peter Nokes, who had confirmed Chris into the church and talked with him many times in those final years. Jim

Capaldi – at first dubious that Chris would have desired a Christian church service at all – was relieved to hear someone who clearly understood his old friend, "The priest that spoke at the funeral – he just said some glowing, wonderful things about Chris, saying that all who met him saw his spirit, that he could connect with everybody – which he did. You could see that he knew Chris, and understood Chris's gift and the spirit he had." At the conclusion of the ceremony it was Jim alone who pushed Chris's coffin into the hearse that would take his body to its final destination, the Lodge Hill Crematorium.

Another ceremony was held there in mid-afternoon. While the church service satisfied the religious rites of passage, it was also typically English; restrained and emotionally controlled. At the crematorium, the repressed feelings of grief were finally loosened. Here many shared their memories, some recalling his unique personality and others the gentleness of his being.

Finally, as the mourners lapsed into a contemplative silence, a tape featuring Chris's music played – Jim Capaldi's "Seagull". The last track on his 1975 album, *Short Cut Draw Blood*, it was a fitting end point on many levels. Actually a pure Traffic song, possibly the last they ever did together back in '74, Jim's emotional lyrics described a man identifying with the freedom of a bird. "Seagull" was an obvious reference to Chris, a point clear to all as the song unfolded. Supported with Steve Winwood's sensitive harpsichord and Chris's own fluttering flute – by the tape's conclusion, nearly all were overcome, with many having a tangible sense of his presence, and as some strongly felt, his liberation.

Among those was the Reverend Peter Nokes, who having officiated many such ceremonies over the years, recalled this one as extraordinary, "It was devastatingly sad, and we all missed him, but there was a kind of joy about the funeral service – it wasn't an unhappy occasion, because I think so many people had rich memories of Chris. It was genuinely a celebration of a very special person. My feeling was that it was very much like a release – the music in the auditorium floating above us. It did feel like Chris's spirit was released from all the difficulties he'd been through – and (was) hovering above and amongst us. The fact is, I must have taken thousands and thousands of funeral services – as a moment, it was quite special."

*

The aftermath of Chris Wood's life played out in ways that were well below the radar of anyone outside of family and close friends. Having been out of the limelight for many years, his passing would rate only the smallest of mentions in the usual 'rock press' publications. And after that – nothing; no tribute album or memorial concert, not a single reporter curious enough to write a story – large or small – about his existence. Even the two biographies of Steve Winwood published since, hold scant information about Chris – a lesson in how quickly even a 'famous' person can dissolve into obscurity.

Clearly troubled that Chris had been both misunderstood and forgotten, Jim Capaldi would dedicate a song (typically "Forty Thousand Headmen") and tell a story about him at every show in his last tours. Having had time to think it over, Jim came to understand Chris's special contribution to Traffic, and he wanted it known. "He was the keeper. He was kind of like the gatekeeper of making sure it never got too twee, too cute, you know? He was always either saying something, or putting his vibe in – playing 'bloo-ehh' on the fucking saxophone somewhere – just to kind of go, 'what the fuck is going on? It's too neat, or too fuckin'…' He always had *that*, which is the mark of geniuses. It is. I can get it all nice – the rose is here, cut the hedges there – get the hedge nice. Chris was like, brilliant. He had such a feel man, such humanity. And Steve, who has such a gift musically – and it is – he is *so* gifted, so special, Steve. If he had an ounce of what Chris had on that side... It's strange isn't it? A strange combination."

Among other friends, his memory would live on in some very tangible ways. Both Graham Broadbent and Stuart Carr would name their first-born sons 'Christopher', in his honor. To this day Vinden Wylde continues to play saxophone, flute and congas in a band in Wales. In the wake of Chris's life being cut so short, Wylde says that he has been spurred on to play "with a terrible resolve", ever since. He also fondly remembers a special tip: "He said, 'Listen to the birds – listen to the blackbirds, because those are the ones with the most beautiful phrases' – he called them flute phrases."

To honor Chris's great love of the Cornwall coast, his family paid for a bench to be installed at one of his favorite places – on a cliff overlooking the sea at Trevone Bay in Padstow, with an attached plate inscribed: "In loving memory of Christopher Wood – June 24, 1944 - July 12, 1983." As if awaiting his return, it continues to sit there to this day.

CHAPTER TWENTY-EIGHT

There is one last great mystery related to Chris Wood – a strange and fittingly enigmatic situation which may never be resolved. After the funeral ceremonies, Chris's cremated remains were buried in the graveyard of St. Laurence's Church. With his ashes placed in a small coffin in the same plot as Jeanette, the two would finally sleep together again; nestled below the black granite headstone Chris had purchased almost two years before.

The story would have ended there, but sometime later it was discovered that the plot actually belonged to another family. In light of the embarrassing and unfortunate circumstance, plans were made to quietly disinter the caskets and move them to another location. But upon digging up the grave, it was discovered that Chris's coffin was in fact, missing. Though a search involving metal detecting machines sweeping a wide area was undertaken, in the end the even more embarrassed church officials had to give up. While the headstone and Jeanette's casket would eventually be relocated, today as then, the whereabouts of Chris Wood's earthly remains, like that of London's ancient *Oswulff's Stone*, are entirely unknown.

('Oregon Trail', Woody Guthrie, 1941)

EPILOGUE

A NEW 'TRAFFIC' AND VULCAN'S RELEASE

With Chris deceased, and Traffic's last live show twenty years gone, by 1994 the band seemed very much to be an artifact of history – surviving only through fans' recollections and recorded music. Yet the saga found a way, in a fashion, to continue a little longer – producing music as well as reanimating some decades-old conflicts.

In 1994, Jim and Steve revived the name 'Traffic', and put out an album – *Far From Home*. With a front cover featuring a stick figure drawing of a flute player, the inner label would dedicate the work to Chris Wood. This was followed by a long U.S. tour (supporting the Grateful Dead on some dates) and then a very brief British leg. Afterward, the unit dissolved with (as was typical for Traffic) no stated plans to return.

This iteration would feature an American musician, Randall Bramblett, assuming Chris's role on flute and saxophone (although he wasn't involved with the album). He might have been the perfect choice. Having successfully fought his own battle with alcoholism, Randall found a strong sense of kinship with Chris (who he never met), a connection strengthened by the receipt of a very special gift – one of Chris's flutes which was given to him by Stephanie Wood.

Bramblett recalled, "The alto flute I keep as a treasured gift. It means a lot to me to be alive and recovering from an illness that took Chris at such an early age. I kind of kept his spirit alive for a while I guess. His influence on me was in giving me permission to try new sounds and melodies. He was quite adventurous and daring even though he didn't have a lot of training. He had great lyrical and tonal originality, (and) wasn't afraid to try something unusual. Most of the time it worked, and many times it provided a hook line for the whole song. I especially like his flute lines on '40,000 Headmen'. That's a very important and haunting line that makes that song really cool."

Uncannily, Bramblett was said to have quit drinking for good while on a tour bus rolling down the road somewhere in the U.S. on July 12th, 1983. He had no idea until much later that it was the same day as Chris's death.

As even this version of Traffic drifted uncertainly into history, Jim would seek to reignite more past sparks by again teaming up with Dave Mason in 1998. With no new musical product to promote, they simply toured, playing favorites in smaller venues across the United States as the 'Co-founders of Traffic'. While both held a desire to bring Steve into the mix as well, when it finally happened the old friction would re-emerge in the blink of an eye. At a gig on February 12th at the Bottom Line in New York, Steve would walk on, near the end of the show, for a cool acoustic/electric "Low Spark" followed by a roaring "Gimme Some Lovin" – which sent the audience into a frenzy. But somehow, "even *that* ended in a fucking disaster," as Dave later put it, when a backstage discussion about an encore song ("Dear Mr. Fantasy") devolved into a heated, unresolved situation over who would play what instrument.

In 2004, as an indication of Traffic's continued stature, the band was inducted into the Rock and Roll Hall of Fame in a ceremony at the Waldorf Astoria Hotel in New York City (with Stephanie Wood accepting Chris's award). While all would get a chance to speak at the podium, when it came to the music, pre-show negotiations *again* found Dave and Steve at odds over the instrumentation for "Dear Mr. Fantasy". Ultimately, Mason would decline to participate. The last ever performance of 'Traffic' thus included the trio of Steve, Jim and Randall Bramblett (on organ). Dave, however, got to play the final card; his now classic "Feelin' Alright?" would serve as the show's closing jam.

Thinking to take advantage of the Hall of Fame momentum, Dave would subsequently talk of his desire for another "real" Traffic reunion with Steve, Jim and himself, but this would never happen; time ran out.

Jim Capaldi died of stomach cancer on January 28th, 2005, only a few months after completing his generous interviews for this book. It was clear to the end that the ember of Traffic still glowed brightly at the core of his identity. One of the last songs Jim would work on was a new arrangement of "John Barleycorn" – done in an up-tempo style, a version of which he performed at shows with Pete Bonas in 2004. Not long after, Pete would write a song called "Come Back My Friend" – about (and for) Chris Wood. Both are unreleased.

EPILOGUE

As for Steve Winwood, since the '94 Traffic album, he has moved far away from the overtly commercial music that typified his early solo career. Now hailed as one of the godfathers of the 'jam band' ethic, his later tours have been built around Traffic-like instrumentation (sax, flute and congas) and more open arrangements. His comeback album, *About Time* (2003), and its follow up, *Nine Lives* (2008) both incorporated these elements. Interestingly, during the sessions for *About Time*, he was also reported to have recorded an excellent version of Chris Wood's "See No Man Girl", but it has not released.

Chris's own unreleased music, especially the album he initially called *Vulcan*, also has a story stretching many years past his death. While it is doubtful the work was ever completed to his satisfaction (the '78 Island rejected version aside), his edits, overdubs and frequent comments to friends indicate this music was of deep significance to him. But tracking it down later was a different matter.

While it is known that Chris went to Island in the early 80's and returned with a pile of thirteen or so reels — two decades later, only a handful of scattered cassettes could be located. With his parents both deceased and Sinewave long shuttered, by then no one associated with the family had any idea where the reels were, or even if they still existed. As such, the possibility of a respectful release of Chris's music looked nearly hopeless.

But one person knew exactly where they were. When interviewed for this book, Vinden Wylde recalled that at the wake held for Chris, at Spindle Cottage, he met Steve Winwood and told him of Chris's experiences at Sinewave. In response Steve would ask, "Where are the tapes?" and express a strong interest in making sure they were accounted for. Soon after, Stephen Wood himself would retrieve the reels from the studio and drive them to Steve's house in Gloucestershire. While both Vinden and Stephen held hopes that Steve might do something with Chris's music, the reels would remain tucked away in Winwood's archives, eventually to be forgotten.

It was only in 2006, after a record label (Esoteric) exhibited interest in releasing the music that Vinden's information was uncovered and followed up. Retrieved from Winwood's tape vault, a few other tapes long ago given to Gordon Jackson for safekeeping were also recovered. With one cassette track used to fill a gap, a version of Chris's musical puzzle was reassembled, completing (as much as possible at the time) his arduous task. Against all odds, on October 27th, 2008, *Vulcan*, Chris Wood's long lost album was finally given its release to the world.

While the CD entered the market with barely a ripple, Chris would have likely been pleased with the review given by *Record Collector*, a U.K. music magazine, which said in part: "*Vulcan* often exhibits a cross-over appeal, integrating Traffic's jazzier influences with a bedrock of Caribbean grooves, that although not always evident, add a broader dimension. There is no doubt that the late Chris Wood was a supremely talented player, with his work having a broad appeal to rock, jazz and world music fans. An exotic dish of fine sounds, more than worthy of the man's memory."

END

Life-line

Name: "Christopher Wood."

Age: "Twenty-Two"

How old do you feel? "Physically, sometimes I feel old. Mentally, very young, but I don't mind about that."

Birthday: "Twenty-fourth of June."

Are you afraid of death?: "Yes."

Why? "The thought of everything just coming to an end. But then, it may not."

Favorite flower: "Buttercups and daisies."

Do you like classical music? "Yes, but I like all different sorts of music."

Do you daydream? "Well, I have nightmares and daymares."

Do you smoke? "Sometimes, in the evening."

What type of foods do you enjoy most? "Simple foods like fruit and sea fish."

What country in the world would you especially like to visit? "China."

Are you patriotic? "Not really."

Ideal girl: "A girl who is honest and understanding and very natural."

Do you love animals? "Yes."

Which animals do you love most? "Monsters (second thoughts, dogs and all house pets)."

Who do you admire? "Someone who is humble and kind."

Who would you like to be other than yourself? "A bird with human functions and a brain."

Ambition: "Happiness for other people."

Personal Statement:

"Here I am trying to write a few words about me, and I don't even know much about myself except what I like at the moment. (Not in order of importance): Traffic, Stephanie Wood, my Mother and Father, several cats, old houses, ghosts, trees, Emily Bronte, summer days, Stourbridge, roads leading south, the sea, beaches, rock pools, Padstow, James, thatched roofs, Dave and Steve, the smell of apple blossoms, earth, fresh sea air, Clancy Brothers, factory, laughing, traveling, Island, Ken, Beatles, children, canes, day, lawn, burial mounds, swallows, rare things, rubies, some totem poles, peaches, butter, colours, the sound of the wind, all instruments, Bob Dylan, dark, lanterns, dawn, dusk, atmospheres in the evening and little things."

('Lifeline' of Chris Wood, written for the Traffic fan-club in 1967 [possibly published in New Musical Express, 1967])

('Vulcan review', Kingsley Abbott, Record Collector, Issue 358, 2009)

235

The Doors Examined by Jim Cherry

Jim Morrison, Ray Manzarek, Robby Krieger and John Densmore. Welcome to the known, the unknown, and the in between. *Welcome to The Doors Examined.*

The Doors remain one of the most influential and exciting bands in rock 'n' roll history, and The Doors Examined offers a unique, expressive insight into the history of the band, their influence on culture, and the group's journey following the death of Jim Morrison in Paris in 1971. It starts at the beginning, on a Venice Beach rooftop, and takes the reader on an invigorating journey, from The Whisky a Go-Go to the Dinner Key Auditorium, The Ed Sullivan Show to Père Lachaise Cemetery.

Comprised of selected acclaimed articles from The Doors Examiner, The Doors Examined also serves up original content that assesses seminal albums, how the group's music has influenced other artists, and key people in the band's history; people like Jac Holzman, Paul Rothchild, Bruce Botnick, and Pam Courson.

The Doors Examined is a must read investigation into one of the greatest rock 'n' roll bands of all time.

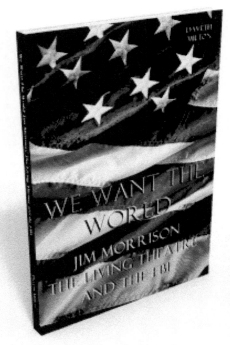

We Want The World: Jim Morrison, The Living Theatre and the FBI by Daveth Milton

"I've always been attracted to ideas that were about revolt against authority… I like ideas about breaking away or overthrowing of established order. It seems to be the road toward freedom." - Jim Morrison.

How could the Establishment not pursue a man who began public life with a statement like that?

Jim Morrison was a songwriter, film maker, poet and singer with The Doors. His opponents saw him as a criminal. And more. In an escalating confrontation over the freedom of America, he was up against men who used law to block justice and fear to halt social change. Those men included the FBI's infamous director, J. Edgar Hoover.

Inspired by true events, this imaginative recreation of history re-opens Morrison's secret FBI dossier to reveal his Establishment opponents. Moving between Jim's image, influences and brushes with the law in Phoenix and Miami, Daveth Milton uses meticulous research skills to assess the extent of the conspiracy against the singer. Part meditation, part rock in the dock exposé, We Want The World provides the ultimate account of Jim Morrison's awkward encounter with the Bureau.

Lightning Source UK Ltd.
Milton Keynes UK
UKHW050230190620
365123UK00010B/74